More Ghosts in the Gallery

ALSO BY DAVID L. FLEITZ
AND FROM MCFARLAND

Cap Anson: The Grand Old Man of Baseball (2005)

Ghosts in the Gallery at Cooperstown: Sixteen Little-Known Members of the Hall of Fame (2004)

Louis Sockalexis: The First Cleveland Indian (2002)

Shoeless: The Life and Times of Joe Jackson (2001)

More Ghosts in the Gallery

Another Sixteen Little-Known Greats at Cooperstown

DAVID L. FLEITZ

McFarland & Company, Inc., Publishers
Jefferson, North Carolina, and London

LIBRARY OF CONGRESS CATALOGUING-IN-PUBLICATION DATA

Fleitz, David L., 1955–
More ghosts in the gallery : another sixteen little-known greats at Cooperstown / David L. Fleitz.
p. cm.
Includes bibliographical references and index.

ISBN-13: 978-0-7864-3133-5
(softcover : 50# alkaline paper) ∞

1. Baseball players—United States—Biography.
2. Baseball players—United States—Statistics.
3. National Baseball Hall of Fame and Museum.
I. Title.
GV865.A1F54 2007   796.3570922—dc22 [B]   2007010795

British Library cataloguing data are available

©2007 David L. Fleitz. All rights reserved

No part of this book may be reproduced or transmitted in any form or by any means, electronic or mechanical, including photocopying or recording, or by any information storage and retrieval system, without permission in writing from the publisher.

On the cover: Smokey Joe Williams, 1915
(National Baseball Hall of Fame Library, Cooperstown, New York)

Manufactured in the United States of America

McFarland & Company, Inc., Publishers
Box 611, Jefferson, North Carolina 28640
www.mcfarlandpub.com

To the memory of my mother, Rosella Kay Fleitz

Acknowledgments

I would like to thank a few people and institutions without whom this book would not have been possible.

The staff at the National Baseball Library in Cooperstown, New York, offered helpful assistance in rounding up photographs for this book, and the Eugene C. Murdock collection of baseball materials at the Cleveland Public Library was invaluable. My membership in SABR (Society for American Baseball Research) came with ProQuest, an online newspaper search engine that has revolutionized research of all subjects, not only baseball. ProQuest makes it possible to find information quickly from home without traveling to a library and plowing through rolls of microfilm. When library resources are needed, I am fortunate to have access to those at Bowling Green State University in my hometown of Bowling Green, Ohio.

Thanks also to Don Thompson, a great-nephew of Sam Thompson, who was a 1974 Hall of Fame inductee and is the subject of one of the chapters in this book. Don, a SABR member, made much information available on his ancestor, and welcomed me at a family gathering in Indiana during the summer of 2006. I was happy to participate in a ceremony unveiling an historic marker honoring Sam's baseball career on that occasion.

Once again, my wife Deborah proved to be a first-rate editor, and I thank her for her editing skills and moral support.

Sources of Statistical Information

Project Retrosheet is an outstanding Internet resource for player statistics, game logs, box scores, and a myriad of other information. Their research is so complete that I have decided to use Retrosheet as a source for the major league statistical data used in the text of this book. The information used here was obtained free of charge from and is copyrighted by Retrosheet. Interested parties may contact Retrosheet at www.retrosheet.org.

For Negro Leagues data, the work of John Holway has been invaluable. Much of the numerical information in the chapters on Hilton Smith, Joe Williams, and Cristóbal Torriente comes from his books, which are listed in this book's notes and bibliography.

Contents

Acknowledgments	vii
Preface	1
1—George Wright	3
2—Jimmy Collins	18
3—Dan Brouthers	33
4—Tommy McCarthy	48
5—Billy Hamilton	64
6—Sam Rice	78
7—Tim Keefe	91
8—Kiki Cuyler	108
9 Joe Kelley	121
10—Mickey Welch	138
11—Sam Thompson	151
12—Amos Rusie	168
13—Arky Vaughan	184
14—Joe Williams	198
15—Hilton Smith	211
16—Cristóbal Torriente	224
Notes	237
Bibliography	243
Index	245

Preface

In 2003, I was writing my first book that focused on little-known members of the Baseball Hall of Fame, *Ghosts in the Gallery at Cooperstown*. As I wrote, I realized that there were many more potential subjects than I could fit in one volume. There were, by my estimation, more than 50 players, executives, and managers in the Hall of Fame that could rightly be labeled as obscure. I chose 16 of them to profile in my first book, but I knew that there was enough material to write a second or even a third work on the same topic.

How could anyone selected for the Hall of Fame not be famous? It seems paradoxical—but even the most serious student of baseball history knows little about many of the men whose plaques adorn the gallery walls. The Hall of Fame has been electing players, managers, executives, and umpires for over 70 years, and during that time shifting standards, changes in voting rules and procedures, and the creation and dissolution of committees have resulted in selections of varying quality. While the annual balloting of the Baseball Writers Association has usually enshrined highly deserving figures, the Veterans Committee, in its several incarnations, has been responsible for almost all of the lesser-known selections, many of which have been widely criticized by the public.

However, as Bill James said in his fine 1994 book *The Politics of Glory*, there is not a man in the Hall of Fame who was not, at the very least, a pretty good player. Some label Tommy McCarthy, an outfielder who played for several teams between 1885 and 1896, as the worst player in the Hall, but he was still a vital component of several pennant winners and made important contributions to baseball strategy, both offensively and defensively. Even the least-deserving Hall of Famers were outstanding players, if not on the level of a Mickey Mantle or a Walter Johnson, and the lesser known status of some Cooperstown honorees does not detract from their accomplishments.

Obscure Hall of Famers appear to fall into several categories:

Those who played in the 19th century. The first professional league was founded in 1871, and the National League began play five years later with teams located in many of the same cities that host major league baseball today. The stars of baseball's early days flourished at a time when newspaper coverage of the sport was in its infancy, and long before radio and television brought the game and its personalities into American homes. Most of the 19th century stars who later gained election to the Hall were long dead by the time of their enshrinement, forgotten save for the lines of statistics they left behind.

Those who died young. More than 20 Hall of Famers did not survive to age 50, and several others lived only a few years more. Some, like Lou Gehrig and Roberto Clemente, are celebrated, while others such as Arky Vaughan and Kiki Cuyler were virtually forgotten after their premature deaths. Vaughan, one of the greatest shortstops of all time, and Cuyler, a star on four pennant winning teams, had been dead for 33 and 18 years respectively before taking their places in Cooperstown.

Those who played for generally unsuccessful teams. Sam Rice is the Washington Senators' all-time leader in many statistical categories, but little was known of him outside of the nation's capital. Amos Rusie never played for a pennant winner, while Arky Vaughan performed for only one, and that as a part-timer near the end of his career. Great players make great teams, but great teams also bring attention to great players.

The stars of segregated baseball. Most fans, myself included, know very little about African American baseball in the pre-integration era. The Hall's first Committee on the Negro Leagues, formed in 1971, brought some of the greatest stars of the pre–1947 black game to public attention, and a second committee named another 17 deserving players and executives to the Hall in 2006. As more research is done on Negro Leagues and pre–Negro Leagues baseball, the lives and careers of many of the segregated game's outstanding performers will come into greater focus.

The life histories of men such as Babe Ruth, Willie Mays, and Henry Aaron are widely known, but the stories behind the less recognizable men in the Hall of Fame also deserve to be told. Sam Rice's triumph over personal tragedy, George Wright's post-career accomplishments as a sports pioneer, and Hilton Smith's fight for recognition are but three of the many compelling narratives contained in this book.

Though their names are not as familiar as those of their more famous brethren, the 16 players profiled herein lived remarkable lives and accomplished much, on the field and off. I found their stories and careers fascinating, and I hope you will as well.

1
George Wright

> "There isn't an infielder in the game today who had anything on George Wright when it came to playing shortstop, and certainly there was none during his time. George fielded hard-hit balls barehanded, gathered them up or speared them when in the air with either hand. He was an expert and accurate thrower, being able to throw with either hand."
>
> —*James (Deacon) White*[1]

In 1936, the Baseball Writers Association of America (BBWAA) held its first election of modern (post–1900) players to the Baseball Hall of Fame. On February 2 of that year, the BBWAA announced that Ty Cobb, Babe Ruth, Honus Wagner, Walter Johnson, and Christy Mathewson would comprise the inaugural induction class of the Hall, which was scheduled to open three years hence in Cooperstown, New York. The Hall had also polled a group of veteran writers to select deserving 19th-century candidates, but the balloting process was fraught with confusion and controversy. Though the writers had been empowered to choose up to five old-time stars to join the moderns in the Hall, not one player managed to gain the required 75 percent of the votes necessary for election.

In response, Commissioner Kenesaw Mountain Landis created a board of six prominent baseball men, including past and present league presidents, minor league executives, and himself, labeling it the Centennial Commission. Landis empowered this panel to identify the major builders and pioneers of the sport from the 19th century, and elect them to the Hall "for outstanding service to baseball apart from playing the game."[2] In December of that year, at the annual league meetings in Chicago, the commission announced its selections. The panel chose managers John McGraw and Connie Mack, league presidents Morgan Bulkeley and Ban Johnson, and George Wright, a star shortstop of the 1860s and 1870s.

A few weeks later, sportswriter Richards Vidmer of the *New York Herald Tribune* dropped a bombshell, suggesting in print that the Centennial Commission had erred in electing Wright to the Hall. The committee, said Vidmer, may have confused George Wright with his older brother Harry, who assembled and managed baseball's first all-salaried team, the 1869 Cincinnati Red Stockings. This legendary nine went undefeated, drew large crowds, and proved that professional baseball could be both profitable and popular. He then moved to Boston, where he built a new ballclub and led it to six pennants in the first eight seasons of professional league play. George was the star of his brother's championship teams, but Harry, the first great baseball manager, was the man who earned the title "Father of Professional Baseball."[3]

In retrospect, the Centennial Commission would have done well to enshrine both Wright brothers. Harry, who did not gain election until 1953, did more than anyone to lay the foundation of baseball as a professional sport, while George was the game's greatest player during the post–Civil War era. Perhaps the committee had intended to choose Harry, but George was a worthy selection nonetheless.

George Wright was born in New York City on January 28, 1847 to Samuel and Annie Tone Wright, who had departed Sheffield, England eleven years before with their first son Harry. They settled in the Harlem section of the city, and Samuel, a cricket player of note in England, took a position as a professional at the St. George Cricket Club. This club, a haven for well-to-do young businessmen seeking recreation and exercise, was the place where Samuel Wright found his calling. He was determined to make cricket as popular a sport in America as it was in his native land.

George Wright in 1869, when he batted .625 for the undefeated Cincinnati Red Stockings. (Library of Congress)

Available land for cricket matches in New York City was scarce, so the club moved across the Hudson River to a new venue, Elysian Fields, in Hoboken, New Jersey. There, Samuel proceeded to groom George and older brother Harry to follow in his footsteps as cricket club professionals. However, that site was also the one where the Knickerbocker Club of New York played the first organized game of baseball in 1845. Elysian Fields was home to the Knickerbockers, Gothams, and other outstanding amateur baseball nines, and the Wright brothers became enthusiastic devotees of this new American sport.

By 1858, the 23-year-old Harry began dividing his time between cricket and baseball, joining the storied Knickerbockers that year as a pitcher and outfielder. Harry was one of New York's leading cricketers as a batsman and bowler (pitcher), though his baseball talent quickly came to the fore as well. He spent five years with the Knickerbockers before joining another prominent team, the Gothams, in 1862. George, 12 years younger, proved to be a natural athlete who excelled at everything he did in both sports. At age 13, the younger Wright joined the St. George junior cricket team, and three years later earned a place alongside his father on the main club, the Dragonslayers. The highly skilled youngster was then appointed to a position as assistant cricket pro at the St. George club.

George left school the following year to train for a career as an engraver, but found his sporting activities much more interesting. He watched the top amateur baseball teams in New York play at Elysian Fields, often filling in for absent players and impressing all with his talent. In 1864, after a stint with the junior Gothams, George was invited to join brother Harry on the varsity. "First I was their catcher," recalled George many years later, "but one day a foul tip struck me in the throat and it hurt so much that I never afterward was able to muster up sufficient courage to catch, and so I went to left field, eventually going to second base and then to shortstop."[4] The multitalented teenager excelled at nearly every position on the field, and drew raves as one of the best ballplayers in New York. In 1865, he left the city to serve as head professional at the Philadelphia Cricket Club, also performing for a leading local baseball team, the Olympics.

In the meantime, Harry was building a reputation of his own in both the baseball and cricket worlds. In August 1865, he accepted a post as head cricket professional and instructor at the Union Club in Cincinnati, Ohio. A year later, the Cincinnati Base Ball Club, which played its games on the Union Club grounds, hired Harry as a pitcher and outfielder. A born leader and organizer, Harry was soon appointed captain of the Union team. He created new batting, pitching, and fielding strategies, many adapted from the cricket field, and eagerly taught them to his charges. By 1867, Harry had put his cricket career on hold to devote all his time to baseball.

George Wright, already one of the top cricketers in America, was soon lauded as the best player in the nation in the rising national pastime. He returned to the Gothams in 1866, but soon left for the Unions of Morrisania, a strong team from a town on Long Island which is now part of the Bronx. In 1867, with the demand for his talents increasing, George became the shortstop and leadoff batter for the Washington Nationals, a team made up of government clerks, mostly with the Treasury Department. Ostensibly amateur, the Nationals were no doubt paid athletes, as they were able to play ball while spending little or no time at their jobs. George, for one, listed his work address as 238 Pennsylvania Avenue, which at the time was a public park.[5] Professionalism, frowned upon by purists of the era, was slowly creeping into baseball.

The Nationals were the first baseball club to take an extended road trip, setting off in July for a series of games against leading Midwestern teams. Stopping in Cincinnati on July 15, they defeated Harry Wright's team by the score of 53–10, and on July 26, a crowd of more than 9,000 paid 50 cents apiece to see the Nationals defeat the Excelsior club of Chicago by a 49–4 count. Their only loss on the tour came in Rockford, Illinois, where the local Forest City squad, behind its 16-year-old pitcher Al Spalding, stunned the visitors with a 29–23 win. The Nationals closed the trip with a 76–14 victory over the Chicago Atlantics, then returned to Washington, where President Andrew Johnson took in a game, staying for all nine innings and showing keen interest in the proceedings.

The Nationals were one of the top teams in the nation, and George Wright was its biggest star. Baseball record-keeping was rudimentary at the time, but one source states that George stroked 186 hits in the 29 games played by the team that season, leading the Nationals in hits and runs scored. He also revolutionized shortstop play. Most who played the position at that time stationed themselves on a direct line between second and third, but George discovered that his strong throwing arm made it possible for him to play farther back, thereby increasing his range, but still be able to throw out runners at first. Within the next few years, all other middle infielders followed his lead, but George was the man who earned the title "King of Shortstops."

George returned to the Unions of Morrisania for the 1868 campaign. The Unions, noting the success of the Nationals' tour the previous year, embarked on a trip of their own and challenged the best teams of the Midwest that summer, winning their first 11 games. After a 41–11 romp over the Chicago Atlantics (in which George scored seven runs), the young shortstop gained a bit of revenge on Al Spalding and Rockford, belting a homer and sparking a 23–17 win over the Forest City club. George and the Morrisania nine did not lose a game until they arrived in Cincinnati, where Harry Wright's club, now called the Red Stockings, surprised the Unions with a 13–12 win, breaking Morrisania's 25-game winning streak. At season's end, the *New York Clipper* awarded medals to the best player in the nation at each position, with George Wright winning the honor as the game's premier shortstop.

The presence of large, enthusiastic crowds throughout the country convinced Harry Wright and the backers of the Cincinnati Red Stockings that an all-professional team could be profitable, so Harry set out to strengthen his team with the best players he could find. He attempted to sign several of the Clipper gold medal winners of the year before, but the man he wanted most was his brother George, who agreed to play for Harry's Red Stockings for the then-impressive salary of $1,400 per year. With six holdovers from the 1868 Cincinnati team, three additions from the crosstown Cincinnati Buckeye club, and George Wright from Morrisania, the Red Stockings became the first all-professional, salaried team in baseball. Stated the *New York Clipper* that spring, "Contestants for the championship will have to keep one eye trained towards Porkopolis."[6]

George, a finely proportioned and compact athlete who stood five feet and nine inches tall and weighed about 150 pounds, decided at this time to stop playing other positions on the field. "I had made up my mind," said George later, "that to be a successful baseball player a man should stick to one position, and so I played at short all the time I was with the Reds, except to pitch a few innings."[7] Harry placed George, his best hitter, in the leadoff spot of the Cincinnati lineup. After a hard training session that spring, in which Harry taught strategy and tactics to his men, the Red Stockings were prepared to challenge the best teams of the East for the national championship.

The Cincinnati club launched their season with a 45–9 win over another Cincinnati nine, the Great Westerns, and compiled 17 consecutive wins in tune-up games against weaker teams. On June 15, they arrived in New York for a contest against the formidable Mutuals. In a particularly low-scoring contest, the Red Stockings defeated their New York rivals by a 4–2 score, staking their claim as the best team in the nation. The next day, they trounced the previously unbeaten Brooklyn Atlantics by a 32–10 score before a crowd of 12,000, then proceeded to Philadelphia five days later and scored a win against the Athletics, by a 27–18 count, before nearly twice as many fans. They completed their eastern tour without a loss in 25 contests, and returned to Cincinnati on July 1 still undefeated on the season.

Though pitcher Asa Brainard, outfielders Andy Leonard and Cal McVey, and third baseman Fred Waterman were also fine players (as was Harry, who patrolled center field and pitched occasionally), George Wright was the recognized star of the team. Statistics for the 57 official games on the schedule reveal that George walloped 49 home runs, belted 339 hits (nearly six per game), scored 304 runs, and batted an unbelievable .625. He powered the Red Stockings to an unprecedented 57–0 record and the undisputed national title, and although the team barely broke even financially (one source says that their profit for the season was $1.39), the Cincinnati fans celebrated their championship. More importantly, the Red Stockings had demonstrated that the future of baseball lay in the professional, not the amateur, game. Other teams quickly moved to follow Cincinnati's lead and built all-salaried nines of their own.

As the game's top player, George made his opinions known regarding new rules to improve the game. At the annual meeting of the National Association of Base Ball Players in December 1869, alarmed by the increasing number of collisions between baserunners and infielders, George proposed that batters be allowed to overrun first base without penalty. The Association agreed

George (left) and Harry Wright with the 1874 Boston Red Stockings. (Author's collection)

and enacted the new rule to take effect the following season, while rejecting a proposal to allow runners to do the same at second and third. The rule survives, virtually unchanged, to this day.[8]

The rise of professionalism occurred faster than anyone could have imagined, for in 1870 the Red Stockings learned that they were not invincible after all. Undefeated after their first 27 games that season, the Cincinnati club faced the Atlantics in Brooklyn on June 14. George, as usual, was the star of the game, fielding flawlessly and scoring two of the seven Cincinnati runs as the Red Stockings and Atlantics battled to a 5–5 tie after nine innings. The Atlantics offered to call the game a draw, but Harry insisted upon seeing it to a conclusion, so the teams carried on into extra innings. Neither team scored in the 10th, but the Red Stockings put two runs across the plate in the top of the 11th to take a 7–5 lead.

George Wright was so sure-handed a shortstop that Brooklyn's Bob Ferguson was determined not to hit a ball in his direction. Usually a right-handed batter, Ferguson turned around and hit from the left side of the plate that day, becoming the first switch-hitter in baseball history. The ploy worked in the bottom of the 11th, when Ferguson singled to right field, far out of George's reach, to drive in Joe Start with the tying run. Moments later, Ferguson scored the winning tally on a single by George Zettelein, handing the Red Stockings their first loss in two years and breaking their 84-game winning streak. Team president Aaron Champion sent a mournful telegram home to Cincinnati that read, "Atlantics 8, Cincinnati 7. The finest game ever played. Our boys did nobly but fortune was against us. Eleven innings played. Though beaten, not disgraced."[9]

Though the Red Stockings remained one of the leading teams in the nation, the loss to Brooklyn destroyed their aura of invulnerability. On July 18 of that year, they nearly lost to the Harvard University nine, trailing by a 17–12 score in the ninth. George Wright saved the day by whacking a bases-loaded double, keying an 8-run rally for a 20–17 win. On July 27 they lost their first home game in two years, dropping an 11–7 decision to the Philadelphia Athletics. They finished the season with six losses, as the Chicago White Stockings and Brooklyn Atlantics each claimed a share of the national championship.

The fickle Cincinnati fans, perhaps spoiled by success, soon lost interest in the Red Stockings. Game attendance fell sharply, and at season's end the club board of directors opted to return to amateur play, disbanding Harry Wright's all-salaried squad. George, now a free agent, was then approached by Boston backers who were interested in entering a team in the first professional league, the National Association, for the 1871 campaign. "The men behind the move sent for me to organize the team," said George, "and I was the first player to be placed under contract. They asked me to become captain and manager, but I declined for the reason that I did not believe a man could be a successful playing manager, and upon my suggestion the Boston club secured my brother Harry from the Cincinnati Red Stockings by telegraph to become manager."[10]

Harry agreed to move to Boston, bringing two more of his Cincinnati players (first baseman Charlie Gould and catcher Cal McVey) to join him and George in the Hub. Harry then signed pitcher Al Spalding, second baseman

Ross Barnes, and outfielder Fred Cone from Rockford. With Dave Birdsall in right, Harry Schaefer at third, and the manager himself in center, the new Boston club promised to be the strongest in the Association. They also appropriated their nickname from their old team; because they wore white uniforms with red hose, as they had in Cincinnati, the new team became the Boston Red Stockings. On January 20, 1871, Harry Wright introduced his team to the public, and the local *Morning Journal* declared, "Boston can now boast of possessing a first-class professional base ball club."[11]

The Boston club almost certainly would have won the first Association pennant were it not for an injury to their star shortstop. In early May, George collided with Harry Schaefer on the infield, suffering a broken leg that kept him out of the lineup for three months. Ross Barnes moved to short, while substitute Sam Jackson covered second, but George's absence devastated the team. The Red Stockings wallowed in fourth place before he returned in early August, sparking the team to 10 wins in its final 12 games and lifting them to second position at season's end. He played in only 16 of Boston's 31 contests that year, but batted .412 and scored more than two runs per game.

This significant leg injury robbed George of his speed, and some say that he was never again as dominant a player. However, he was still one of the stars of the game. Jim O'Rourke, who joined the Boston club two years after the accident, was nonetheless impressed. "George Wright never had any equal as a fielder, base runner and batsman," he said, "combined with heady work of a quality never accredited to any ball tosser. All his qualifications taken together, he was really in a class by himself, and I do not know of a ball player today who ever was entitled to be considered in the same breath with him."[12]

Henry Chadwick, the most influential sportswriter in the nation, agreed. "George Wright is generally regarded as a model base-ball player, especially in his responsible position of short-stop; and until he injured his leg he had no equal in the position," wrote Chadwick in the *New York Clipper*. "He is a jolly, good-natured youth full of life and spirit, up to all the dodges of the game, and especially is he noted for his sure catching of high balls in the infield, and for his swift and accurate throwing. At the bat, too, he excels; while as a bowler, fielder, and batsman, in cricket, he ranks with the best of American cricketers."[13]

He was a wizard at strategy. Recognizing the value of the double play as a defensive weapon, George devised new tactics in which he and the second baseman would share coverage of the bag depending on where the ball was hit and how many men were on base. He also reputedly invented the trap play at this time as well. George would often allow a popup to fall to the ground with runners on base, then pick up the ball and force the runners at their subsequent bases for double and triple plays. The infield fly rule, which ended this practice, would not become part of baseball law for another two decades.

On September 14, 1872, he displayed a variation on the trap play, stunning the Philadelphia Athletics by catching a fly ball in his hat. George knew that the batter, Fergy Malone, was not out, since hat catches were illegal, but Athletic baserunners Al Reach and Cap Anson froze in confusion and were easily retired on force plays. The Athletics complained so loudly about the unusual tactic that the umpire decided to ignore the play, sending Reach and Anson back to their bases and allowing Malone to bat again. George had the rulebook on his side, but the arbiter was more concerned about the unhappy Philadelphia fans than in strict interpretation of the rules and regulations. The Boston club let the matter slide. "If there was one thing we were careful about," said George, "it was in protesting decisions made by the umpires. My brother Harry always would insist that we say nothing. Let the other fellows kick was our rule. I have always found that a successful team does the same thing."[14]

Healthy again in 1872, George hit .337 and retained his title as "King of Shortstops" as Boston swept to the pennant. With Al Spalding on the mound, George Wright at short, and stars such as three-time batting champion Ross Barnes in the field, the club dominated the Association almost as thoroughly as the Cincinnati nine had conquered its rivals several years before. "Break up the Bostons!" was a common refrain around the league, but the Wright brothers paid it no heed. George batted .388 in 1873, led the league in triples in 1874, and cleared the .300 mark each year as the Red Stockings followed their 1872 pennant with three more championships in a row. The 1875 team, one of the greatest in baseball history, went 71–8 and won all 37 of its home games, finishing 18 and a half games ahead of its nearest rival and making a mockery of the pennant race.

The 1874 season was notable for an unprecedented in-season trip to England by the Boston and Philadelphia clubs. Harry Wright had long dreamed of introducing baseball to his native country, so he and Spalding arranged for the Red Stockings and Athletics to play both baseball and cricket during a three-week excursion to the British Isles in July and August of that year. The tour was a financial failure, as the British showed little interest in baseball, but the cricket matches garnered attention. Few of the ballplayers had ever played in, or even seen, a cricket match, so Harry and George gave their fellow tourists a crash course in the nuances of the game. They preached the virtues of defensive batting and "proper form," though Al Spalding, Cap Anson and others simply advanced to the bat and walloped the ball as far as they could, much to the amusement of their hosts. Still, the Americans, with Harry handling the bowling chores, managed to defeat a leading British cricket team by a 107–105 score.

George, an ambitious sort, recognized that the growth of baseball represented a keen business opportunity, so in 1871 he began a sporting goods business, one which occupied much of his time and energy during the next several years. Though Harry awarded his brother a contract to make uniforms for the Boston club, George's company was slow to turn a profit. However, the fledgling business received a boost in 1875, when a Harvard University player named Fred Thayer invented the first catcher's mask. George bought the patent for the protective device from Thayer and began manufacturing it, along with other baseball equipment. One item that proved unsuccessful was a creation of George's, a flat-sided bat used for bunting, which he promoted, then dropped after a few years.

George moved permanently to Boston during the 1870s, married Abbaria (Abbie) Coleman, and produced two sons and two daughters. He spent his spare time at the Longwood Cricket Club in Brookline, a well-to-do suburb of the city, where he continued his cricket career as perhaps the premier bowler and batsman in the sport. Though cricket never became a popular pastime in the United States, George continued to play it at the highest level long after the conclusion of his baseball career.

After a ten-year reign as the "King of Shortstops," George Wright began to decline as a player. His batting average fell to .299 in 1876, Boston's first season in the new National League, as the Red Stockings fell all the way to fourth place. They were supplanted by the upstart Chicago White Stockings, which had built its championship team by signing pitcher Al Spalding, second baseman Ross Barnes, catcher Cal McVey, and infielder Jim (Deacon) White away from Boston. However, White returned to the Hub for the 1877 campaign, and the Red Stockings recovered, capturing the next two National League flags despite George Wright's steadily decreasing performance at bat.

George hit only .276 in 1877 and .225 in 1878, and some attributed his slide to the introduction of the curve ball. Only a few pitchers, such as William (Candy) Cummings and Bobby Mathews, had thrown the pitch earlier in the decade, but by 1876 more hurlers had mastered the tricky delivery. George never learned to hit the curve effectively, and some say that the pitch drove him away from the plate in fear of being hit in the head. He was still a fine fielder, leading the league in assists and double plays in 1876 (though Harry moved him to second base in 1877 to make room for Ezra Sutton at short), but George began to look for new challenges as he passed his 30th birthday.

He discovered such a challenge in a city only a short distance from Boston. The Providence Grays had joined the league in 1878, finishing a strong third under Tom York, but the team owners offered the manager's job to George Wright for the following year. George accepted the post, inserted himself into the lineup at shortstop, and stunned the league by winning the pennant by five games over brother Harry's Boston club. However, he wished to return to Boston and tend to his growing sporting goods business, which had been renamed Wright and Ditson with the addition of partner Henry Ditson. He gave up the field leader's post after the season, and remains, to this day, the only major league manager to win a pennant in his first, and only, season at the helm.

George acquired another, albeit unwanted, distinction when he became the first player in baseball history to fall victim to the reserve clause. The

1—George Wright 13

George's last major league team, the 1882 Providence Grays. Manager Harry Wright sits in the middle of the photo, with George seated next to him with arms crossed. (Author's collection)

National League magnates had instituted this piece of contract language, which allowed each team to "reserve" the services of five players on its roster for the following season, after the 1879 campaign. Providence had offered George a contract for 1880 that included a sizable pay cut, though he had led the team to the pennant the year before, and the shortstop wanted out. However, the Grays put George on its reserve list, rejecting all trade offers from other teams. Though the Worcester team offered Providence $1,000 merely to negotiate with George, the Grays would not give up his rights, and were unable, or unwilling, to work out a deal with the Boston club. George refused to report to the Grays that spring, so Providence began the 1880 season without him.

The Wright brothers, believing the reserve rule unfair, challenged it on May 29. Harry wanted his brother in the lineup that afternoon when the Red Stockings played league-leading Chicago, so he wired the Providence team president to request George's release for one game. The Grays assented, and George appeared in uniform that day for Boston at his customary shortstop position. Chicago manager Cap Anson protested Wright's participation, but George scored two runs and led Boston to an 11–10 victory, breaking Chicago's 13-game winning streak. "George hit the ball about Wright yesterday," said the *Boston Globe*.

League president William Hulbert, who was also the owner of the White Stockings, acted quickly. He ordered George out of uniform, lest other teams copy the practice and loan out stars to their rivals, thereby throwing pennant races into chaos. Hulbert allowed Boston's disputed victory to stand, but refused to permit George to play for any team other than Providence. The reserve rule had withstood the first of many challenges, and George Wright spent the remainder of the 1880 campaign on the sidelines.

As Providence declined to reserve George for 1881, he was free to return to Boston, though he played only seven games due to an increased amount of time spent in business pursuits. The following year, Harry left the employ of the Boston club after 11 seasons and signed to lead George's former club, the Providence Grays. George, now 35, accompanied his brother to Rhode Island, but batted only .162. His speed was gone, as he managed to hit only one double and two triples all season long. Harry, who led the Grays to a second-place finish, chose to remain in Providence for one more campaign, but George announced his retirement from the game at season's end.

George might have sensed that his career was coming to a close on August 17, when the Grays and the Detroit Wolverines played the longest scoreless game in baseball history up to that time. The teams failed to score in 18 frames before Providence outfielder Charley Radbourn slugged a game-ending homer in the 19th for a 1–0 victory. Three innings earlier, George made a bid to win the contest when he belted a drive over center fielder George Wood's head. The ball rolled through an open outfield gate and into the street beyond as the aging Wright chugged around the bases. Wood dashed into the street, retrieved the ball, ran back into the field of play, and relayed the ball back to the infield. The throw to the plate beat the sliding George, and catcher Charlie Bennett tagged him out to keep the contest a scoreless tie.

Following his retirement, George focused on his family and his sporting goods company, though he made one more foray into baseball. In 1884, a St. Louis millionaire named Henry V. Lucas decided to form a new major league, which he called the Union Association. Lucas awarded a Boston franchise to George, who hired former player Tim Murnane as manager and then set to work signing players for the new team. Wright and Ditson won the contract to produce balls, uniforms, and equipment for the league, and George looked forward to a boost in business as a result. Unfortunately, the league collapsed after only one season, and George Wright's brief career as a baseball team owner was over.

His Boston teammate, Al Spalding, had followed George's lead and founded a sporting goods company of his own in 1876, and by the mid-1880s A. G. Spalding and Company had achieved a near-monopoly of the baseball equipment market. George realized that he needed to diversify his merchandise to survive in the business, so he investigated the possibility of offering equipment for sports other than baseball. One day, he picked up a British sports catalog and saw a set of clubs for the game of golf, with which George was totally unfamiliar. He ordered some, but as he had no idea of how the game was played, the equipment languished on a store shelf for several months.

One day, a Scotsman spotted the clubs and offered to buy them, if a suitable course on which to play could be found. There were no golfing facilities in New England at the time, though George expressed keen interest when the visitor sketched a layout of a golf course on a pad of paper and promised to send a book on the game and its rules. This arrived a few weeks later, and George set out to familiarize himself with the game.

Though the retired baseball player was still an active cricketer, retaining his position as perhaps the finest bowler and batsman in the nation, George became enthralled by golf. He and a group of friends attempted to construct some holes and play the new game in Boston's Franklin Park one day, but a policeman stopped them, insisting that they obtain permission before doing so. George procured a permit from the Boston Parks Commission, after some initial resistance, and on December 10, 1890, he and three friends created nine short holes with tomato cans set into the ground to serve as cups. They had created the first golf course in New England, and George posted the best score of the foursome that day, shooting a 59 over nine holes.

The *Boston Herald* was unimpressed, noting, "The royal game of golf was played on local grounds yesterday, for the first time in the history of the city," but "spectators were conspicuous by their absence."[15] However, the sport's popularity grew almost as quickly as baseball's had three decades earlier. Within a few short years, golf courses sprang up all over the eastern part of the country, and George Wright received a great deal of credit for the sport's introduction. Some have dubbed him the "father of American golf," while George told a United Press reporter in 1926 that he was "the man responsible for the general introduction of the Scotch game into this country."[16] This may be an exaggeration, but George did play a major role in its development in New England.

More importantly, golf gave a much-needed boost to Wright and Ditson, which became the leading provider of golfing equipment in America during the 1890s. Though the Spalding monopoly gained control of George's company after Henry Ditson's death in 1889, the firm retained a measure of independence and continued to prosper. At first Wright and Ditson sold only imported equipment, but a few years later Spalding decided to manufacture golf balls and clubs, which George then sold under the Wright and Ditson label. It was an arrangement that proved beneficial, and profitable, for both companies.

Another opportunity came in 1894, when Wright and Ditson branched out into winter sports. Ice polo, played with rounded mallets and a rubber ball, had become popular on New England college campuses, while Canadians extolled the virtues of ice hockey, with bladed sticks and a flat puck. In December 1894, George assembled an ice polo team, made up of students from Harvard, Brown, and Yale, to travel to Canada and play both sports. After watching a few contests, George recognized that hockey was the superior game, so he set his company to work promoting the Canadian sport and manufacturing its equipment. By the dawn of the 20th century, hockey had supplanted ice polo in popularity, with George Wright providing a major impetus to its growth in the United States.

George's cricket career finally ended in 1900, when the Longwood club disbanded its team, but soon afterward he helped introduce another popular sport to the American public. His sons Beals and Irving had become enthusiastic tennis players, and Beals, a fine athlete like his father, won gold medals in singles and doubles at the 1904 St. Louis Olympic Games. He followed up that victory with three consecutive United States championships in doubles, in addition to the national singles title in 1905. George, sensing another boom on the horizon, promptly made Wright and Ditson the leading American manufacturer of tennis rackets, balls, nets, and other related equipment. His products, especially George Wright signature rackets, spread tennis to all corners of the nation.

Harry Wright had passed away in 1895 at age 60, but George outlived his brother by more than three decades. Prosperous in business and respected as New England's premier sportsman, George played golf, gave interviews to sportswriters, and continued to follow the sport that made him famous. "Baseball is on a higher moral plane than it has ever been before," he said in 1915. "This can be attributed to the umpires. So long as they are given full charge of the field the game will remain clean. Baseball has no limits and I expect to see interest in it steadily increase with the years to come."[17] In 1905, at the request of his old Boston teammate and later business associate, Al Spalding, George agreed to serve on the Mills Commission, which investigated the origins of baseball and ultimately identified Cooperstown, New York as the birthplace of the national game. Mistaken though it was, this finding later resulted in the establishment of the Hall of Fame in that small upstate New York town.

George was widowed in 1913, but remained healthy and active long past his 80th year. He spent his winters in South Carolina and summers in Boston, where he played golf and remained in control of his sporting goods company well into the 1930s. In 1935, George became the oldest living major league player, and in 1937 the American and National Leagues honored him with their Number One gold lifetime pass, which he held until he died on August 21 of that year at the age of 90. Three months later, a special committee named George Wright and four others to the Hall of Fame.

The text on George Wright's Hall of Fame plaque is one of the most succinct of any in the gallery at Cooperstown. The plaque reads:

GEORGE WRIGHT
STAR OF BASEBALL'S FIRST
PROFESSIONAL TEAM, THE
CINCINNATI RED STOCKINGS OF 1869.

1—George Wright

GREAT SHORTSTOP AND CAPTAIN OF CHAMPION BOSTONS IN NATIONAL LEAGUE'S PIONEER YEARS.

Despite the abbreviated nature of the text, George made major contributions, not only to baseball, but to American sports in general. He was baseball's first great star, defining the shortstop position for all who succeeded him, and set new standards for performance at the bat. The key performer on the legendary 1869 Cincinnati team, he played for seven major league pennant winners, and led one as a manager. George Wright was also the nation's premier cricket player, as well as a golfer of distinction who created the first nine-hole course in New England and played a major role in introducing the game to the American public. He founded a sporting goods company, Wright and Ditson, which pioneered the manufacture and sale of golf, tennis, and hockey equipment, making those sports available to the masses. Few, if any, Hall of Famers have built a lifetime record of accomplishment to compare to that of George Wright, one of the greatest ballplayers, and all-around sportsmen, in American history.

2

Jimmy Collins

> "With a swoop like that of a chicken hawk, Collins would gather up the bunt and throw it accurately to whoever should receive it. The beauty about him was that he could throw from any angle, any position on the ground or in the air."
> —*1902 Spalding's Official Base Ball Guide*

The National Baseball Hall of Fame and Museum opened its doors to the public for the first time on June 12, 1939. During the previous three years, the Baseball Writers Association of America had selected 12 players as recipients of baseball's highest honor, while two committees added 13 more names to the list. The twenty-five men so named (11 living, 14 deceased) were distributed fairly evenly among the different defensive positions on the field. There were six pitchers, two first basemen, two second basemen, two shortstops, one catcher, and four outfielders. The remaining inductees included league presidents, early managers, and other pioneers of the game.

There was one position, however, that did not have an honoree in the Cooperstown shrine. Neither the baseball writers nor the two special committees had selected a third baseman. John McGraw, elected to the Hall in December 1937 by the Centennial Commission, played third base during the 1890s, but was chosen for his accomplishments during his 30-year tenure as manager of the New York Giants. None of the 25 men honored that day were selected as a third baseman, and the Hall came into existence without one.

Jimmy Collins, an Irishman from Buffalo, New York, was widely considered to be the greatest third sacker in baseball history up to that point. A solid hitter and brilliant fielder, particularly in handling bunts, Collins compiled a .294 lifetime batting average in a career that lasted from 1895 to 1908. Such luminaries as Babe Ruth, Connie Mack, Ty Cobb, and others had proclaimed Collins to be the greatest third baseman of all time. Still, Collins received only 58 of the 226 votes in the first election by the baseball writers in 1936 and, inexplicably, saw his total fall each year after that. In the 1939 balloting, Collins finished in 18th place.

Collins, who at the time was 69 years old and living in retirement in Buffalo, was disappointed by the scant support, but expressed hope of eventually gaining election to the Hall. The museum decided in 1939 to hold ballots every three years instead of annually, and during that interval several prominent sportswriters decried the absence of third basemen in the Hall and pushed for Jimmy's election. However, Collins gained only 68 of 233 votes in the 1942 balloting, finishing in 14th place. Rogers Hornsby, with 182 votes, was the only new electee.

The old ballplayer then looked hopefully to the next election three years hence, but did not live to see his plaque in Cooperstown. He died on March 6, 1943, and his death vaulted his name back into the headlines, giving a boost to his candidacy for the Hall. His vote total rose to 121 in 1945, good enough for eighth place in the balloting but still well shy of election; however, the Hall's Permanent Committee came to the rescue. On April 25, 1945, the panel elected Jimmy Collins and nine other 19th century stars to the Hall of Fame.

Jimmy Collins with the Beaneaters in 1899. (National Baseball Hall of Fame Library, Cooperstown, N.Y.)

James Joseph Collins was born in Niagara Falls, New York on January 16, 1870, the second son of Anthony Collins, an Irish immigrant who worked as a railroad policeman, and the former Alice O'Hara. Anthony moved the family a few miles south to Buffalo in 1872, and there Jimmy attended school and played ball with his brothers and the sons of other transplanted Irish.

Baseball was a significant part of life in Buffalo during Jimmy's teenage years. His hometown hosted a National League team, the Bisons, from 1879 to 1885. After some initial success, that ballclub folded after a seventh-place finish in 1885, but the team soon resurfaced in the International League. The city maintained a presence in the high minors for nearly a century afterward. Buffalo's most prominent citizen, Grover Cleveland, was on a first-name basis with the Bison players during his tenures as Erie County sheriff and mayor of Buffalo. Cleveland's election as President of the United States in 1884 put an enthusiastic baseball fan in the White House for the first time.

More importantly for Jimmy Collins, Buffalo was a hotbed of semipro and amateur baseball during the young man's formative years. Jimmy played while attending St. Joseph's Institute in Buffalo as a business student. A right-handed batter and thrower, he earned a reputation on the sandlots for his hard hitting and fielding ability at third base and shortstop. He soon became one of the most sought-after sandlot players in Buffalo, though for several years he resisted all professional offers. Instead, he graduated from St. Joseph's and took a job with the Lackawanna Railroad. In 1893, his play came to the attention of the manager of the Buffalo Bisons of the Eastern League, Jack Chapman, who offered the young man a contract. Jimmy hesitated, but agreed only after his supervisor at the railroad promised to rehire him if he failed as a ballplayer. Thus reassured, Jimmy signed to play for his hometown team.

The Bisons had finished well below the .500 mark in 1892, and Chapman put Collins at shortstop and hoped that the popular local boy would energize his team. It did not happen immediately, as Jimmy struggled in the field. He batted .286, but played erratically at short, compiling a fielding percentage of .854. By mid-season Chapman moved Collins to the outfield. Still, the Bisons improved by eight games in the standings and finished the season in fourth position, only five and a half games out of first place. In 1894, Collins spent the entire season in the outfield and produced a .352 batting average, leading the league with 198 hits and 34 outfield assists. The Bisons dropped a notch to fifth place, but Jimmy Collins established himself as a solid major league prospect.

Providence manager Billy Murray was impressed with Collins and recommended him to Frank Selee, manager of the Boston Beaneaters of the National League. Selee was intent upon rebuilding his Beaneaters, who had won three consecutive pennants from 1891 to 1893 but fell apart in 1894. Selee trusted Murray's judgment, and in November of 1894 the Boston club bought Collins' contract from Buffalo for $500. He began his career in Boston as a right fielder, sharing the outer garden with future Hall of Famers (and fellow Irishmen) Hugh Duffy in left field and Tommy McCarthy in center.

The 25-year-old rookie, who stood five feet and eight inches tall and weighed 160 pounds, got off to a rough start with the Beaneaters. He hit poorly, struggling to keep his average above the .200 mark, and his erratic play in the field earned boos from the frustrated Boston fans. Selee decided that his young prospect needed to mature in a less stressful environment, so on May 17 of that year Selee loaned Collins to the Louisville Colonels, one of the National League's second-division teams. The transaction was recorded as a sale, with Boston receiving $500 for Collins' release, but the agreement stipulated that the Beaneaters could reacquire Jimmy later in the season for the same amount.

Collins began his stint with Louisville in the outfield, but on May 31, 1895, third baseman Walter Preston made four errors while fielding bunts in a 16–6 loss to the Baltimore Orioles. Louisville was mired in a 15-game losing streak at the time, and manager John McCloskey was desperate. Knowing that his new acquisition had begun his professional career as a shortstop,

McCloskey prevailed upon Jimmy Collins to fill in at third on a temporary basis. Collins later recalled that Louisville first baseman Dan Brouthers, a former Oriole who had seen Collins play the year before in the Eastern League, suggested the rookie as a likely candidate for the third base job.

The Baltimore players, especially master bunters Willie Keeler and John McGraw, fairly salivated at the prospect of driving another Louisville infielder to the bench, but Jimmy Collins refused to be intimidated. Some say that Hugh Jennings, the Baltimore shortstop, patted Jimmy on the back and promised that the Orioles would bunt no more that day. "That's all right, Hughie," replied Collins. "Bunt 'em down to me and I'll show you something!"[1]

Collins had waited for a chance to return to the infield, and had already hatched a plan to defeat the Oriole bunting attack. "I came to the conclusion there was only one solution to this bunting game," said Collins many years later. "A third baseman had to give himself a chance to get those fast guys. Once around the circuit, you knew who would bunt and who wouldn't. You knew McGraw and Keeler were bunters. So I played them on the edge of the grass."[2] Most third sackers played much deeper, closer to the outfield, but Collins was eager to demonstrate a new approach to playing the position.

McGraw was the first Baltimore batter after Collins' shift to third, and dropped a bunt down the base line. Collins amazed the Orioles when he charged in, scooped up the ball with his bare right hand, and gunned a powerful underhanded throw to first. McGraw was surprised to see the throw beat him to the bag by several feet. Willie Keeler, a faster runner, tried the same thing, but Collins repeated the maneuver, retiring Keeler by a step. Recalled an older Collins, "I had to throw out four bunters in a row before the Orioles quit bunting that afternoon." Louisville lost the game, but Jimmy Collins was the star of the contest. On that afternoon in Baltimore, Collins unveiled a revolutionary new way to play third base.

Collins also hit well for Louisville, compiling a .279 average, but his fielding caught the attention of every other team in the league. After a game in Boston, in which Collins threw out 11 bunters without an error, the Beaneaters decided to bring him back. Louisville offered to pay a sizeable amount to keep him, but Frank Selee was adamant. He traded his veteran third sacker, Billy Nash, to the Phillies and installed Jimmy Collins as the new Boston third baseman for the 1896 season. Tim Murnane, the former player and *Boston Globe* sportswriter, knew a future star when he saw one. "Just one word of warning might not be amiss," wrote Murnane to the Boston ownership that November. "Never lose your hold on young Collins."[3]

Collins was a man who knew his true value, and he held out for a larger salary before reporting to the Beaneaters that spring. The three Boston owners, known as the Triumvirs, were notoriously tight-fisted when it came to player salaries, but Collins threatened to go home to Buffalo if his price of $2,000 per year was not met. Jimmy held an advantage in the negotiations, since the Triumvirs had already traded Billy Nash and had no other third baseman ready to take over. Besides, though Jimmy had played only one season in the National League, many observers agreed with one Beaneater who called Collins "the best in the business" at third for his magnificent fielding prowess. On April 1 the two sides agreed on a contract for $1,800, and Jimmy reported for work.

Bunting was all the rage in the National League at the time, and frustrated managers had searched for a way to neutralize the practice. Pitchers had taken responsibility for fielding bunts in past years, but the pitching distance was lengthened to its present dimension of 60 feet and six inches before the 1893 season. This new infield configuration provided more room for an talented bunter to ply his trade, and small, fast hitters such as Baltimore's Willie Keeler and Cleveland's Jesse Burkett pushed their batting averages well over the .400 mark by taking advantage of the bunt.

Third basemen played even with or behind the bag at the time, mostly because they feared sharp line drives. Jimmy Collins, however, had exceptionally quick reflexes, and could stand much closer to the plate and still stop a hard liner. Playing in such a fashion may have reduced his range, but the Boston shortstop, Herman Long, was able to cover large amounts of ground and could go to his right and snare balls that eluded Collins. The team of Collins and Long sealed off the right side of the diamond, giving the Beaneaters the best defensive infield in the National League.

However, the Beaneaters almost lost their new star during the seventh game of the 1896 campaign. In a game at Baltimore on April 23, Collins slid awkwardly into second base while trying to avoid a collision, and caught his toe on the bag. The force of his slide twisted his ankle severely, and he was carried off the field and taken to a nearby hospital. The ankle was not broken, but the injury kept him out of the Boston lineup for more than six weeks. Boston finished in fourth place that season, partly because Joe Harrington, Jimmy's replacement at third, batted only .197 and was overmatched in the field. Collins returned in June and compiled a credible .296 average in his first full season for Boston.

Jimmy was healthy again as the 1897 season dawned, and the Beaneaters were finally ready to regain the National League title that they had won with regularity early in the decade. With defensive wizard Fred Tenney taking over the first base spot, Boston presented one of the greatest infields in history with Collins at third, Herman Long at short, and Bobby Lowe at second. New right fielder Chick Stahl batted .354, while Collins came into his own as a hitter with a .346 average and 132 runs batted in. The Boston club batted .319 as a team and defeated the defending champion Orioles in a close race for the pennant. The 1898 team was even better, as the Beaneaters won 102 games (becoming the first major league team to win 100) and rolled to another championship. Jimmy Collins, now a certifiable hitting star, led the league with 15 homers and 284 total bases while batting .328.

Other third basemen did their best to emulate the Boston star, but Jimmy Collins ruled as master of third base play for the next several seasons. Few could match his quick reflexes, strong throwing arm, and intuitive prowess. Cleveland's Bobby Wallace, a former pitcher, moved to the infield in 1897 and established himself as the second-best third sacker in the game, but he and Collins stood head and shoulders above their contemporaries, with Collins firmly in the lead. By 1898, Collins' third full season in Boston, many observers were already proclaiming him the greatest third baseman of all time.

Jimmy was also the most popular player in the lineup. Boston fans, many of them sons of immigrants like Collins himself, loudly cheered the exploits of stars with Irish names such as Collins, Duffy, and McCarthy. Jimmy was a personable and handsome bachelor, friendly with the fans and the best in the game at his position, and enjoyed the loyalty and adulation of his fellow Irishmen. Perhaps only John L. Sullivan, a Bostonian who was then the heavyweight boxing champion of the world and a frequent visitor at Beaneater games, stood higher in the esteem of local sports fans than did Jimmy Collins.

The Boston dynasty, having won five pennants from 1891 to 1898, began to crumble in 1899. Injuries to center fielder Billy Hamilton and starting pitcher Kid Nichols, combined with a general aging of the roster, doomed the Beaneaters to a distant second place finish that season, though Collins set a record for fielding chances at third (601) that stands to this day. The team fell to fourth in 1900, as money troubles and player discontent with the frugal Boston management reached a boiling point. When the new American League opened for business that year, many players looked to the new circuit for better pay and working conditions. After functioning as a minor league for one year, the American League decided to compete with the senior circuit on an equal basis in 1901 and began raiding National League rosters for players.

One of the most sought-after men in baseball was the best third baseman in the game, Jimmy Collins. Now 31 years old, Jimmy had often expressed his frustration with the Triumvirs and the National League's $2,400 salary limit. He was open to new opportunities, and Connie Mack, one of the new league's main recruiters, discussed the matter with Jimmy in February of 1901. The American League operated a team in Buffalo, and perhaps Jimmy would have been interested in a managing position there. However, the new league moved the Buffalo franchise to Boston to do battle with the established Beaneaters of the National League. If Jimmy could be induced to throw in his lot with the new circuit, the American League might prove a success.

Charles Somers, the main financier of the emerging league and backer of the new Boston entry, offered Jimmy a position as manager and third baseman. Jimmy quickly accepted, signing a contract that called for a reported salary of $3,500 and 10 percent of all team profits above $25,000. Collins told the local papers that the Triumvirs "have always treated me nicely and paid every cent that their obligations called for, but I saw a chance to better myself and took it and I can name 50 others that will do the same thing."[4]

Collins' departure was a mortal wound to the National League in general and the Beaneaters in particular, as Jimmy was the most popular ballplayer in Boston. His presence alone conferred legitimacy on the new ballclub, which was variously called the Invaders, Somersets (after Somers) and Americans in its early years.[5] Most importantly, he brought the Irish fans of Boston with him to the new league. The American League dominance of the Boston baseball scene began on the day of Collins' signing and continued until 1953, when the National League team capitulated and moved to Milwaukee.

Somers and Collins selected a uniform style (blue letters and stockings, to contrast with the red worn by the Beaneaters) and went to work securing players during the early months of 1901. They scored their biggest coup by signing Cy Young, the best starting pitcher in the game, for $3,000 a year. Collins further damaged the Beaneaters when he convinced his former teammates Buck Freeman, Ted Lewis, and Chick Stahl to follow him to the new league. Jimmy managed the new Boston Americans to second place in 1901, behind Charles Comiskey's Chicago White Sox, as Young posted a 31–12 record and Collins led the attack with a .332 average and 108 runs scored. Collins also earned $18,000, an unheard-of salary in those days, from his profit-sharing arrangement with the team. The Boston Americans outdrew the fading Beaneaters at the box office by a wide margin.

Pitcher Ted Lewis quit the team after the 1901 season to attend divinity school, but Collins corralled another Beaneater hurler, right-hander Bill Dineen, to take his place. With a solid rotation of Young, Dineen, and right-hander George Winter, the pitching appeared solid, but depth became a problem as the 1902 team dropped a notch to third. Oddly enough, Collins' team was handicapped by the generosity of its own management. Philadelphia Athletics manager Connie Mack had signed several stars away from the Phillies of the National League, but lost them when the Phillies went to court to void the contracts. Mack was desperately short of pitchers, and Boston team president Charles Somers gave three second-line Boston hurlers (Bert Husting, Fred Mitchell, and Howard Wilson) to the Athletics. Mitchell and Wilson provided Mack with much-needed depth, while Husting won 14 games and helped Eddie Plank and Rube Waddell pitch the Athletics to the pennant.

Jimmy, who could have used Husting and the others in Boston, recognized that his team needed more pitching to support his starters. He failed in a bid to sign Vic Willis, the curveball artist who was the sole remaining good pitcher on the Boston National League team. Shortly afterward, the two leagues declared a truce and the cross-league raiding came to an end. Jimmy was stuck with his current roster, and with George Winter, the third starter, ill for most of the 1903 season, Collins planned to count on Tom Hughes, a right-hander recently acquired from Baltimore, and Norwood Gibson, a rookie from Notre Dame.

The 1903 campaign began as the tightest race yet seen in the new league. The Boston Americans (other nicknames, such as Puritans, had fallen by the wayside) stood in fifth place at 15–15 on May 26, but were only two and half games behind the league leading White Sox. The last-place Washington Senators were only seven games back, and the summer promised a wild race with every team in contention. However, an 11-game winning streak vaulted Boston into first. Another 9–1 run at the end of June opened up a 3-game lead over the Athletics, and by Labor Day the race was over. Collins' men held an 11-game lead by then, and another 11–1 streak pushed their lead to 15 games. The team clinched Boston's first American League pennant on September 17 with a 14–3 win over Cleveland.

Jimmy's decision to put more work on Tom Hughes' shoulders paid off, as "Long Tom" won 20 games for the

Collins as manager of the Boston Americans. (National Baseball Hall of Fame Library, Cooperstown, N.Y.)

first time in his career. Bill Dineen went 21–13, Norwood Gibson 13–9, and Cy Young led the league in wins with a 28–9 record. Jimmy batted a solid .296, while right fielder Buck Freeman led in homers and runs batted in. Catching injuries were a problem all year, with Duke Farrell playing in only 17 games and Lou Criger batting .192, but rookie Jake Stahl, no relation to Chick, provided solid support.

Both the Boston Americans and the Pittsburgh Pirates of the National League ran away with their respective pennants, and in early September representatives of the two clubs signed an agreement to play the first championship series between the leagues. It was called the World Series, a best-of-nine contest for the championship of the world, and captured the imaginations of fans across the nation. Jimmy Collins liked the idea of a World Series. "I should not be surprised to see post season games each fall," said the Boston manager, "as long as there are two big leagues.... They give the public a high article of base ball and enable the championship teams to pick up a bit of prize money for the cold winter."[6] Collins, a player himself, recognized that his men looked forward to extra pay as well as the chance to defeat the rival league. The Boston player contracts expired on September 30, so the team management needed to make satisfactory arrangements with its players if the championship series were to become a reality.

Those details were more problematic than anyone could have imagined, and the first World Series almost never took place. Pittsburgh owner Barney Dreyfuss promised his team's entire share of the gate receipts to his players, but Boston team president Henry Killilea offered only 50 percent to Collins' men. They "yelled murder," said Collins later, "and it was useless to argue with them." The players demanded at least 75 percent, but the two sides eventually agreed to a 60–40 split of the proceeds. The grumbling among the Boston players continued, however, and the bad feelings engendered by the controversy lingered through the Series and beyond.[7]

The first three games took place at the Huntington Avenue Grounds in Boston. On October 1, Collins sent Cy Young out to face the Pirates in the first game of the modern World Series in front of a standing-room only crowd of 16,242 fans. The Pirates silenced the crowd with four runs in the first inning and cruised to a 7–3 win behind their star pitcher, Deacon Phillippe, assisted by four Boston errors. "That's only one game," said Collins to the papers. "We've rid ourselves of a lot of bad baseball, and Cy won't give us another game like that one again."[8] Bill Dineen evened the Series with a three-hit shutout the next day (before a smaller crowd of 9,415), but the third game turned out to be one of the most raucous in Boston baseball history. The crowd of 18,801 broke through the ropes in the outfield and interfered with the fielders; eventually, the umpires decided that any ball hit into the surging crowd would be called a ground rule double. The Pirates hit five of them and, though Jimmy Collins stroked two hits and scored both Boston runs, the Pirates defeated Hughes 4–2 behind Phillippe.

The two teams traveled to Pittsburgh on Sunday, October 4, and a rainout on Monday gave Pirate starter Deacon Phillippe an extra day of rest.

Phillippe pitched the fourth game on Tuesday and defeated Dineen by a 5–4 score. The Pirates held a 5–1 lead late in the game, but the Americans scored three times in the ninth and almost pulled the game out. This boded well for the Bostonians; though they trailed in the Series three games to one, they did not give up the fight. They whipped the Pirates 11–2 on Wednesday behind Cy Young, then took a 6–3 win on Thursday to even the Series at three games apiece.

The critical seventh game was postponed by the Pirate management on Friday because of cold weather (and, perhaps, to give Phillippe another day of rest) and more than 17,000 packed the Pittsburgh ballpark on Saturday to see Phillippe face Young. It was an error-filled game, with groups of fans standing in the outfield as obstacles to the fielders, but the Americans belted five triples (one by Collins) and scored a 7–3 win.

Another rain delay postponed the eighth game until Tuesday, October 13, and Bill Dineen was ready to end the Series. "I want to get back to Syracuse," said Dineen. "I got a lot of things I want to do. This thing has gone far enough." The Pirates sent Deacon Phillippe to the mound for the fifth time, but three Pittsburgh errors led to two Boston runs in the fourth and another in the sixth. Boston catcher Lou Criger killed one rally when the Pirates had Honus Wagner at second and Tommy Leach at third with one out. Criger bluffed a throw to second, then threw to Jimmy Collins at third to catch Leach off the bag. Dineen ended the game by striking out Wagner as Boston won the game by a 3–0 score, capturing the first World Series.

Boston retained most of its personnel in 1904, but this pennant race was as close as the 1903 race was a runaway. The New York Highlanders emerged as a challenger when right-hander Jack Chesbro started throwing his new creation, the spitball, in earnest. The Highlanders also enjoyed some preferential treatment from the American League itself. The circuit wanted a strong contender in New York, and in mid-season league president Ban Johnson prevailed upon the Boston ownership to send its hard-hitting left fielder, Patsy Daugherty, to New York for utility infielder Bob Unglaub. This move damaged the Boston offense, leaving a hole in the outfield. There is no evidence that manager Jimmy Collins approved of, or even knew about, the trade until after it happened.

Once again, Collins' team was hampered by its own management, but the Americans rode the pitching of Cy Young (who threw a perfect game against the Athletics on May 5) and battled the Highlanders down to the wire. The season ended on October 10, 1904, in one of the most memorable games yet played in the new league, as Bill Dineen faced 41-game winner Jack Chesbro in the first game of a doubleheader. New York needed to win both games to clinch the flag, while Boston would take the pennant with only one victory. The score was tied in the ninth when Chesbro, no doubt exhausted after pitching 464 innings that season, heaved a wild pitch with Boston's Lou Criger on third base. Criger scored the winning run, and the Americans won their second pennant in a row.

Collins and his players were disappointed when the owner of the National League champion New York Giants declared that his club was "content to rest on its laurels" and refused to play a World Series against the Americans. However, Boston's fan club, the Royal Rooters, presented a silver trophy to Jimmy and his men. "The players did it all," said Collins modestly. "I had a great team of ballplayers to manage; they did everything I asked of them."[9] Jimmy Collins stood at the pinnacle of his fame in Boston, but the 1904 pennant represented the last high point of his career. The Americans aged rapidly and slumped badly in 1905, mostly due to a weak offense. Jimmy, at age 35, batted only .276 but led the team in that category as the Americans dropped to fourth place.

Management was once again a problem. General Charles H. Taylor, publisher of the *Boston Globe*, purchased the team in 1904 and installed his son, John I. Taylor, as team president. The younger Taylor shocked Collins in early 1905 when he traded young outfielder George Stone to St. Louis for the 36-year-old Jesse Burkett. It was an awful trade, as Burkett hit poorly and retired at season's end, while Stone led the league in hits in 1905 and won the batting title in 1906. Taylor received so much criticism for the Burkett-Stone trade that he refused to make any more deals for the next two seasons, saddling Jimmy Collins with an old team and leaving open no avenue for improvement.

The 1906 season was even worse, as Boston fell to last in the American League amid criticism of Collins' management, not only in the local newspapers but also in the executive suite. John I. Taylor stopped talking to his manager during the 1905 season, and Jimmy became increasingly frustrated with the situation. Collins was also coping with an ankle injury that kept him out of the lineup that year for all but 37 games. The Americans, aging and injury-riddled, endured a 20-game losing streak in May that buried them in the league basement. The club won only six of its first 35 games as attendance fell and player morale dissolved.

Unable to play the field, Collins began managing from the bench in street clothes, much to the irritation of John I. Taylor. The relationship between the popular manager and the team president deteriorated swiftly, and when Jimmy took an in-season vacation in August, leaving the team in charge of Chick Stahl, Taylor decided that enough was enough. On August 28, 1906, he suspended Collins and named Stahl to succeed him as manager. The season mercifully ended in early October with the Americans in last place, 45 and a half games behind the pennant-winning Chicago White Sox.

Several other American League teams, including the Philadelphia Athletics, offered to take Collins off Taylor's hands, but in December Taylor announced that Collins would return as a player, under Stahl's management, in 1907. Chick Stahl and Jimmy Collins were best friends and roommates on the road, and had played together since 1897, Stahl's rookie season with the Beaneaters. Stahl was a quiet, intense individual who had been, like Collins, a longtime bachelor until his recent marriage to a Boston woman. Stahl did not want the manager's job, but decided to take it to help pull the team out of its rut. Before accepting, Stahl asked for the reinstatement of his friend Collins as a player, a request with which Taylor agreed to comply.

Collins looked forward to the 1907 season, telling the *Boston Globe* that "it has been the pleasure of the management to place 'Chick' Stahl in charge, and they no doubt made an excellent move."[10] However, Stahl appeared to be having difficulty handling the added responsibility. He seemed preoccupied and distant at spring training in West Baden, Indiana, and complained of splitting headaches. He was not acting like his usual self, and on March 25 he surprised everyone when he tendered his resignation to team president Taylor. After some discussion Taylor convinced Stahl to withdraw his resignation and continue as manager, but the new field leader was noticeably unhappy. No one was prepared for what happened a few days later.

On the morning of March 28, Chick Stahl was in his room at West Baden, preparing for practice. He had been suffering from a bone bruise and had obtained a bottle of carbolic acid to rub on the injury. At about 9:50, Stahl stepped into Jimmy Collins' room next door and drank from the bottle of acid. He staggered back into his own room and collapsed on the bed as Collins, walking down the hall, noticed his distress. Collins shouted down the hall for help, and he and infielder Bob Unglaub tried to save their manager and teammate. "I'm sorry, boys," gasped Stahl. "It drove me to it." Those were his last words, and 20 minutes later Chick Stahl, still in his Boston uniform, was dead.

The baseball world recoiled in shock at Stahl's suicide, and no one seemed to understand what Stahl meant by his cryptic last words. Not until years later did the public learn that the recently-married Stahl had been threatened with a paternity suit by a woman he knew before meeting his wife. Stahl killed himself rather than face the ruin of his reputation and perhaps his baseball career as well. He had mentioned suicide several times in the previous few weeks, though no one took the remarks seriously. Stahl was buried in his home town of Fort Wayne, Indiana, three days after his death.

John I. Taylor appointed Cy Young as manager of the Americans, but the veteran pitcher did not want the job and agreed to serve only until a replacement could be found. On April 19, Taylor dropped another surprise on the baseball world. He named George Huff, a college coach from the University of Illinois, as the new field leader. Huff had never played professional ball, and his inexperience doomed his chances for success. He resigned after only eight games and was succeeded by Bob Unglaub.

Jimmy Collins was nearing the end of his career. At age 37, he batted a respectable .291, but his power was nearly gone and he was slowing down in the field. On June 7, 1907 his Boston career came to a halt when Taylor traded the veteran third baseman to the Athletics for infielder Jack Knight. The Boston players gave Collins a farewell dinner at a local hotel, and Jimmy revealed a surprise of his own before leaving town. He announced that he planned to marry Sara Edwina Murphy of Boston in a few weeks. The confirmed bachelor would soon become a family man, with two daughters joining the Collins family over the next few years.

As for John I. Taylor, he made up for his mistakes and left his imprint on Boston baseball after Jimmy Collins left the team. In December of 1907, Taylor decided to drop the blue-and-white uniforms worn by the team since 1901, replacing the color scheme with one that featured bright red letters and stockings. Taylor told the newspapers that his team would henceforth be known as the Red Sox. A few years later, Taylor spearheaded a drive to build a new ballpark for his team. The facility was located in a part of town known as the Fens. "It's in that section of Boston, isn't it?" said Taylor. "Then call it Fenway Park." In 1912, the year Fenway Park opened, Boston won the pennant and defeated the Giants in the World Series.

Jimmy Collins finished the 1907 season with the Athletics, but the team was undergoing a youth movement, and a 22-year-old from Maryland named Frank Baker was primed to take over at third base. Jimmy batted only .217 in for the Athletics in 1908, and on December 11 manager Connie Mack handed Collins his release. Jimmy finished his major league career with a .294 average and 1,999 hits in 1,726 games played. For nearly three decades after Jimmy's retirement, almost every old ballplayer who picked an all-time All-Star team put Collins at third base.

Jimmy hoped to remain in baseball, so he inquired about buying the Buffalo Bisons of the Eastern League. The team was for sale, but the owners demanded too much money, so Jimmy accepted a position as playing manager of the Minneapolis Millers of the American Association. It was a pitcher's league—Minneapolis outfielder Mike O'Neill won the batting title at .296—but the 39-year-old Jimmy batted a solid .273 and led the Millers to a third-place finish and a large attendance increase. Still, he missed the East, and when his old Boston teammate Hugh Duffy left Providence of the Eastern League to manage the Chicago White Sox, Duffy suggested Collins as his replacement. Now 40, Jimmy hit only .224 and managed Providence to a 61–92 season. In 1911, the team was in last place when Jimmy was fired in June, never to play or manage again.

Though Jimmy had lived in an apartment in Boston during the baseball season, he had always spent the offseason months in his hometown of Buffalo. Upon his retirement in 1911, he and his family returned to Buffalo and remained there for the rest of Jimmy's life. Jimmy was well off from his baseball savings, and had invested heavily in real estate. He also served as president of the Buffalo Municipal League, one of the nation's largest amateur baseball programs, for 22 years. He reportedly refused a salary for that position, serving without pay for more than two decades. The Collins family lived well until the early 1930s, when the Depression wiped out most of Jimmy's net worth, but the old ballplayer never complained. He took a job with the Buffalo parks department, working until he was nearly 70 years of age.

He traveled to Boston every now and then to visit old friends and see the Red Sox play at Fenway Park and the Braves (the former Beaneaters) at the South End Grounds. Collins, who once led the National League with 15 homers in a season, expressed shock when he saw Babe Ruth blast two long four-baggers in one game. His friend and former teammate, Jim Delahanty, turned to the surprised Jimmy and said, "I guess it's a little livelier than the one we used, eh, Jimmy?" Collins recalled that he hit only two homers in his first professional season, and "when I saw the first one go over the fence, I was so surprised I nearly fell over second base."[11]

Collins with the Minneapolis Millers, 1910. (Library of Congress)

Baseball had entered a new era, one in which power was more important than speed and defense, but Jimmy Collins was still the universal choice of sportswriters and veteran ballplayers as the greatest third baseman of all time. Ruth named Collins to his all-time All-Star team, though the Babe never actually saw Jimmy play; he relied on the testimony of teammates and writers who still raved about Collins' third base play long after he left the game. Tim Murnane of the *Boston Globe* saw all the greats and put Collins at the head of the list. "Collins was always graceful," said Murnane. "Bill Bradley [of Cleveland] would get twice the applause on the same play Collins made easy." One of Jimmy's contemporaries, Detroit's Bill Coughlin, said simply, "Third base was put into baseball for Collins."[12]

After several Hall of Fame elections passed without anointing Jimmy Collins (nor any other third baseman), the *Buffalo Evening News* began a campaign to put the long-retired local hero in Cooperstown. Though the baseball world had long since passed him by, Jimmy was still enormously popular in his hometown, and schoolchildren learned that the three most famous Buffalonians were two Presidents (Millard Fillmore and Grover Cleveland) and baseball's greatest third baseman.

The movement gained steam during the winter of 1942–43, as such respected sportswriters as Arthur Daley of *The New York Times* and others took up Jimmy's cause. Jimmy appreciated the attention, but was characteristically modest in evaluating his own abilities. When asked to name his personal all-time All-Star team, he left the third base slot blank. "I couldn't choose among [Bill] Coughlin, [John] McGraw, [Lee] Tannehill, [Bill] Bradley, and Wid Conroy," he explained.[13]

The old ballplayer was still in good health as he passed his 70th birthday, but in February of 1943 Collins sustained an injury when he fell on an icy sidewalk near his Buffalo home. He soon developed pneumonia and, after a brief rally, died on March 6, 1943 at the age of 73. Survived by his wife and two daughters, Jimmy was buried at Holy Cross Cemetery in Lackawanna, New York, outside of Buffalo. Two years later, he became the first third baseman elected to the Hall of Fame.

Despite his presence on almost everyone's all-time All-Star team, Jimmy Collins received little attention from the Hall of Fame electors when the balloting began in 1936. He had been retired from the game for 28 years by then, and many of the voters had never seen him play. For many observers, hitting statistics are the key to greatness, and Jimmy Collins posted good, but not great, numbers at the bat. Men such as Ty Cobb, Nap Lajoie, and Honus Wagner boasted lifetime batting averages far above the .300 level, while Jimmy, who played mostly during the dead ball era, posted a .294 mark. Collins retired in 1908 with 1,999 hits, a total that compares unfavorably to Lajoie, Wagner, and others in the 3,000-hit club. Ty Cobb, for example, stroked more than twice as many hits as Jimmy Collins. Jimmy had revolutionized the third base position, but his hitting stats undoubtedly worked against his candidacy for baseball's highest honor.

The Permanent Committee of the Hall of Fame was roundly criticized for many of the 21 selections it made in 1945 and 1946, and some of those old-time players now appear to be less than overwhelmingly qualified for the honor. However, no one, then or now, disputes the election of Jimmy Collins. There may have been greater third basemen, such as Mike Schmidt, George Brett and Eddie Mathews, but Collins was the man who showed all who followed him how to play the position. He was a good hitter, a great fielder, a World Series-winning manager, and a defensive innovator who changed the way the game is played, and he richly deserves his plaque in Cooperstown.

3

Dan Brouthers

"Brouthers really was a great hitter, one of the most powerful batters of all time. Big Dan in his prime, against the present-day pitching and the modern lively ball, would have hit as many home runs as anybody. I don't think I ever saw a longer hitter."
—*John McGraw*[1]

Some of the most prominent players in the Baseball Hall of Fame spent their entire careers with only one team. Though Babe Ruth, Willie Mays, and Hank Aaron all switched uniforms towards the end of their major league days, star performers such as Lou Gehrig and Mickey Mantle remained with their original clubs without ever being sold or traded away. The record for the greatest number of seasons with the same team is 23, shared by Carl Yastrzemski of the Boston Red Sox and Brooks Robinson of the Baltimore Orioles, while Al Kaline, Mel Ott, and Stan Musial, to name a few, enjoyed long careers under a single employer.

The same cannot be said of one of early baseball's greatest sluggers, a well-traveled first baseman named Dan Brouthers. During a 19-year major league tenure that began in 1879 and ended in 1904, Brouthers played for 10 different teams. From 1888 to 1896 he performed in three leagues for seven distinct franchises, all in the space of nine years. He was sold four times, released three times, and traded once during his career, and on three occasions his current team disbanded at season's end. Though a journeyman pitcher named Mike Morgan holds the all-time revolving team record, having appeared with 12 of them in a career that ended in 2005, no man in the Hall of Fame donned more major league uniforms than Dan Brouthers.

Though he bounced from team to team, Brouthers was one of the game's most valuable performers during the late 1800s. A power hitter at a time when home runs were rare, he hit the ball harder and farther than any of his contemporaries while winning five batting championships and playing for four pennant winners. He compiled a lifetime batting average of .342, the ninth-highest mark in history, and regularly led his league in slugging percentage and extra-base hits. One of the most popular players of his time, Dan Brouthers was posthumously elected to the Hall of Fame on April 25, 1945.

Brouthers in a Buffalo uniform, early 1880s. (National Baseball Hall of Fame Library, Cooperstown, N.Y.)

3—Dan Brouthers

The third of five children, he was born Dennis Joseph Brouthers on May 8, 1858 in Sylvan Lake, New York, a hamlet of fewer than 100 people in the Hudson River valley. His parents, Michael and Annie, left Ireland during the early 1850s and settled in Dutchess County, where Michael went to work as a printer. Before long, Dennis and his family moved to Fishkill, a larger town a short distance away, and then a few miles north to Wappingers Falls, a village of about 3,000 people just south of Poughkeepsie. Members of the family, who appeared on the federal census as Bruder or Bruther, pronounced their surname "Broo-thers."

Wappingers Falls took its name from the spot where Wappingers Creek emptied into the Hudson River. During the mid-19th century, dozens of textile mills and other factories sprang up in Dutchess County along the Hudson, eager to utilize the power generated by the falls. Incorporated in 1871, the town grew quickly, providing work for many immigrant families, including the Brouthers clan. As the population increased, baseball became a popular pastime, and amateur teams with names like the Monitors and the Actives played each other as well as nines from nearby villages. Dennis, a big boy for his age, was one of the most enthusiastic ballplayers in town. He spent his teenage years in Wappingers Falls, playing ball and attending school until the age of 16.

The future major leaguer was known to all as Dan, and it did not take him long to become "Big Dan." He matured so quickly that he looked ungainly on the baseball field, though he was unwilling to let this lack of grace inhibit his love for the game. The muscular Dan grew to six feet and two inches tall, weighing well over 200 pounds, and was the largest man in practically every game he played. He learned to control the movements of his large body, and by the mid-1870s had earned a place as a pitcher for the Actives, the main town team in Wappingers Falls.

Dan, who batted and threw left-handed, played amateur and semipro ball in and around Dutchess County for several years, but his career nearly came to a premature end one day in 1877. While playing for the Actives on July 7 against a team called the Clippers of Harlem, Dan rounded third and headed for home, intent on scoring a run. He slammed into catcher Johnny Quigley with such force that he knocked the ball from the catcher's hand to tally the run. Quigley, however, was rendered unconscious in the collision, having suffered a severe head injury. He died on August 12, and the guilt-stricken Brouthers vowed never to play baseball again.[2]

Dan changed his mind during the winter of 1877–78, and by spring was back in uniform as a pitcher and first baseman for a team in Stottsville, New York, about 50 miles up the Hudson River from Wappingers Falls. In 1879 he played for the Lansingburg (New York) Haymakers, and was noticed by Horace Phillips, manager of the National League Troy Trojans. Phillips quickly signed Brouthers, and on July 23, 1879, Dan made his major league debut.

The 21-year-old rookie made two starts as a pitcher for Troy, both of which proved disastrous. On July 30 he lost an 8–0 decision to the Boston Red Stockings, defending champions of the National League, and on August 21 suffered a 16–0 drubbing at the hands of the same team. Dan relieved in one other game, but his 0–2 record and 5.57 earned run average impressed nobody, and his pitching career was over almost before it began.

In contrast, Brouthers exhibited promise as a hitter. His .274 average led the team, and he hit the only four home runs tallied by the Trojans that season. One came in a game at Cincinnati on July 19, when a line drive that looked like a sure double rolled through a hole in the center field fence. He fielded passably at first base, but his contributions could not lift the Trojans out of last place. Phillips, the man who signed Dan, was replaced by Bob Ferguson in August, and the Trojans finished the season 35 and a half games behind the pennant-winning Providence Grays.

Dan did not return to Troy at the beginning of the 1880 season, playing instead for a National Association team in Baltimore until that club disbanded in late June. A new team in Rochester, called the Hop Bitters, absorbed four of the recently released Baltimore players, including Dan. This ballclub lasted only a few months before it, too, collapsed, and Brouthers closed the season with three games in Troy. The Trojans had four future Hall of Famers in its lineup in Tim Keefe, Mickey Welch, Buck Ewing, and Roger Connor, and team management did not choose to put Dan on its five-man reserve list for the 1881 campaign. He was unable to sign with another National League club, and his baseball career appeared to be stalled in its tracks.

Dan began the next season with a minor league nine in New York City, but a National League team, the Buffalo Bisons, needed another hitter and signed Dan in late May. This was the break that Brouthers needed, and he made the most of the opportunity. He batted .319, and despite his late start led the league in home runs with eight and in slugging percentage with .541. Playing mostly in left field, Dan combined with three other hard-hitting Bisons—catcher Jack Rowe, first baseman Jim (Deacon) White, and center fielder Hardy Richardson—to form the fearsome "Big Four." These great hitters comprised one of the earliest "Murderer's Rows" in baseball history.

The Bisons, managed by veteran third baseman Jim O'Rourke, played at Riverside Park at the corner of Fargo and Rhode Island streets. Riverside was a small ballpark, located about four blocks from the Niagara River, near the present site of the Peace Bridge that connects Buffalo to Fort Erie, Ontario. Its outfield fences stood only 210 feet from the plate down the lines, but the power alleys increased quickly to over 400 feet, leaving plenty of room for Dan and the other Bison batters to hit doubles and triples. Pitchers generally disliked the Buffalo ballpark, but hitters looked forward to playing there.

The Bisons drew slightly less than 500 fans per game in 1880, not enough to properly support a National League team, though the club attracted a few influential fans. The most notable was Erie County sheriff Grover Cleveland, who in 1881 became mayor of Buffalo and, only four years later, President of the United States. Cleveland, an enthusiastic baseball supporter, was on a first name basis with the Bison players. Buoyed by the hitting exploits of Dan Brouthers and the rest of the Big Four, the 1881 team played before about 750 fans per game, but attendance was still below the league average, and the question of Buffalo's ability to maintain a major league ballclub remained unresolved.

While the Big Four (and another hard-hitting Bison, future Hall of Famer Jim O'Rourke) took care of the offense, the Buffalo pitching effort was mainly the responsibility of one man. Jim (Pud) Galvin was a stocky right-hander who earned his nickname, so it was said, because he turned opposing batters into pudding. Galvin had starred with the minor league Bisons of 1878, remaining with the team when it moved into the National League the following year. He regularly pitched more than two-thirds of the innings for the Bisons each season, and in 1883 completed 72 of his 76 starts, winning 46 of them. One of the great pitchers of the era, in 1889 Galvin became baseball's first 300-game winner.

The "Big Four" continued their attack on National League pitching in 1882, but no one belted the ball harder than Dan Brouthers. He was one of the biggest and strongest men in the game, with only Chicago's Cap Anson and Troy's Roger Connor rivaling him in size, and his line drives frightened the barehanded infielders of the time. Other players called Dan "the man with the wagon-tongue bat," when he swung with his powerful arms and shoulders. He struck out only rarely for a slugger, hitting the ball frequently enough to lead the National League in on-base percentage for six consecutive years beginning in 1881.

In 1882, at age 24, Dan broke out as a star. He hit .368 to claim the batting title from Cap Anson, who had won it in two of the previous three seasons, and his .547 slugging percentage was the best in the league by far. Dan now equaled Anson as the preeminent slugger of the game, and his hitting was a crucial factor in Buffalo's third-place finish in the pennant race. The primitive reserve rule in effect at the time allowed each National League team to retain five men from year to year, and the Bison management did not hesitate. They designated the Big Four and pitcher Pud Galvin as their five best, and most irreplaceable, players.

Brouthers made headlines with his powerful batting, prompting the *Boston Globe* to explain his hitting style. Dan, said the paper, "is certainly the greatest slugger in the league. Dan goes to the bat to hit that ball, and few men can size up a pitcher as he can.... Brouthers is a left handed batsman and his position at the bat is not as clean as Anson's. Dan gets close to the plate with his feet well apart, and set firm. Unlike Anson, who cracks the plate with his bat to see if it is sound, Dan keeps swinging his bat back and forth.... This man can hit a high or low ball, and will seldom let go at one out of his reach....

"Like Anson, Brouthers would remain on the field all day hitting, if he could get someone to toss him the ball. He swings his body, and when he does catch the ball square no man can drive one farther."[3] The Boston fans found that out on August 18, 1882, when Dan smacked a homer over the right field fence in the fifth inning. The ball traveled so far that it could not be found afterward, and the contest proceeded with a ball that had been removed from the game earlier.[4]

As a fielder and baserunner, however, Dan's size worked against him. Though he was fast enough (or hit the ball far enough) to reach double figures in triples in almost every season, he took a great deal of ribbing for his alleged slowness afoot. One paper claimed that "ladies fainted and grown men cried" when Dan surprised the crowd one day by stealing second base. At first base, he did not cover much ground, though he caught the ball well in those days of barehanded fielding. One sportswriter complimented Dan by saying, "Brouthers comes pretty near having made more assists than any other first baseman. He is great on throws to the pitcher when the latter covers the bag." Another columnist replied, "In other words, Brouthers is awful slow in getting back to the base."[5]

Despite the powerful hitting of Dan Brouthers and the pitching of Pud Galvin, the Bisons were unable to mount a serious challenge for the pennant. They finished third in the league in 1881 and 1882, then fell to fifth the next year despite Galvin's 46 wins. Brouthers continued his hot hitting, winning the batting title for the second time in 1883 with a .374 mark, and leading the league in slugging percentage, triples, and runs batted in. On July 20 Dan went six for six in a 25–5 pounding of the Philadelphia Quakers; on the same day, Jack Rowe and Hardy Richardson earned inside-the-park home runs when the Quaker outfielders lost the ball in the tall outfield grass. However, the team's efforts were inconsistent, as illustrated by a 31–7 loss to Chicago on July 3 for the worst defeat in Buffalo baseball history. The Bisons rallied for five runs in the ninth inning to salvage some pride and lessen the severity of the humiliating defeat.

The Buffalo club tried everything, even new uniforms, in an effort to boost its popularity. In 1882 they played in brown and white uniforms at home and lavender blue on the road, and the following year donned blue shirts and pants with red and white hats. Pud Galvin hated the blue pants, complaining that they made his rear "resemble the back end of a hack," but management hoped the colorful attire would appeal to the fans. It was a constant struggle, for the Bisons continued to draw between 650 and 800 fans per game during the early 1880s, while the average National League team attracted two to three times that number.

During his early years in professional baseball, Dan resided in Wappingers Falls, and would continue to do so for the next several decades. He married Mary Ellen Croak in 1884 and started a family that eventually produced two sons (Leo and Addison) and two daughters (Margaret and Lillian). Dan's mother had died during the 1870s, but his father Michael continued to work as a printer. Following his retirement, Michael moved in with Dan and Mary Ellen, spending the remainder of his life under his son's roof.

The owner of the land that Riverside Park sat upon opted not to renew the team's lease agreement after the 1883 season, so the Bison management was obliged to build a new park. The costs of its construction further crippled the team financially, and local interest waned in the early part of the season after injuries to Brouthers and Galvin caused the Bisons to lose 11 of their first 15 games. Dan led the league in slugging percentage again and set a new team record with 14 homers, but the Bisons finished third, 19 and a half games behind the leaders.

The Bisons finally lost the attendance battle in 1885, after Pud Galvin started the season poorly and the team dropped quickly out of contention. The players missed manager and third baseman Jim O'Rourke, sold to the Giants in a salary move, and by mid-season Galvin, too, was gone, sold to Pittsburgh. The Bisons languished in seventh place and, although Dan Brouthers swatted the ball at a .359 clip and led the league in slugging, the club teetered on the edge of insolvency. Their per-game attendance was less than a third of the league average, and major league baseball in Buffalo was doomed.

Though no longer possessed of Galvin and O'Rourke, the team owned a highly coveted quartet of hitters in the Big Four. Rather than simply disband at season's end, the Buffalo owners chose a more radical course. On September 16, 1885, a month before the official end of the season, team management sold the entire ballclub to one of their National League rivals, the Detroit Wolverines. The price tag was $7,000 and included every man on the roster, though the Wolverines were interested solely in the Big Four and intended to release all the other players. Brouthers, Rowe, White, and Richardson immediately quit the Bisons and boarded a train for Detroit, where they expected to appear in the lineup for the Wolverines the next day.

This transaction, as one might expect, raised a howl of protest from the other National League teams, who saw the move as a threat to the integrity of future pennant races. After a quick round of consultations among league executives, president Nick Young decreed that the Big Four would not be allowed to play for Detroit until the beginning of the next campaign, and ordered Buffalo to finish the season as best it could. Dan returned to Wappingers Falls, New York, while the rest of the Big Four also abandoned the team, and the decimated Bisons finished the season with 16 consecutive losses. Except for a brief turn in the Players League in 1890 and another in the Federal League in 1914 and 1915, Buffalo never again hosted a major league club.

The Detroit Wolverines, on the other hand, was a team on the move. It had been one of the sad-sack franchises of the league from its inception, but in 1885 team president Frederick K. Stearns, a pharmaceutical magnate, began to buy players in an attempt to turn the club into a contender. Rookie outfielder Sam Thompson, purchased earlier that year from Indianapolis, and pitcher Charles (Lady) Baldwin, bought from Milwaukee, had already strengthened the lineup and helped the team move from last place to sixth by season's end. The addition of the Big Four suddenly gave Detroit the best offense in the National League, turning the Wolverines into instant contenders.

Center fielder Ned Hanlon, a canny baseball strategist, served as field captain of the Wolverines, but the sudden infusion of offense changed the focus of the team to pure slugging. Manager Bill Watkins placed his best hitters at the top of the lineup without regard for traditional roles, with Hardy Richardson in the leadoff spot, Dan Brouthers hitting second, Jack Rowe third, and holdover Sam Thompson in the cleanup position. There wasn't much speed on the Detroit roster, but Watkins was not concerned with manufacturing runs with sacrifice bunts, stolen bases, and clever base-running. He figured to use his powerful hitters to pound Detroit's opponents into submission, and before long the out-of-town newspapers regularly referred to the Detroit team as the "Sluggers."

The biggest sluggers on the ballclub were Dan Brouthers, the muscular first baseman, and Sam Thompson, the power-hitting right fielder. Both swung the bat with great force, paying little attention to the nuances of "scientific" hitting, protecting the plate, and other such strategies. Brouthers, a bit larger and heavier than Thompson, hit the ball harder than anyone in the league, and his tape-measure blasts elicited gasps from fans and opposing players alike. On September 10, 1886, Dan walloped three homers in a game against Chicago, adding a single and a double for good measure. Though the Wolverines lost that day by a 14–8 score, Dan drove in four runs and scored four times, and his 15 total bases broke Cap Anson's National League record.

Chicago was still the class of the league, despite the hitting exploits of Brouthers and the Wolverines, but the White Stocking management broke up their ballclub after the 1886 campaign. This move opened the door for the Wolverines to challenge for the pennant. Each of the Big Four contributed, but Dan Brouthers batted .419 (in a year in which walks counted as hits), finishing only two points behind Cap Anson for the batting title. The baseball magnates had decreed that four strikes, not three, would constitute a strikeout in 1887, and the extra strike increased offensive production league-wide. The hard-hitting Wolverines benefited from this change most of all. Sam Thompson drove in a record 166 runs, Dan scored 153 times, and the Wolverines held off the Philadelphia Quakers (later called the Phillies) for the pennant, capturing Detroit's first and only title in the National League.

The Wolverines contracted to meet the St. Louis Browns, champions of the American Association, in a 15-game "World's Series" in October, but Brouthers played in only one of the contests. Bothered by a sprained ankle, he remained on the sidelines as his Detroit teammates defeated the Browns, 10 games to 5, to claim the championship of the baseball world. Brouthers, always an honest sort, felt badly that he was unable to play. He offered to give his winner's share of $200 to his teammates, a gesture that was declined with thanks by the other Wolverines.

Detroit's victory represented a defeat for "scientific" baseball, as the Wolverines, for the most part, simply overwhelmed their opponents with offense. The championship also belied the notion that a team could not simply buy a pennant, as Detroit's purchase of Brouthers and others from the failed Buffalo club proved that such an action was possible. Team president Frederick Stearns, apparently believing that there was no such thing as too much offense, even tried to buy Cap Anson from the White Stockings late in the season. He offered $10,000 to Chicago for Anson's services as playing manager, though the Wolverines already owned a slow, power-hitting first baseman in Dan Brouthers. "Of course I would not think of letting Brouthers go," said Stearns. "I could play one of the two men in the outfield."[6] Chicago turned down the offer.

However, Detroit faced an uphill battle to repeat in 1888. Several other teams, including Anson's Chicago club, appeared to have improved, and the rules-makers decided to restore the three-strikes-and-out rule that remains to this day. Dan did not like the change. "The rules were all right and should be let alone," complained Brouthers. "The rules as they were made the batting more free. Taking off that fourth strike, however, throws the work back on the pitcher and catcher again, and reduces the chance for batting the ball. The young players had some chance as the rule stood before, but they have no chance now. You will find that I am right about it, too. A batter has no chance now. He has to go right in and make a rush at the ball, and first thing he knows, why, he is out."[7]

One highlight of the 1888 season was a visit to the White House. Grover Cleveland, the Buffalo native and baseball fan then completing his first term as President, often welcomed teams when they came to Washington to play the Senators. The Detroit club visited the chief executive in June, and Cleveland regaled the players with tales from his Buffalo days. He inquired about one of his idols, pitcher Pud Galvin, who by 1888 was playing for Pittsburgh. "Galvin was a great favorite of mine in Buffalo," remarked the President. Turning to Brouthers, President Cleveland asked, "Do you keep up your hard hitting?" "I try to," said Brouthers.[8]

The Wolverines failed to repeat, though Dan was not at fault. The restoration of the three-strike rule put a damper on offense, and batting averages fell after the league decided to stop counting walks as hits. The Wolverines suffered the most under the new rules, as Brouthers was the only one of the six .300 hitters in the 1887 Detroit lineup to match the feat in 1888. Injuries to Hardy Richardson and Sam Thompson, coupled with player dissatisfaction with manager Bill Watkins, resulted in a long losing skid in August that dropped the

Wolverines from contention. The Detroit ballclub, always on the edge financially, lost money profusely in 1888, and by September it was clear that the team would not survive another year. The Wolverines fell to fourth place in what turned out to be their final National League season.

As happened in Buffalo three years before, the Detroit owners decided to disband and sell its stars around the league. Jack Rowe and Deacon White, however, purchased the Buffalo club in the International League and intended to play there; unfortunately, the Wolverines management still owned their playing rights and, under the reserve rule, could assign them to any team it chose. The owners sold Sam Thompson to Philadelphia for $5,000 and peddled Rowe and Pete Conway to Pittsburgh for a reported $7,000, none of which went to the players themselves. White objected vigorously—"no man is going to sell my carcass unless I get half," he snarled—but in the end the reserve rule won out. Rowe and Conway went to Pittsburgh for the 1889 season, while five Detroit players, including Brouthers, White, and Richardson, were sold to Boston for $30,000.

A Gypsy Queen cigarette card of Dan Brouthers, 1887. (Library of Congress)

The reserve clause and player sales were two of the thorny issues that prompted many National League players to form the first baseball trade union during the late 1880s. Called the Brotherhood of Professional Base Ball Players, it was founded in 1885 by nine New York Giants and quickly gained support from other teams. Dan Brouthers joined the Brotherhood, along with three of his Detroit teammates, in May of 1886, and was elected vice-president of the organization the following year. He took a leading role in the coming "baseball war," as part of a Brotherhood committee (with John Ward and Ned Hanlon) that met with league magnates in 1888 to iron out a dispute concerning player releases.

Dan's new team, the Boston Beaneaters, was operated by three owners called the Triumvirs. They had tried to follow Detroit's lead and buy the necessary parts of a pennant-winning team, acquiring popular catcher Mike (King)

Kelly from Chicago in 1887 for a record $10,000, and purchasing star pitcher John Clarkson a year later from the same team for the same amount. Now, with half of the Big Four on board in Brouthers and Richardson (White had refused to report, forcing the club to trade him to Pittsburgh), the Beaneaters hoped to make a move, but fell short at season's end. Dan compiled another outstanding hitting season while Clarkson won an amazing 49 games, but the team had little depth, and lost the pennant by two games to the New York Giants.

During the 1889 season, the officers of the Brotherhood, including Dan Brouthers, made plans to form their own league. Called the Players League, this new circuit promised to abolish the reserve clause, offer the players ownership in their own teams, and remove artificial restrictions on salaries. Immediately after the close of the season, in which Dan batted .373 and won his third National League batting title, Brouthers and most of the other Beaneaters signed contracts to play for the new Boston entry in the Players League. Only pitcher John Clarkson and catcher Charlie Bennett, offered large sums of money by the three Boston owners, opted to remain with the National League ballclub.

The new Boston Players League team, called the Reds, was managed by perhaps the most unlikely field boss in major league history. Mike (King) Kelly, the most popular player in the game during his tenure with Cap Anson's Chicago pennant winners, was a legendary drinker and carouser. He loved playing practical jokes on his teammates, and his after-curfew exploits were legend in the baseball world. He had even been disciplined during the 1889 campaign for playing ball while drunk, and his failure to stay in condition was one of the key factors in the Beaneaters' narrow loss of the pennant. Still, Kelly was the most charismatic player of his era, and was admired by his teammates. He had proved his loyalty to the Brotherhood when he turned down an offer of $10,000, a huge sum at the time, to remain in the National League.

Brouthers, too, could have profited handsomely by turning his back on the infant league (as had Mickey Welch, a founder of the Brotherhood), but he was an officer in the union and, like Kelly, believed in the cause. He must have held strong convictions, because Dan, by all accounts, was one of the most frugal players in the game. In 1889 he had promised to play in Buffalo with Deacon White and Jack Rowe for $4,000 per year, but when Boston offered $5,000, Dan changed his mind, much to White's consternation. "I didn't sign any paper to stick with the crowd," explained Dan. "I merely gave my word."[9] Some said that Dan received his salary each fall in silver dollars, which he put in a sack and buried on his farm in Wappingers Falls.

Kelly enjoyed teasing the good-natured Brouthers about his thriftiness. Dan, who did not generally trust banks, kept small amounts of money in many different financial institutions around the league. One day Kelly charged into the locker room and bellowed, "The Boston Savings Bank has busted, Dan!"

Brouthers, so the story goes, ran shrieking out of the room and onto the field before he realized that Kelly was pulling his leg. Big Dan laughed, then bought a round of drinks for Kelly and his teammates. Kelly was so surprised that Dan spent a dollar to buy a round that he kept the bill and framed it.[10]

Though Kelly was no disciplinarian, the Boston nine was the strongest club in the Players League, and rode the bats of Hardy Richardson (who drove in 146 runs) and Dan Brouthers (who hit .330) to the pennant. However, the Players League collapsed after only one season, with most of the Reds moving to the Boston team in the American Association, the remaining rival of the National League. This team, also called the Boston Reds, won the Association pennant as Dan captured his fourth batting title at .350 and led the league in slugging average and on-base percentage.

The Association, too, folded after the 1891 season, and Dan wound up with the Brooklyn Bridegrooms (later known as the Dodgers), winning his fifth batting title in 1892. Unfortunately, his performance suffered the following year due to an illness that kept him out of the lineup until late May. He appeared in only 77 games for the sixth-place Bridegrooms. Manager Dave Foutz wanted to play first base himself, and the Brooklyn management considered releasing Brouthers outright at season's end. Instead, they worked out a trade with Baltimore that proved to be one of the most one-sided in baseball history. On January 1, 1894, the Bridegrooms traded Brouthers and little-used outfielder Willie Keeler to the Orioles for third baseman Billy Shindle and outfielder George Treadway.

Keeler, a diminutive right fielder, became an immediate star in Baltimore, batting .371 while teaming with young standouts such as John McGraw, Joe Kelley, and Hugh Jennings to lead Baltimore into pennant contention. Brouthers, whose career was supposedly over, found new life in Baltimore. He took over at first base and added a necessary jolt of power to the lineup, leading the team in runs batted in with 128 and batting .347. Shindle and Treadway contributed little to Brooklyn, while Brouthers and Keeler played key roles on the suddenly improved Baltimore team. The Orioles won the pennant in 1894, the first in Baltimore baseball history, and the fourth of Dan Brouthers' career.

Dan could still swing the bat effectively. On May 4, 1894, he walloped a homer off Brooklyn left-hander George Sharrott that soared over the right field fence at the Baltimore ballpark. Contemporary accounts, possibly exaggerated, stated that the ball landed some 500 feet away, rolling another 200 feet before it came to rest. John McGraw called it the longest hit he had ever seen, and many baseball historians consider Brouthers' blast the longest home run of the 1890s. Orioles team president Harry von der Horst celebrated the occasion by retrieving the ball and having it gilded and framed, while the embarrassed Brooklyn team released Sharrott that evening. Dan's mighty blow ended the left-hander's career, as Sharrott never again pitched in a major league game.

"I am feeling better than I have for years," said Dan to the *Brooklyn Eagle*.

"I would rather retire from the business than play for Brooklyn again. Not that I wasn't treated right, but the fact is I couldn't hit safely there. The wind is so strong in the Eastern park outfield that I couldn't hit at all. Every time I sent a ball up in the air that should have gone away out over the fielders' heads the wind held it back and it dropped into the man's hand. It was enough to disgust anybody. Here in Baltimore nothing stops a ball and it goes every time it is hit. That's why I like Baltimore."[11]

The 1894 season was Dan's last hurrah in the National League. The aging first baseman hit well during spring training in 1895, belting the longest home run ever seen on the grounds in Raleigh, North Carolina, but once the regular season began, Dan's slowness in the field became a liability for the Orioles. "Brouthers is and always has been the poorest fielding first baseman in fast company," complained the *Washington Post*. "A low throw nearly always gets away from him, and he is going backward so fast in batting that it is very doubtful if he would be able to get to .300 this or any other year."[12] A new first baseman, George (Scoops) Carey, was not much of a hitter but possessed superior fielding skills, and the Orioles decided that Carey's glove was more important to them than Dan's bat. Brouthers saw action in only five games for the Orioles, and on May 8, 1895, Dan's 37th birthday, the Orioles sold him to the last-place Louisville Colonels for $500.

The former star was not interested in playing for the Colonels. He compiled a .309 average over 24 games, then went home to Wappingers Falls in mid-June to take care of his wife Mary Ellen, who was seriously ill. Mary Ellen recovered, but Dan never returned to Louisville, and at season's end the Colonels sold him to the Philadelphia Phillies for $500. Sam Thompson, Dan's former teammate with the Detroit Wolverines many years before, was the Philadelphia right fielder, and the team hoped that the two aging sluggers would pile up the runs by taking aim at the short right field fence at the local ballpark, the Huntingdon Avenue Grounds.

"Big Dan" and "Big Sam" were together again, but their reunion did not last long, for by mid-May it was clear that Brouthers was finished as a player. The *Chicago Tribune* claimed that Dan was "striking out with alarming frequency," though he fanned only 11 times that season, but Dan was no longer a terror at the plate. Though he batted .344 for the Phillies, his slugging average was down, and his poor defensive play and slowness on the basepaths were more pronounced than ever. The Phillies were going nowhere, languishing in the bottom half of the standings, so on July 4 manager Billy Nash handed Dan his 10-day notice of release. In mid-July Dan packed his bags, left the team, and returned to Wappingers Falls, where he owned and operated a small hotel. In early August, the Phillies signed Napoleon Lajoie, a 22-year-old rookie from Rhode Island, to fill Dan's place at first. More than 40 years later, Lajoie preceded Dan into the Hall of Fame in Cooperstown.

Dan's departure from the game elicited a mixture of regret and pity from his peers. Veteran first baseman Roger Connor of St. Louis, for one, declared that he would leave the game on his own terms, explaining that "there will be no Dan Brouthers about my quitting."[13] Brouthers appeared to be the classic example of a player who held on too long, as his remarkable 1894 season in Baltimore was his only good showing in the previous four years. Had the designated hitter existed during the 1890s, Dan might have been able to remain on a major league roster, though his lack of speed would still have presented a problem on the bases. At any rate, except for a brief appearance several years later, Dan's major league career was finished.

Within days of his severance from the Phillies, Dan signed to play for Springfield of the Eastern League, where in 1897 he walloped minor league pitching for a .415 average, winning the batting title. The pitchers caught up with him eventually, and after stints at Toronto in 1898 and Rochester in 1899 he decided that it was time to hang up his spikes. "I am satisfied that I have seen my best days on the diamond and am ready to quit," wrote Dan in his letter of resignation. "When I received manager [Al] Buckenberger's telegram from Worcester last week asking me to join the Rochester team, I hesitated for four days before replying. I finally decided for Rochester, but I can't hit them square on the nose, as I did once.

"I know that I am not satisfactory to the Rochester team and I do not want you to keep me a moment longer. I am going home to Wappingers Falls to run my little hotel.... The days of Big Dan are over, I guess. I have enough of this world's goods to keep me going until I die."[14]

Dan managed his hotel and helped raise his family for a few years, but the lure of the diamond was still strong. In 1902 he reportedly volunteered to sign with New London of the New England League, promising to refund his entire salary if he failed to bat .300. In 1903, when Dan was 45 years old, the Hudson River League formed a new team in nearby Poughkeepsie, and the veteran could no longer resist. He played in 15 games for Poughkeepsie that year, batting .300, and in 1904 played the full season and won his second minor league batting title, and seventh overall, with a .373 average.

Dan's fine performance with Poughkeepsie attracted the attention of his old friend and Baltimore teammate John McGraw, now manager of the New York Giants. McGraw's team had clinched the 1904 pennant in early September and subsequently declined the opportunity to play the American League champions from Boston in a World Series. McGraw wanted to entertain the New York fans in the waning days of the 1904 season, so he invited Brouthers to play a few games for the Giants. Dan happily agreed, appearing at first base on October 3 against St. Louis at the Polo Grounds and pinch-hitting a day later. Dan failed to get a hit in five trips to the plate, but the small crowd cheered his presence after an absence of eight years from the major league scene.

He returned to Poughkeepsie for the 1905 season, but not even Dan could put off the inevitable as he neared his 50th year. His average fell to .295, and after seven games for another Hudson River League team in Newburgh the following year, he called it quits and resumed his business pursuits in Wappingers Falls. Unfortunately, Dan was a better ballplayer than a businessman, and financial problems prompted him to seek another position in the baseball world. John McGraw, learning of his friend's distress, hired Dan as a scout and unofficial advisor early in 1907. Dan and wife Mary Ellen then moved to Manhattan, where they lived for the next 20 years.

McGraw trusted his old teammate's judgment, relying on Dan for evaluations of young ballplayers seeking to play in the majors. Brouthers was instrumental in signing Fred Merkle, Larry Doyle, Buck Herzog, and other future Giant stars over the next few seasons. During the early 1910s, McGraw assigned Dan to duties as a night watchman and also put him in charge of the press box at the Polo Grounds. McGraw held a soft spot in his heart for old ballplayers, and Dan was joined by several National League stars of the 1880s and 1890s, including Amos Rusie, Arlie Latham, and Mickey Welch, in the employ of the Giants. "Dan's getting old," wrote McGraw in his 1923 autobiography, "but will always have a job."[15]

Brouthers worked at the Polo Grounds until the late 1920s. He was past 70 years of age when he retired and moved to East Orange, New Jersey, where he and his wife spent their declining years with their daughter Margaret and her family. Dan died at age 74 on August 5, 1932 of a heart attack, while Mary Ellen, after a two-year illness, passed away only two weeks after her husband. They were buried in St. Mary's Catholic Cemetery in Wappingers Falls. In 1971, on the 100th anniversary of its incorporation, the town of Wappingers Falls dedicated a monument in a local park to its most famous athlete. The marker stands next to a youth baseball diamond called Brouthers Field.

Dan Brouthers was a power hitter at a time when power hitting was often held in low regard. The 19th century was an era of so-called "scientific" baseball, featuring one-run strategies and the hit-and-run, and many writers decried "slugging" as a crude and unenlightened way to play the game. The 1896 *Spalding Guide* complained about "that rutting class of slugging batsmen who think of nothing else when they go to the bat but that of gaining the applause of the 'groundlings' by the novice's hit to the outfield of a 'homer,' one of the least difficult hits known to batting in baseball, as it needs only muscle and not brains to make it."[16] Though the fans admired power-hitters like Dan Brouthers, many sportswriters denigrated them.

Despite the criticism he received from the advocates of strategic, low-scoring baseball, Dan was a valuable player because of, not in spite of, his slugging. Though he was slow on the bases and a mediocre fielder at best, his batting prowess made him of the greatest stars of his era and an obvious choice for the Hall of Fame.

4

Tommy McCarthy

> "The best man in the business at the trapped-ball trick was Tommy McCarthy. He had the play down pat, and on more than one occasion saved his team by resorting to it. I recall one game in which McCarthy had the opportunity of using the play twice, and on both occasions he made a double play out of it, and Wilbert Robinson was the victim each time."
>
> —*John McGraw*[1]

On June 12, 1939, when the Baseball Hall of Fame opened its doors to the public for the first time, 25 players, managers, and executives were honored at its inaugural ceremony. Over the next few decades, both the Baseball Writers Association of America and several incarnations of the Veterans Committee selected new men for Hall enshrinement, albeit slowly. Not until 1964 did the number of inductees pass the 100 mark, and by 1969, when Stan Musial and Waite Hoyt gained entry, the roster boasted 114 names.

The Hall's population began to grow quickly after that. Fifty-five new members joined during the 1970s, and in 1988 Willie Stargell became the 200th man to gain election to the Cooperstown museum. The number passed the 250 mark in 2001, and 2006 saw the induction of the largest class in history. The baseball writers selected Bruce Sutter in January of that year, and in February a special committee, empowered to weigh the merits of Negro Leagues and pre–Negro Leagues players and executives, surprised many observers when it designated 17 new members of the Hall of Fame. At the end of 2006, there were 278 plaques in the museum gallery.

While the Hall of Fame continues to expand, critics have focused attention on the more questionable selections of the past, most of which were made by the Veterans Committee and its predecessors. Some players with short careers (Elmer Flick, Addie Joss, Ross Youngs) or unimpressive statistics (Rube Marquard, Jesse Haines) have been selected while other, perhaps more deserving candidates have been shut out. Tommy McCarthy, an

Opposite page: **An Old Judge cigarette card of Tommy during his brief time with the Philadelphia Quakers (later Phillies), 1887. (Library of Congress)**

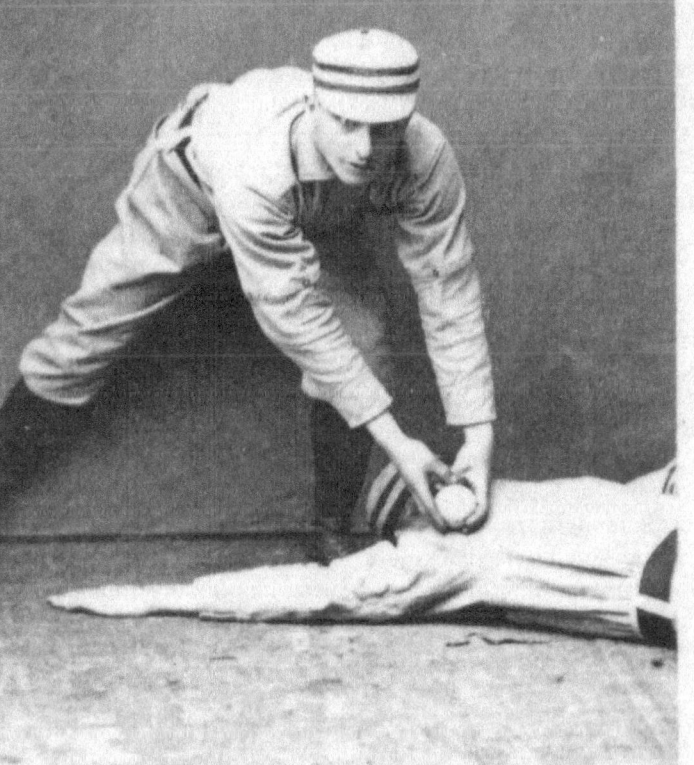

outfielder who posted a .294 average in the American Association and the National League from 1885 to 1896, is often cited as one of the Hall's most glaring missteps. He played only 1,222 major league games (some members of the Hall participated in more than 3,000) while his statistical record is distinctly unimpressive.[2]

Chicago sportswriter Eddie Gold asked in 1995, "Who is Thomas Michael Francis McCarthy and why is he in the Hall of Fame?"[3] Bill James described McCarthy's presence in the Hall as the result of "a fluke or off-the-wall type of nomination,"[4] while columnist John B. Holway of *The New York Times* labeled McCarthy an "imposter" among the greatest players in the Cooperstown museum.[5] Many Internet chat rooms devoted to baseball roundly condemn McCarthy's election in 1946 by the Permanent Committee (later called the Veterans Committee) as a mistake, and some writers suggest that he be removed from the roster. Various Hall committees have made many controversial selections through the years, but Tommy McCarthy is often derided as the least deserving member of the Hall of Fame.

McCarthy's statistical record does not mark him as an obvious honoree, and no one seriously suggests that he belongs on an equal footing with all-time greats such as Willie Mays or Hank Aaron. Nonetheless, McCarthy was an influential early ballplayer. A strategic innovator and a key player on several winning teams, his contributions to the game convinced the Permanent Committee to name him, along with 10 other 19th-century players, to the Hall of Fame on April 23, 1946, 24 years after his death.

Thomas Francis Michael McCarthy was the son of Irish immigrants. Born to Daniel and Sarah McCarthy on the south side of Boston, Massachusetts on July 24, 1863, he grew up in a neighborhood teeming with recent refugees from poverty and famine in Ireland. This area, which the locals call Southie, is overwhelmingly Irish and Catholic to this day. Baseball was the most popular pastime among its young boys, and Tommy McCarthy loved to play ball. Small and fast, with a fine throwing arm, he performed on sandlots all over South Boston, excelling against much older players.

After finishing grammar school in 1877, the teenager combined work and baseball over the next several years. He worked as a clerk in a clothing store while playing for the company team (the Bundle Boys), and made his reputation as a fine pitcher, hitter, and outfielder. His skills were much in demand, and in the early 1880s he was offered a job with the Chickering Piano Works in Boston. Tommy labored in the piano factory and pitched for the Chickering baseball team, one of the leading amateur nines in the city, for a reported salary of $18 per week.

Tommy was 21 years old in 1884, a season in which the demand for talented players was high. That year, a St. Louis entrepreneur named Henry Lucas created his own league, called the Union Association, as a rival to the established National League and American Association. Lucas awarded a franchise to Boston under the management of George Wright, the great shortstop of the 1860s and 1870s, and Tim Murnane, a former ballplayer who later became a renowned sportswriter for the *Boston Globe*. Murnane scoured the city for players to fill his roster, and happened to see Tommy McCarthy pitching for the piano company team one day. Duly impressed, Murnane signed McCarthy to a contract.

Baseball historians disagree on the question of whether the Union Association was a true major league or not, but Tommy McCarthy found the competition too fast for him. Murnane put Tommy in left field and placed him in the leadoff spot in the lineup, but the newcomer went hitless in his first game on July 10 against the famous one-armed pitcher Hugh Daily. McCarthy batted only .215 in 53 games, and late in the season he pitched in seven contests, losing them all. The Union Association collapsed at season's end, leaving Tommy's professional future in doubt, until the National League's Boston Beaneaters decided to give him a trial for 1885.

Tommy failed to impress his new team, batting only .182 in 40 games, and drew his release before the halfway point of the season. He spent the remainder of the 1885 campaign at Haverhill in the New England League, and then signed with the Philadelphia Quakers (later called the Phillies) of the National League. He performed no better for the Quakers, batting below the .200 mark in brief appearances in 1886 and 1887. Though he hit well at Brockton of the New England League in 1886, batting .330, Tommy realized that he would not make the majors on talent alone. He would need to use his intelligence and creativity to carve out a place in the game for himself.

Fortunately, Tommy found a manager who could harness the young player's talents. Frank Selee, manager of the Northwestern League team in Oshkosh, Wisconsin, signed Tommy early in 1887 and installed him in right field. To utilize Tommy's keen running ability, Selee urged him to bunt whenever possible, and with practice he became the best bunter in the league. Base stealing became McCarthy's specialty; he pilfered 69 sacks that year in 80 games, though advancing a base on a fly ball also counted as a stolen base in that era. Tommy blossomed under Selee's tutelage, batting .389 for the pennant-winning Oshkosh ballclub.

Perhaps Tommy's greatest contribution came on the defensive side. McCarthy played an extremely shallow right field, occasionally resembling a fifth infielder. He often became involved in rundown plays between first and second, which sometimes ended with McCarthy tagging out the baserunner at first. Tommy may also have developed his most famous maneuver, the trap play, in Oshkosh. If a batter hit a short fly ball to right with runners on base, Tommy would either trap the ball on the short bounce or purposely drop it. The confused runners would freeze on the basepaths, and Tommy would peg the ball back to the infield and begin a series of force plays. Double plays, or even triple plays, would result.

Selee nurtured and developed several future major league stars in Oshkosh, including William (Dummy) Hoy, a deaf-mute center fielder for whom Selee created a system of signs to keep track of balls, strikes, and outs. Hoy, like McCarthy, was a fast runner who grew into a skilled bunter and base-stealing threat. Pitcher Tom Lovett, who later threw a no-hitter for Brooklyn in the National League, posted a 20–2 record for Oshkosh, leading the circuit in earned run average. Ten other men from that team wound up playing in the major leagues at some point during their careers, but Lovett, Hoy, and McCarthy were the club's biggest stars. At season's end Selee relocated his entire Oshkosh franchise to Omaha and the Western Association, but Hoy moved on to Washington, while Tommy McCarthy signed to play for the St. Louis Whites, a new ballclub that was created as a farm team for the St. Louis Browns of the American Association.

The Browns' owner was an eccentric German immigrant named Chris von der Ahe, a portly man in loud checkered suits who called himself "Der Boss President." When von der Ahe, a St. Louis saloon owner, discovered that many of his customers were baseball fans, he bought a franchise in the American Association in 1882. He knew precious little about baseball, but was perceptive enough to put his first baseman, Charlie Comiskey, in charge. Comiskey, only 24 years old when he took the reins of the Browns, was a born field leader and judge of talent, and in 1885 the team won the Association championship. They played Cap Anson's National League pennant winners, the Chicago White Stockings, in a contentious post-season World Series that ended in a tie. This series established the Association as the equal of the older National League, at least in the minds of Comiskey and the St. Louis fans. The Browns repeated as champions during the next two seasons, winning the World Series against the White Stockings in 1886 and losing a 15-game postseason match against Detroit in 1887.

Von der Ahe, who once commissioned a statue of himself to decorate the outside of the ballpark, was known for his outlandish behavior, but began to alienate his players with fines and punishments for behavioral infractions, real or imagined (he once fined third baseman Arlie Latham for singing during a game). Angered by the World Series loss to Detroit, von der Ahe stunned the Association by decimating his roster. Bob Caruthers and Dave Foutz, who alternated between the pitching box and right field, were dispatched to Brooklyn for $14,000 in cash, while outfielder Curt Welch, catcher Doc Bushong, and shortstop Bill Gleason were traded or sold. The eccentric owner then took a vacation to Europe, leaving Comiskey to fill five of the nine spaces in the starting lineup.

Comiskey went to work, signing Harry Lyons to play center, with Bill White at shortstop, Jocko Milligan at catcher, and pitcher Elton (Icebox) Chamberlain to pick up the slack left by the departures of Foutz and Caruthers. He had not yet filled the right field slot when the Browns played an exhibition

Tommy McCarthy with the St. Louis Browns. (Library of Congress)

series in St. Louis against the Whites in late April. Tommy McCarthy saw the occasion as a chance to impress the parent club. He dropped bunts, stole bases, and displayed his defensive wizardry so well that McCarthy never played a regular season game for the Whites. Comiskey offered Tommy a promotion to the Browns, one which the 25-year-old outfielder immediately accepted.

Von der Ahe preferred big, tall ballplayers, and reacted strongly upon seeing McCarthy for the first time. To his dismay, he noticed that his new right fielder stood only five feet seven inches and weighed 155 pounds. "Ach!" he spat at Comiskey. "Dat Tommy can't play big ball."[6] He pressured Comiskey to release McCarthy, but the manager stuck to his guns, retaining the newcomer in right. Comiskey's faith was rewarded as McCarthy, usually batting sixth in the St. Louis lineup, batted .274, stole 93 bases, and helped the Browns to their fourth consecutive American Association pennant.

Comiskey was a defensive innovator, having been the first to design infield plays where the pitcher covered the first-base bag, and McCarthy was his kind of ballplayer. Tommy brought the trap play with him to St. Louis, and he and Comiskey refined it further, creating new ways to catch runners off base on popups and short fly balls. Tommy led the league in 1888 with 44 outfield assists and 12 double plays, both incredibly high totals for a right fielder, mostly by employing variations on the trap play. He was so successful at this that, a few years later, baseball introduced the infield fly rule to prevent such deception.

Tommy also discovered a novel way to prevent runners from advancing on longer fly balls. The rules in the 1880s allowed a baserunner to tag up and advance when the outfielder gained possession of the ball. When a batter hit a fly to right field, Tommy simply kept the ball airborne as long as possible, batting it in the air and juggling it in his hands while running toward the infield. He did not yet have possession, so the runners were forced to maintain their positions until McCarthy finally caught the ball in the middle of the diamond. This tactic frustrated opposing players and managers, and the league magnates changed the rules a few years later to allow baserunners to advance immediately when the ball touched any part of the outfielder's person.

St. Louis was, like Boston, stocked with Irish-American fans, and Tommy McCarthy quickly became one of the most popular players on the Browns. In his fifth game for St. Louis, on April 23, 1888, Tommy scored the winning run against Cincinnati by stealing second, third, and home in quick succession. On May 6, he made a key play against Louisville when he slipped in from right field and joined a rundown, tagging the runner out at first base. On July 17, he stole six bases in a game, stroked five hits, and scored three runs in a 10–3 victory over Kansas City. *The Sporting News* praised the rookie outfielder in June, stating that "there is no better base runner in the country."[7] The season, however, ended in disappointment as the New York Giants defeated the Browns in a 10-game World Series that October, but Tommy McCarthy established himself as the newest St. Louis star.

Though McCarthy played ball more than 1,000 miles from his hometown, he continued to make his permanent home in South Boston. He became a family man, marrying a woman named Margaret McCluskey, seven years younger than he, during the late 1880s. The couple produced three daughters during the next five years.

In 1889, Comiskey moved McCarthy to the second spot in the St. Louis lineup, directly behind the speedy Arlie Latham. Tommy called upon his bunting skill to move Latham around the bases, but soon developed the fake bunt, pulling his bat back at the last moment and rifling a liner past the charging corner infielders. After every team in the American Association was victimized by the maneuver, first and third basemen began to play farther back to give McCarthy additional room to drop bunts and race to first. Von der Ahe stopped complaining to Comiskey about Tommy's small stature, and the Bostonian became the best second-place hitter and most feared bunter in the circuit.

The Browns vied with the Brooklyn Bridegrooms (later known as the Dodgers) all year for the pennant, and in September the St. Louis club traveled to Brooklyn for a key three-game series. The contest on Saturday, September 7, turned out to be one of the wildest affairs on record. The Browns, after taking a 3–2 lead in the sixth inning, complained to umpire Fred Goldsmith that it was too dark to continue. Goldsmith refused to stop the game, so Comiskey instigated several arguments and other delays in the action as the sun approached the western horizon. Chris von der Ahe, in the meantime, slipped out to a grocery store and bought a box of candles, which the Browns lit and arranged around their bench. Fans tossed beer mugs at the candles, staring some papers on fire, and causing a near panic before the players stamped the fire out. Somehow, the two teams completed the seventh and eighth innings, but Tommy McCarthy nearly started a riot when fans observed him soaking the game ball in a bucket of water before the Bridegrooms went to bat in the ninth.

Brooklyn put its leadoff batter on base after St. Louis catcher Jocko Milligan, who complained that he could not see the pitch in the approaching darkness, dropped a third strike. While Milligan and Comiskey argued again with the umpire, the baserunner stole second. Enraged, Comiskey ordered his team off the field, whereupon Goldsmith forfeited the contest to the Bridegrooms. The fans then threw beer mugs at the St. Louis players, aiming many of their missiles at McCarthy. Ultimately, the Browns required a police escort back to their hotel.

This disputed game marked the beginning of a series of disagreements that cost the Browns a chance at their fifth consecutive pennant. The Browns refused to play the next day, resulting in another forfeit loss, while the final game of the series was rained out. The Browns were now five games behind Brooklyn and seemingly out of the pennant chase, but a 12-game winning streak later that month put them back in contention. Though only one forfeit loss was counted against St. Louis after a long period of controversy and negotiation, Brooklyn held on to win the flag by two games, with the remaining September forfeit accounting for part of the margin of victory.

The 1889 pennant race was the last hurrah for the St. Louis Browns under the ownership of Chris von der Ahe. After season's end, the first baseball trade union, the Brotherhood of Professional Base Ball Players, set up their own Players League in competition with the established National League and American Association. Charlie Comiskey, the architect of the Browns' success, left St. Louis to join the new league as manager of a ballclub in his hometown of Chicago. Von der Ahe then turned to the man whom the papers were already calling "the trickiest player in the business," and named Tommy McCarthy as manager of the Browns for 1890.

Almost every team in the Association was compelled to find new players in 1890, but the situation was particularly dire in St. Louis. Most of von der Ahe's stars had departed for the Players League, with only McCarthy, pitcher Jack Stivetts, shortstop Shorty Fuller, and center fielder Clarence Duffee remaining from the 1889 team. By signing some minor leaguers and promoting a few bench-warmers into regular roles, McCarthy managed to assemble a viable ballclub to open the season. However, von der Ahe was an impatient owner, and after 22 games, with the team in fourth place, "Der Boss President" dismissed Tommy as manager on May 19. Five managerial changes followed during the 1890 season, with McCarthy taking over again for a five-game stretch in August, but the constant turmoil took its toll. Tommy found it difficult to practice his on-field trickery with an inexperienced supporting cast, though he hit .350 and led the league in runs scored, and the Browns ended the season well out of the pennant race.

After the Players League collapsed after one season of operation, Comiskey returned to lead the Browns for the 1891 campaign. Unfortunately, von der Ahe had grown more quarrelsome in Comiskey's absence, and the magic of the pennant-winning years was gone. Tommy McCarthy put together another excellent season, with a .310 average and 127 runs scored, but the Browns finished a distant second to the Boston Reds in what turned out to be the final season for the American Association. The circuit folded after the 1891 campaign, though von der Ahe managed to salvage his franchise and move it into the National League. However, the St. Louis players had had enough of their prickly owner, and on October 29, 1891, Comiskey, McCarthy, and almost the entire team revealed their intentions to play for other National League clubs in 1892. Tommy, perhaps the most sought-after Browns player, signed with his hometown team, the Boston Beaneaters.

Von der Ahe responded to Tommy's defection with his usual flair. Believing that McCarthy owed him money from unpaid fines, the team president hired a burglar to raid Tommy's hotel room in St. Louis late in 1891. The thief stole $19 and a gold watch from Tommy's pants pocket, and von der Ahe marked the disputed debt as paid in full.[8]

Tommy chose to sign with Boston not only because he was born there, but also because the move reunited him with Frank Selee, his former Oshkosh manager. Selee, after winning pennants at Oshkosh in 1887 and at Omaha in

1889, had become manager of the Beaneaters for the 1890 season. He built the club into a solid contender, mostly by promoting minor league stars such as pitcher Kid Nichols and infielders Herman Long and Bobby Lowe. In 1891 Selee's team won the National League pennant in a tight race with the Chicago White Stockings. The 1892 race promised to be tougher, because the National League had absorbed the best players from the now-defunct American Association, and almost every club had improved itself over the winter.

McCarthy was not the only new man on the Beaneaters. Selee signed a teammate of McCarthy from the Browns, Jack Stivetts, who won 33 games and was the best pitcher in the Association in 1891. Selee also managed to attract perhaps the best young player in baseball, center fielder Hugh Duffy, who batted .336 and led the Association in runs batted in for the pennant-winning Boston Reds. Duffy, like McCarthy, was a New Englander, a first-generation Irishman, and a quick-witted man, who believed in using brains rather than brawn to win games. Duffy stood five feet and seven inches tall, as did McCarthy, and Cap Anson had once pronounced him too small to play major league ball. A powerful hitter and outstanding fielder, Duffy spent the remainder of his career proving Anson wrong. He and McCarthy were so perfectly matched that the Boston papers began calling them the "Heavenly Twins," a nickname that lasted. This collaboration between Duffy and McCarthy set the tone for the Beaneaters over the next several seasons.

Tommy brought his bag of tricks to Boston, and he and Duffy promptly went to work on devising new strategies on both offense and defense. Perhaps the most notable maneuver the two friends developed was the hit-and-run play. This tactic, in which a runner on first starts for second at the moment the pitcher releases the ball, trusting the batter to put the ball on the ground, was devised as a way to stay out of the double play and advance a runner from first to third on a single. Though some observers were surprised by the play, it had been a part of baseball strategy for many years; the *Chicago Tribune* described an almost identical tactic used by manager Al Spalding with the White Stockings in 1877.[9] However, most managers during that era thought the maneuver too risky. They would simply order a sacrifice bunt with a runner on first, giving up an out in order to put a man in scoring position on second.

Frank Selee did not believe in giving up outs, and with Duffy and McCarthy in his lineup, he could play the hit-and-run game with confidence. The Beaneaters still used the sacrifice bunt in 1892, Tommy McCarthy's first season with Boston, mainly because pitchers dominated the game that year. In 1893 the league magnates moved the pitching box back ten feet, to its current distance of 60 feet and six inches from the plate, and hitting made a remarkable comeback. The league batting average, only .247 in 1892, jumped to .280 in 1893 and .309 the following year. With hitting suddenly made easier, the hit-and-run became a valuable weapon for teams that mastered it, and no ballclub executed the play better than the Beaneaters.

The "Heavenly Twins" did not invent the hit-and-run, but they and the other Boston players contributed their own refinements. With Duffy on first and McCarthy at bat, Duffy might begin a steal attempt, then scamper back to first. In this fashion, the Beaneaters could ascertain which infielder was assigned to cover the bag on a real steal attempt. Duffy would light out for second on a later pitch, while McCarthy drove a grounder in the hole vacated by the covering infielder. This ploy moved Duffy on third with McCarthy on first, and the next batter would repeat the maneuver, grounding a single through the hole to score Duffy, with McCarthy advancing to third. The Beaneaters, most of whom were fast runners with good bat control, might perform several hit-and-run plays in a single inning.

John Ward, captain of the New York Giants, expressed amazement at the offensive brilliance of the Boston ballclub. "I have never, in my twelve years experience on the diamond, seen such skillful playing," said Ward in 1893. "McCarthy is the chief schemer. He is the man who has introduced his new style of play into the team and he has been ably assisted by Nash, Duffy, Long, Lowe, and Carroll. These men have the utmost confidence in one another's ability to carry out instructions, and they work together as one man. 'Team-work in the field' used to be a prime factor in a pennant-winning team, but now 'team-work at the bat' is the latest wrinkle and the Bostons have it down fine."[10]

Selee's Beaneaters won the pennant in 1891, the year before Duffy and McCarthy arrived, but the newcomers added a jolt of energy, keeping the team on top of the National League. Tommy McCarthy batted only .242 in 1892, but scored 119 runs and stole 53 bases, while Hugh Duffy led the team in batting with a .301 mark and pitchers Jack Stivetts and Kid Nichols posted identical 35–16 records. The Beaneaters won mostly with defense, as the outfield of McCarthy in right, Duffy in center, and Bobby Lowe in left turned in one spectacular fielding play after another.

The 1892 season was played on a split schedule, with the victors of the first half slated to face the second-half champions in an October playoff for the pennant. Boston earned its place in the post-season series by winning the first half. The Beaneaters finished second to the Cleveland Spiders in the second half, but Boston was clearly the best team in the league, and swept through the Spiders in October. The first game of the post-season series, played on October 17 in Cleveland, ended in a scoreless tie after 11 innings, but the Beaneaters won the next five games in a row to win the pennant. Duffy batted .462 and McCarthy .381 to lead the Beaneaters to a series sweep.

The 1893 season, with its surge in offense, radically changed the baseball landscape, and the Beaneaters were primed to take advantage of the new conditions. Selee moved Bobby Lowe from left field to second base, replacing the light-hitting Joe Quinn, and installed Tommy McCarthy in left and Cliff Carroll in right. Lowe teamed with shortstop Herman Long to create one of the best double-play combinations in the league, while Carroll's move to right field strengthened the outfield defense. Tommy, who turned 30 years old in 1893, had battled weight problems during the off-season and was already beginning to slow down in the field and on the basepaths. No longer "Little Mac," he weighed about 180 pounds by this time, and covered less ground in the outfield with each passing season. Despite his disappearing speed, Tommy's batting average jumped to .346 in 1893, and he retained his place in the lineup directly behind Duffy where he could execute the hit-and-run to perfection.

The newspapers lauded the Boston ballclub for playing "scientific" baseball, and the Beaneaters developed a few new tactics in the early 1890s. Duffy and McCarthy, assisted by such able baseball strategists as Herman Long, Bobby Lowe, and captain Billy Nash, grew proficient at stealing signs from other teams. A Boston runner, standing on second base, could read the catcher's signals to the pitcher and relay them to the batter using a series of whistles. All the Beaneaters learned to steal signs, but Tommy McCarthy was the acknowledged master. Another strategy that appeared during this time was the delayed steal, in which a runner caught the opposition by surprise by setting out for the next base as the catcher tossed the ball back to the pitcher. Tommy, who most likely invented the delayed steal, earned so much credit for his strategic acumen that the papers of the time often referred to a smart play as a "Tommy McCarthy."

The Pittsburgh Pirates mounted a minor challenge to the Beaneaters late in the season, but the outcome of the 1893 pennant race was never in doubt. Hugh Duffy batted .363, the fourth-best mark in the league, while Herman Long scored 149 runs and Kid Nichols led the pitching staff with a 34–14 record. The Philadelphia Phillies led the circuit in runs scored, hits, home runs, and batting average, but mediocre pitching left them in fourth place, 14 games out of first. The Beaneaters were a more balanced team, breezing to the flag by five games and dominating the league so thoroughly that newspapers across the nation cried, "Break up the Bostons!"

Hugh Duffy and Tommy McCarthy, so similar in background and playing styles, became more than teammates during this time. Tommy had always wanted to operate his own bar, as did many players of the day, and in 1894 he and Duffy opened a place called "Duffy and McCarthy" on Washington Street in Boston's south side. The place began as a billiard room and bowling alley, since the two ballplayers had not yet been approved for a liquor license. The establishment became popular with Southie residents and baseball fans, sponsoring bowling and billiard teams that played in organized leagues around the city. In September 1895, the teammates gained a liquor license, and expanded the business to include a bar.

On the field, the hitting revolution came to full flower in 1894. During that season, the Boston Beaneaters became the highest-scoring team in baseball history, tallying 1,220 runs in 133 games for an average of 8.6 per contest.

Boston hit .331 as a team, which was only the third-best figure in the National League; the Phillies, with their outfield of three .400 hitters, led with a .349 team mark, trailed by Baltimore at .343. No team, however, could match the speed and baserunning of the Beaneaters. Tommy batted .349 and scored 118 runs in 1894, while Hugh Duffy put together one of the greatest seasons in baseball history with a record .440 average, leading the league with 18 homers and 145 runs batted in.

Unfortunately, the Beaneaters suffered through a season plagued with difficulty. Catcher Charlie Bennett, a skilled handler of pitchers and a fixture on the team for the previous several seasons, was run over by a train in January of 1894. He survived, but his crippling injuries permanently ended his baseball career. On May 15, a game between the Beaneaters and the Baltimore Orioles ended in a fire that gutted the Boston ballpark and spread through the south side of the city, destroying 170 homes and businesses. The Beaneaters played in temporary grounds until a new, smaller park was hastily constructed. Pitchers Kid Nichols and Jack Stivetts turned in solid performances, but the lack of capable starting pitching behind them began to tell as the season wore on. Boston led the league by two games in late August, but four losses in five games dropped them back. They finished the 1894 campaign in third place, eight games behind pennant-winning Baltimore.

On August 15, 1894, McCarthy both started and ended one of the strangest fielding plays of the decade. With two on and nobody out in the ninth inning, Pittsburgh batter Bill Merritt hit a short fly ball to McCarthy in center. Tommy, playing in place of the injured Duffy, called "I got it!" then let the ball drop. He threw to Bobby Lowe, who stepped on second for a forceout and then tagged the runner going from second to third. Third baseman Billy Nash saw that Merritt was not on first and tagged that base, but McCarthy had noticed that Merritt had touched first, then wandered back to the plate area in the general confusion. The batter was not yet out, so McCarthy called for the ball and tagged Merritt out at home to complete the triple play. This play sent the game into extra innings, and the Beaneaters went on to win it in the eleventh.

The National League rules committee had been receiving complaints about McCarthy's trap play for several years, and perhaps the attention paid to this unusual triple play convinced the league that those criticisms were valid. In early 1895 the committee decreed that a batter would henceforth be called automatically out if he hit a pop-up on the infield with a runner on first base and less than two outs. This new wrinkle in officiating was called the infield fly rule, and exists relatively unchanged to this day. The new rule took the trap play away from McCarthy, who often caught infield pop-ups from his position in shallow left field, and left the Boston club with one less defensive weapon. From 1895 on, McCarthy played left field in a more conventional manner.

Boston hoped to contend again in 1895, but Selee's dynasty of the early part of the decade began to unravel. Several of the key Beaneaters, including the 32-year-old McCarthy, were slowing down, and Tommy arrived at spring training at least 15 pounds heavier than he had been at the end of the previous season. The onetime "Little Mac" now tipped the scales at nearly 200 pounds, and his teammates gave him the nickname "Pudge." His poor conditioning was probably responsible for a leg injury that dogged him all year. The Beaneaters, usually a fast-starting team, struggled near the .500 mark for the first month of the new season, and by May the Boston club was mired in seventh place in the 12-team National League.

Internal rifts, exacerbated by the team's poor performance, began to erupt with regularity. *The Sporting News* had reported rumors that the Beaneaters were divided into cliques, with the Irish Catholics such as Duffy and McCarthy opposing the Protestant players, and the issue came to a head in late May. An on-field dispute between McCarthy and pitcher Jack Stivetts led to a hotel-room fistfight in Louisville. Frank Selee tried to keep the disagreement out of the papers, with little success, and tension surrounded the ballclub all season long.

In the meantime, the friendship between Duffy and McCarthy began to fray. Duffy was still one of the stars of the game, leading the team in batting, hits, and stolen bases, while Tommy's production was curtailed sharply due to injuries and excess weight. Both ballplayers were aggressive, competitive men, and Tommy's decline as a player strained the relationship between the two friends. Also, the prospect of sharing the operation of a business may have proved too much for their temperaments to handle. At any rate, Duffy and McCarthy began to argue off the field, affecting their play during the games. The Beaneaters, distracted by internal battles, finished in fourth place in 1895, their worst showing since the Players League season of 1890.

McCarthy, once one of the fastest and sharpest players in the game, had declined considerably. Frank Selee believed in the value of speed, both at bat and in the field, and "Pudge" McCarthy, who stole only 18 bases in 1895, could no longer provide it. Selee desired a younger and faster lineup, so he made a few key trades. He sent his aging third baseman and captain, Billy Nash, to Philadelphia for the speedy center fielder Billy Hamilton, brought rookie third sacker Jimmy Collins (whom the Beaneaters had farmed out earlier) back from Louisville, and signed several youngsters, including catcher Marty Bergen and pitcher Fred Klobedanz. The arrival of Hamilton pushed Hugh Duffy to left field and left no room for Tommy McCarthy, so in November 1895 Selee sold McCarthy's contract to the Brooklyn Bridegrooms for $6,000.

Fortunately, the rift between the "Heavenly Twins" did not last. Duffy and McCarthy decided to end their business partnership amicably, with Tommy buying out his partner and operating the bar and bowling alley on his own. This settlement was completed in late 1895, and the two resumed their friendship, which lasted for the rest of their lives. Tommy continued to manage the bar and bowling alley for more than a decade afterward.

Tommy pondered retirement from the playing field, telling the *Boston Globe* that he was tired of the game, but chose to report to the Brooklyn club for one more season. Perhaps he realized that his bar business depended upon his baseball popularity; as sportswriter Tim Murnane, Tommy's old manager from the Union Association more than a decade before, put it, "McCarthy has, no doubt, discovered by this time that if he keeps his promise to give up playing ball that the baseball public will soon forget him and his new change of base."[11] His tenure in Brooklyn was an unhappy one, as Tommy did not get along with manager Dave Foutz, a former St. Louis Brown whom Tommy had replaced in right field nine years earlier. Shuffling between the starting lineup and the bench, the aging outfielder batted only .249 for the ninth-place Bridegrooms.

Though Brooklyn continued to carry McCarthy's name on its reserve list (and would do so until 1902), Tommy's major league career was over. He decided not to report for spring training in 1897, and in June Tim Murnane reported that Tommy had given up the game for good. Family issues most likely played a major role in McCarthy's decision to leave the sport, as his wife Margaret had died suddenly that year at the age of 27, leaving him with three young daughters to raise. McCarthy, who never remarried, focused his energies on his business and left baseball behind, though the Dodgers offered him a contract for 1898. "I guess baseball is through with me," said Tommy in March of that year, "though it is not for lack of opportunity that this is so.... I find it will be impossible for me to give any attention to league ball next season. My business requires all my time until the hot weather comes, and even then I could not well be away."[12]

McCarthy took care of his daughters and managed his business, but was never far from the game. He played a few semipro games, despite his expanding waistline, and coached baseball at Holy Cross during the early 1900s, followed by a stint at Dartmouth and, later, at Boston College. When Cap Anson and a group of investors made an unsuccessful attempt to create a new major league, a revived American Association, in 1900, McCarthy was the main backer of a proposed Boston franchise. When his bowling alley and bar eventually closed, he returned to the game as a scout for the Cincinnati Reds for four seasons. In 1914 he scouted for his old team, the Boston Braves, the club formerly known as the Beaneaters. The Braves won the World Series that season, and Tommy received a share of the credit. In 1918 he managed the Newark Bears of the International League and inserted himself, at age 55, as a pinch hitter a few times. He held this position for only one season, after which he became a scout for the other local team, the Red Sox.

Tommy was not yet sixty years old, but his health began to deteriorate during the early 1920s. He had grown portly, with well over 200 pounds on his small frame, and during the winter of 1921 he was stricken with pneumonia in both lungs. He traveled to Florida to recover in a warm climate, but an attack of malaria weakened him further. After returning to Boston in early 1922, his illnesses forced him to relinquish his duties as scout for the Red Sox. He was cared for by his three daughters, who still lived with him in South Boston, but doctors discovered cancer that summer. He failed rapidly, and died on August 5, 1922 at the age of 59. He was buried at Calvary Cemetery in Roslindale, a suburb of Boston, and Hugh Duffy, his old friend and teammate, served as one of his pallbearers. Duffy, who died in 1954, was buried in the same cemetery, not far from his fellow "Heavenly Twin."

Tommy McCarthy was one of the most popular ballplayers of the 1890s. Hall of Fame director Ken Smith described him as "a consistent hitter, a wonderful hit-and-run exponent, and a good base runner," while longtime executive Bob Quinn stated that McCarthy and Hugh Duffy were "the most talked-about players of their day."[13] Nonetheless, McCarthy's claim to Cooperstown enshrinement is not evident in his statistics. He played only nine full major league seasons, compiling a batting average of .294 in a high-average era, and was finished as a player by age 33. He led his league in only one major offensive category, pacing the weakened American Association of 1890 in stolen bases. He amassed only 1,451 hits during his career (not counting his Union Association total), more than 80 percent of which were singles, and his slugging percentage is the lowest of all outfielders in the Hall of Fame. Some modern observers label Tommy McCarthy the least qualified player in the Hall, and surely his statistics do not compare with those of most of his fellow Cooperstown honorees.

It appears that McCarthy was elected in 1946 not for his statistical achievements, but for his contributions to baseball strategy. He revived the hit-and-run as an important offensive tactic, probably invented the delayed steal, and was directly responsible for several rules changes, most notably the infield fly rule. He may have been the first man to stand on second base and relay the catcher's signals to the batter, and his variations of the trap play terrorized opposing base runners until the National League rules committee took steps to prevent him and other outfielders from using it. Tommy McCarthy was a good, not great, player, but his reputation as one of the outstanding strategists and innovators of the game's early days paved his way to Cooperstown.

5

Billy Hamilton

> No one was more popular with the patrons of the game [in Philadelphia] than Billy Hamilton. He is the best run-getter that ever played ball, and his base stealing has been a feature of the Philadelphia's team's play since he joined the club in 1890. Many are the crowds that Hamilton has sent away from the grounds at Broad and Huntingdon streets satisfied that they had received their money's worth, despite the fact that the visiting team won the game. There is a dash about his play that inspires the spectator.
>
> —*Boston Globe, 1895*[1]

From 1951 to 1955, the Baseball Writers Association of America selected 13 new members of the Hall of Fame in its annual balloting (including such stars as Joe DiMaggio, Mel Ott, and Jimmie Foxx) while another eight players, umpires, and executives were chosen for induction by the Committee on Veterans. Perhaps the institution's administrators decided that the population of the Hall was growing too quickly, for beginning in 1956 they empowered the Baseball Writers Association to elect new members in even-numbered years only, while the Veterans Committee was relegated to meet in the odd years.

After the writers chose slugger Hank Greenberg and shortstop Joe Cronin in 1956, the flow of new Hall of Famers significantly abated. The Veterans Committee elected two men in 1957, outfielder Sam Crawford and manager Joe McCarthy. No one gained the required 75 percent of the votes for election on the writers' ballot in 1958, with base-stealing specialist Max Carey leading the tally with 51 percent, and in 1959 the veterans' panel chose only one man, former Brooklyn outfielder Zack Wheat. In 1960, the writers once again failed to elect anyone, leaving the Hall with only one new member in a three-year period. Since there were no new inductees that year, the annual ceremony at the museum in Cooperstown that summer was only 15 minutes long.

The candidacy of Max Carey, who at the time held the post–1900 National League record for stolen bases in a career with 738, passed from the writers to the Veterans Committee in 1960, and Carey immediately became a favorite to gain election at the 1961 meeting of that panel. While studying Carey's qualifications, the committee also examined the statistics of an earlier base-stealing great, the man who held the pre–1900 record for career steals. Billy Hamilton, who played from 1888 to 1901, batted .344 during his career (as opposed to Carey's .285 mark), stole more than 900 bases, and scored runs at a faster rate than any player before or since. None of the panel members had seen Hamilton play, as he had retired from the game 60 years before, but his numbers were so impressive that on January 29, 1961, the committee elected both Max Carey and Billy Hamilton to the Hall of Fame. Carey was still healthy and active at the age of 70, but Hamilton had been dead for more than 20 years.

Though *The Sporting News* had, six months earlier, listed both men as worthy candidates for the Hall of Fame, Arthur Daley of *The New York Times* was unimpressed. "This

Hamilton in 1889, his second season with the Kansas City Cowboys. (Library of Congress)

department fails to get excited by this double election [of Carey and Hamilton]," wrote Daley. "Neither is a [Ty] Cobb or a Babe Ruth or a Walter Johnson. The lesser players are starting to make it and that is fundamentally unsound. The conviction here is that admission standards should be kept high and rigorously enforced. The Hall of Fame is a privileged sanctuary and should be kept that way."[2]

William Robert Hamilton, the son of Scottish immigrants Samuel and Mary Hamilton, was born in Newark, New Jersey on February 16, 1866. Billy was the first of two children, the other being his sister Mary, born two years later. By 1870 the Hamilton family had settled in Clinton, Massachusetts, an industrial town of about 3,000 people in Worcester County. Situated in the central part of the state, Worcester County was the hub of the Massachusetts textile industry, and Clinton was dominated by several large factories that produced gingham, rugs, carpeting, and similar products. There Samuel Hamilton found work in a textile mill. Billy became a fine athlete in school, reportedly running the 100-yard dash in ten and three-quarters seconds, but by the time he was 14 years old, he had quit and joined his father in the mill.

Billy, a left-handed batter and a right-handed thrower, excelled in the semipro leagues around Clinton during his teenage years, though few could have predicted that he would find fame in the professional game. The young man stood only five feet and six inches tall at his full adult height, and though he weighed 165 pounds, his thick, muscular legs made him appear heavier. However, those powerful legs became his greatest asset. He was an incredibly swift runner, and was usually the fastest man on the field in any game he played. He learned to use his speed to beat out bunts, steal bases, and cover large amounts of ground in the outfield. Billy Hamilton was more interested in playing ball for a living than in spending his life as a textile worker, and he realized that his speed was his ticket out of the mill.

By 1886, when Billy was 20 years old, he began to draw notice from professional teams. Some sources say that he signed with the Waterbury club of the Eastern League that season, though his name does not appear in the team's box scores; perhaps he played under an assumed name. We do know that he played for Lawrence of the New England League in 1887, and that on July 26 of that year the money-losing team moved to Salem to finish the season. The 1888 campaign found Billy playing center field for Worcester, also in the New England League, where he batted .351, scored 71 runs, and stole 76 bases in only 61 games. His offensive prowess marked him as a future star, and in July of that year the Worcester club sold his contract to the Kansas City Cowboys of the American Association, then one of the two major leagues.

The Cowboys were the weakest team in the Association, and were already buried in last place when the young outfielder joined them. Billy's first day in major league ball was not a positive experience. On July 31, Billy played right field against the Philadelphia Athletics, batting leadoff and going hitless in four trips to the plate against veteran pitcher Gus Weyhing. At least Billy performed no worse than any of his teammates, as Weyhing pitched a no-hitter against the hapless Cowboys that day.

The 22-year-old rookie played in 35 of the remaining 58 games that season for Kansas City, batting .264 and stealing 19 bases for the last-place club. Eager to make a good impression, Billy attempted to steal bases at almost every opportunity, only to get picked off with regularity by the experienced major league pitchers. In one series against Baltimore, lefthander Matt Kilroy caught Billy off first base three times. Manager Sam Barkley ordered him to quit trying to steal until he had studied the pitchers better. In mid-September, former Detroit field leader Bill Watkins replaced Barkley as manager and gave Billy the green light once again. On September 18, Billy stole four bases and scored five runs in an 11–3 victory over Cleveland, and he was on his way.

Hamilton displayed enough promise to be hired as Kansas City's regular right fielder and leadoff batter for the 1889 season, and he rewarded manager Watkins with a .301 average and a league-leading 111 steals. His totals cannot be compared to those compiled in the present day, since stolen bases then included advancing on fly balls or taking extra bases on errors. Still, Billy's 111 thefts were 20 more than the second-highest total in the Association that season and marked him as one of the rising stars of the game. Kansas City moved up a notch to seventh place, in large part due to the inept Louisville team falling behind them, but the ballclub lost money and disbanded at season's end. Billy Hamilton was one of the team's most coveted assets, and on January 7, 1890 the Kansas City owners sold his contract to the Philadelphia Phillies for $5,000.

The Phillies (who up to 1889 had been known as the Quakers) were harmed, as was nearly every other National League team, by the Players League revolt of 1890. Most of the 1889 Phillies had deserted the club and signed with the new league, though the team managed to woo back such key performers as home run champion Sam Thompson, pitcher Kid Gleason, and catcher Jack Clements. Manager Harry Wright, perhaps the most respected figure in baseball, and team owners John I. Rogers and Al Reach filled the holes on the roster with minor-league imports and acquisitions from other teams. Wright installed Billy Hamilton as the left fielder and second-place hitter for the Phillies, with rookie center fielder Eddie Burke in the leadoff spot.

Billy quickly let the Philadelphia fans witness both his strengths and his weaknesses. On the basepaths, the 24-year-old Hamilton "tried to steal everything in sight, including the umpire," as one paper put it. He took large leads against pitchers and catchers who, it must be said, had not yet refined the art of holding runners close to the bag. His spectacular slides brought cheers from the fans and resulted in his nickname, "Sliding Billy." He had the go-ahead to steal at any time, not that he needed any encouragement. "Hamilton's work on the basepaths was spectacular; he delighted in stealing bases," said his outfield mate, Sam Thompson, years later. Thompson, who played a few games for the Detroit Tigers many years later with a young Ty Cobb, claimed that Hamilton was "more daring and reckless" than Cobb.[3] In mid-

May, manager Wright switched Hamilton and Burke in the lineup, with Billy now batting leadoff.

Billy's speed and bunting skill kept his batting average above the .300 mark, but his fielding was sorely lacking. Billy led the league in outfield errors in 1890, and his fielding percentage of .882 was one of the worst in the league. He chased the ball well enough, but dropped flies and poor throws plagued him all season long. One Philadelphia sportswriter complained in May that Billy "omitted to close his hands properly at different times" after he committed two errors in a game against Brooklyn.[4] Despite these shortcomings, Billy batted .325 and led the National League with 102 steals for the third-place Phillies.

The Players League refugees came streaming back to the National League following the demise of the new circuit, and the best-hitting outfield in major league history was complete with the return of Ed Delahanty to the Phillies. "Big Ed" was a native of Cleveland who joined the Phillies in 1888 and jumped to Cleveland's Players League entry in 1890. He was a muscular, hard-hitting left-handed batter, and while he was not much better in the outfield than Billy, he owned a stronger throwing arm. Wright put Delahanty in center field for the 1891 season, though he also played several games at first base. Hamilton, Delahanty, and right fielder "Big Sam" Thompson were mediocre at best in the field, but their hitting and run-scoring were unmatched in the National League.

Hamilton's defensive play improved in 1891, with his error total dropping and his fielding percentage on the rise, but his main contribution to the Phillies lay in his offense. He captured the league batting title with a .340 mark that year, while leading the circuit in hits (179), runs scored (141) and stolen bases (111). Billy was a disruptive force, particularly with his ability to frustrate opposing pitchers by fouling off their deliveries until he found one to hit or drew a walk. He was the perfect leadoff man, getting on base in more than 45 percent of his plate appearances that season and putting himself in position to be knocked in by sluggers Delahanty and Thompson.

Though the Philadelphia pitching was too weak for the team to mount a serious challenge for the pennant, the offensive fireworks drew fans to the Huntingdon Street Grounds and made the flashy Billy Hamilton one of the most popular players on the team. In 1892 all three outfielders batted over .300, with Billy leading the way at .330, and in 1893, after the pitching distance was lengthened by ten feet, their batting averages soared. Billy's outfield defense had improved as well, and in 1893 Harry Wright, in his final season as manager, moved Billy to center field and sent Ed Delahanty to left. Billy remained in center for the remainder of his major league career.

Not always popular with his opponents, Billy shared some of the qualities and personality traits of Ty Cobb, a later center fielder who also set records for stealing bases. Both men took pride in their play, refused to settle for mediocrity, and paid close attention to their own statistics. Hamilton, like Cobb, was intense, driven to succeed, and took losing poorly. Also like Cobb, Billy was careful with his money, and the free-spending Ed Delahanty often teased Billy regarding his frugality. Billy replied, "I have everything I want, and I don't see why I should throw away my earnings to prove I am a good fellow." A few years later, financial reversals caused Delahanty to change his tune. "I take my hat off to [Billy] now," said Delahanty. "Hamilton was right and I was wrong."[5]

Unlike many ballplayers of the era, Hamilton worked hard to keep himself in fine condition, and though he held out for a higher salary almost every spring, always reported to training camp in playing shape. With his short frame and stocky build, he did not look much like an athlete; pitcher Kip Selbach once remarked that Billy "is built on the same lines as an old-fashioned ink bottle [and] looks about as fast as a Quaker Sabbath in Philadelphia."[6] Perhaps his physical limitations drove him to succeed, for he played the game with a laser-like focus, intent on getting to first base and working his way around the bases to home plate by whatever means presented itself.

Billy employed an unusual batting stance. A left-handed batter, he stood as far away from the plate as possible, so much so that fans and opposing players often asked him, "Why don't you step up to the plate now?" Billy paid no attention and took a position with his feet almost parallel to the pitcher, his right foot forward and his left, with most of his weight on it, acting as a pivot. From this extremely closed stance he could wheel around and bunt, or step forward to line a pitch through the infield. Cy Young called Billy "the most difficult of men to pitch to, for he stood way back and stepped in to meet the ball. It is, of course, natural to pitch to the man rather than to the plate, and Billy had most of us pitchers in the hole."[7] Hamilton was also a keen judge of the strike zone, leading the league in walks five times and earning another nickname, "Good Eye Billy."

His posture in center field was even more atypical. Billy relied upon hearing the crack of the bat to determine where the ball would travel, so he stood facing left field, watching the batter out of the corner of his left eye, with his left ear pointed toward the plate and his hands behind his back. The left field area in Philadelphia's Huntingdon Street Grounds was huge, while right field was tiny, so Hamilton depended on Sam Thompson to cover right while his stance helped him get a jump on balls hit to left-center. At five feet and six inches tall, Billy looked like a schoolboy compared to the towering men beside him, Ed Delahanty in left field and Thompson in right, but he used his speed to cover tremendous amounts of ground. He regarded every fly ball as catchable, and while his fielding was erratic, he made up for the occasional dropped fly with spectacular diving catches. His primary failing was a poor throwing arm; baseball historian Bill James wrote that Hamilton owned the weakest outfield arm of the 1890s.

Proud of his status as the king of National League base stealers, Hamilton endured criticism as a "record player" who cared more for his statistics than for the team. "Billy Hamilton ... is what I would call a kleptomaniac," said Tom Brown of the Senators in 1896. "All he thinks of is stealing bases, and he will steal without the least provocation. I have seen Billy take the toughest kind of chances, and make or attempt to make steals when a stolen base wasn't necessary. It doesn't make any difference to him how often he is thrown out. His only ambition in playing ball is to lead the league in stolen bases.

"I remember a game between the St. Louis Browns and Phillies to illustrate Billy's mania for stealing bases. He had stolen four during the game, and as he walked off the field to the visiting players' bus he yelled to me, 'What do you think of me, Tom? Four stolen bases today. That makes 45 this year.' Yet he didn't stop to think that his reckless base running was responsible for the loss of that game to the Phillies."[8]

Baseball scholars do not know how many times Billy was tagged out while trying to steal, as statistics on times caught stealing were not kept until the 20th century, but newspaper accounts indicate that his rate of success was remarkably high. As *The Sporting News* reported in 1898, "[Hamilton] has got base stealing down to a science, and no player succeeds in the attempt so often in proportion to times attempted. His slide is wonderful, and often he gets away from the fielder when the latter has the ball in hand waiting to touch him."[9] They called it the "fadeaway slide," and while Billy may not have invented it, he was its most skilled practitioner. Billy's baserunning exploits frustrated and embarrassed his opponents, and contributed to his lack of popularity among the players. One day, during a game against the Cleveland Spiders, third baseman Chippy McGarr became so angry at Hamilton that he picked up the diminutive Phillie, carried him to the stands, and tossed him over the railing and into the seats.

If anyone needed confirmation of Billy's value to the team, they received it in 1893. Billy was on his way to another outstanding season in early August, and the Phillies stood in second place after three double-digit drubbings of the Senators by scores of 22–7, 14–7, and 21–8. Hamilton had recently complained of not feeling well, and his health grew worse as he tried to play despite fever and fatigue. On August 10, a doctor diagnosed Hamilton with a serious case of typhoid fever and ordered him out of the lineup. Billy played no more that season, and in his absence the Phillies fell quickly out of the race, going 19–26 the rest of the way and settling into fourth place.

Manager Arthur Irwin, who succeeded Harry Wright, scoured the minors for pitching prospects before the 1894 season started, but the result was the same. The Phillies displayed the most incredible hitting attack ever seen in the game, with all members of the outfield batting .400 or better, but finished in third place due to mediocre pitching. Thompson, who missed a month after finger surgery, hit .407 and drove in 141 runs, while Delahanty batted .407 and substitute Tuck Turner turned in a .416 average. As for Billy Hamilton, he rode the crest of the offensive explosion to score 192 runs, the highest total ever achieved in the major leagues, and one that has never been surpassed, or seriously challenged, to this day. Hamilton also became the first player ever to reach base on more than half of his plate appearances in a season, and his on-base percentage of .523 stood as a record until Baltimore's John McGraw passed it four years later.

The official statistics at season's end gave Billy a batting average of .399 on 223 hits in 559 trips to the plate. He missed the .400 circle by one hit, and regretted for the rest of his life that he could not beat out one more roller or one more bunt. Later statisticians have since revised the numerical records of long-ago games, correcting errors and discrepancies, and determined that Billy actually had 220 hits in 544 trips, putting his average at .404. Though major league baseball, and the Baseball Hall of Fame web site, still list Billy's 1894 average at .399 (with 196 runs scored), the researchers at Retrosheet and Total Baseball put Billy in the .400 class with his outfield mates, long after his death.

Billy's 1894 season was remarkable in many ways. From July 6 to August 2, he scored at least one run in 24 consecutive games for the hot-hitting Phillies. On August 31, he tied George Gore's 13-year-old major league record with seven stolen bases, leading the Phillies to an 11–5 win over the Senators. He also compiled a 36-game hitting streak, the longest in Phillies team history until Jimmy Rollins matched the feat at the end of the 2005 season. Still, Billy quarreled with manager Arthur Irwin, a traditionalist who believed in the sacrifice bunt, even when Billy was at bat with the eighth- or ninth-place hitter on first base. Billy, for his part, could not understand why a speedy .400 hitter would be expected to purposely make an out to move a much slower runner up one base. With offense at its highest level in baseball history, Hamilton would have better served the team by swinging away or drawing a walk, but Irwin was unyielding. Player and manager bickered endlessly, with Irwin complaining to the papers that Billy was a "disorganizer."

Nonetheless, offensive production was not the Phillies' main problem. Despite their .400-hitting outfield, Billy's new major league records for runs scored and on-base percentage, and Sam Thompson's incredible standard of 1.43 runs batted in per game, mediocre pitching doomed the team once again. The Baltimore Orioles and Boston Beaneaters, who eschewed the sacrifice bunt for the more rewarding hit-and-run, finished ahead of Philadelphia in the pennant race. The 1895 season brought more of the same, as Billy hit .389 and led the league with 97 steals and 166 runs scored, Thompson drove in 165 runs, and Delahanty batted .404, but the Phillies were never a contender. They finished third, nine and a half games behind Baltimore and seven in back of the Cleveland Spiders.

The Phillies were stagnating, and team owners Rogers and Reach decided that a change was in order. They faulted the management of Arthur Irwin, notwithstanding the fact that the Philadelphia pitching was perennially unequal to the task of holding down the opposition. They desired a new field leader, and were willing to trade one of their hard-hitting outfielders to obtain one. On November 14, 1895, in one of the worst trades in Philadelphia baseball history, the Phillies sent Billy Hamilton to the Boston Beaneaters for third baseman Billy Nash, who replaced Irwin as manager of the ballclub.

Billy expressed regret at leaving, while the Beaneaters were happy to greet him in Boston. Manager Frank Selee had won the pennant with the Beaneaters each year from 1891 to 1893, but the ballclub had finished out of the race during the previous two seasons. Left fielder Tommy McCarthy, once one of the premier base stealing threats in the league, had slowed down and was no longer a force at the top of the lineup. Selee, who believed in the value of speed (and, fortunately for Billy, preferred the hit-and-run to the sacrifice), sold McCarthy to Brooklyn, tapping Hamilton as his replacement. Selee moved Hugh Duffy, one of the best hitters in the game, from center field to left to make room for Billy in the outfield. Most observers believed that Boston received the better end of the trade, and one Philadelphia paper warned the fans, "That [Hamilton] will be missed both by the team and the patrons of the game is a certainty, and the majority will censure Messrs Reach and Rogers for agreeing to his transfer to Boston."[10]

Billy soon grew to love playing for the Beaneaters, as Boston was only an hour by train from his home in Clinton, Massachusetts. Billy had married a local girl named Rebecca Carr in 1888, and by 1896 had three daughters, named Ethel, Mildred, and Ruth. A fourth daughter, Dorothy, was born in 1904, completing the family. Though Billy played ball in Philadelphia and then Boston, the Hamiltons made their home in Clinton for more than three decades, and Billy often took the train to Clinton on off-days during the season. When Billy played in Kansas City, Rebecca often traveled from their home in Massachusetts to see him play, even when she was pregnant, for Billy believed that his play improved when he saw her in the stands. In later years, Rebecca brought their children by train to Boston and other cities to watch their father play ball. "I was dad's shadow," said daughter Ruth many years later. "I followed him around the circuit like a puppy."[11]

Frank Selee, seeking to replace the aggression that Tommy McCarthy had once brought to the ballclub, put Billy in the leadoff spot and gave him free rein on the base paths. Billy's speed and enthusiasm energized the Boston lineup, and his .365 average and 152 runs scored led the Beaneaters to a fourth place finish in 1896. In 1897, Selee promoted two young pitchers, right-hander Ted Lewis and left-hander Fred Klobedanz, to regular roles in support of the staff ace, Kid Nichols, and suddenly Boston owned the best starting pitching in the league. Jimmy Collins, a 24-year-old third baseman, and defensive-minded first baseman Fred Tenney solidified the infield, while rookie Marty Bergen took over as the regular catcher. Boston, with Billy Hamilton front and center, was now the most balanced team in the National League. After a strenuous battle with the defending champion Baltimore Orioles, the Beaneaters won their first league title since 1893, making Billy a pennant-winner for the first time in his career.

Billy was now the centerpiece of a new all-star outfield with Hugh Duffy in left and rookie Chick Stahl, who batted .354 and scored 112 runs, in right. Hamilton was a major contributor to the championship team, as he led the league with 152 runs scored and 105 walks. On September 27, in the final contest of a three-game series with Baltimore with the pennant on the line, Billy swatted four hits, scored three runs, and stole two bases in a 19–10 win that virtually sewed up the flag for Boston. The Beaneaters wound up winning the pennant by two games over the Orioles.

There was no World Series then, but for four years in the 1890s the first and second-place teams in the National League met in the post-season Temple Cup series. Held on the heels of the exciting pennant race, the Temple Cup match-up was anticlimactic. The Boston and Baltimore players had decided beforehand to split their winnings, so the teams played listlessly before small crowds. Billy saved the first game for Boston with two spectacular diving catches in center field, but the Orioles won the next two contests. In the fourth game, Billy went hitless and dropped an easy fly ball by Jack Doyle in the sixth inning, letting in a key run in a 12–11 Baltimore victory. Selee benched Billy for the final game, a sloppy affair won by the Orioles before a few hundred fans, as pitcher Jack Stivetts played center field.

The Baltimore and Boston players each received about $250 after dividing their shares of the revenue from the series, but the then-common practice of splitting the proceeds removed all incentive to win and disappointed the fans. The Temple Cup series was so poorly played and sparsely attended that Baltimore team president Harry von der Horst complained, "This convinces me that the whole Temple Cup business has been a farce, and I shall offer a resolution—that the trophy be refunded to Mr. Temple [the donor] with thanks." The National League agreed, and the 1897 Temple Cup series was the last.

Perhaps Billy was eager to finish the series and return to Clinton, where one of his favorite hobbies awaited him. The diminutive ballplayer was a fan of trotting horses, and his size and athleticism made him a perfect candidate to drive the animals on professional tracks. On October 16, only five days after the last game of the Temple Cup series, Billy drove two winning races at the Clinton track. He continued to perform as a driver for several years afterward at tracks in Clinton and Worcester, after the conclusion of each baseball season.

The Beaneaters repeated as champions in 1898, but Hamilton began to show signs of aging. He had based his career almost entirely on his speed, and his legs were beginning to wear down after taking a pounding for more than ten years at the major league level. A sprained knee limited him to 110 games of the 152 on the schedule, though Billy batted .369 and scored 110 runs. A more serious injury in 1899, a tendon problem in his lower leg that developed after he wrenched his knee while sliding in early May, shortened Billy's season and put his career in jeopardy. He played only 84 games in 1899 and saw his batting average fall to .310, with his stolen base total dwindling to 19.

Billy's inevitable decline was symptomatic of the aging Beaneaters. Pitcher Kid Nichols, left fielder Hugh Duffy, and shortstop Herman Long all battled injuries and ineffectiveness in 1900, and the team suffered another loss when catcher Marty Bergen committed suicide in January of that year (Billy Hamilton and Connie Mack were the only ballplayers to attend Bergen's funeral). Billy, at age 34, managed to play the entire season without a serious injury, batting .333 but with only 34 stolen bases. Frank Selee still batted him in the leadoff slot, but his days of scoring more than a run per game were long over. He was slowing down noticeably, and the Beaneaters fell down the standings, settling in sixth place.

When the American League began play in 1901, most of the Boston stars (including Duffy, Stahl, and Collins) bolted to the new circuit, leaving Frank Selee with a shell of a team. Jimmy Collins, manager of the new American League team that would become known as the Red Sox, wanted the popular "Sliding Billy" to move to the new league with him, but Billy turned down all offers and remained with the Beaneaters for one more season. He was now 35 years old, and advancing age sent his batting average below the .300 mark for the first time since 1888. He managed to steal only 20 bases in 101 games for the seventh-place Beaneaters, and at the end of the 1901 season he requested and received his release from the team owners. Approached by several American League teams to play in 1902, Billy turned down an offer from Washington Senators manager Tom Loftus and declared that his major league career was over.

Few observers paid attention to lifetime statistics and career records 100 years ago, but Billy Hamilton's numbers marked him as one of the greats. He retired as baseball's all-time leader in walks, a distinction he held until Eddie Collins passed him in 1922. His .344 career batting average is the eighth-highest of all time, and his on-base percentage of .455 is surpassed only by Ted Williams, Babe Ruth, and John McGraw. Hamilton's total of stolen bases, once recorded as 937 and later revised to 912, stood as a major league record until Lou Brock of the St. Louis Cardinals ended his career in 1979 with 938 steals. One cannot compare stolen base records of the 1890s with those of the present day, as mentioned before, but Hamilton's totals far outpaced those of all other players of his time.

The Boston papers had labeled Billy "the best run-getter that ever played ball," and his run-scoring totals were perhaps his most impressive statistics. Billy still holds the record for runs scored in a season, and his 1894 total of 192 is 15 more than his nearest competitor, Babe Ruth of the New York Yankees, who crossed the plate 177 times in 1921. During his 14 years in the majors, Billy scored 1,690 runs in 1,506 games, and his average of 1.06 runs per game is the highest figure ever recorded. Only three men (Hamilton and fellow 19th-century stars Harry Stovey and George Gore) scored more than one run per game during their careers, and no modern player comes close to matching the feat. The highest figure among players active in 2007 belongs to Alex Rodriguez of the Yankees, whose career average of runs per game stood at 0.78 at the beginning of the season.

Billy was gone from the majors, but not yet from the game. In June of 1902 he was hired to manage and play for the New England League team in Haverhill, Massachusetts, a manufacturing city about 30 miles north of Boston. The Haverhill club was a listless outfit, holding sixth place in the eight-team league, but Billy promised to shake things up. He called the team the Hustlers, put himself in center field, and pushed his charges to play the game as he did. Billy was a demanding manager, described in the papers as a "hard loser," but by August the Hustlers had crept up the standings to second place, where they finished the season. Billy remained with Haverhill for three seasons, playing on a part-time basis in 1902 and 1903 and becoming a full-timer in 1904. His 1903 team finished last, but Billy led the team to the pennant in 1904, winning the batting title with a .412 average and leading the league in stolen bases and runs scored at the age of 38.

Billy Hamilton in 1900, his next-to-last season with the Boston Beaneaters. (National Baseball Hall of Fame Library, Cooperstown, N.Y.)

This success at Haverhill led to a position at Harrisburg in the "outlaw" Tri-State League, outside the boundaries of organized baseball, but disputes with the team owners and player discontent over Billy's managing style led to his ouster in mid-1906. The old ballplayer then returned to Haverhill, where he played and managed until 1908, winning another batting title. He spent the next two seasons with another New England League team, the Lynn Shoemakers, before he finally retired as a player after the 1910 campaign. During this period, he battled an old National League opponent, Jesse Burkett, the former Cleveland outfielder who was probably the second-best leadoff batter in the game during the 1890s. Burkett owned, managed, and played for the Worcester club of the New England League, and the two feisty old-timers became good friends as well as rivals.

Billy spent the 1911 and 1912 seasons scouting for his old team, the former Beaneaters (who became the Braves in the early 1910s), then managed for Fall River and Springfield in the New England League in 1913 and 1914. In 1916, Jesse Burkett sold his Worcester ballclub to a group of investors that included Billy, who moved his family to Worcester and managed the team for one season. Billy sold his interest in the club in March of 1917 and never returned to the game, though he and wife Rebecca resided in Worcester for the rest of their lives. The old ballplayer, too young to retire at age 51, then obtained a position as a production foreman at a local leather manufacturing plant, where he worked until the early 1930s. His daughters all married, and before long Billy and Rebecca welcomed two granddaughters into the family.

While many other retired ballplayers maintained close contact with the game, Billy Hamilton seemed to fade away. He appeared every now and then at baseball functions in Boston, including a benefit game at Fenway Park for the late pitcher Christy Mathewson in May of 1926, but for the most part Billy stayed out of public view. He enjoyed reliving the old days with other old players living in Worcester, including friend and rival Jesse Burkett, as well as spending time with his family. He rarely, if ever, spoke to sportswriters, and as the years passed, memories of his record-setting performances grew dimmer.

The old ballplayer was a proud man, and although he shied from the spotlight, he wanted his records to be respected. He was unhappy that modern statisticians discounted his base-stealing exploits due to the different scoring rules of the 1890s, and grew upset when newspapers and magazines published articles that named Ty Cobb as the greatest base stealer of all time. In 1937, after one such account appeared in *The Sporting News*, Billy sent a hand-written response to the paper. "I was and will be the greatest stealer of all times," proclaimed the long-retired ballplayer. "I stole over 100 bases in many years and if they ever recount the record I will get my just reward."[12]

This impassioned letter was Billy's last hurrah, as he was already fighting heart disease. Mostly confined to bed for the last year of his life, Billy died at home in Worcester on December 16, 1940 at the age of 74. He was survived by his wife Rebecca, who lived until 1957, as well as four daughters and two grandchildren. On July 24, 1961, 21 years after Billy's death, three of his children represented him at his Hall of Fame induction ceremony in Cooperstown.

Billy Hamilton was the master of the fadeaway slide during his playing days, but his "fadeaway" from the spotlight was so complete that few recognized his name when he finally gained admittance to the Hall of Fame. Bill James, who ranked Hamilton as the ninth-best center fielder of all time in his book, *The New Historical Baseball Abstract* in 2000, remarked on the anonymity of the man who called himself "Sliding Billy." "Hamilton was completely invisible in the literature of the sport up to 1960," wrote James, "and was not elected to the Hall of Fame until 1961. He left no legend behind him, no stories, no anecdotes.... Hamilton was eventually elected to the Hall of Fame purely on the overwhelming quality of his numbers. Even now, in books about nineteenth-century baseball, he is often not mentioned at all, and is never presented as a fully-formed character."[13]

Billy Hamilton may be one of the least familiar players in the Hall of Fame, but he was the greatest base stealer and leadoff man of 19th century baseball. His record for runs scored in a season, which he has held for more than 110 years, appears to be unbreakable, and his incredible statistics reflect his value to his teams. The most important aspect of baseball, on offense, is to score runs, and Hamilton did so with a frequency unmatched by any other player in baseball history. Though sportswriter Arthur Daley may have disagreed, the selection of Billy Hamilton was fully justified and well deserved.

6

Sam Rice

> "I played against Sam Rice for 15 years. That's how you get to know a ballplayer. You know more about the fellow you're playing against than the man you're playing with. You see the hits he grabs away from you, and you see the many ways he beats your team. That's what leaves you impressed."
>
> —*Ty Cobb*[1]

The original Washington franchise of the American League was one of the least successful teams in baseball during the 60 years of its existence. Popularly known as the Senators (though its official team nickname was Nationals from 1905 to 1955), the ballclub finished either last or next to last in the standings in 24 seasons, and won only three pennants and one World Series before moving to Minnesota at the conclusion of the 1960 campaign. Of the eight ballclubs that constituted the initial lineup of American League teams in 1901, only the hapless St. Louis Browns (who relocated to Baltimore in 1954 and became the Orioles) were less fortunate, on the field and at the gate, than the Senators.

As one might expect, the Senators produced fewer star players than did more accomplished outfits such as the New York Yankees. The greatest Senator of all was undoubtedly Walter Johnson, the right-handed pitcher who set a 20th-century record with 417 wins and was one of the first five men elected to the Hall of Fame in 1936. Though a few Hall of Famers (including Tris Speaker and Al Simmons) played briefly in Washington at the end of their careers, Walter Johnson remained as the only lifelong Senator in Cooperstown for nearly three decades.

The career leader in nearly every batting category for the Washington team was a small, fast right fielder named Edgar (Sam) Rice. A converted pitcher, Rice moved to the outfield and, though he did not play his first major league game until he was 25 years old, spent 20 seasons in the American League, all but the last in Washington. He leads all Senators in games played, runs, hits, doubles, triples, and runs batted in, and stands second in batting average and stolen bases. He retired from the game in 1934 with 2,987 hits, only 13 shy of the magic 3,000 mark. Since career records were not so significant then, and as Sam was a team player who cared little for personal glory, he never considered coming back for a 21st campaign merely to join the 3,000 hit club.

Though Sam Rice compiled a .322 career batting average and led his team in almost every offensive category, he drew scant support for the Hall of Fame for many years. He received one vote in the 1938 election, then was not mentioned again until 1949, when three writers cast ballots for him. His totals began to rise during the 1950s after Ty Cobb and other baseball luminaries publicly offered their support, and in 1960 Rice finished second in the balloting with 53 percent of the vote, 75 percent being necessary for election. "Sure, I want to be in Cooperstown," remarked Rice to *Washington Post* reporter Shirley Povich. "Who wouldn't? I've got my bags packed for the ceremonies, if they want me."² He slipped a bit in 1962 when Bob Feller and Jackie Robinson appeared on the ballot for the first time and siphoned off some of the votes, but he still cleared the 50 percent line. By the rules of the Hall then in effect, the candidacy of Rice, who had been retired from the game for 28 years, then passed to the Committee on Veterans, which elected Rice and three others to the Hall on January 27, 1963.

At the time, Sam Rice was a 72-year-old retiree living on a farm in Ashton, Maryland, not far from Washington, with his third wife Mary and stepdaughter Christine. When asked for his reaction, the old ballplayer was modest in his assessment of his own worthiness for the honor. "Oh, it's fine," said Rice to the newspapermen, "but I can't say I'm too thrilled about it. If it were a real Hall of Fame, you'd say Cobb, Speaker, Walter Johnson, Babe Ruth, Lou Gehrig and a few others belonged and then you'd let your voice soften to a mere whisper." However, he expressed his gratitude at the induction ceremony that summer. "I don't think there are words to use on a day like this," he said. "It's the biggest thing any of us can have."³

Edgar Charles Rice was born on a farm near Morocco, Indiana, to Charles and Louise Rice on February 20, 1890. Morocco, a small town of about 1,300 people in Newton County, lies about five miles from the Illinois state line and about 65 miles south of downtown Chicago. Edgar attended grammar school in Newton County, where friends remembered him as a good athlete and fast runner with a strong throwing arm. The oldest of three children, Edgar worked at odd jobs and played amateur ball in the area during his teenage years.

When he was 18, Edgar married a girl named Beulah Stam and moved with her to Watseka, Illinois, about 30 miles west of Morocco. Edgar and Beulah produced a son and a daughter in short order while he toiled as a laborer. He managed to pursue baseball in his spare time. Despite his small stature—he was only five feet and nine inches tall and weighed between 140 and 150 pounds—he was a fine right-handed pitcher on the Watseka town team and hoped for a career in professional ball. From 1909 to 1911 Edgar made several unsuccessful attempts to sign on with teams in Indiana and Illinois, but in early 1912 his luck appeared to change. He received an offer to try out for a

Central Association club in Galesburg, Illinois, and in April of that year Edgar drove his wife and two children to Morocco to stay with his parents while he pursued his dream.

Sam Rice in a Washington uniform, which he wore for 19 of his 20 major league seasons. (National Baseball Hall of Fame Library, Cooperstown, N.Y.)

During his absence, tragedy struck the Rice family, changing Edgar's life forever. On April 21, 1912, a series of powerful storms ripped through eastern Illinois and western Indiana. The storm front produced tornadoes, one of which touched down in Morocco at about six-thirty in the evening. The tornado slammed into the Rice farmhouse, instantly killing Edgar's mother, two sisters, wife, and both of his children. Charles Rice, Edgar's father, survived the initial destruction but died nine days later of his injuries. In one horrific blow, Edgar's entire family was gone. He returned to Morocco to oversee the funerals and settle accounts, but there was nothing left for him there. Following his father's death, he left his hometown and wandered the country for the next year or so.

Though Edgar played a few games for a team in Muscatine, Iowa that summer, he seemed to lose interest in professional ball. He reportedly worked in a distillery in Louisville for a while, found employment as a farm laborer somewhere in the Midwest, and performed odd jobs wherever he could find them. In 1913, perhaps in an effort to distance himself from the tragedy, he traveled to Virginia and joined the United States Navy. He served as a fireman aboard the *USS New Hampshire* and saw battle during the Mexican incursion of 1914, in which American troops occupied the city of Vera Cruz in response to hostilities arising from revolution in Mexico. The battleship had a baseball team, and Edgar pitched for the ballclub later that summer while the ship was stationed at Guantanamo Bay in Cuba.

By mid-1914 some of Edgar's enthusiasm for baseball had returned, and during a furlough from the Navy he tried out for a Virginia League team in Petersburg, Virginia. The owner of the club, a man named Doc Lee, was so impressed with the 24-year-old Edgar that he secured the young man's release from the Navy and put him in the starting rotation. Petersburg was a poor team, finishing in fifth place in a six-team circuit, but Edgar won nine of his 11 decisions that year. In 1915 he posted an 11–12 log for the last-place ballclub and made a mark as a hitter, batting over .300 while splitting time between the mound and the outfield.

The Petersburg club struggled to make ends meet, and Doc Lee was forced to borrow $600 from Clark Griffith, manager of the Washington Senators of the American League, in early 1915. Unable to repay the debt, Lee urged Griffith to accept the right-handed pitcher and part-time outfielder instead, suggesting the Edgar Rice might be a success in the major leagues. Griffith, who no doubt despaired of ever receiving payment on the $600 loan, agreed, taking Edgar's contract in lieu of the debt. At age 25, Edgar Rice was now a major league ballplayer.

Upon his arrival in Washington, Edgar Rice received a new name. Griffith was notoriously bad at remembering names, and when he told the local newspapermen that he had procured a new player from the Virginia League, the reporters asked what the man's first name was. Griffith could not remember and replied "I don't know. Sam, I think." The local papers reported the next day that "Samuel Rice" was the newest member of the Senators. "When a newspaper writer calls you Sam," said Griffith to his new pitcher, "you turn around and answer him, because that's the name I gave you."[4] Edgar never bothered to correct the mistake, and from then on, he was Sam Rice to reporters, fans, and teammates.

Perhaps the newest Senator embraced his new name as a way to put the catastrophe of three years before even further in the past. He never mentioned the tragedy to his teammates, many of whom played with him for more than a decade, never knowing that he had been married and widowed as a young man. He was a quiet individual, friendly enough but never boisterous, and reserved. "He was a very nice man, Sam was," said legendary *Washington Post* columnist Shirley Povich. "But a bit of a loner."[5]

The Senators had traditionally been one of the American League's worst teams, though they had rallied to finish second, second, and third during the previous three seasons. Their major asset was right-hander Walter Johnson, the best pitcher in baseball, who had won the Most Valuable Player award in 1913 with a 36–7 record, and followed it in 1914 with a 28–18 mark. Johnson was almost a one-man pitching staff, and Griffith hoped that Sam Rice might lighten the load, giving Johnson adequate support as a reliever and sometime starter. Sam made his debut against Chicago on August 7, 1915, pitching one and two-thirds relief innings in a 6–2 loss. His first start came on September 7 and resulted in Sam's first (and only) major league win, a 7–4 complete-game decision over the last-place Philadelphia Athletics.

Clark Griffith noticed that his new pitcher had the makings of an outstanding hitter. In his limited action, Sam exhibited the ability to hit the ball squarely, belting three singles in eight plate appearances for a .375 average and hitting well in practice. Griffith, a former pitcher himself, recognized that Sam's fastball was mediocre at best, but his steady hitting and speed could be put to better use in the lineup on a daily basis. When the 1916 season began, Griffith shuttled Sam between the mound and the outfield.

Sam pitched only five times for the Senators in 1916, and his pitching career came to an end in Detroit on June 4. The Tigers led by a 3–2 score after eight innings, but the Senators tied the score with a run in the ninth. Griffith sent Sam to the mound to preserve the tie, but with a runner on first, pitcher George Dauss walloped a triple over right fielder Clyde Milan's head to win the game for the Tigers. The embarrassed Rice stormed into the dugout and confronted his manager. "[Dauss] was probably the worst hitting pitcher in baseball," recalled Sam years later. "When Dauss got that hit, I came to the bench and ripped off my toe-plate and told Griff, he was managing the team then, 'I'm no pitcher if this guy can get a hit off me. Tomorrow, put me in the outfield.'"[6] Sam pitched a few more times, but from then on he was an outfielder.

The Senators finished in seventh place in 1916, but Clark Griffith was beginning to assemble the pieces of what he hoped would be another first-division team. In September 1915, about a month after Sam made his debut, Griffith obtained Joe Judge from Buffalo of the International League. Judge first played in the outfield, but Griffith soon put him at first base despite the fact that Judge was only five feet and eight inches tall. Judge turned into a .300 hitter and a fine fielder, remaining with the Senators for 18 seasons. Judge and Rice became fast friends, rooming together on the road and, several years later, buying row houses next door to each other in the Petworth area of Washington, not far from the ballpark. However, during the first few years of his baseball career, Sam still made his residence in Watseka, Illinois.

By 1917 Sam was a full-time right fielder, showing the Washington fans what they could expect from him in the future. He batted .302 that season and led the team in nearly every offensive category, with 35 stolen bases, 77 runs scored, and 69 runs batted in. Sam was never a home run threat—he hit only 34 during his career, 21 of which were inside-the-park blows—and he hit no homers at all in 1917. However, the fences in Washington's National Park, which became Griffith Stadium in 1920, were so far away that few Senators tried to hit home runs. In fact, Sam never managed to hit a ball over the fence in his home park during the 19 seasons he spent with the Senators. All nine of his career homers in the Washington ballpark were inside-the-park shots. The spacious outfield was suited for players who hit doubles and triples in the gaps and down the lines, and Sam Rice became an expert at this style of hitting.

His routine at the plate was well known to Washingtonians, who saw him perform it for nearly two decades. Sam would exit the dugout swinging two bats, toss one aside, knock the dirt out of his spikes with the other, and step in to meet the pitcher. He'd crowd the plate, standing at the front of the batter's box, then step into the pitch and drive it on a straight line. Sam almost never swung at the first pitch, which was "worth only his scorn," as Shirley Povich one stated. "Why worry about the first pitch?" explained Rice. "If it's no good, you're ahead of [the pitcher]. If he gets over a good pitch, you can be sure he'll come back with it again, and you're laying for him."[7]

He hit to all parts of the field, but specialized in driving sharp line drives through the middle of the diamond. One day, after a Cleveland pitcher knocked him down with a fastball, Sam forced both the pitcher and his successor out of the game with liners off their legs. He was the epitome of the small, fast singles hitter, though his speed enabled him to stretch singles into doubles and doubles into triples. His throwing arm, strengthened from years of pitching, helped him throw out 26 runners from right field in 1917, and though opponents soon stopped challenging him, he still compiled double figures in assists in almost every season.

His career was interrupted, as were many others, by World War I. Sam was 28 years old in 1918, barely falling within the eligible draft age, and when the military quota for Watseka, Illinois was raised that spring, he received a draft notice, previous Navy service notwithstanding. Sam requested a six-month delay in reporting, but was turned down, so he joined the Army in April. Stationed at Fort Terry in Connecticut, Sam received two furloughs that summer and managed to participate in seven games for the Senators, batting .348, before shipping out to France. Sam attained the rank of sergeant before returning home at war's end and rejoining the Washington ballclub.

The Senators were still far from achieving contender status, but right field was in capable hands. Sam, who batted .321 for the seventh-place club in 1919, was so consistent and durable that his teammates dubbed him "Man-o-War," after the famous horse that nearly won the Triple Crown of racing that year. His speed and two stints in the military may also have influenced the choice of nickname. In 1920, when Griffith moved him to center field, Sam hit .336 and led the league in stolen bases with 63, no small feat in a circuit with Ty Cobb, Eddie Collins, and other fast runners. In typically quiet fashion, Sam waited until the season ended before springing a surprise on his teammates. He married Edith Owens, an Indiana native, on October 23, 1920, and moved from Watseka to the Washington area, where he remained for the rest of his life.

Griffith retired from managing and assumed the presidency of the team after the 1920 campaign, and the Senators went through four managers during the next four seasons. George McBride, a Washington shortstop since 1908, led the team to fourth place in 1921 and was replaced by another old-time Senator, Clyde Milan, who saw the team fall back to sixth the following year. Griffith then hired Donie Bush, who was too abrasive for the players' taste and lasted only one season before Stanley (Bucky) Harris, a 26-year-old second baseman, took the reins in 1924. Through it all, Sam rarely missed a game, batting over .300 (except for a .295 mark in 1922) and staying among the league leaders in hits, doubles, and steals. He was a good center fielder, but excelled more in right, and after the 1922 season Sam moved back there on a more or less permanent basis. Several sportswriters, especially those in Washington, proclaimed Sam to be one of the most valuable players in the American League, but his unostentatious play and reticent nature made him perhaps the least-appreciated star of his era.

Not much was expected of the Senators in 1924, and hardly anyone thought they could challenge Babe Ruth and the New York Yankees for the pennant with the inexperienced "Boy Manager," Bucky Harris, at the helm. However, Clark Griffith had finally assembled a strong ballclub around veteran pitcher Walter Johnson and .300 hitter Sam Rice. First baseman Joe Judge, who hit .308 in 1924, anchored a solid infield that included manager Harris at second, Roger Peckinpaugh at shortstop, and Ossie Bluege at third. Leon (Goose) Goslin, a hard-hitting run producer, played left field, with Sam Rice in right and a platoon of Earl McNeely and Nemo Leibold in center. Veteran Herold (Muddy) Ruel handled the catching chores. On the pitching side, the 37-year-old Johnson anchored the staff, but received excellent support from second-line starters Tom Zachary and George Mogridge, with reliever Fred (Firpo) Marberry chipping in with 15 saves and 50 appearances.

The Senators now possessed enough depth to battle the powerful Yankees on even terms, though they did not rise above the .500 mark until mid-June. In fifth place on June 18, but only three and a half games out of first, the Senators ran off a 10-game winning streak and shot into the lead. Four losses to the Yankees in a five-game set in early July brought the New Yorkers within one game, and the upstart Senators drifted back to second before a 12–2 spurt in late August brought them back into a virtual tie with the Yankees on August 25. In the most important series of the season, a four-game set held at Yankee Stadium from August 28 to August 31, the Senators won three of the contests to extend their lead to two games. Two losses to Detroit in mid-September tied the race again, but eight wins in their next nine games overwhelmed the Yankees and clinched the pennant, Washington's first major league flag of any kind.

Much of the credit for the Senators' success belonged to the Washington right fielder. Sam Rice batted .334 in 1924, and on August 23 began a 31-game hitting streak, the longest in team history, during the hottest part of the pennant race. He batted .402 during the streak, in which the Senators won 23 of the 31 games, and on August 28 Sam belted five hits in an 11–6 victory over the Yankees that started the Senators on their charge to the pennant. By the time the streak ended against the St. Louis Browns on September 26, Washington held a two-game lead which it never relinquished. Walter Johnson, who led the league with 23 wins and six shutouts, won the Most Valuable Player award, but Sam Rice's contributions at the bat were crucial to the team's winning effort.

Sam, perhaps worn out from the demanding pennant race, batted only .207 with six hits, all singles, in the seven-game World Series against the New York Giants that fall, but good pitching and a measure of luck aided the Senators. Walter Johnson dropped the first game despite striking out 12 Giants, but the Senators took game 2 behind Tom Zachary. The teams traded wins over the next four games to tie the Series and force a seventh game, which was played in Griffith Stadium on October 10. The Giants led Game 7 by a 3–1 count in the eighth before Washington loaded the bases, and a bad-hop single by Bucky Harris over third baseman Fred Lindstrom's head brought home two runs, tying the game. Sam Rice, who went hitless in five trips to the plate that day, then grounded out to end the inning.

Johnson entered in the ninth and gave up a one-out triple to Frank Frisch, but the veteran pitcher kept the Giants off the board, sending the game into extra innings tied at 3. In the bottom of the twelfth, Muddy Ruel popped up with one out, but Giants catcher Hank Gowdy tripped over his mask and dropped the ball. Given another chance, Ruel whacked a double down the left field line. Johnson then reached first on shortstop Travis Jackson's error, with Ruel holding at second, bringing Earl McNeely to the plate. McNeely hit a grounder to third, and once again the ball took a bad hop and skipped over Lindstrom's head as Ruel dashed home with the winning run. The Senators, against all odds, had won their first, and only, World Series title.

The Senators, with Sam batting .350 and Goslin, Harris and others continuing their outstanding play from the year before, repeated as champions in 1925. It was a much easier race, as the Yankees fell to seventh place due to internal strife and the absence of Babe Ruth from the lineup for weeks at a time. The Philadelphia A's, building around young stars such as Lefty Grove and Al Simmons, provided the main challenge as the two teams sparred all season long. Tied for the lead on August 25, the Senators then won eight in a row while the A's collapsed and fell out of the race, as Washington won its second consecutive pennant by eight games. Sam Rice, still hitting the ball soundly at the age of 35, pounded out 227 hits that season, and his 182 singles set a new American League record that lasted until Kansas City's Willie Wilson bettered it in 1980.

As defending champions, the Senators were regarded as favorites going into the World Series against the Pittsburgh Pirates, and Sam Rice played a pivotal role. He drove out a record-tying 12 hits, all singles, during the Series, and his two runs batted in gave the Senators a victory in the first game in Pittsburgh. The Pirates won the second contest, and the third game, played at Griffith Stadium before President and Mrs. Calvin Coolidge and more than 36,000 fans, put Sam at the center of a controversy that raged for nearly 50 years afterward.

The Pirates held a 1–0 lead in Game 3 before Sam singled in the third inning, was sacrificed to second, took third on a fly ball, and scored on a double by Joe Judge to tie the game at 1. The teams traded the lead a few more times before the Senators scored twice in the seventh to take a 4–3 advantage. Sam had started the game in center field, but when Joe Harris pinch-hit for right fielder Nemo Liebold, manager Bucky Harris sent Earl McNeely to center and moved Sam to right to start the eighth inning. The first two Pirates went out in the eighth, but Earl Smith belted a long fly to right-center that Sam chased all the way to the fence. Sam leaped against, and over, the fence, and he and the ball both disappeared into the crowd. After an agonizing wait of at least 10 seconds (some onlookers claimed it was 15 seconds or more), Sam emerged from the crowd with the ball secure in his glove.

The umpires declared Smith out, precipitating a wild protest on the part of the Pirates. Manager Bill McKechnie claimed that the Washington fans caught the ball and passed it back to Rice, but the umpires did not witness that. The Senators insisted that Sam caught the ball and, with no evidence to the contrary, the decision stood. McKechnie protested to the baseball commissioner, Judge Kenesaw Mountain Landis, who was present at the game, but Landis stated that he could not overrule a judgment call made by the umpires. The Pirates were retired in the eighth and failed to score in the ninth, and the Senators won the game to take a two games to one lead in the Series.

The Pirates eventually won the Series in seven games, but the mystery of Sam's catch remained a source of controversy for decades. Some Pittsburgh fans, sitting in the bleacher seats that day, swore out affidavits claiming that Rice had dropped the ball, while a number of Washington fans filed legal papers of their own that stated the opposite. When Judge Landis asked Sam if he had, indeed, made the catch, Sam replied, "Judge, the umpire said I did." Landis thought it over for a minute, then said, "Sam, let's leave it that way."[8] The commissioner advised Sam to proffer that explanation when queried about the matter in the future, and so he did for the rest of his life. He kept the mystery alive by never telling anyone, not even family or teammates, what really happened, and the play became one of the most famous and controversial in World Series history.

The Senators finished in the first division over the next several seasons, but the Yankees won three pennants in a row beginning in 1926, and the Athletics took the top spot each year from 1929 to 1931. The Senators slowly changed personnel; Walter Johnson pitched his last game in 1927, while Goose Goslin was traded to the Browns in 1930 and Bucky Harris went to Detroit after the 1928 season. Sam Rice, along with first baseman Joe Judge, remained into the 1930s. "Day in and day out," wrote Francis Stann of the *Washington Star-News*, "Rice was the most consistent of the Washington hitters.... Plaudits went to Goose Goslin and Bucky Harris and Walter Johnson and Joe Judge, but Sam was quietly lining out his base hits, stealing when it was appropriate and, during his and the Senators' heyday, scoring 100 runs a year."[9]

Sam Rice kept hitting the ball effectively despite his advancing age, and in 1930, when he was 40 years old, he hit .349 with 207 hits and 121 runs scored. Not until 1996, when Paul Molitor achieved the feat, did another major leaguer rack up 200 hits in a season at that age. Sam was still the most consistent Senator at the plate, though his stolen base totals dropped each season, and some believed that he could play forever. On July 19, 1932, the Senators held "Sam Rice Day" at Griffith Stadium, presenting Sam with a check for $2,235.09, a new Studebaker automobile, an engraved trophy, a silver tea service, an electric clock, a wrist watch, and a set of golf clubs. President Herbert Hoover sent a letter of congratulations which read in part, "You have given all of us who love baseball so much pleasure that you have richly earned the honor of a 'Sam Rice Day.'" Rice, with his usual reticence, gave a speech in which he said only, "Thanks, folks. This is the greatest day in my baseball career."[10]

However, not even Sam Rice could slow the march of time, and by 1932 he was a part-time player and pinch-hitter, batting .323 in 106 games, only 69 of which were in the field. The Senators won an unexpected pennant in 1933, beating the Yankees by seven games, and giving the 43-year-old Sam a chance to play in one more World Series. He batted once in the third game and stroked a pinch-hit single. The Senators lost the Series in five games to the New York Giants, and his appearance in the fall classic turned out to be Sam's last in a Washington uniform. On January 9, 1934, Clark Griffith gave Sam his unconditional release.

Sam pondered retirement from the game at age 44, but his old friend and teammate Walter Johnson was managing the Cleveland Indians at the time and offered Sam a job as a pinch-hitter and spare outfielder. Sam signed with the Indians in February, earned a place on the team in spring training, and batted a respectable .293 in his 20th season of major league ball. He finished the season with 2,987 career hits, only 13 shy of the magic 3,000 circle, but decided that he had played enough baseball. Johnson wanted him to return to the Indians in 1935, but Sam instead announced his departure from professional baseball.

The old ballplayer now turned his attention to business pursuits. He and his wife Edith, who had no children, operated a successful chicken and egg farm near Ashton, Maryland called "Sam Rice's Chicken Hatchery" for more than a decade. They sold the business in 1945, and Sam raised pigeons and dabbled in real estate, increasing his land holdings with the passing years. A fine left-handed golfer, he played several times a week and entered tournaments in the Washington area. He still refused to give a straight answer when asked about the catch he made in the 1925 Series, sticking with the same reply—"the umpire said I caught it"—that served him well for many years. He even turned down an offer of $2,500 from a national magazine to tell the inside story. Sam,

Sam at the plate, late in his career. (National Baseball Hall of Fame Library, Cooperstown, N.Y.)

who usually shunned the spotlight, seemed to enjoy the attention, and his coy reluctance to resolve the question fueled the controversy further, keeping it, and him, in the public eye.

Edith Rice died on November 7, 1957 after 37 years of marriage, and in December of 1959 Sam married a widow named Mary Kendall and gained two stepdaughters. Christine, the younger of the two, took Sam's last name. "Daddy was the kindest, most considerate man I've ever known," said Christine Rice many years later. "He helped so many people along the way. He reminded me of Gregory Peck, the actor. But he never talked about himself much. He kept it all inside—the catch, his life before baseball.

"It was only by accident that we found out about the storm."[11]

One day in the mid-1960s, after Sam had been elected to the Hall of Fame, a newspaper reporter sat down with him and wife Mary and asked about the tragedy that had happened in Morocco, Indiana, more than 50 years before. Sam tried to change the subject, but the reporter persisted, and the truth soon came spilling out. Apparently, Mary had no idea that she was the third, not the second, Mrs. Rice. Sam had buried his personal sorrow so deeply in the past that he had not told Mary or his stepdaughters about the family he lost in the tornado in 1912. Though mentions of the loss had appeared in print every now and then, the details were largely unknown by the public until long after Sam's death.[12]

Sam held on to his other huge secret, the catch in the 1925 World Series, for the rest of his life, but perhaps the revelation of his personal tragedy convinced him to come to grips with the on-field controversy in some way. He still refused to say definitively whether he caught the ball or not, but in 1965 he attended the annual Hall of Fame banquet in Cooperstown and told his fellow inductees that he had written a letter that explained the truth. Lee Allen, the Hall historian, had suggested the idea to Sam, who thought it over and agreed that it was a good way to resolve the question. Sam wrote the letter, sealed it in an envelope, and gave it to Hall director Paul Kerr with instructions not to open it until the ballplayer's death.

Sam's old team, the Senators, moved to Minnesota in 1960, but the American League put an expansion team in the nation's capital in 1961. Sam watched the new Senators every now and then on television, though his stepdaughter Christine explained, "He said that watching baseball made him tired, because when the players were running, he was running alongside them."[13] Sam was more interested in golfing, bowling, and talking about old times with teammates such as Joe Judge and Nick Altrock, who resided in the Washington area. He lived comfortably, especially after selling some of his farmland to developers, who built an upscale housing development called Sam Rice Manor, which exists under that name to this day.

He and Mary attended the Hall of Fame induction ceremonies at Cooperstown almost every summer, though Sam began to slow down after passing his 80th birthday. In July of 1974, both Sam and fellow Hall of Famer (and

Maryland resident) Lefty Grove attended the ceremonies that enshrined Mickey Mantle, Whitey Ford, and Sam Thompson. Both men were ill, Sam with cancer and Grove with eye problems, but they walked arm in arm all weekend, each man supporting the other. It was the last visit for both, as Grove died in May of 1975, while Sam Rice passed away on October 13, 1974, at the age of 84. He was buried in Woodside Cemetery in Brinklow, Maryland.

Three weeks later, on November 4, 1974, Hall of Fame director Paul Kerr held a press conference and opened the letter that Sam had given him nine years earlier. The letter, written in longhand, illuminated the 49-year-old mystery of the catch Sam made in the 1925 World Series, and read as follows:

> Monday, July 26—1965
> It was a cold and windy day—the rightfield bleachers were crowded with people in overcoats and wrapped in blankets, the ball was a line drive headed for the bleachers towards right center, I turned slightly to my right and had the ball in view all the way, going at top speed and about 15 feet from bleachers jumped as high as I could and back handed and the ball hit the center of pocket in glove (I had a death grip on it). I hit the ground about 5 feet from a barrier about 4 feet high in front of bleachers with all the brakes on but couldn't stop so I tried to jump it to land in the crowd but my feet hit the barrier about a foot from top and I toppled over on my stomach into first row of bleachers. I hit my adams apple on something which sort of knocked me out for a few seconds but McNeely arrived about that time and grabbed me by the shirt and pulled me out. I remember trotting back towards the infield still carrying the ball for about half way and then tossed it towards the pitchers mound. (How I have wished many times I had kept it.)
> At no time did I lose possession of the ball. "Sam" Rice

Sam added a postscript:

> P.S. After this was announced at the dinner last night I approached Bill McKechnie (one of the finest men I have ever known in Baseball) and I said Bill you were the mgr of Pittsburgh at that time, what do you think will be in the letter. His answer was, Sam, there was never any doubt in my mind but what you caught the ball: I thanked him as much as to say, You were right.[14]

Sam Rice would probably have entered the Hall of Fame long before he did had he returned to Cleveland in 1935, played for a few weeks, then retired after stroking his 3,000th hit. His longtime friend, Walter Johnson, was managing the Indians at the time and probably would have allowed Sam to pursue membership in the 3,000-hit club. However, playing for personal glory was not Sam's style. He was the epitome of the quiet, efficient team player, a type that is valuable to his ballclub but attracts little attention from Hall of Fame electors. Fortunately, the oft-criticized Veterans Committee made an excellent choice when it tapped Sam in 1963. Perhaps no other member of the Hall of Fame overcame as much personal sorrow, or earned as much respect from teammates and opponents alike, as did Sam Rice. His legacy of tragedy and triumph is one of the great stories of American sports.

7

Tim Keefe

> "[Tim Keefe] is one of the most perfect gentlemen who ever played ball. Eighteen years he pitched, and who ever heard of him having a row or quarrel on the field, with either an umpire or another player? And his honesty is unquestionable."
> —*An unidentified Chicago opponent, 1896*[1]

During the late 1950s, the Hall of Fame Committee on Veterans met every two years and was allowed to select up to two old-time ballplayers for induction. Such players as Sam Crawford, Max Carey, and Zack Wheat were chosen from 1957 to 1961, when the committee met on an annual basis. Two men were selected in 1962 (Bill McKechnie and Edd Roush) and in 1963 the Hall instructed the committee to pick as many as four 19th-century and early 20th-century players. This it did, selecting John Clarkson, Sam Rice, Eppa Rixey, and Elmer Flick for membership in January of 1963.

At that time, there were still fewer than 100 men in the Hall of Fame, and sportswriters across the nation decried the backlog of deserving candidates still on the outside of the Cooperstown museum. To alleviate this logjam, the Hall allowed the Committee on Veterans to choose up to six men during its next election. On February 2, 1964, the panel filled its quota by selecting pitchers Burleigh Grimes and Red Faber, outfielder Heinie Manush, manager Miller Huggins, and two 19th century stars, pitcher-turned-infielder John Montgomery Ward and pitcher Tim Keefe. The six honorees were joined by Luke Appling, elected a few weeks later by the Baseball Writers Association, and comprised the largest Hall induction class since the enshrinement of eight men in 1953.

Paul Kerr, secretary of the Veterans Committee, contacted the newly-elected players and their families by phone and informed them of their election. Three of the new inductees—Manush, Faber, and Grimes—were still living and received the news directly from Kerr. The committee secretary managed to locate a surviving brother of Huggins, who died in 1929, and the 86-year-old Katherine Ward, widow of John, who died in 1925. Tim Keefe, however, presented a problem for the Hall of Fame. The star pitcher of the New York Giants during the 1880s had died in 1933 in his hometown of Cambridge, Massachusetts. Keefe, a widower at the time of his death, left no children, and neither Paul Kerr nor Hall historian Lee Allen were able to locate any surviving relatives, in Cambridge or anywhere else.

Fortunately, the publicity surrounding Keefe's election to the Hall reached two of his relatives. A few days following the announcement, a woman named Paula Brodbine called *Boston Globe* writer Harold Kaese. Miss Brodbine explained that she and her sister Ann were nieces of Tim Keefe, and happened to live in the same house in Cambridge in which Keefe had spent his final years. The sisters owned a family scrapbook documenting their uncle's baseball career, which they offered to donate to the Hall of Fame, and wished to represent their relative at the ceremony. Kaese relayed this information to Allen and Kerr, and on July 27, 1964, Paula and Ann Brodbine looked on as Tim Keefe took his place in the Hall of Fame.

Timothy John Keefe, born in Cambridge, Massachusetts on New Year's Day 1857, was the second son of Patrick Keefe, a carpenter, and the former Mary Leahy. Patrick and Mary Keefe had left Ireland a few years before, settling in Cambridge among dozens of Irish families named Keefe or O'Keefe. Patrick named his second son after his two younger brothers, Timothy and John, who worked as laborers in Cambridge.

Tim Keefe was four years old at the outbreak of the Civil War. His father, according to family lore, was working on a construction project south of the Mason-Dixon Line at that time. Arrested by Confederate soldiers, Patrick Keefe was offered a choice between service in the Southern armed forces and internment in a prison camp. Patrick refused to fight, as his two brothers had joined the Union army, so he spent the war in custody, making bullets in a prison factory. His brothers both died in battle during 1862, while Patrick remained in prison. Eventually repatriated, he returned to Cambridge after an absence of several years.[2]

Patrick Keefe came home and resumed a family life that would eventually produce seven children, but he was profoundly changed by the war. Determined to make a success of his son Tim, the namesake of both of his beloved brothers, Patrick demanded that his son immerse himself in mathematics, science and business, and it frustrated the elder Keefe that Tim, an intelligent boy and a good student, nonetheless preferred to play baseball. Tim's father derided baseball as a waste of time and talent, and father and son quarreled endlessly over Tim's enthusiasm for the sport.

Despite the friction at home, Tim Keefe managed to play ball whenever possible, and by the early 1870s the right-hander was gaining notice as a fine amateur ballplayer. Baseball was a popular pastime in Cambridge, a suburb of Boston and the home of Harvard University, and some of the region's leading amateur clubs performed there. In 1874, the 17-year-old Tim earned a position on the Franklin Junior club in Cambridge. Over the next few years, he pitched and played third base for such teams as the Mutuals and Our-Boys of Boston, and the Tremonts of Cambridge. By 1878 he was a semi-professional, playing for a highly-regarded independent club in Clinton, Massachusetts alongside future major league umpire John Gaffney. Tim followed his stint at Clinton with an engagement as a pitcher in Westborough, where he quickly earned recognition as the best young hurler in New England.

Tim was not the only first-generation Irish-American baseball star in Cambridge. A jeweler's son named John Clarkson, four years younger than Tim, was also an outstanding right-handed pitcher in local amateur circles. Clarkson played high school ball in Cambridge and later pitched for the Beacons and the Hyde Parks, two of the leading clubs in Boston. Clarkson was one of five ballplaying brothers, three of whom made the major leagues. Clarkson's cousins Mert and Walter Hackett were Cambridge boys who played on amateur clubs in the Boston area, as were catcher Barney Gilligan and outfielders Joe Kelley and Patrick (Cozy) Dolan. All eventually made a mark in major league ball, and Clarkson and Kelley later gained enshrinement in the Hall of Fame.

Tim Keefe with the Giants during the 1880s. (National Baseball Hall of Fame Library, Cooperstown, N.Y.)

Underhanded pitching was the norm in baseball until 1872, when the rules were changed to allow pitchers to release the ball from anywhere below the waist. Tim Keefe, who stood five feet ten inches tall and weighed about 180 pounds, developed a sidearm delivery that not only put the ball over the plate with speed, but, more importantly, was endlessly repeatable. Tim recognized that proper mechanics of pitching were crucial in avoiding arm strain and fatigue, and the young right-hander was one of the first to approach pitching from a scientific point of view. Control, not velocity, was the prime objective of the pitcher, in Tim's opinion. "Learn control first," he said. "Worry about speed and curves later." Nonetheless, Tim Keefe packed a lot of speed on the ball, and his delivery produced one of the best fastballs in the semipro ranks.

Tim's work at Clinton and Westborough drew attention, and in 1879 he entered the professional game, playing in Utica and New Bedford (where he was managed by Jim Mutrie, who would play an important role in Tim's career) before landing on a National Association team in Albany, New York. He began the 1880 campaign in Albany, where he posted a 7–9 record for a poor team but recorded an excellent earned run average of 1.73. The Albany team folded in July of that year, but Bob Ferguson had been watching the 23-year-old Tim. Ferguson was the manager of the Troy Trojans of the National League, who played only a few miles from Albany, and was impressed with the intelligent young pitcher. He signed Keefe to a contract which provided a salary of $300 per month. Tim, who had learned carpentry from his father and listed his occupation on the United States census that year as a cabinetmaker, was now a major league baseball player.

The Troy team was a good hitting ballclub, with future stars such as Roger Connor and Buck Ewing in the lineup, but their fielding was less than stellar. Tim pitched his first game in the National League on August 6, 1880, defeating Cleveland by a 4–2 score, but multiple errors led to losses in several of the games he pitched afterward. He started 12 games for Troy in 1880, completing them all, and while posting a 6–6 record, he also produced a microscopic 0.86 earned run average. Bob Ferguson had been looking for a new pitcher to complement Troy's main starter, curveball specialist Mickey Welch, and the manager recognized that the fastball-throwing Tim was the perfect candidate. The Trojans were allowed to reserve contract rights to five players after the 1880 season, as mandated by the primitive reserve clause in effect at the time, so Ferguson protected both Welch and the newcomer Keefe.

Keefe was still learning how to pitch, as evidenced by his 18–27 record in 1881, but proved his durability by completing all 45 of his starts. Mickey Welch also completed every game he pitched that season, and between them the two pitched every inning for the Trojans that year without once needing a reliever. Keefe and Welch, who posted a 21–18 log, thus began a partnership that lasted for most of their careers. Though different in temperament, as Welch was a fun-loving and outgoing family man while Tim was quiet, studious, and single, the two pitchers became fast friends.

Troy was the smallest city in the National League, and its unsuitability as a major league market became more acute during the 1882 campaign. The Trojans, with Keefe winning 17 and losing 26 while Welch stumbled to a 14–16 record, had settled into seventh place by September, and a late-season series against Worcester drew six fans to one game and 18 to another. The Troy management, after several years of financial struggle, disbanded its team at season's end, as did the Worcester ownership group. When the Troy players became free agents, a New York baseball entrepreneur named John B. Day swooped in to sign the best performers. Day, owner of the independent New York Metropolitans, proposed to create a new team, the Gothams, to represent New York in the National League, and also to move his "Mets" into the rival American Association. New York, which had not been represented in either league in 1882, would have a team in each circuit in 1883.

Day signed six Trojan players, making sure to grab both Troy pitchers,

Welch and Keefe, before any other team could make a higher offer. Day then split the duo, putting Welch (along with Roger Connor, Buck Ewing, and Pat Gillespie) on the Gothams and placing Tim Keefe and Bill Holbert on the Metropolitans. Holbert had been Keefe's personal receiver for Troy, catching nearly all the games Tim pitched. The Metropolitans, managed by Tim's old New Bedford field boss Jim Mutrie, had been a good independent team, and now, with Keefe, Holbert, and fine hitters like Dave Orr and Tom (Dude) Esterbrook, the ballclub appeared to be one of the better nines in the American Association.

The Metropolitans played, as did the Gothams, at the Polo Grounds in upper Manhattan. The Polo Grounds contained two baseball fields, with the Gothams playing on the west side of the complex and the Mets on the east. It was here that Tim Keefe reached stardom as one of the top starting pitchers in the Association. He pitched 68 games for the Mets in 1883, completing all of them, and posted a 41–27 record as the Mets finished their first season in the American Association in fourth place. Tim struck out a league-leading 361 batters, and led the league in games, complete games, and innings pitched (with an astounding 619). On July 4, Tim threw both ends of a doubleheader against Columbus, giving up only one hit in the first game and two in the second. He won the contests by scores of 9–1 and 3–0.

By 1883, Tim had perfected a weapon that gave him an advantage over the batters. He had learned to throw what the papers called the "slow ball," the pitch we now know as a change of pace. Other hurlers had thrown off-speed pitches in previous years, but Tim learned to deliver his slow pitch with the same motion that he used to throw his impressive fastball. The resulting deception made Tim the strikeout king of the Association. His 361 strikeouts obliterated the previous single-season record, set by Larry Corcoran in the National League in 1880. Other pitchers rushed to copy Tim's "slow ball," and by the end of the 1880s most major league pitchers had a version of Tim Keefe's invention in their arsenals. It appears that Tim threw a variety of change-ups, as some contemporary accounts describe a Keefe pitch that did not rotate on its way to the plate; perhaps Tim not only pioneered the change of pace, but the knuckleball as well.

Keefe racked up impressive strikeout totals, mainly because he tried to whiff as many batters as possible. He believed that each strikeout reduced the amount of pressure on the defense by giving the fielders less work to do (and less opportunity to make errors behind him). After pitching in front of a poor fielding team such as the Troy Trojans for three seasons, perhaps Tim adopted this tactic as a self-preservation measure. Other pitchers, most notably his fellow Cambridge native John Clarkson, believed in letting the batter hit the ball and allowing the fielders to do their work. Clarkson, however, performed for the Chicago White Stockings, one of the best fielding teams in baseball, and enjoyed the luxury of a good defense supporting him. Tim, whose New York teams were only average at best on defense, continued to strike out batters in bunches, and in 1888 he became the first major league pitcher to strike out 2,000 men during his career.

On a personal level, Tim was reserved and studious, not given to drinking or raucous partying. He was one of the more handsome New York ballplayers, with a pair of intense eyes set behind a bushy mustache, but refrained from the dating scene until he was nearly 30 years of age. The press called the outgoing Welch "Smiling Mickey," but the nickname "Smiling Tim," though it appeared sometimes in print, did not do justice to Keefe's demeanor. "Sir Timothy," a more appropriate moniker for the gentlemanly pitcher, soon came into popular usage. He was one of the most temperate and well-behaved ballplayers in the game, and Mickey Welch later remarked that he never once saw Keefe argue with an umpire. Tim also became a respected teacher of pitching, and coached baseball at Harvard, Yale, or Princeton almost every spring during the 1880s and 1890s.

Keefe was all business on the field, said fellow hurler "Long John" Healy, who called Keefe "the greatest pitcher who ever stepped into a box." Keefe relied on his excellent control, but "there was no sentiment about him," said Healy. "I've seen him drive batter after batter back from the plate. If [Keefe] could not intimidate him by twisting the ball around his neck or almost cutting his belt off, [Keefe] would soak him good and hard.... If there were three balls and no strikes on the batter, Tim would not waste any time with him.... Tim would plant the next ball into his ribs."

"How could a batter do any good under these conditions?" continued Healy. "His whole attention would be directed toward dodging the ball and Tim would have a picnic with him. Tip O'Neill and the other sluggers on the old Browns were pygmies when Keefe was in the box. I heard Tip say one day that he'd give a season's salary if he could knock a ball through Tim Keefe's body."[3] However, Tim greatly feared hitting a batter in the head with his fastball, and in 1887 he was so distraught after doing so that he admitted himself to a sanitarium for a brief time.

Though the Gothams (who later became the Giants) played at the Polo Grounds until 1957 and won 17 National League pennants, the Metropolitans were the first major league flag-winner in New York. The 1884 Mets, with Tim Keefe winning 37 games and striking out 334 batters, won the American Association pennant by six and a half games over the second-place Columbus Buckeyes. At season's end, Mets manager Jim Mutrie challenged the National League winners, the Providence Grays, to a best-of-five matchup for the world championship. The Providence ballclub agreed, and the New York fans were treated to the first "World's Series" in baseball annals.

Providence won the National League flag on the mighty arm of Charley Radbourn, a right-hander who pitched almost all the games for the Grays during the last half of the season and won an incredible 59 games that year. The series, which began at the Polo Grounds on October 23, started poorly for the

Mets. Keefe, rattled by the absence of his regular catcher Bill Holbert, hit two batters in the first inning. Both came around to score, and Radbourn dominated the New Yorkers for a 6–0 win. The next game progressed in a similar fashion, when the Grays, helped by a few bad calls by the umpire, defeated Keefe again, this time by a 3–1 score.

The New York fans quickly lost interest in the spectacle, and when the Providence players saw only 300 fans at the Polo Grounds on October 25, they refused to play the third game. The series might have collapsed at that point, but Mutrie convinced the Grays to play by allowing them to choose the umpire, a right usually enjoyed by the home team in that era. The Grays agreed, and then made a brilliant strategic move. They appointed Tim Keefe to serve as umpire, removing him from the lineup and forcing the Mets to put a rookie named Buck Becannon in the pitcher's box. Predictably, the Grays rocked Becannon for 12 runs in only six innings, and clinched the championship with a 12–2 victory.

The Mets did not draw well in 1884, despite their Association pennant, and John B. Day realized that the National League Gothams carried more status with the New York fans than did the Mets. Accordingly, Day decided to move two of his best players, pitcher Tim Keefe and third baseman Dude Esterbrook, from the Mets to the Gothams for 1885. The contracts of both men expired after the 1884 season, but Day could not simply transfer them from one team to another. Under league rules, players were not permitted to sign with another team for 10 days following the expiration of their contracts, though they were allowed to negotiate with any or all other major league teams during the waiting period. Day did not want other teams to contact his two stars, so he sent Keefe and Esterbrook on vacation to Bermuda. Keefe and Esterbrook rode a steamship to the island, enjoyed themselves on the beach for ten days, then voyaged back to New York and signed to play for the Gothams in 1885.

Tim Keefe was already planning for life after baseball. As the weekly magazine *Sporting Life* reported, "The New York club, in traveling about the country, began to notice that as soon as they reached their hotel in any city they happened to be visiting, Keefe retired to his room, shut himself in and wasn't seen again excepting on the ball field. This conduct puzzled the club for a long time, until it was discovered that the big pitcher was studying shorthand, and studying it seriously too."[4] While many of his New York teammates partied at night, Tim managed to familiarize himself with business topics such as bookkeeping and shorthand. He put this knowledge to use in 1884, when he and pitcher Buck Becannon organized their own sporting goods company. Called Keefe and Becannon, the firm produced bats, balls, and other baseball equipment, selling merchandise at a store at 157 Broadway in Manhattan.

Tim's move to the National League team, by now known as the Giants, reunited him with his old friend and Troy pitching partner Mickey Welch.

Welch and Keefe again shouldered almost the entire pitching load, with Welch assuming the role of staff ace with a 44–11 record and an earned run average of 1.66 in 55 games. Tim pitched 46 games, completing all but one while posting a 32–13 record. They were the best pitching duo in the National League, and the Giants challenged for the pennant for the first time, falling only two games shy of the Chicago White Stockings at season's end.

The most notable development of 1885 may have been the one that occurred at season's end. Professional ballplayers had been dissatisfied with management for several years, and grew even more disgruntled after the National League and the American Association agreed to set a maximum player salary of $2,000 beginning with the 1886 campaign. The reserve clause, which had allowed teams to reserve five players each year at its inception in 1879, expanded to cover most of the roster by 1886, and the players resented the near-total control exercised by ownership over their livelihoods. John Ward, shortstop and captain of the Giants, was an outspoken foe of the status quo in baseball, and proposed that the National League players organize a trade union, the first of its kind in sports. On October 22, 1885, Ward, Keefe, and seven other Giants formed the first chapter of the new union, which they called the Brotherhood of Professional Base Ball Players.

Ward, who had received a legal education and later became a successful lawyer, was elected president of the organization, and Tim Keefe, the self-taught businessman and shorthand expert, became its secretary-treasurer. Keefe kept a ledger with the minutes of meetings, financial records, and membership data of the Brotherhood, and also wrote the constitution for the union in longhand. Keefe wrote, "We, the undersigned, professional base-ball players, recognizing the importance of united effort and impressed with its necessity in our own behalf, do form, ourselves this day into an organization to be known as the 'Brotherhood of Professional Base-Ball Players.' The objects we seek to accomplish are: To protect and benefit ourselves collectively and individually; To promote a high standard of professional conduct; To foster and encourage the interests of the game of Base Ball."[5]

The page contained the signatures and addresses of nine New York Giants: Ward, Keefe, Joe Gerhardt, Buck Ewing, Roger Connor, Dan Richardson, Mickey Welch, Mike Dorgan, and Jim O'Rourke. Though the league magnates ignored Ward, Keefe, and their union, the National League players reacted positively to this development, and within one year the Brotherhood grew to include over 100 members and boasted chapters in every league city.

Mickey Welch was the number one pitcher for the Giants in 1885, but Tim Keefe took the top spot the following year and held it for the next several seasons. Welch and Keefe once again pitched nearly all the innings for the Giants in 1886, making all but one start for the club, and Keefe compiled one of his greatest seasons, leading the league in innings pitched (535), games started (64) and complete games (62) while posting a 42–20 record. Welch chipped in with a 33–22 mark, but the Giants settled into third place early on and never managed to climb above pennant-winning Chicago and the hard-hitting Detroit Wolverines. The New Yorkers were only four games out of the lead on August 27, but a nine-game road losing streak to St. Louis, Chicago, and Detroit left them 13 games back and well out of the race.

The National League season grew longer each year (the Giants played 112 games in 1885, 124 in 1886, and 138 by 1888) and teams found that they now required more than two starting pitchers. The Giants looked for pitching help to assist Keefe and Welch, but the 1887 squad fell back to fourth place as six other hurlers failed to provide support. Keefe (35–19) and Welch (22–15) performed well, but the other pitchers combined for a total of 11 wins and 20 losses. Second line pitching held the Giants back, and would continue to do so until a new starter or two emerged. Perhaps Tim realized this as well, for he demanded a significant pay increase before the start of the 1888 season. He had been earning $3,000 per year for three seasons in a row, but after a brief holdout John B. Day raised his pay to $4,000, the highest salary on the club.

The 1888 campaign started poorly for the Giants, as Tim Keefe suffered from his own inconsistency and poor Giants fielding early on. *The Sporting News* declared in early July, "Keefe's work so far this season has not been by any means up to the standard, but he is not to blame for half the defeats, as he has received poor support."[6] Two of his starts in May ended in ties, and his record stood at 8–6 in late June after he lost four of six decisions. The Giants struggled with injuries, but the team managed to hold onto fourth place, six games behind league-leading Chicago.

Tim finally turned his season around, starting one of baseball's historic winning streaks. The Giants sat in third place, three and a half games out of first, on July 19, but won 18 of their next 19 games to burst into the league lead by 7 games on August 10. Tim Keefe was the biggest reason for the surge, as he won 19 starts in a row from June 23 to August 10, breaking Charley Radbourn's four-year-old record of 18 consecutive wins. Keefe's record winning streak was tied by Rube Marquard, also of the Giants, in 1912, but has never been surpassed. Tim finally lost a game (to Chicago) on August 14, when shortstop John Ward was unable to play and replacement Gil Hatfield committed two costly errors. The 19-game streak boosted his record to 27–6, best in the National League, and only John Clarkson, by now pitching for Boston, rivaled Keefe as the premier pitcher in baseball.

For the first time in his career, Keefe was able to rely on someone other than Mickey Welch to carry the pitching load. The Giants finally found relief in the person of Ledell (Cannonball) Titcomb, a fastball pitcher who spelled Keefe and Welch and made enough starts to keep the two main hurlers fresh. Thus supported, Keefe won 35 games in 1888, his sixth consecutive campaign with 30 wins or more, and led the league in earned run average, shutouts (8) and strikeouts (335). Tim was the first pitcher to strike out 300 men in a season three times, a feat that was not matched until Sandy Koufax of the Dodgers compiled his third 300-strikeout campaign in 1966.

The Giants were the premier team in baseball in 1888, and also the most fashionable, thanks to Tim Keefe. His sporting goods company, Keefe and Becannon, was growing, and gained an important boost when Tim designed a new uniform for the ballclub and convinced team owner John B. Day to adopt it. Tim's creation featured an all-black uniform with "New York" in white letters on the front. Some called them "funeral uniforms," but they looked sharp and set the Giants apart from other teams. Keefe and Becannon also began producing bicycles and goods for other sports during the late 1880s, as Tim Keefe became not only a star athlete, but also an entrepreneur.

Keefe on an Allen & Ginter baseball card in 1887. (Library of Congress)

The Giants coasted to the 1888 pennant, their first in the National League, and Tim Keefe used the October World's Series as a personal showcase. The Giants faced the St. Louis Browns, perennial champions of the American Association, in a 10-game matchup with Tim's old Clinton semipro teammate John Gaffney serving as umpire. Keefe dominated the overmatched Browns, pitching four complete games and allowing only two earned runs, as the Giants won six of the first eight games. St. Louis won the last two meaningless contests against the New York second-stringers, but the Giants were the champions of the world.

The city of New York celebrated this victorious season, but the Brotherhood grew ever more frustrated with the baseball owners during the late 1880s. Albert Spalding, owner of the Chicago ballclub, took his White Stockings and a group of National League all-stars (which included Brotherhood president

John Ward) on an around-the-world exhibition tour in late 1888. With Ward out of the country, the league owners passed a new salary classification plan, under which each player would be assigned a letter grade from A to E and have his salary fixed accordingly, from $1,500 for an E player to $2,500 for one at the A level. The players were outraged, including Keefe, whose salary would drop sharply under the new guidelines. The Brotherhood suspected that Spalding may have invited Ward on the tour to keep him away from the controversy; at the very least, the magnates certainly took advantage of his absence.

Keefe criticized Spalding's proposed scheme, and dropped a hint as to the plans of the Brotherhood. "I won't say what the Brotherhood will do, but we will move," he remarked. "There is one thing certain, [that] they won't classify as many men this fall as they think. Why, this talk about [league president] Nick Young classifying men is rot. The clubs send in the salaries, and he puts them in categories to correspond."[7] However, Keefe's animosity toward Spalding apparently extended beyond the National League. Spalding was also the leading sporting goods magnate in the nation, having absorbed or bought out other players-turned-entrepreneurs such as Al Reach, George Wright, and others during the previous few years. Spalding was fast building a near-monopoly in the sporting goods field, while Keefe and Becannon fought for a piece of the booming market.

Some National League players supported the idea of a general strike, but Ward returned from Europe in early 1889 and quelled such talk. He, Keefe, and the Brotherhood board had already set plans in motion to create a new league, to be called the "Players National League," which would take the field for the 1890 season. Ward had discussed this vision with his fellow ballplayers during the world tour, though Keefe's ledger book reveals that the possibility had been raised as early as 1887. Ward, Keefe, and the Brotherhood board spent the 1889 season negotiating with financiers, identifying playing venues, and enlisting players in the coming baseball war, all the while hiding their intentions from the National League owners.

Tim Keefe was a busy man as the 1889 campaign approached. He held out in a salary dispute for the first two weeks of the season, threatening to quit the game and attend to his sporting goods business if the Giants offered him less than $5,000 per year. He remained in Cambridge that spring, coaching the Harvard baseball team, until settling for a $4,500 salary and returning to the Giants in early May. Tim had also started dating a young widow, Clara Gibson Helm, the sister of John Ward's wife Helen Dauvray, a well-known actress of the time. Tim, an intensely private sort, tried to quell the talk of his romance, but the news soon became public. He and Clara married on August 19, 1889, making Tim Keefe not only John Ward's teammate, but also his brother-in-law. Though John and Helen Ward divorced a few years later, Tim and Clara Keefe enjoyed a successful marriage.

Tim's holdout cost him a chance at his seventh consecutive 30-win season, but his 28–13 record and Welch's 27–12 log boosted the Giants into the pennant chase once again. Cannonball Titcomb was gone, but another fastball hurler, Ed (Cannonball) Crane, won 14 games in a supporting role while Hank O'Day won nine of his ten decisions. The Giants, with the league's best starting rotation, battled the Boston Beaneaters down to the last weekend of the season. John Clarkson handled most of the pitching load for Boston, winning 49 games and pitching 620 innings, but the team of Welch and Keefe, supported by Crane and O'Day, proved superior. Clarkson lost his last start of the season, and a chance to win his 50th game, to Pittsburgh on October 5, while Keefe pitched a 5–1 win at Cleveland to clinch the Giants' second consecutive pennant. Tim pitched only one game during the World's Series against Brooklyn, which the Giants won easily behind Crane and O'Day.

John B. Day sponsored a banquet for his players at the end of the Series, but the mood there was somber. News of the Brotherhood's upcoming break with the National League had leaked, and Day's ballclub stood to become one of the coming baseball war's most prominent casualties. The New York players genuinely liked Day, one of the friendliest and fairest of National League owners, but the Brotherhood course had already been set. Any chance of reconciliation was lost in September of 1889, when Albert Spalding, the most powerful magnate in the National League, refused to meet with the Brotherhood to discuss their differences. Keefe, increasingly radical in outlook, later characterized Spalding's snub of the players as "the crowning point to the arrogant despotism of these dictators, and the players revolted at the contemptuous disregard of their rights as men and laborers."[8]

On November 4, 1889, at a meeting in New York of the organization's officers and chapter presidents, the Brotherhood adopted a manifesto, which it soon made public, and released an outline of its plan to create a new league. The document, which was probably written mainly by Ward and Keefe, decried the ever-growing reserve clause and player sales between teams. "Players have been bought, sold, and exchanged as though they were sheep instead of American citizens," it stated. The new Players League promised to do away with the reserve clause and the salary classification system, while each team would be operated by a board consisting of both the financial backers and the team's own players. Profits were to be divided between owners and players, and all teams would receive an equal share of gate receipts.

Ward and Keefe produced a pamphlet detailing the new league's aims, and Keefe wrote an article that gave credit to the Brotherhood for eradicating features such as "the selling and buying of players, the reserve rule and the classification system," and claimed that the Brotherhood was "forced by the arbitrary actions of the National League to secede from the latter organization." Keefe continued:

"The only conclusion that a thoroughly informed and fair minded person can reach ... is that [the Brotherhood] has benefited and will continue to benefit and elevate the game in the future far more than the braggart National League ever claimed to have done in the past.... In the day when the National League had a chance to show what it cared for the game when not associated with its own profit, the National League's exhibition was a mean and miserable one. No means, however dirty and enervating, were not called into play to wreck the Brotherhood and its kindred organization, the Players' National League. Both stand and will live on to a glorious old age."[9]

In short order, almost all the National League players (except for Cap Anson, Jack Glasscock, and a few others) quit the established circuit and joined the newborn Players League. Ward, president of the new circuit, became manager of the Brooklyn entry, while Buck Ewing signed on to manage the New York ballclub. Tim Keefe, Roger Connor, and almost all the other Giants stars moved over to Ewing's team, which contained five of the nine founding members of the Brotherhood. Surprisingly, Mickey Welch resigned from the Brotherhood and opted to stay with Day's club for a large increase in salary and a three-year no-cut contract. Ward was angered by the "defection," but Keefe took a more forgiving view, and he and Welch remained friends.

Keefe profited personally from the formation of the new league. His company, Keefe and Becannon, won the contract to produce the official Players League ball, as well as bats, uniforms, and other equipment for the circuit. Some observers objected, since Keefe was an officer of the Players League (and John Ward's brother-in-law), but Ward explained that Keefe's firm earned the three-year deal by submitting the lowest bid. Probably at Ward's insistence, Keefe and Becannon produced a lively baseball, a sure way to appeal to the fans by increasing offensive production, and the "Keefe ball" became famous around the nation.

The New York Players League club also called itself the Giants, since the team contained most of the Giant stars of the world championship seasons, but the papers called them the "PL Giants" or "Ewing's Giants" to differentiate them from Day's National League team. Adding to the confusion, the Players League club built a new ballpark next to the Polo Grounds. Since the rival leagues scheduled games on the same dates, fans in each stadium could watch the action in the other all season long. On June 4, crowds in both parks cheered as Tim defeated Boston for the 300th win of his career. He was the second pitcher in history to reach that plateau.

Ewing's Giants boasted a solid four-man rotation with Tim Keefe, Hank O'Day, Cannonball Crane, and veteran John Ewing, but the club drifted along in fourth place for most of the season. The club was blessed with fine hitters such as Buck Ewing and league home run champ Roger Connor, but the pitching (possibly due to the lively Keefe ball) failed to keep pace. Tim pitched well, with a 17–10 record through mid-August, and appeared headed for a 25-win season before disaster struck on August 19. During practice that morning, he misjudged a line drive and broke the index finger on his pitching hand while

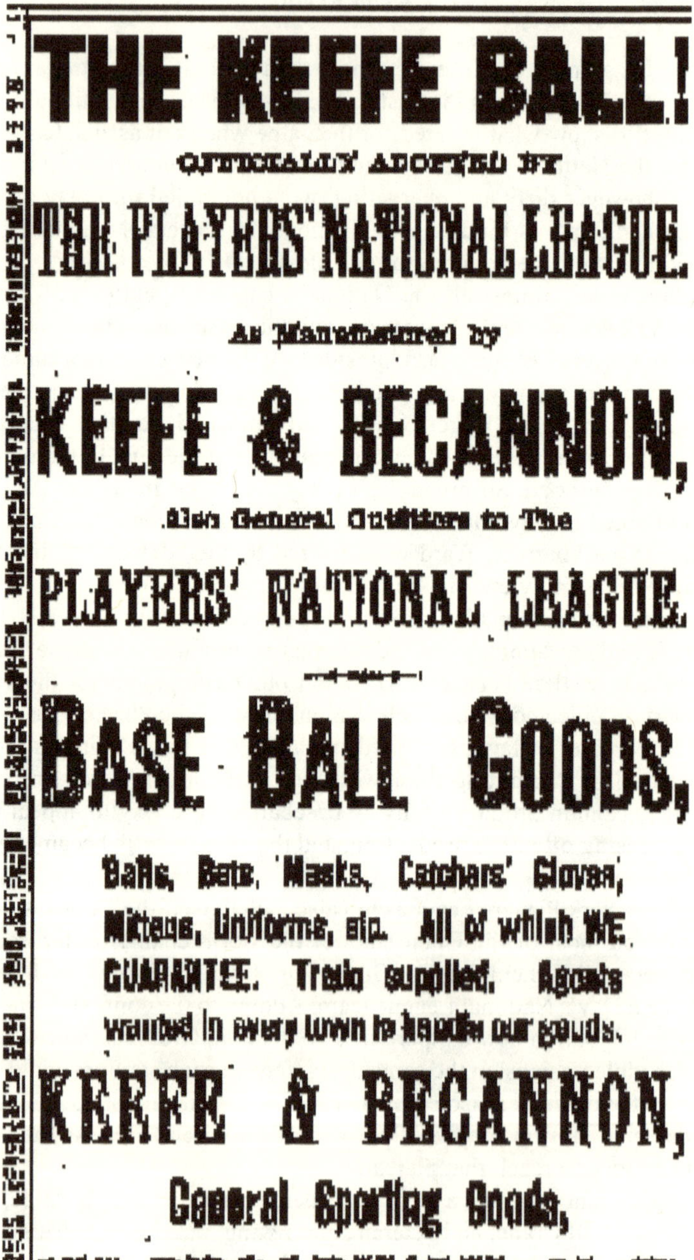

THE KEEFE BALL!

OFFICIALLY ADOPTED BY

THE PLAYERS' NATIONAL LEAGUE.

As Manufactured by

KEEFE & BECANNON,

Also General Outfitters to The

PLAYERS' NATIONAL LEAGUE.

BASE BALL GOODS,

Balls, Bats, Masks, Catchers' Gloves, Mittens, Uniforms, etc. All of which WE GUARANTEE. Trade supplied. Agents wanted in every town to handle our goods.

KEEFE & BECANNON,

General Sporting Goods,

157 BROADWAY, N. Y.

An 1890 add for the Keefe ball, used by the Players League in its only season of operation. (Author's collection) trying to catch it. It was a painful injury that required surgery, and started the Giants on a freefall out of the pennant race. Tim tried to pitch again on September 8, but lasted only one inning, walking four and throwing two wild pitches while giving up five runs to Boston. Tim did not pitch again in 1890, and the PL Giants finished in third place, eight games behind Boston.

Tim spent the last month of the 1890 season making plans to improve the PL Giants for 1891, but the Players League was already on its last legs. Both the National League and Players League teams in New York lost money, and Day's Giants required an emergency infusion of cash from Albert Spalding and his associates in August to stave off total collapse. However, Ewing's ballclub was in no better shape, and the team's financial backers were willing to cut a deal. They sold their holdings to the National League in November, combining the two New York teams into one and, in effect, cutting the heart out of the Players League. Within weeks the new circuit, and the Brotherhood itself, were dead and gone.

Tim Keefe was outraged, and not only because his work as a founder and officer of the Brotherhood had been nullified. Keefe and Becannon's three-year contract to provide balls and equipment for the Players League was now worthless. This deal was the linchpin of the firm's business, and Tim threatened to sue the Players League for breaching the agreement. Nothing came of his threat, and though Keefe and Becannon tried to continue operations, the company soon folded, casting Tim's financial security in doubt. Two years later, when several of his teammates considered holding out as a group for higher salaries, Tim advised against the move. "I was in [a strike] once," said the pitcher sadly, "and it cost me everything I was worth."[10]

Tim returned to the National League Giants in 1891, but he was 34 years old, an advanced age for a pitcher in that era. His place as the main hurler for the Giants was assumed by Amos Rusie, a 20-year-old fastballer who won 29 games for the National League Giants in 1890. Tim battled for playing time with Mickey Welch, Hank O'Day, Cannonball Crane, and others, and the lack of steady work kept him rusty all year long. To exacerbate matters, Albert Spalding's brother Walter was now a major stockholder in the Giants, and Keefe, as an officer in the now-defunct Players League and a business rival of Spalding's sporting goods company, found himself out of favor with team management. Tim pitched in only eight games for the Giants in 1891, winning two and losing five, and in late July he asked for, and received, his release.

Insisting that he could still pitch, Tim signed with the Philadelphia Phillies two weeks later. He won only three of his nine games for the Phillies that year, but worked to bring his arm back into shape over the winter and appeared at spring practice in 1892 in fine playing condition. Settling in as the third starter on Harry Wright's team, Tim made 38 starts, compiled a 19–16 record, and led the Phillies staff in earned run average. Unfortunately, the league magnates decided to increase the pitching distance from 50 feet to 60 feet and six inches for 1893, and Tim's pitching suffered. He allowed more than four earned runs per game that season, and the Phillies did not want to pay a high salary to a fading pitcher. Tim was released in August after posting a 10–7 record, and his major league career was over. At the time of his retirement, he was baseball's all-time leader in strikeouts (a distinction he held until Cy Young passed him in 1907) and his total of 342 victories put him in second place on the all-time list behind Jim (Pud) Galvin.

Keefe continued his college coaching duties each spring for several years, but needed to find a new line of work after the collapse of his sporting goods firm. He decided to apply for a position as an umpire, and the National League hired him in August of 1894. Keefe was widely admired for his integrity and knowledge of the sport, and the league hoped that Tim would command the respect of the players and add a touch of dignity to the conduct of the games.

However, the decade of the 1890s was the worst era in baseball history for the arbiters. Arguing, brawling, forfeits, and general mayhem were the rule at the time in the National League, and even as respected a figure as Tim Keefe found himself on the receiving end of abuse. He was criticized in newspapers and magazines for indecisiveness and inconsistency, and eventually even the fans at the Polo Grounds booed their former pitching hero on a regular basis. Keefe worked hard at his job, but reached his breaking point in St. Louis on July 7, 1896. After a series of ugly arguments with both the Giants and the Browns that day, Keefe walked off the field in the fifth inning and submitted his resignation to league president Nick Young.

Keefe pulled no punches in explaining his actions. "Baseball has reached a stage where it is absolutely disgraceful," complained the retired pitcher. "It is the fashion for every player engaged in a game to froth at the mouth, and emit shrieks of anguish whenever a decision is given which is adverse to the interests of the club to which he belongs.... This continual senseless and puerile kicking at every decision has been infinitely trying to me, and I have been considering for some time whether I had not better resign. I can apparently please nobody."[11]

A friend asked Tim about his future plans. "I don't know," replied Keefe. "I need the money, but I can't stay in a business that makes my friends abuse me and mistrust me. I can't have people whom I have had for associates for years pass me up when they meet me, and so I am going to resign."[12] Oddly enough, Keefe then took a position as an umpire in the Eastern League, where he remained for the next two seasons. His umpiring career ended when he suffered a separated shoulder in an on-field accident in 1897, so Tim left the game and opened a real-estate business in Cambridge, Massachusetts.

Tim Keefe sold real estate in his hometown over the next few decades, paying scant attention to major league baseball. He sometimes visited with his old teammate and friend Mickey Welch, who lived in Holyoke, and attended a few contests with Welch at Fenway Park in Boston, but otherwise showed little interest in the game. In 1912 a reporter asked the 55-year-old Keefe if modern baseball was faster than in the old days. "I have seen so few games in recent years," replied Tim, "that I am unable to make a fair comparison."[13] He did, however, offer his opinion that the old Chicago shortstop Ed Williamson was the greatest player of all time, while fastballer Charlie Sweeney was the most outstanding pitcher.

By 1920 Tim, now a widower, lived in Cambridge with two of his sisters, Katherine and Mary. There he remained, little noticed by the baseball world, until he died of a heart attack on April 24, 1933, at the age of 76. He was buried in the Cambridge Cemetery under a marker that includes the names of his uncles, Timothy and John, who died in the Civil War. Mickey Welch, one of his last surviving teammates from the Giants of the mid-1880s, stated simply that his longtime friend was "one of the finest gentlemen that ever played ball."

Tim Keefe is nearly forgotten today, though his name came to the forefront when Roger Clemens won his 300th major league game in 2003, and again when Greg Maddux crossed the 300-win barrier in 2004. On both occasions, "Sir Timothy," one of the 22 members of the 300-win club, surfaced briefly in the nation's newspapers and quickly disappeared again. His obscurity is unworthy, because Tim Keefe was a great pitcher who led the New York Giants to their first two pennants, set records that still stand, and developed the change of pace pitch that nearly all hurlers employ to this day. Keefe's pitching accomplishments, as well as his work in organizing the first baseball trade union, made him one of the giants of early baseball. He earned, and deserves, a prominent place in the history of the game.

8

Kiki Cuyler

> "Cuyler is a wonder, one of those all around players that you don't see very often. He can field and hit and run bases. He is fast as a flash and has a great throwing arm.... In any case, he's the best young outfielder who has broken into baseball for many years."
> —*Fred Clarke, 1925*[1]

Many people who wander through the gallery at the Baseball Hall of Fame in Cooperstown, New York, have never heard of Hazen (Kiki) Cuyler.

Cuyler, an outfielder for the Pirates, Cubs, Reds, and Dodgers who hit .321 during his career, played for five pennant winners, hit the double that won the 1925 World Series, and excited National League fans with stolen bases and inside-the-park home runs. Kiki, whose nickname was pronounced "Kai-kai," was one of the most famous and popular players of his era, but died in 1950 at age 51 and fell from public awareness. Voted into the Hall by the Veterans Committee in 1968, he remains in such obscurity that most fans who read his plaque call him "Kee-kee." Old-time fans and baseball history buffs wince at the mispronunciation, for though Cuyler is mostly forgotten today, his 18-year career was filled with highlights, and deserves to be remembered.

Hazen Shirley Cuyler was born on August 30, 1898 in Harrisville, Michigan, a town on Lake Huron in the northeast part of the state's Lower Peninsula. Hazen's parents, George and Anna Cuyler, were both natives of Canada from German and Irish stock. George Cuyler played semipro ball in Canada before he and his wife moved to Michigan in the mid-1880s and settled in Harrisville, the seat of the sparsely populated Alcona County. Most of the residents were farmers, fishermen, or lumber mill workers, but George was a bookkeeper who worked as a recorder of deeds at the local courthouse. He later became the director of a fish hatchery and, in his sixties, a probate judge in Alcona County. George and Anna had two children, Hazen and his older sister Edna.

Hazen, known to his friends and teammates as "Cuy," was a good student and a star athlete at the county high school, excelling in baseball, football, basketball, and track. Polite and shy, perhaps due to a stutter that remained for his entire life, Hazen did not smoke, drink, or carouse, neither during his

Kiki Cuyler with the pennant-winning Chicago Cubs in 1929. (National Baseball Hall of Fame Library, Cooperstown, N.Y.)

teenage years nor in adulthood. The clean-cut youngster earned an appointment to the United States Military Academy at West Point following graduation, but after three months decided that military life was not a good fit. He returned to Michigan, married his high school sweetheart Bertha Kelly, and went to work as an automobile roof assembler at a Buick Motors plant in Flint, about 150 miles from Harrisville.

The plant sponsored a baseball team, and "Cuy" quickly became the star of the ballclub. A right-hander in the field and at bat, he was five feet and ten inches tall, weighed about 180 pounds, and was the strongest and fastest ballplayer in the industrial leagues that competed in Flint and Detroit. He also starred as a guard on the company basketball team, but after posting incredible numbers as a pitcher and outfielder for Buick Motors, the Bay City Wolves of the Michigan-Ontario League signed the 21-year-old Cuyler to a professional contract in 1920. He compiled a .317 average, with 16 triples, in 1921, and in September of that year the Bay City club sold his contract to the National League Pittsburgh Pirates.

The Pirates placed Cuyler in their lineup for one late-season game, in which he went hitless, and then farmed the youngster out to Charleston, South Carolina of the South Atlantic League, where Cuyler hit .309 in 1922 and showed his remarkable speed with 15 triples. In 1923 he played for Nashville of the Southern League, where he earned an automobile, presented by Commissioner Kenesaw Mountain Landis, as winner of the circuit's Most Valuable Player award. Cuyler batted .340 with 114 runs scored and convinced the Pittsburgh management that he was ready for the major leagues. He played in 11 contests for the Pirates at the end of the 1923 season, batting .250, and set his sights on making the major league roster in 1924.

The nickname "Kiki" preceded him to Pittsburgh, as the ballplayer once explained. "When I was a boy," he said, "my friends would call me Cuy and this name clung to me. When I went to Nashville, it was Cuy this and Cuy that and the newspapers finally picked it up, spelling it Ki. It got so every time I went for a fly ball the shortstop would yell Ki and the second baseman would pipe up immediately with another Ki. It caught on with the fans, and in no time they were calling me Kiki."[2] Some say, however, that his stutter caused him to say "Kiki" when he told people his last name. Wherever the nickname came from, it stuck with him for the rest of his life.

Kiki Cuyler, after three successful minor league seasons and three brief stints with the main club, was still considered a rookie at the age of 25. He was ready to crack the starting lineup for the Pirates, a perennial first-division team that was not quite talented enough to break the dominance of the defending champion New York Giants. The Giants had won the league title for three years running, and the Pirates hoped that their new outfielder could help end the Giants' run at the top of the league.

Assigned to left field by Pirate manager Bill McKechnie, Cuyler paid dividends immediately. He belted doubles and triples into the spacious outfield at Pittsburgh's Forbes Field and surprised the fans with his speed and skill on the bases. He opened the season in a left field platoon with incumbent Carson Bigbee, but by May Cuyler had driven the veteran to the bench, claiming the position on a full-time basis. On August 9 Kiki belted six hits in a 16–3 romp over the Phillies, boosting his average above the .370 mark.

Cuyler, always eager to improve himself, found a fine base-stealing tutor in center fielder Max Carey, a fixture in the Pirate outfield since 1911 and a ten-time National League stolen base champion. Carey, the Pittsburgh field captain, instructed the rookie in leading off a base, avoiding pick-offs, and sliding around a tag. Cuyler, who ultimately supplanted Carey as the fastest man in the National League, proved to be a quick learner. He finished fourth in the batting race at .354, second in stolen bases (behind Carey) with 32, and hit 16 triples. There was no official Rookie of the Year award in 1924, but many newspaper columnists labeled Cuyler as the game's outstanding new player that year.

After only one full season in the major leagues, Kiki was already one of the most popular members of the Pirates. Despite a prominent nose, he was a handsome man with wavy black hair and a ready smile. At the plate, he copied the stance of perennial batting champion Rogers Hornsby, who stood far back in the batter's box and stepped forward into the ball. "I can watch a curve better from that position," Cuyler once explained. "When a spitball pitcher is on the slab, I an inclined to move up a little in the box."[3] He swung the bat hard, like Babe Ruth, and his strikeouts were sometimes as spectacular as his hits. Few home runs were hit at Forbes Field, as the fences were too far away, but Kiki belted doubles and triples down the lines, made spectacular catches in the outfield, and raised enormous clouds of dust when he slid into bases. Kiki brought excitement to the ballclub, and former Pittsburgh manager Fred Clarke told *Baseball* magazine that Cuyler "might become a second [Ty] Cobb."

By 1925, the Pirates were ready to challenge the aging Giants, winners of the previous four pennants, while Kiki Cuyler prepared to burst into stardom. He compiled the finest season of his career that year, setting team records with 144 runs scored and 220 hits. His 369 total bases established a standard which no Pirate, not even Roberto Clemente or Willie Stargell, has ever surpassed. Kiki carried the team on his back during the early months of the season, which saw the Giants rush out to an early lead and the Pirates jump into contention with a 24–9 spurt in June and July. The Giants and Pirates traded the lead until early August, when the New Yorkers suffered through a six-game losing streak to leave the Pirates in first by five games. Pittsburgh held first place for the remainder of the season, winning the flag by eight games for their first pennant since 1909.

With 18 homers, 102 runs batted in, and a .357 average, Kiki served as the primary offensive weapon for Bill McKechnie's Pirates in 1925. In September the second-year star belted 10 consecutive hits to tie a league record, and on August 28 he stunned a Philadelphia crowd with two inside-the-park homers in the same game. He stole 41 bases and hit eight inside-the-park homers, while his 26 triples led the league, and stands today as the second highest total of modern National League history. Had Rogers Hornsby of the Cardinals not batted .403 with 42 homers, Kiki Cuyler would probably have won the Most Valuable Player award.

Kiki used the World Series against the Washington Senators that fall as his personal showcase. The Senators won the first game in Pittsburgh behind Walter Johnson, but Kiki delivered a victory in the second contest with a two-run homer in the eighth inning off spitball specialist Stanley Coveleski. Washington won the next two games to surge ahead three games to one, but the Pirates took the next two to even the Series and force a decisive seventh contest. On a rainy afternoon at Forbes Field, the Senators took an early 4–0 lead before the Pirates managed to narrow the gap to one run after seven innings. In the eighth, with rain turning the field to mud, the Pirates tied the score when Earl Smith and Carson Bigbee doubled in succession. After Eddie Moore walked and Max Carey reached base on an error, Kiki strode to the plate to face Walter Johnson.

Cuyler made the sign of the cross, then belted a Johnson fastball down the first base line. Washington outfielder Goose Goslin claimed that the ball was foul, but the umpire ruled it fair as Bigbee and Moore crossed the plate, giving the Pirates a 9–7 lead. "It wasn't fair at all," complained Goslin more than 40 years later. "It was foul by two feet. I know it was foul because it hit in the mud and stuck there."[4] The umpires disagreed, and the hit made Kiki the hero of the Series. The Senators went down quickly in the ninth, and the Pirates were champions of the world.

The Pirates probably should have repeated as champions the following year, as Kiki delivered another outstanding season and newcomer Paul Waner, a left-handed line drive hitter, batted .336 and claimed the right field job (with Kiki alternating between left and center). However, the team imploded with internal turmoil in August. Fred Clarke, who had managed Pittsburgh from 1900 to 1915, returned as coach and vice-president of the club and took a place on the bench, where he offered unsolicited advice to manager McKechnie. Max Carey, team captain, had been slumping, and Clarke advised McKechnie to replace him in the lineup. "Put in the bat boy," sneered Clarke. "He can't be any worse."[5]

Several of Carey's teammates reported this exchange to their captain, and before long Carey and other players accused Clarke of trying to undermine McKechnie. Six Pirates signed a petition requesting Clarke's removal from the bench, which brought team management into the dispute. Owner Barney Dreyfuss supported Clarke against the players and dealt with the problem by releasing outfielder Carson Bigbee and pitcher Babe Adams outright, while Carey was stripped of his captaincy and dealt to Brooklyn. The Pirates, in first place when the disagreement occurred, fell to third and remained there as the Cardinals swept to the pennant.

McKechnie, despite being only one year removed from a world championship, was fired after the 1926 season and replaced by Donie Bush, a hard-nosed disciplinarian who had spent most of his career in the American League. Bush's appointment signaled the beginning of the end for Kiki in Pittsburgh, as Bush decided to move his star player to left field and bat him second in the lineup. Cuyler, a free-swinging hitter, was uncomfortable in the second slot, and earned the wrath of his new manager when he complained publicly about the assignment. Kiki had recently won a new $12,000 contract after bitter negotiations, which made him unpopular with management, and his season started poorly when he tore ligaments in his leg in May while sliding against the Cardinals. He returned to the lineup in June, but his hitting lacked its usual power, and before long Cuyler and manager Bush were barely on speaking terms.

"The whole thing began, I think," said Kiki later, "...when Bush instructed me to change my style of leading off second base. He wanted me to face the pitcher instead of leading with my back to the second baseman [as Carey had taught]. Then Bush decided to change the lineup and I was made to hit second. I did it and tried my best, but I have never been a successful second man. When I tried it, the ball went straight to some fielder for a double play and the whole team started dubbing me 'double.'"[6]

The situation was complicated further when Lloyd Waner, Paul's younger brother, joined the team and hit well during Kiki's absence from the lineup. Bush viewed Lloyd as a better fielder than Kiki and was reluctant to put Cuyler back into regular action. "I admit Cuyler had a great arm," recalled Bush. "But he was inclined to throw the ball in from the outfield so high that the infielders couldn't cut off the throw and prevent runners from advancing from first or second base. I had spoken to him about it several times."

On August 6, Kiki failed to slide into second to break up a double play against the Giants. Bush levied a $50 fine and benched him. A few days later, Cuyler missed a cutoff man from left field with a high throw. Bush snapped, "Won't you ever learn to throw the ball low?"

"If you don't like the way I play," replied Cuyler, "get someone else."

"I will," said the manager, and Kiki played only sparingly for the remainder of the season.[7]

The Pirates, in the thick of the pennant race, left their best player on the bench as a disciplinary measure. "I had great respect for Cuyler as a player," stated Bush. "He always was in top shape physically. His only trouble was his bullheadedness. If he had apologized to me, I would have put him back in the lineup." Several Pirate players signed a petition asking Bush to reinstate Cuyler, but the manager refused to yield. In September, with Clyde Barnhart unable to play due to injury, Bush called up Adam Comorosky from the minors rather than put Kiki back on the field. "It had to be that way," insisted Bush. "I had to maintain discipline."[8]

Even without Cuyler, the Pirates won the pennant behind the hitting of the Waner brothers, with Lloyd and Paul hitting .355 and .380 respectively. They entered the World Series against perhaps the greatest team of all time, the 1927 New York Yankees. This fearsome lineup included Babe Ruth, Lou Gehrig, and a "Murderer's Row" of outstanding hitters. Kiki was desperate to play against the Yankees, and tried to say all the right things to mollify his manager. "If [Bush] had put me in," said Kiki, "it would have looked like he was backing water. I don't blame him for the way he handled the situation."[9] Still, Kiki remained firmly chained to the bench. Though the Pittsburgh fans chanted "We want Cuyler!" during the first game in Forbes Field, Bush would not budge, and the Yankees overwhelmed the Pirates in four straight games.

Kiki received a full Series share of $3,985.48, but knew his days were numbered in Pittsburgh. He wrote a column for a Pittsburgh newspaper, detailing how the Pirates would continue to win pennants with an outfield consisting of him and the Waner brothers, but team owner Barney Dreyfuss was not interested in retaining Kiki. Perhaps he felt that Cuyler was expendable, as the Pirates had won the pennant without him, while others have suggested that the emergence of Lloyd Waner made Dreyfuss reluctant to pay the salaries of three star outfielders. At any rate, Dreyfuss entertained offers from several National League teams, including the Cubs, Giants, and Dodgers. The Chicago Cubs won the bidding war, acquiring Kiki on November 28, 1927 for infielder Sparky Adams and outfielder Pete Scott. After Kiki's departure, the Pirates would not win another pennant until 1960.

Chicago manager Joe McCarthy was also a disciplinarian, but he and Kiki established a friendship that lasted for the rest of Cuyler's life. McCarthy had taken charge of the Cubs in 1926, after the team had finished in last place the previous year. His leadership moved them immediately into the first division, with fourth-place finishes in 1926 and 1927. McCarthy was skilled at taking men rejected by other teams (including former Giant Hack Wilson and ex-Indian Riggs Stephenson), and turning them into productive ballplayers. McCarthy planted Kiki in right field and put him in the third position in the Chicago lineup, where Cuyler felt most comfortable. Kiki was a happy player once again, and though an ankle injury caused his average to drop to .285 in 1928, he led the league in stolen bases for the second time with 37.

He became as popular with the Chicago fans as he had been in Pittsburgh, and forged strong ties with his teammates. Several of the Cubs loved to sing as much as Kiki did, and during his first season in Chicago, Cuyler formed a quartet with outfielders Hack Wilson and Cliff Heathcote, and catcher Gabby Hartnett. Kiki loved music, perhaps because his stutter disappeared when he sang, and friends remember him as a tenor with a fine voice. "He had a beautiful voice," said Johnny Pesky, who played under Cuyler many years later. "He'd sing all the time, sing in the showers, sing in the locker rooms.... He'd sing the Lord's Prayer. He's sing show tunes."[10] He was also a good dancer. The Cubs trained at Catalina Island off the coast of California each spring, and Kiki won the annual waltz contest held there for several years in a row.

Despite his penchant for music and dancing, Kiki was a serious individual. He was sensitive to newspaper criticism that he, the prototypical five-tool player, did not have the drive to become another Ty Cobb. He had feuded with Donie Bush in Pittsburgh, not due to an overdeveloped ego, but because Bush put him in an unfamiliar role as a second-place hitter in the lineup. He hated to be embarrassed, and gained a reputation as a worrier, though he denied it. "I consider that I conduct my life on a rather level plane," explained Cuyler. "Of course I feel better when the Cubs are winning and I am helping them do it than I do when things go bad. But I do not believe that worry is the cause of slumps which I have had come on me from time to time."[11] Still, on a team of hard drinkers and nightlife enthusiasts, Kiki Cuyler stood out for his sober, serious approach to the game.

He was also not frivolous about his hobbies. He spent the winter months fishing and hunting in the woods of Michigan and Ontario, but upon his return to training camp one spring, he found that some of his teammates did not believe the stories he told about his moose-hunting exploits. Kiki, well aware that outdoorsmen often exaggerate their conquests, was determined to show his teammates that he was telling the truth. He bought a movie camera and carried it with him on subsequent hunting trips, bringing the filmed record of his adventures to camp to prove his veracity.

Cuyler was healthy again in 1929, and the Cubs rode his hot bat into contention. The team received a boost when it acquired the league's best hitter, second baseman Rogers Hornsby, from the Braves, and a lineup with Hornsby (.380), Stephenson (.362), Cuyler (.360) and Wilson (.345 with 159 runs batted in) comprised the most powerful hitting attack in the league. The Cubs traded the lead in the pennant race with Kiki's old team, the Pirates, until mid-July, when the Pirates stumbled and the Cubs pulled away from the pack. Kiki, still the fastest man in the league, won the stolen base crown for the third time, and the Cubs won the pennant, their first since 1918, by ten and a half games.

After his humiliating benching of 1927, Kiki had finally returned to the World Series, this time against the Philadelphia Athletics. The A's won the first two games at Wrigley Field in Chicago, but the Cubs took the third contest in Philadelphia as Kiki drove in the winning tallies with a two-run single in the sixth inning. This set up one of the most embarrassing losses in Series history in the fourth game. The Cubs held a 7–0 lead after six innings, and added another score in the seventh on a single by Cuyler, his third hit of the day. Incredibly, the Athletics roared back with 10 runs in the bottom of the inning, aided by Hack Wilson's loss of two fly balls in the sun. The game, which appeared well in hand for the Cubs, was lost by a score of 10–8, and the Series ended when the Cubs lost the fifth and final game two days later.

Despite the disappointing loss, Kiki Cuyler had reestablished himself as one of the league's brightest stars. He was 31 years old but still a speedy baserunner, mainly because he worked hard during the winter months to keep in shape. Kiki still lived in Harrisville, his hometown, where he pursued his love of hunting and fishing. He played basketball for a team that represented a Pontiac auto plant in Flint, and also captained a squad of cagers that toured the Midwestern states and challenged professional teams, beating many of the top clubs in the nation. Kiki's non-smoking, alcohol-free lifestyle set him apart from many of his Cub teammates, most notably the hard-drinking Hack Wilson, but Cuyler was determined to set a good example for his children, eight-year-old Harold and newborn Kelly June.

The 1930 Cubs missed Rogers Hornsby, who sat out most of the season with ankle problems, but Kiki turned in a great year, scoring 155 runs, driving in 134, and batting .355. Hack Wilson compiled an even better one, with 56 home runs and a still-standing record total of 191 runs batted in, as the hard-hitting Cubs led the league in homers and scored more runs than any team except the Cardinals. The Cubs remained in the pennant hunt all season, but fell two games shy of the Cardinals in the end. Team ownership blamed manager Joe McCarthy for the failure to repeat as champions, prompting McCarthy's resignation during the last week of the season. McCarthy wound up with the Yankees, who won eight pennants and seven World Series titles under his guidance.

Following the 1930 season, Kiki enjoyed a lucrative, but brief, career on the stage. He and his singing mates Wilson, Heathcote, and Hartnett were offered a four-week contract to play vaudeville stages in the Chicago area during the month of October, with Kiki receiving $1,500 per week, Wilson $2,000, Hartnett $1,250, and Heathcote $400. When the quartet reported for rehearsals, two days before the first performance, the promoters discovered that while Heathcote (the only one of the four who could read music) and Cuyler possessed good voices, the other two men could not carry a tune. "It hurts me to reveal," said Kiki years later, "that during the four weeks of our engagement neither Gabby nor Hack sang a note, just stood there and moved their lips while two professionals, screened behind them, sang with Cliff and me. And even though they didn't have to sing, they said they'd never worked so hard for their money in all their lives."[12]

McCarthy was replaced as manager of the Cubs by Hornsby, who proved unpopular with his charges. Hornsby, whom historian Lee Allen had described as "frank to the point of being cruel and subtle as a belch," banned eating, card playing, and singing in the clubhouse. He even tried to bar players from reading or going to movies in the belief that such activities strained the eyes. It did not take long for Hornsby, who was no longer playing regularly, to alienate his men, especially Hack Wilson. The hard-drinking Wilson hit only 13 homers and drove in 61 runs in 1931 after setting league records in both categories the year before. Though Cuyler held up his end, with a .330 average and 110 runs scored, the Cubs dropped to third place in 1931.

Despite the absence of Cuyler for the first seven weeks of the 1932 campaign after he broke a bone in his right ankle during spring training, the Cubs jumped into the pennant race despite widespread resentment of Hornsby's management style. By August the team had reached the breaking point, the volatile situation fueled by rumors that Hornsby had borrowed large sums of money from his players to support a gambling habit. On August 3, with the Cubs in second place, the Chicago owners fired Hornsby and put first baseman Charlie Grimm in charge. Grimm, who accompanied Cuyler and his quartet on the banjo and preferred a much looser rein than Hornsby, proved such a popular choice that the Cubs won their first game under his management by a 12–1 score over the Phillies.

The Cubs immediately began playing inspired baseball, and in late August a 14-game winning streak vaulted them into first place by a 7-game margin. The 12th game of that streak, played in a steady rain at Wrigley Field on August 31, may have been Kiki's greatest as a Cub. The Cubs trailed the Giants by a 4–3 score in the ninth, but Kiki, with two out, singled home Frank Demaree to tie the game. With rain falling harder, the Giants scored four times in the tenth for a 9–5 margin and retired the first two Cubs in the bottom of the inning, before Mark Koenig homered and Sam Taylor singled. Base hits by Billy Herman and Woody English scored Taylor to make the score 9–7 and brought Cuyler to the plate. Kiki, who had already hit safely four times that day, belted a homer into the right field stands to win the game by a 10–9 count.

The Cubs won the pennant under Grimm's leadership and prepared for a date with the New York Yankees in the World Series. It proved to be no contest, as the Yankees won the first two games in New York by scores of 12–6 and 5–2. The Series then returned to Wrigley Field, where the Yankees opened up a 4–1 lead before a two-run homer by Kiki Cuyler in the third closed the gap to a single run. That set the stage for Babe Ruth's legendary "called shot" off Charlie Root in the fifth inning, followed by an even longer homer by Lou Gehrig that put the game out of reach. The Cubs surrendered meekly the next day, and the Yankees completed a four-game sweep of the Series.

Kiki hit well during spring training in 1933, raising hopes that the Cubs could repeat as pennant winners, but disaster struck on March 29. During an exhibition game in Hollywood, Kiki slid awkwardly into second base on a steal attempt, shattering the fibula of his right leg. This injury, which the doctors called a "comminutive fracture," caused a three-inch piece of bone to break completely away. He missed nearly half the season, not returning until July, and when he finally re-entered the lineup his speed was gone forever. He managed to steal only four bases in 70 games, and his sudden decline was a blow to the Cubs, who finished in third place. Kiki played well in 1934 and stayed in the lineup for the entire season (though one Chicago paper professed to be waiting for his "annual leg injury"), but his base-stealing days were over, and the Cubs repeated their third-place showing.

Still one of the most popular players in Chicago, Kiki won a fan vote to start the All-Star Game in right field. The first All-Star contest had been held at Comiskey Park in Chicago the previous year, and proved so popular that the two leagues opted to make it an annual affair. Kiki, whose injury kept him from participating in the first contest, batted twice in the 1934 game at the Polo Grounds in New York. He grounded out in the first inning and lined out to center in the fourth before giving way to Mel Ott in the fifth. Though the Giants' Carl Hubbell made headlines by striking out five of the game's greatest hitters (Ruth, Gehrig, Foxx, Simmons, and Cronin) in succession, the American League won the contest by a 9–7 score.

Kiki with Cincinnati late in his career. (National Baseball Hall of Fame Library, Cooperstown, N.Y.)

Kiki led the National League in doubles with 42 in 1934, but turned 36 late that season and showed signs of age. Leg injuries had robbed him of his most important asset on the ball field, his speed, and he struggled at the plate early in 1935. The Chicago outfield was crowded, with Frank Demaree returning after a year's layoff and Fred Lindstrom arriving during the off-season from the Pirates. Both Demaree and Lindstrom were much younger and faster than Cuyler, and Kiki found himself relegated to the bench. He was batting .268 with only three stolen bases when the Cubs, in a cost-cutting move, stunned Kiki when they handed him his outright release on July 3.

Suddenly a free agent, Kiki was contacted by several teams during the July 4 holiday. The Chicago White Sox of the American League expressed interest, but Cuyler reportedly demanded a salary of $14,000, with a $5,000 signing bonus, a price that proved too high for the Sox. The Cincinnati Reds, whose slugging outfielder Chick Hafey had retired unexpectedly a few weeks before, were willing to pay Kiki more than any other team, so he signed with the Reds on July 5. He batted only .251 for Cincinnati during the remainder of the campaign while his former team, the Cubs, swept to the pennant but lost to Detroit in the World Series. Kiki rebounded to .326 in 1936, but his performance declined again in 1937 after he suffered a broken cheekbone in another spring training accident. It soon became apparent that his playing career was coming to an end. Kiki wanted to manage the Reds, who fired manager Charlie Dressen with two weeks to go in the season, but the team owners hired Bill McKechnie and released Cuyler in early October.

Kiki spent the winter seeking another major league position, and finally found one in January, when the Brooklyn Dodgers signed him as a part-time coach, pinch-hitter, and extra outfielder for the 1938 campaign. The oldest player in the National League that season, Kiki shared the spotlight with Babe Ruth, whom the Dodgers had hired as a coach in a bid to draw fans to Ebbets Field. Kiki batted .273 in limited action for the sixth-place Dodgers, and at season's end the 40-year-old decided to call it quits. He left the major leagues with a .321 lifetime batting average in 1,879 games. Once again he hoped to be considered for his team's managing job after Burleigh Grimes was dismissed, but Dodger president Larry MacPhail hired Leo Durocher instead.

Cuyler realized that he needed to prove himself as a manager in the minors before he could land a major league job, so he accepted a position as field leader of the Chattanooga Lookouts, a farm team of the Washington Senators, in the Southern Association. The Lookouts, under Kiki's guidance, won the regular season league title in 1939, though they lost in the first round of the playoffs. Kiki led the team to a fourth-place finish the following season, then left in August of 1941 to rejoin the Chicago Cubs as a coach under his old friend and teammate Jimmy Wilson. Cuyler stayed with Wilson and the Cubs until the end of the 1943 season.

While Kiki managed in Chattanooga, his son Harold decided that he, too, wanted a career in professional ball. Kiki recognized that his son did not have the physical tools to succeed in the game, and tried to dissuade him. "I had to leave the major leagues because my legs have gone back on me, and that's why I'm through as a player," said Kiki to his son. "But I'll race you a hundred yards. If you beat me, I'll say it's all right for you to go ahead. If I beat you, you'll give it up." They raced, Kiki beat Harold by a comfortable margin, and the boy gave up his dream of playing baseball.[13] He joined the United States Army shortly thereafter.

Kiki made his own contribution to the war effort in 1944 when he captained a unit that organized baseball games for military personnel. He then returned to the Southern Association to manage the Atlanta Crackers, winning pennants in 1945 and 1946. Kiki still yearned for a chance to manage in the majors, but no offers materialized, so he spent two more less-successful years in Atlanta before Joe McCarthy, his old manager with the Cubs, invited him to join the coaching staff of the Boston Red Sox in 1949. He performed the job well, though the Red Sox lost the pennant by one game to the Yankees, and Cuyler looked forward to returning to Boston in 1950.

Though Kiki had always kept himself in fine physical condition, he was troubled by varicose veins and circulation problems in his legs, no doubt caused by the severe leg injuries he endured during his playing career. He suffered a heart attack, possibly due to a blood clot that formed in his legs, while fishing near his home in northern Michigan on February 3, 1950. Taken to a small hospital in Alpena, his condition deteriorated so rapidly that his doctors decided to transfer him to University Hospital in Ann Arbor, some 200 miles away. On

February 11, doctors put the retired ballplayer in an ambulance for the long trip to Ann Arbor, but another heart attack struck en route. By the time the ambulance arrived at its destination, Kiki Cuyler was dead at the age of 51. He was buried in St. Ann's cemetery in Harrisville, survived by his wife Bertha and two children.

On January 23, 1968, the Baseball Writers Association named Joe Medwick to the Hall of Fame. Five days later, the Veterans Committee met in New York and emerged with two new honorees. One was Kiki Cuyler, and the other was Leon (Goose) Goslin, the former Washington outfielder who opposed Kiki in the 1925 World Series. Goslin was the better-known of the two, having returned to the public eye two years earlier after being interviewed by Larry Ritter for the influential baseball book *The Glory of Their Times*. Goslin also drew more notice that Cuyler because he was still alive, in good health, and willing to talk to sportswriters and television news crews. Cuyler, on the other hand, had been dead for 18 years. His widow represented him at the induction ceremony in Cooperstown that summer, but Kiki appeared to be an afterthought that day as press attention focused on living inductees Goslin and Medwick. Even today, Cuyler's name is rarely mentioned when the greats of the game are discussed.

The Sporting News summed up the general feeling about Cuyler shortly after his death in 1950. "A model on and off the field—he didn't drink or smoke—Cuyler had only one flaw that kept him from being ranked with the leading immortals of the game," said the paper. "He lacked the ruthlessness that might have carried him to great heights and made his record even more brilliant."[14] Perhaps that assessment is true, but Kiki Cuyler still managed to enjoy an outstanding career while earning a reputation as a gentleman. He was not the second Ty Cobb after all, but he accomplished more than enough to merit inclusion in the Hall of Fame.

9

Joe Kelley

> "Joe had no prominent weakness. He was fast on the bases, could hit the ball hard and was as graceful an outfielder as one would care to see. He covered an immense amount of ground and had that necessary faculty, so prominent in [Tris] Speaker and others, of being able to place himself where the batter would be likely to hit the ball."
> —*John McGraw, 1923*[1]

"This is the ultimate glory of baseball."

So said Commissioner Bowie Kuhn on August 9, 1971 in his opening remarks at the Hall of Fame induction ceremony in Cooperstown. It was a pivotal day for the institution, as all eyes were focused on the first inductee from the world of segregated African American baseball. Leroy (Satchel) Paige, elected by a special Committee on the Negro Leagues, opened the doors of the Hall to players who were barred from major league baseball before the color line was broken in 1947. Seven others were enshrined that afternoon, but Paige was the man who commanded all the attention.

Almost unnoticed by the crowd, a 72-year-old railroad executive from Silver Spring, Maryland, Joseph Kelley Junior, shared the stage with Paige, Kuhn, and the rest. His father Joe Kelley had been one of the great players of the 1890s, compiling a .317 career batting average over a 17-year career and playing a key role on five pennant winners in Baltimore and Brooklyn from 1894 to 1900. Kelley was forgotten by fans and baseball historians alike until the Committee on Veterans lifted him out of obscurity by electing him 28 years after his death. His son accepted his plaque from Commissioner Kuhn, and after his brief (but posthumous) moment in the spotlight, Joe Kelley faded from memory. To this day, his name is one of the least familiar in the Cooperstown museum.

He was born Joseph James Kelly in Cambridge, Massachusetts on December 10, 1871, the son of working-class parents who, like many of their neighbors, were Irish immigrants. Joe, who changed his last name to Kelley in adulthood, attended school, worked alongside an older brother in a carting and hauling business, and played sandlot ball with other first-generation Americans of Irish parentage.

This picture appeared on the cover of the Baltimore Herald on October 3, 1894, after the Orioles won the first of three consecutive pennants. Joe Kelley is shown at left. (Author's collection)

Cambridge was a hotbed of baseball, and by the time Joe was a teenager, the city had already produced Irish-American major league stars such as Tim Keefe and John Clarkson. More than a dozen other Cambridge lads had earned places in pro ball, and Joe Kelly was determined to follow their lead. He practiced with the Harvard University team and starred in the fast semipro leagues in Boston, but yearned to play for the nearest National League team, the Boston Beaneaters. In 1889 and 1890, he wrote to several professional teams requesting tryouts while playing for the Woven Hose, a team sponsored by a local textile factory, as a pitcher, shortstop, and outfielder. In 1891, just shy of his 20th birthday, Joe Kelly signed his first professional contract with Lowell of the New England League.

A right-handed batter and thrower, Joe joined the Lowell club as a pitcher, but hit so well that he decided that his future lay in the outfield. Joe stood five feet and 11 inches tall and weighed 190 pounds, and was a fine natural athlete who demonstrated good speed and a keen batting eye. He batted .344 at Lowell, and in July of 1891 realized his dream when the Boston Beaneaters purchased his contract.

Frank Selee, a good judge of talent, was the Boston manager, and young Kelly might have prospered under Selee's tutelage. However, the club was in a state of flux when Joe joined it. The Beaneaters were locked in a bitter, winner-take-all competition with the Boston Reds, the American Association club managed by former Beaneaters star Mike (King) Kelly. The two organizations battled for fan loyalty and newspaper space, and it was clear that both could not coexist. One of the competing ballclubs would drive the other out of business, and Selee was focused on survival, not player development, during the summer of 1891.

Joe played in 12 games for the Beaneaters, flashing signs of brilliance. On July 27, in his first major league game, he singled off New York Giants pitcher Mickey Welch, then belted two hits the next day off Tim Keefe. His work at the bat moved the *Boston Globe* to say, "Young Kelly is a natural born hitter."[2] On August 26, his triple was the only Boston hit off Pittsburgh hurler Mark Baldwin in a 6–1 loss. Joe batted only .244 for Boston, but his speed and strong throwing arm provided a glimpse of his potential. He was inconsistent in the outfield, though improving, and looked like a solid outfield prospect.

Unfortunately for Joe, the war between the Beaneaters and the rival Reds took a decisive turn in late August. Mike Kelly, the most popular player in the game, quit the Reds and rejoined the Beaneaters for the last six weeks of the season. This move decimated the Reds, leading to their demise and, at season's end, the American Association itself. The Boston players heard the news as they finished a road trip in Pittsburgh and, predictably, were thrilled with the return of their superstar. To make room, the Beaneaters, perhaps reluctantly, were obligated to release the other Kelly. Joe "seemed a little weak in the field, but was all right at bat," said the *Boston Globe*. "The opinion prevailed that the gentleman would be allowed to go when the team returned home."[3] Upon his arrival in Boston, Joe was informed that his services were no longer required. He returned to the Boston semipro leagues, where he finished the 1891 campaign while awaiting his next opportunity.

With the demise of the Association after the 1891 season, the number of major league teams dropped from 16 to 12, leaving fewer positions available for a young player to fill. Joe Kelly signed with Omaha, Frank Selee's old team, in 1892, and began to reclaim his status as a prospect, batting .330 before the Omaha club sold him to the Pittsburgh Pirates for $500 in June. Joe, perhaps still disappointed with his failure to stick with Boston, hit poorly for Pittsburgh, and the Pirates sent him and $2,000 to the Baltimore Orioles in exchange for outfielder George Van Haltren on September 5, 1892.

Van Haltren, a six-year veteran, was a much more accomplished player than Joe Kelly at this stage, but the last-place Orioles were eager to trade him away. Van Haltren had begun the season as manager of the club, but was dismissed after the team dropped 10 of its first 11 games. Ned Hanlon took over in early May, but Van Haltren remained on the roster and criticized the new manager's decision making. Hanlon had already sized up Joe Kelly as a raw talent with great potential, and though the trade appeared to be a lopsided one in Pittsburgh's favor, Hanlon was pleased to gain Joe and drop Van Haltren. "I had my eye on Kelly for a long time," said Hanlon to the *Baltimore Sun*. "I think it is better to have a good, steady ballplayer than to have a great player who, for some reason, does not play as well as he should."[4]

Joe was eager to succeed, and exhibited his resolve by working with Hanlon in the spring of 1893. Hanlon was well qualified to teach the nuances of center field play, having manned the same position for the champion Detroit team of 1887, and being regarded as one of the smartest players of his era. Hanlon brought Joe to the Baltimore ballpark each day, sometimes as early as eight in the morning, for individual lessons. The manager hit fly balls and line drives to Joe by the hour, as Joe gradually learned to handle the position. The local newspapers appreciated his hard work and started referring to him as "Kelley," a spelling that reportedly carried higher status back in Ireland. Joe liked the name, perhaps because it set him apart from the more famous Mike Kelly, and called himself Joseph James Kelley for the remainder of his life.

The Orioles failed to break the .500 mark in 1893, but Hanlon had already assembled some of the pieces of a future championship team. At shortstop was John McGraw, a 20-year-old who battled opponents and umpires with a ferocity rarely seen in the game to that point. The veteran Wilbert Robinson manned the catching position, while 24-year-old infielder Hugh Jennings arrived in mid-season from Louisville, where he batted only .136 but impressed Hanlon with his potential. Joe Kelley, Hanlon's star pupil, absorbed his manager's teachings well enough to bat .305 in 1893, score 120 runs, and steal 33 bases. Joe played well in center field, but later that year Hanlon put the newly-acquired Steve Brodie there and moved Kelley to left, where he remained for the next several seasons.

Baltimore fans waxed enthusiastic about their newly-successful team, with Joe Kelley becoming one of their favorite ballplayers. Some considered Joe the most handsome of the Orioles, with his cleft chin and brownish-blond hair parted in the middle. He appeared taller than his five feet and eleven inches, as his larger-than-life behavior contributed to that image. Joe Kelley was a cocky, confident lad, friendly with the fans but rough and argumentative with umpires and opponents. He also drew female fans, who sat behind their favorite player in the left field bleachers. Before long, left field in the Baltimore ballpark became known as "Kelleyville" after the popular outfielder. Joe, cognizant of his appeal and more than a little vain, carried a small mirror in his back pocket to check his appearance during games.

The Orioles rose from last place in 1892 to eighth the following season, and a key trade with Brooklyn filled in two more pieces of Ned Hanlon's puzzle. On January 1, 1894, the Orioles sent infielder Billy Shindle and outfielder George Treadway to the Dodgers for outfielder Willie Keeler and first baseman Dan Brouthers. Once again the baseball world believed that the Orioles had received the worst of the deal, as the little-used Keeler stood only five feet and four inches tall and the 36-year-old Brouthers, once baseball's greatest power hitter, was regarded as washed up. However, Hanlon wanted more speed and power in his lineup, and Keeler and Brouthers provided both. Keeler, a brilliant bunter and swift base-stealer, became Joe Kelley's best friend on the team and joined McGraw, Jennings, and Robinson to form a solid core of talent for the rising ballclub.

The young Orioles were a gifted bunch of athletes, but the key element of their success was a willingness to do anything to win. They were the rowdiest, most ill-behaved team that baseball had yet seen, verbally (and sometimes physically) abusing umpires, tussling with opponents and hostile fans, and generally making life miserable for the rest of the National League. McGraw, the Baltimore field captain, was the game's nastiest player, whom one reporter labeled "a rough, unruly man" who "has the vilest tongue of any ballplayer." McGraw often tripped opposing baserunners, grabbed their belts, or even tackled them as they rounded third. Only a single umpire was present to keep order during the 1890s, and McGraw knew that one man could not watch every player on the field simultaneously.

Joe Kelley and most of his teammates took their lead from McGraw. They deliberately ran into first basemen on close plays, hoping to dislodge the ball and be called safe. They hid extra baseballs in the long outfield grass, a stunt that backfired one day when an opponent hit a liner to right center and both Willie Keeler and Steve Brodie returned balls to the infield. They spiked opponents, threw at batters' heads, and treated umpires so badly that several of them refused to work Baltimore games. Predictably, many contests degenerated into brawls, some of which resulted in fan riots. It was an intentionally dirty way to play baseball which drew condemnation from all quarters. Umpire John Heydler summed it up when he complained, "The Orioles were mean, vicious, ready at any time to maim a rival player or an umpire, if it helped their cause. The things they would say to an umpire were unbelievably vile, and they broke the spirits of some fine men."[5]

The Orioles played in this fashion, negative as it was, since it proved to be a winning strategy. McGraw, Kelley, Jennings, and the others were so focused on winning, no matter the price, that they put their opponents on the defensive from the first pitch of a contest to the last. Every National League player knew that he was in for a battle, not a game, whenever he played Baltimore. The Orioles brimmed with talent, but their aggressiveness on the field gave them an additional, albeit distasteful, competitive edge.

Kelley, McGraw, Jennings, and Keeler, whom the Baltimore papers dubbed the "Big Four," pushed each other to greater levels of excellence. They refined plays such as the hit-and-run and double steal, and maintained discipline without waiting for manager Hanlon to do so. "Hanlon didn't have to scold or punish a player for failing to do his part," said McGraw. "We attended to that ourselves.... Woe betide the player who failed us! His life on the bench was not a pleasant one. He never forgot the roasting and never failed to deliver one if somebody else failed."[6] Joe most likely received such a roasting on May 30, 1893, when Pittsburgh first baseman Jake Beckley caught Kelley off base with the oldest stunt in the book, the hidden ball trick.

Joe Kelley did not garner as many headlines as McGraw, but he was the most well-rounded, and probably the best player on the team. Keeler, Jennings, and McGraw were high-average hitters with little power, but Joe was an expert both at scoring runs and driving them in. In 1894, when slugger Dan Brouthers batted in 134 runs from the cleanup spot, Joe hit next in the lineup and drove home 111 more. Joe's .393 average and .602 slugging percentage set new club records in 1894, and he thrilled the fans with circus catches in the outfield. Though Kelley indulged in alcohol and asked for salary advances too often for Hanlon's taste, the manager thought so much of his prize pupil that he named Joe assistant captain, an honor that carried an extra $200 in pay.

Though Joe, as a left fielder, was not as close to the umpire on defense as were McGraw and Jennings, he copied McGraw's style and became one of the circuit's leading umpire abusers. Kelley was always primed to argue, especially over balls and strikes, and soon the umpires came to loathe Kelley almost as much as the despised McGraw. In most seasons during the 1890s, Kelley led the Orioles in ejections and fines. "[Kelley] has had more fines inflicted by umpires this season than any other player in the league," remarked the *Washington Post* in 1896. "He would not be so obstreperous if they came out of his own pocket."[7] Since Hanlon and the Baltimore team ownership paid all the fines, Kelley, McGraw, and the rest were free to play their highly aggressive brand of baseball without fear of economic reprisal.

Kelley's competitive streak resulted in one of the most bizarre on-field incidents of the 1890s. One day, a delegation of fans from Joe's hometown of Cambridge presented him with a gold watch prior to the game. Joe handed it to the clubhouse man, who passed it off to umpire George Burnham for safekeeping. During the contest, Joe began arguing with Burnham, who took as much abuse as he could stomach and then, following the custom of the era, pulled out a watch and gave Kelley one minute to return to his position. Joe slapped the timepiece out of Burnham's hand, stomping on it until the umpire informed Joe that he had destroyed his own watch. The episode earned the umpire a new nickname, and he was called "Watch" Burnham ever after.[8]

The Orioles, who finished in eighth place in 1893, pulled off one of the most amazing ascents in baseball history the following season. They won their first four games, then announced their arrival on April 25 in a game against

Boston. Trailing by a score of 3–1 after eight innings, the Orioles rocked pitchers Kid Nichols and Jack Stivetts for 14 runs in the ninth and won the game 15–3. They charged into the league lead and held it until late July, when a seven-game losing streak dropped them into second place, five games behind the Beaneaters. They battled through August and then, beginning on August 26, put together an 18-game winning streak that vaulted them back into the lead. On Labor Day, September 3, they trounced Cleveland by scores of 13–2 and 16–3 as Joe Kelley belted nine hits and scored seven runs in the two games. Keeler and Brouthers had seven hits apiece and McGraw five, while Joe's nine for nine performance in a single day has never been matched in baseball history.[9]

Brouthers provided the power while Keeler and McGraw supplied the speed, but Joe Kelley was the man who sparked the Orioles to their first pennant. He batted .541 in the last 30 games of the season, playing sensational ball in the outfield while leading his team in batting, slugging, doubles, and walks. With Kelley leading the charge, the Orioles romped to the pennant and a berth in the post-season Temple Cup series against the New York Giants, who edged out Boston for second place.

The Baltimore players showed little interest in the Temple Cup, which pitted the first and second-place teams in a best-of-seven October series. Since there was only one major league at the time, there was no true World Series, and Baltimore considered the Temple Cup match a poor substitute. They demanded a 50–50 split of gate receipts between the two teams (rather than 65 percent for the winning team as stipulated in the rules) and, when their request was denied, made individual deals with the New York players to split their winnings evenly. Kelley paired off with Giants pitcher Amos Rusie, while the other Orioles also found partners among the Giants. By the time the series began, all the players had agreed to divide their post-series checks equally.

This arrangement removed all incentive for either team to win, and the Temple Cup was noted for its display of dull, listless baseball. Though the Orioles were heavy favorites, the Giants ran off four consecutive wins behind pitchers Rusie and Jouett Meekin, winning the Cup before small crowds. Joe Kelley counted himself fortunate to have teamed up with Rusie, as the Giants pitcher left $204 (the difference between the winning and losing shares) for Joe at his hotel after the last game of the match. No other Giant lived up to his word, as all (except Rusie) reneged, keeping all their winnings for themselves. This episode caused great antagonism between the two ballclubs, which lasted for years afterward and gave a bitter edge to their on-field disputes throughout the 1890s.

Despite the loss in the Temple Cup, the Orioles were favored to repeat as pennant winners in 1895. This proved to be a much tougher race, and they struggled early in the season. Dan Brouthers' hitting and fielding fell off dramatically, and in May Hanlon sold the aging slugger to Louisville and put rookie George (Scoops) Carey on first base. Hanlon then moved Joe Kelley to the cleanup spot in the lineup, where Joe became the leading run producer for the Orioles. Later that season, after John McGraw was sidelined with tonsillitis, the versatile Kelley became the new Baltimore leadoff man. He ended the season with 148 runs scored, 134 runs batted in, and a .365 average as the Orioles rode another hot streak in September to their second consecutive pennant. They lost the Temple Cup to Cleveland, four games to one, in October.

By 1895, Joe Kelley had become one of the best all-around players in the game. He hit for average and power (his 10 homers in 1895 set a new team record), but was speedy enough to bat leadoff and be a serious base-stealing threat. He exuded confidence, but with a touch of arrogance, making him a natural leader. He also, to the disbelief of many, boasted that he could hit with any bat. "It makes no difference to me what kind of bat I have," said Joe in 1897. "For instance, I often grab the first bat I come across when I go up to the plate. Muggsy McGraw uses a light stick and Jake Stenzel has a heavy one, but I'm liable to take any one of the miscellaneous lot that falls in my way."[10] Few believed him, but such was his self-assurance.

The battling Orioles had an easier time of it in 1896, winning the pennant by nine and a half games over second-place Cleveland, then getting serious in October for the first time and sweeping the Temple Cup series in four straight. McGraw, ill with typhoid fever, played in only 18 games that year, but Kelley took his place at the top of the lineup and produced a .364 batting average, with 148 runs scored and a league-leading 87 stolen bases. McGraw's absence made Joe the temporary captain of the Orioles, and he took a more prominent role on the field, especially in regard to arguing with umpires. Joe liked the role of team captain, and perhaps it was at this time that he began making plans to manage his own ballclub in the future.

The Orioles staged one of their most notorious battles one day when McGraw was not present. On April 4, 1896, Baltimore played an exhibition game against a club in Petersburg, Virginia, a mill town with a reputation for toughness. The home plate umpire, a Petersburg man, made such egregiously bad calls all day that the Orioles demanded his removal in the seventh inning. A Petersburg player took this opportunity to punch Hugh Jennings, and a riot broke out. Kelley, Jennings, and the rest of the team fought their way out of the ballpark and made it to their hotel, but another row exploded in the lobby between Kelley and the umpire. By the time this second brawl ended, police issued arrest warrants for Kelley and two others, but the ballplayers slipped out of the hotel and beat it out of town ahead of an angry mob.

The young Oriole stars were close friends on and off the field. Following the 1896 Temple Cup series, Keeler, Kelley, Jennings, McGraw, and pitcher Arlie Pond boarded a passenger ship, the *St. Paul*, for a voyage to Europe. They visited London, Paris, and Brussels, enjoying the Old World that their parents had left behind before returning home in early December. In March of 1897, when McGraw married a Baltimore girl, Jennings served as best man while Keeler and Kelley were groomsmen. McGraw and Jennings coached baseball together at St. Bonaventure University in the off-seasons, while McGraw and Wilbert Robinson co-owned a bowling alley in Baltimore. Perhaps no team in the National League was as close as the Orioles.

However, the young ballplayers were marrying and starting families. Joe Kelley had always spent the winter months in Cambridge, but after the 1896 season he remained in Baltimore for the first time. He had been dating Margaret Mahon, the daughter of a powerful Baltimore political figure named John J. Mahon. Known around town as "Sonny," Mahon was a key player in city government and the Democratic Party hierarchy, and the ambitious young ballplayer would find his contacts useful in the future. Joe and Margaret married on October 26, 1897, with Willie Keeler as best man. Joe and his new bride spent their honeymoon traveling the western states with a baseball tour organized by Boston manager Frank Selee. The couple returned to Baltimore in December and set up housekeeping, and over the next few years Margaret produced two sons, Ward and Joseph Junior. Joe Kelley, a native of Cambridge, Massachusetts, made Baltimore his permanent home.

The Orioles might have continued their reign in 1897, but the Boston Beaneaters, after a spirited pennant race, kept Hanlon's men from winning an unprecedented fourth consecutive National League championship. Joe, returned by Hanlon to the cleanup spot, drove in 118 runs and hit .362, while Willie Keeler won the batting title at .424 and new center fielder Jake Stenzel hit .343 and led the league in doubles. Though Joe professed confidence in the Orioles ("We'll win the pennant, all right. Boston doesn't frighten us a bit," he proclaimed in July)[11], the Beaneaters edged Baltimore at season's end, though the Orioles exacted a measure of revenge by winning its second consecutive Temple Cup.

Much to Ned Hanlon's annoyance, Kelley, Jennings, and Keeler held out together during the spring of 1898. Kelley had been receiving the National League maximum salary of $2,400, with an extra $200 tacked on for his duties as assistant captain, but wanted more. He threatened to quit the game and join his brother in a hauling business in Cambridge if he was not granted his desired salary. Hanlon was in no mood to pay, as the Orioles had lost money in 1897, and the looming Spanish-American War threatened to take public attention away from baseball. The two sides remained at an impasse until four days before the season opener, when Kelley finally signed for a $100 raise. Keeler and Jennings soon came to terms as well, and the Orioles were ready to recapture the pennant.

Nonetheless, the new season did not go smoothly for the Orioles. Attendance dropped sharply for the second straight year, partly due to the war but also, perhaps, because Baltimore fans were jaded after losing the pennant in 1897 after three consecutive titles. Only 6,500 fans attended the home opener in April, and by midseason crowds numbered only in the hundreds during the week. When Hanlon traded center fielder Jake Stenzel to the Browns for Ducky Holmes on June 10, he moved Joe from Kelleyville in left to center and installed Holmes in left. This move energized the team (though a confrontation between Holmes and New York Giants owner Andrew Freedman resulted in Holmes' suspension in July) and the Orioles made a charge, but finished in second place again, six games behind Boston.

The 1898 season marked the end of an era in Baltimore baseball. Rumors abounded that the ballclub, which had finished first or second for five consecutive seasons but lost money in the last three, might be sold or disbanded. Joe Kelley waited impatiently for news during the winter of 1898–99, and it finally materialized in February when the owners of the Brooklyn Dodgers bought the Orioles outright and transferred the best Baltimore players to Brooklyn. Ned Hanlon, who wound up as president of the Baltimore club and manager of the Brooklyn entry simultaneously, took Joe Kelley, Hugh Jennings, Willie Keeler, and six other Orioles with him to the Dodgers. John McGraw and Wilbert Robinson stayed behind in Baltimore (where the 26-year-old McGraw became the new manager), so Hanlon appointed Kelley as field captain. Hanlon's arrival also resulted in a new nickname for the club, as the papers dropped the name Dodgers and began calling the team the Superbas, after a popular vaudeville act.

Joe did not want to go to Brooklyn, as he and his wife had recently purchased a home in Baltimore. He hoped to follow McGraw's example and become a manager, but Hanlon's presence as president and part owner left no room for advancement with the Brooklyn team. Kelley begged Hanlon to send him to Washington, which was close to Baltimore and needed a manager, but the cellar-dwelling Senators did not have enough talent to trade for a star like Joe. Willie Keeler, a Brooklyn native, was thrilled with the move to the Superbas, but Joe realized that he was stuck in Brooklyn and decided to make the best of it. He threw himself into his duties as field captain and waited for an opportunity to manage.

Brooklyn had finished in tenth place in 1898, but the infusion of talent from Baltimore suddenly made the Superbas the class of the National League. The outfield of Kelley, Keeler, and holdover Fielder Jones was the best in the circuit, and while Hugh Jennings was unavailable most of the season due to injury, Bill Dahlen arrived in a trade from Chicago to solidify the infield. The Superbas, with Kelley batting .325 and leading the team in runs batted in, won the 1899 pennant easily with an eight-game bulge over second-place Boston.

Though Joe Kelley, as captain of the Superbas, received a large amount of credit for the Brooklyn championship, he still wanted to return to Baltimore. However, the National League dropped four teams after the 1899 campaign, and the Orioles (along with the clubs in Cleveland, Washington, and Louisville) were relegated to the sidelines. John McGraw was shunted off to St. Louis, where he and Wilbert Robinson spent an unhappy year with the newly-named Cardinals, while Kelley and Keeler returned to Brooklyn to play again under Ned Hanlon's leadership. The Superbas won the pennant again the following year, as Joe led the team in runs batted in and batted .319.

Joe had begun his professional career as a shortstop, and by 1900 was eager to return to the infield. He may have believed that it was easier to serve as captain of the Superbas as an infielder, or perhaps he wanted to preserve his legs as he approached his 30th year. At any rate, Joe played 13 games at third base in 1900 and, after Hugh Jennings was sold to the Phillies in June, 32 games at first. Joe preferred first base to the outfield, and in 1901 he remained there for the entire season, with newcomer Jimmy Sheckard taking over in left.

Joe Kelley in 1899, his first season with Brooklyn. (National Baseball Hall of Fame Library, Cooperstown, N.Y.)

The Superbas failed to win their third consecutive pennant, finishing third as Joe Kelley compiled a solid, but not spectacular, season. Most likely he was distracted by the chance to return to Baltimore, where John McGraw managed a new edition of the Orioles in the American League, which began play in 1901 as a rival to the established National circuit. Though both Joe Kelley and his friend Willie Keeler had declined American League offers that spring, the new league looked more promising after surviving its inaugural season. Additionally, Joe's father-in-law John J. Mahon bought a large share of stock in the Orioles and became club president. The new league launched a campaign to sign National League stars, and though Keeler elected to stay in Brooklyn, Joe Kelley quit the Superbas and signed with McGraw's Orioles in 1902.

A highly-regarded veteran and still an outstanding player, Joe became captain of the Orioles and received some stock in the team, though his homecoming was short-lived. McGraw, who continued the umpire-baiting and rowdiness that had brought the Orioles success during the previous decade, ran afoul of American League president Ban Johnson, who had promised "clean baseball" to the American public. Johnson and McGraw sniped at each other in the papers all year long, and by mid-season McGraw was angling to return to the National League. The New York Giants had offered him a $10,000 salary to switch allegiances, but McGraw was not solely interested in managing the Giants. He wanted to destroy the American League and drive it, and Ban Johnson, out of business. The Orioles were a lost cause anyway, losing money and languishing in the second division. McGraw hatched a scheme, enlisting Joe Kelley and John Mahon to help facilitate it. "Someone would be left holding the bag," said McGraw later, "and I made up my mind it wouldn't be me."[12]

On June 28, Kelley and McGraw abused umpire Tommy Connolly so viciously during a game against Boston that Connolly forfeited the contest. Johnson promptly suspended both men indefinitely, threatening to drive McGraw out of baseball and declaring, "Rowdyism will not be tolerated in the American League ... and the men who disregard the organization rules must suffer the consequences."[13] McGraw used his time away to confer with the owners of the New York Giants, and on July 7 quit the Orioles and signed with the Giants, thus throwing the Baltimore club into turmoil. During this time, Mahon had acquired 201 of the 400 outstanding shares of Oriole stock by buying up those owned by McGraw, Kelley, Wilbert Robinson, and several small investors. With a majority of the team under his control, Mahon then sold the ballclub to New York Giants owner Andrew Freedman, giving the National League full possession of an American League team. Freedman, in turn, released Joe Kelley and eight other Orioles from their contracts, making them free agents. This act decimated the Baltimore club and dealt a near-fatal blow to the upstart league.

It was a brilliant and cold-blooded scheme, but Mahon, Kelley, and McGraw may have overplayed their hand. The Orioles, left with only six players, could not play their next scheduled game, which gave Ban Johnson the opportunity to declare the franchise forfeited to the American League. Johnson kept the Orioles alive until the season's end, using players borrowed from other league teams, and in 1903 he moved the club to New York to create the team that later became the Yankees. McGraw managed the Giants for the next 30 years, winning ten pennants and three World Series, while several other former Orioles found stardom during the next few seasons. The ultimate loser in the episode was the city of Baltimore, which waited until 1954 to host another major league team.

Joe Kelley, like McGraw, profited from the deal. John Mahon had demanded a managerial role for his son-in-law as a condition of the complicated multi-team transaction, and John T. Brush, a part-owner of the Giants who also controlled the Cincinnati Reds, had long coveted Kelley as a manager. Brush and Freedman were willing to give Mahon and Kelley what they wanted, and on July 17 Kelley signed a contract to manage and play for the Reds. The only obstacle to the pact was Brooklyn manager Ned Hanlon, who claimed ownership of Kelley's baseball rights. Joe had quit Brooklyn and signed with Baltimore after the 1901 season, but Hanlon had kept Kelley's name on the Brooklyn reserve list for 1902. Nonetheless, the return of Kelley to the National League represented a victory for the senior circuit, and the other National League owners convinced Hanlon to drop his objections to the arrangement.

The Reds also signed former Oriole Cy Seymour, a hard-hitting pitcher-turned-outfielder, who joined the team that same day. However, Joe did not immediately report to Cincinnati. He traveled instead to Boston, met with several members of the Boston American League team, and attempted to lure them back to the National League. Joe ultimately failed in this endeavor, so he went to Cincinnati and took over as manager of the Reds on July 31.

The Reds had been a chronically underachieving team since joining the National League in 1890. They had not yet won a pennant, and a series of bad trades (especially the deal that sent future pitching star Christy Mathewson to New York for a sore-armed Amos Rusie) had eroded their talent base. The team languished in the second division early in 1902 under popular former player Bid McPhee, who resigned in early July amid rumors that Kelley was negotiating to take his job. The club was listless and disorganized, but Joe had waited patiently for an opportunity to manage, and eagerly went to work.

Joe Kelley was still, at age 30, one of the best players in the league, and put himself in the cleanup spot in the lineup while playing wherever needed in the infield and outfield. He wanted to play first base, but that position was the domain of one of the Reds' few stars, the colorful Jake Beckley, a poor fielder but a .300 hitter who was popular with the fans. Kelley saw time at short, third, and second base, while Cy Seymour and another ex-Oriole, Mike Donlin, filled two spots in the outfield and immediately raised the team's level of play. Joe also could count on one of baseball's best young players, right fielder Sam Crawford, who led the league with 16 homers the year before and ended his career 15 years later as baseball's all-time leader in triples. Kelley managed the team to a 36–26 record and lifted the Reds to fourth place by season's end.

The new manager made sure that the Cincinnati players and fans knew he had lost none of his feistiness. On October 4, 1902, the Reds were scheduled to play the last game of the season in Pittsburgh, but a rainstorm left standing water on the field. Kelley wanted the contest called off, but Pittsburgh owner Barney Dreyfuss, unwilling to disappoint a large crowd, ordered the game played. Kelley showed his disdain by putting the worst thrower on the team, Jake Beckley, on the mound for the Reds, letting pitcher Rube Vickers try his hand at catching, and placing other Reds at unfamiliar positions. Vickers suffered six passed balls and did not even bother to chase wild pitches, while Beckley allowed eight runs in only four innings as the game degenerated into a farce. The Pirates won by a score of 11–2, but Kelley had made his point, while Dreyfuss was obliged to offer refunds to placate the angry fans.

Joe managed the team for three more seasons, and although the Reds won more games than they lost each year, they never challenged for the pennant.

The loss of Sam Crawford to the American League after the 1902 campaign hurt the ballclub, and the departures of two more steady .300 hitters shortly after put a crimp in the team's offense. Mike Donlin hit .351 in 1903 but was too wild off the field for Kelley to handle, so the Reds traded him to McGraw's Giants a year later. Jake Beckley, still a good hitter, was sent to St. Louis at season's end to make room for Kelley at first base. Joe batted only .281 as a full-time first sacker in 1904, and the Reds finished in fourth place, 18 games behind the pennant-winning Giants.

Kelley, now in his mid-30s, began his inevitable decline as a player. In 1905, though Cy Seymour hit .377 to capture the batting title, Joe returned to the outfield and hit only .277. The Reds ended the season in fifth place, and team ownership dismissed Joe as manager and replaced him with his old Baltimore and Brooklyn boss, Ned Hanlon. Retained by Hanlon as a player, Joe batted only .228 in 1906, and in December of that year the Reds released him, apparently ending his major league career.

Joe was a determined individual, and was still convinced that he could succeed as a field leader. He searched for a job in organized ball, and in January of 1907 agreed to manage the Toronto Maple Leafs of the Eastern League. Playing on a part-time basis at first base and in the outfield, Joe hit .322 and led the Maple Leafs to the pennant. He loved Toronto and was eager to stay there, but his success worked against him. As an active player, he was subject to the major league draft, so in December of 1907 the Boston club of the National League put in a claim for Kelley's services. Joe was not interested in returning to the National League, but the rules of the player draft were clear, and he had no choice but to report to Boston.

Ironically, the Boston team was the same one that Joe had dreamt of joining as a child, and the first major league club that he had played for 17 years earlier. Known as the Beaneaters in the 1890s, the club was called the Doves (after owner George Dovey) in 1908, and would change its nickname again before adopting the name Braves in 1911. The Doves, one of the worst teams in baseball, had finished in seventh place in 1907 and held little hope for 1908, but Dovey was an optimist. He signed Joe Kelley to a two-year contract to manage the club.

Kelley brought the talent-poor Doves home in sixth place, but the impatient Dovey fired him in December of 1908. This dismissal precipitated a bitter dispute over the money owed Kelley for the second year of his contract. Kelley threatened to sue, but the league brokered a settlement, and he discarded plans for legal action. He then returned to Toronto, where he managed the Maple Leafs until 1914 and won another Eastern League pennant in 1912. He stopped playing after the 1910 campaign, but during the following season brought his best friend, Willie Keeler, to Toronto for a last hurrah in professional ball. Keeler, at age 39, batted only .277 for the Maple Leafs and, finding himself unable to cover right field adequately, quit after 39 games.

In 1915, Joe left Toronto to take a scouting position with the New York Yankees. He was respected for his baseball knowledge, and proved to be a tough but shrewd judge of young talent. Though not yet 50 years old, Joe followed the example of many old ballplayers and severely criticized the generation of athletes that followed his. He often remarked that the men he played with in the 1890s were far superior to players of the present day. Joe was not an easy man to impress, and one year did not recommend a single minor league player for his bosses to sign. The Yankee co-owner, Colonel T. L. Huston, praised Joe for his pickiness, declaring that Kelley had saved the team a large amount of money by not signing players who would turn out to be failures.

Joe grew less patient with young players as he aged, perhaps because the salaries earned by the later generation (especially Babe Ruth, whom the Yankees acquired in 1920) dwarfed those of Kelley's day.

Kelley as manager of the Toronto Maple Leafs in 1910. (Library of Congress)

On one occasion, a reporter asked him if modern baseball had changed substantially since the 1890s. "Yes," replied Joe. "On the first and fifteenth of the month." Another time, someone asked the old Oriole if there was any department in which 1920s-era players surpassed the old-timers. "Only one," said Kelley. "Playing golf."[14]

Miller Huggins, who had played second base for Kelley on the Reds more than a decade before, became the Yankee manager in 1918. Huggins, a brilliant field leader who had learned his trade from both Kelley and Ned Hanlon, had trouble handling the hard-drinking Babe Ruth, and assigned Kelley as Ruth's keeper one spring. Joe was assigned to pick up Ruth at his home in Baltimore, keep him out of the bars, and deliver him safely to Florida for spring training. Huggins waited in Florida for the arrival of his star player, but several days went by with no sign of either man. Finally, Huggins received a collect call from Ruth, who was still in Baltimore. "It's that old guy, Kelley," said the Babe. "I can't get him on the train. He met some old pals here and doesn't want to leave." Ruth ended up transporting Kelley to spring training, not the other way around.[15]

Joe's last job in the majors came in 1926 when his old Baltimore teammate Wilbert Robinson, manager of the Brooklyn Dodgers, hired Kelley as his third base coach. The Dodgers were an easy-going, second-division team, and outfielder Babe Herman recalled Kelley's performance in Larry Ritter's *The Glory of Their Times*. One day, Herman hit a liner in the gap which the outfielder bobbled, but Kelley tried to stop Herman at second. Herman made it to third anyway, but Kelley stopped him again, though Herman could easily have scored. Standing on third base, Herman asked Kelley why he gave the stop sign.

"Babe," said Kelley, "I want to tell you something. Without my glasses, I can't even see who's pitching. But I won't wear glasses on a ball field."

"Why not?" asked Herman.

"Pride!" replied the coach. Joe Kelley, at age 54, was still concerned about his appearance.[16]

Joe left baseball after the 1926 season and remained in Baltimore, where he utilized his father-in-law's political contacts to gain a seat on the Maryland State Racing Commission. The job was not a demanding one, and Joe lived an easy life with his wife and children. He attended annual reunions of his old Baltimore Oriole teammates, though their ranks were beginning to thin. Willie Keeler died in 1923, Hugh Jennings in 1928, McGraw and Robinson in 1934, and Hanlon in 1937, making Joe Kelley the last survivor of the old Oriole stars. After an illness lasting more than a year, Joe died of cancer on August 14, 1943 at age 71, and was survived by wife Margaret and two sons. He was buried at New Cathedral Cemetery in Baltimore, not far from the graves of McGraw, Robinson, and Hanlon.

The Baltimore Orioles of the 1890s bulldozed the rest of the National League on their way to three consecutive pennants, and while their hyper-aggressive style of play won them few friends, no one could deny their success. By 1945, nine years after the first group of players was elected to the Baseball Hall of Fame, five Orioles—McGraw, Keeler, Robinson, Brouthers, and Jennings—had been inducted into the Cooperstown shrine. Joe Kelley, perhaps the most talented and versatile man on the team, was bypassed by the Veterans Committee and remained outside the Hall for three decades. Not until 1971, when the Hall electors looked at Kelley's statistics and saw a man who starred for five pennant winners, was a consistent .300 hitter, and was equally at home as a cleanup batter and a leadoff man, did they place Joe in Cooperstown. Ironically, one of the seven men enshrined with Kelley that day was Jake Beckley, whom Kelley had traded away from Cincinnati 67 years before.

Kelley may be one of the least well-known players in the Hall, but he was also a key performer for one of the greatest teams in baseball history. The Orioles, successful though they were, might not have won three National League pennants (and two post-season Temple Cup series) without Joe Kelley in their lineup. He was the best player on an outstanding team, and as such Kelley earned his place in the Hall of Fame.

10

Mickey Welch

"Welch, of the New Yorks, is always smiling. He plants his right foot forward and scrapes a pile of dirt, then expectorates, and a moment later wipes the perspiration from his brow, when suddenly he doubles up and throws with all his might. Batters say that he is the best pitcher in the league."

—*Brooklyn Eagle, 1888*[1]

August 6, 1973 was a hot and steamy day in Cooperstown, New York. The annual induction ceremony for the Baseball Hall of Fame took place on that Sunday afternoon, and it proved to be one of the most emotional days in the history of the institution. Inductee Warren Spahn, the longtime pitching star for the Braves, was interrupted during his acceptance speech by the sight of a man in the audience suffering a heart attack. The stricken man was Spahn's brother-in-law, and a shaken Spahn had to be persuaded to continue his speech while medical personnel provided assistance to his relative. The day was also notable for the appearance of Vera Clemente, widow of the late Pittsburgh star Roberto, who was elected to the Hall in a special ballot after his death in a plane crash eight months before. Mrs. Clemente's speech drew both applause and tears when she called her husband's induction "Roberto's last triumph."

The ceremony was broadcast live in Puerto Rico, Clemente's homeland, and the demands of television prompted Hall officials to relegate the afternoon's most obscure inductee to the last spot on the program. That final honoree was Mickey Welch, who won more than 300 games during his career and led the New York Giants to its first two National League pennants in 1888 and 1889. "Smiling Mickey" Welch had been one of the most popular athletes in New York, but was forgotten by everyone except the baseball historians who wondered why a man with so many wins had not yet been enshrined in the Cooperstown museum. The members of the Veterans Committee had, in previous years, elected all the other members of the 300-win club to the Hall. Now, though he appeared to be no more than an afterthought on the program, Mickey Welch finally joined the Hall of Fame 32 years after his death.

The pitcher was born Michael Francis Walsh in the Williamsburg section of Brooklyn, New York, on the Fourth of July in 1859. He was the son of John

Joseph Walsh, a blacksmith who immigrated to New York from Nenagh in County Tipperary, Ireland a few years before, and his wife Bridget. Brooklyn was always known as the City of Churches, but it may well have been the City of Baseball Fields as well. The city was baseball-crazy during the 1860s, when Mickey Walsh grew up, and it seemed that nearly every vacant lot was covered with boys and young men playing ball.

The hub of Williamsburg baseball was the Union Grounds, built by a man named William Cammeyer at Lee and Marcy avenues, and opened in 1862. Cammeyer had the foresight to construct a baseball ground enclosed by a fence, the first in the nation. The closed grounds made it possible for Cammeyer to charge admission to games, a development that turned the pastime into a business and eventually paved the way for the professional game. The Brooklyn Eckfords, one of the leading amateur teams in the nation, played at the Union Grounds, and in 1868 another famous team, the New York Mutuals, moved from their base in Hoboken, New Jersey to Cammeyer's field.

A boy named William (Candy) Cummings grew up in Williamsburg and taught himself to throw the curveball, baseball's first, during the 1860s. Some of the game's earliest stars, such as Cummings, Bob Ferguson, Lip Pike, and Al Reach played for such outstanding Brooklyn teams as the Eckfords, Atlantics, Stars, and Excelsiors. Many young men who grew up to become famous ballplayers learned to play, as did Mickey Walsh, on the Williamsburg streets and lots. It was a tough neighborhood, and as Mickey told a newspaper reporter many decades later, "we turned out ball players and fighters galore in those days."[2] Williamsburg was a baseball proving ground, and Mickey made a name for himself there during the formative years of professional ball.

Mickey Walsh did not grow to be a big man, even for the era. At five feet and eight inches tall and 160 pounds, he was sturdy and owned a strong and durable right arm. He utilized an underhanded pitching delivery, as required by the rules of the time, and during his teenage years learned to put spin on the ball. He was never a power pitcher, and though his fastball was more than adequate, he was obliged to rely more on brains than brawn. "I was a little fellow," said Mickey, "and I had to learn to use my head. I studied the hitters and I knew how to pitch to all of them, and I worked hard to perfect my control. I had a pretty good fast ball, but I depended chiefly on a change of pace and an assortment of curve balls."[3]

Every boy in Williamsburg, it seemed, yearned to be a professional ballplayer, but Mickey's pitching ability made him stand out. In 1878, at age 18, he signed a contract to pitch for an independent (non-league) team in Poughkeepsie, New York. The team, called the Volunteers, paid Mickey $45 per month. Statistics from that era are sketchy, but one source states that he threw his array of underhand curveballs well enough to post a 16–6 record for the Volunteers. He started the 1878 season with a team in Auburn, New York, but soon left the state for a position as a pitcher for a strong National Association team in Holyoke, Massachusetts.

Mickey Welch with the pennant-winning Giants in 1888. The caption of the card refers to him as "Welsh," his original family name. (Library of Congress)

It was during this time that Mickey's last name morphed into Welch, though no one knows the reason. Perhaps a newspaper misspelled his name in a box score, or maybe Mickey wished to distinguish himself from several other Holyoke residents who shared the common Irish name of Michael Walsh. Whatever the reason, the pitcher was known as Mickey Welch for the remainder of his baseball career, though many of his closest friends called him Mike. He married a local girl named Mary Whelihan, and the two decided to make their home in Holyoke and raise a family there.

Mickey became one of the stars of the Holyoke team, but he was by no means the only good player on the roster. The first baseman was a future major leaguer from Waterbury, Connecticut named Roger Connor, who walloped home runs over the right field fence and into the Connecticut River. Holyoke conducted bitter rivalries with other clubs, especially the nine from Springfield, which was managed by a legend of the Brooklyn baseball scene named Bob Ferguson. In a hard-fought 1–0 win for Holyoke against Springfield that year, Ferguson complained loud and long about Mickey's pitching. "It is claimed that Welch's delivery was wholly illegal and unfair," said the Springfield newspaper the next day, but the umpire disagreed and the victory stood.[4]

Ferguson was a fighter, but he admired the pitching skill of his fellow Brooklyn native. When "Old Fergy" became manager of the Troy Trojans of the National League in 1880, he brought with him several National Association stars who had impressed him. At Ferguson's insistence, the Trojans signed both Mickey Welch and Roger Connor, and both young men made their major league debuts with Troy in May of 1880.

The National League, at the time, did not have teams in New York or Philadelphia as the clubs representing those cities had been expelled from the circuit following the 1876 season. The league did, however, feature teams from Troy, New York, and Worcester, Massachusetts in its eight-team lineup. Troy and Worcester were the smallest cities in the league, and struggled to compete against the better-financed ballclubs in Chicago and Boston, and the defending champions from Providence. The Troy Trojans played some of their games in Albany to draw more fans, but financial stability was always an uphill struggle.

Perhaps Mickey did not realize how demanding the Troy fans could be until he pitched his first major league game against Worcester on May 1. He lost the contest by a 13–1 score, giving up 11 hits and throwing three wild pitches, and the *Troy Press* was so shocked that it suspected Welch of drunkenness. "Rumor has it that Welch has been dissipating," said the paper, "and charges will be preferred against him in a day or two."[5] Nothing came of the threat, and he defeated Worcester four days later, winning the first of his 307 career victories.

The Trojans boasted several future stars in its 1880 lineup, none more important than the curveball artist from Brooklyn. Mickey Welch was the main starting pitcher for the Trojans that season, while Frank Larkin was the "change pitcher," but after Larkin lost his first six starts, Welch began pitching nearly every game. In August another rookie, right-hander Tim Keefe, arrived to replace Larkin, but Mickey still started 64 of the 83 games on the Troy schedule. His durability allowed him to complete all 64 of his starts, compiling a 34–30 record. With Welch throwing more than three-fourths of the innings for the team, the Trojans surprised the rest of the league by finishing in fourth place.

Pitchers dominated the National League in 1880. In that era, the hurler stood inside the "pitching box" with a front line only 45 feet from home plate, and was allowed to take several steps before throwing the ball. Although only underhanded or below-the-waist sidearm pitching was legal, batters found it difficult to hit a ball thrown from so short a distance. In 1881 the box was moved back five feet, to a distance of 50 feet, a change that restored some balance to the pitcher-batter confrontation.

Some pitchers, such as Charley Radbourn, took running starts inside the six feet by six feet pitching box, but Mickey Welch threw the ball after a two-step motion. "Facing the batsman, Welch advances the left foot, holding the ball at his breast," said a newspaper of the era. "With a characteristic hop he shifts his weight from his right foot to his left, delivering the sphere in the act."[6] He threw a fastball and a curve, and also introduced the "reverse curve," which was later labeled a fadeaway and is now known as a screwball. Welch may have been the first to throw the pitch, and some credit him with inventing the delivery that made later stars like Christy Mathewson, Carl Hubbell, and Fernando Valenzuela famous.

Tim Keefe had pitched well in the late stages of the 1880 season, completing all 12 of his starts and winning six of them, so the Trojans entered the 1881 season with Keefe and Welch alternating as starting pitchers. The two men pitched every inning between them for Troy that season, as Welch completed all his 40 starts and Keefe finished all 44 of his. Welch posted a 21–18 record, while Keefe went 18–27 for the Trojans. On July 4, his 22nd birthday, Mickey pitched both ends of a doubleheader against Buffalo and won both games. Unfortunately, Troy was a poor fielding team, and despite the presence of catcher Buck Ewing, another future star whom Ferguson had signed from Rochester, the Trojans finished in seventh place.

Mickey Welch, perhaps the most durable pitcher in the league, had started 104 games during his career up to that point and completed them all. This remarkable streak ended during the first month of the 1882 campaign. Mickey's arm was sore, probably from overuse, and he lost his first game to Providence by a 17–1 score. In his next start, Boston blasted him for 18 runs before Buck Ewing came in and finished the contest. Mickey had finally failed to complete a game, but after a two-week layoff, Welch defeated Boston 1–0 on May 23 and scored the only run of the game. He battled a tired arm and a sore ankle all year long, finishing with a 14–16 record in 36 games.

The Trojans suffered a rash of injuries in 1882 and settled back into seventh place. Attendance was so poor in the league's smaller cities that both Troy and Worcester withdrew from the circuit at season's end. The National League finally recognized the desirability of maintaining teams in New York and Philadelphia, and an entrepreneur named John B. Day offered to organize a new squad to represent the largest city in the nation. Day owned the New York Metropolitans, a leading independent ballclub, and most people figured that he would move that club into the National League. Instead, Day put the "Mets" into the rival American Association and built a new team, the Gothams, for the National circuit.

The dissolution of the Troy franchise made its players free agents, and Day quickly moved to grab the best Trojans for himself. In quick order, Day signed first baseman Roger Connor, pitchers Mickey Welch and Tim Keefe, catchers Bill Holbert and Buck Ewing, and outfielder Pat Gillespie. He sent Keefe and Holbert to the Metropolitans, while the other four landed with the Gothams. Day also acquired pitcher John Ward from Providence to assist Welch, and signed another hurler in James (Tip) O'Neill, who later made a name for himself as a hitter and an outfielder.

The New York Gothams made their National League debut on May 1, 1883, at the Polo Grounds in upper Manhattan, and Mickey Welch was given the honor of pitching the team's first game. More than 10,000 fans, including former President Ulysses S. Grant, watched Welch defeat Boston by a 7–5 score. The Gothams won their first three games, but a 1–13 skid dropped them to last place by Memorial Day. Welch finished the season at 25–23, while the sore-armed Ward divided his time between pitching and the outfield and went 16–13. Buck Ewing led the league in home runs with 10, and the Gothams finished in sixth place in their first National League season.

Pitching was not Mickey's only responsibility. "On the days when I wasn't pitching," said Welch, "I used to ride out ahead with [manager Jim] Mutrie in a two-seated hack and he'd put me watching the turnstiles. And when John Ward and I were the main pitchers ... we'd take turns playing center field, too. When he pitched, I played center and when I pitched, he played center."[7] Mickey played 38 games in the outfield in 1883, batting .234 and contributing 30 runs batted in.

Jim Mutrie, who supervised both the Metropolitans and the Gothams as Day's assistant, was a born showman. "He was a fine feller, a grand man," said Mickey late in life. "He stirred up interest. He'd stand on the steps at the park with his high hat and fancy coat and as the crowd came in or went out he'd be shaking his cane and shouting 'We are the people!' He'd stand up in the hacks in other cities and shout it as we drove to the ball parks with the rooters for the other team hootin' at us."[8] Mutrie's battle cry, "We Are the People," became the unofficial team motto during the 1880s.

The 1884 season was an up-and-down ride for Mickey. On August 23 Buffalo's Dan Brouthers, one of the biggest and strongest men in the National League, drove a shot off Mickey's hip. Mickey walked around in pain for more than 20 minutes, assisted by a doctor, before he could continue the game. Three days later, Cleveland pitcher John Harkins threw a fastball that struck Mickey in the head, rendering him unconscious. As *The New York Times* reported, "After making a few spasmodic kicks he regained consciousness, and was assisted to his feet, but was unable to pitch."[9] Welch made his next start against Cleveland on August 28, and set a record by striking out the first nine batters he faced. That record stood until Tom Seaver, pitching for a later incarnation of the New York Mets in 1970, fanned ten men in a row. Mickey did not celebrate his feat for long, because on September 4 another muscular hitter, Chicago's Cap Anson, drove a liner off the pitcher's head.

The Gothams moved up to fifth in 1884, while the Metropolitans won the American Association pennant. However, the Gothams captured the attention of fans and sportswriters, while the Metropolitans played to small crowds despite their on-field success. The National League carried greater status than the Association, and John B. Day decided to pour his energies into one team instead of two. He reinforced the Gothams by moving pitcher Tim Keefe and third baseman Dude Esterbrook over from the Metropolitans, once again uniting Mickey Welch and Tim Keefe as a one-two pitching punch.

Before the 1885 season began, Mickey made a demand upon the team owners. He had started more than half of the Gothams' games in 1884, winning 39 and completing 62 of his 65 starts, and had often pitched two complete games in successive days. He found little support, with John Ward playing almost full-time in the field and second-string pitcher Ed Bagley posting a 12–18 log, and feared wearing himself out at an early age. He refused to sign his contract for 1885 unless it contained a clause that prevented him from pitching two days in a row. Such a clause was unprecedented, but with Keefe joining the team, the owners agreed. John B. Day and Jim Mutrie lived up to the agreement, and at no time in 1885 did Mickey pitch two days in succession.

The Gothams acquired several new players and a new nickname that season as well. Keefe, Connor, and several other men on the team were tall, and manager Mutrie called them "My big fellows! My Giants!" one day. From then on, the New York team in the National League was known as the Giants, and the club, which now plays in San Francisco, uses the moniker to this day.

The tandem of Welch and Keefe nearly pitched the Giants to the pennant in 1885. Mickey used his array of curveballs and change-ups to post a remarkable 44–11 record, completing all 55 of his starts and striking out 258 men. From July 18 to September 4, he won 17 games in succession, falling one win short of Charley Radbourn's National League record. Keefe was nearly as good, with a 32–13 log and a 1.58 earned run average. The Giants battled all year long, and not until the last weekend of the season did Cap Anson's Chicago White Stockings nose out the Giants by two games for the flag. It was the Giants' best performance to date, and New York's .759 winning percentage would have been good enough to win any pennant in the 20th century.

Welch and Keefe were, by now, considered two of the three best pitchers in the game, and only Chicago's John Clarkson (who went 53–16 for the pennant-winners) stood with them atop the pitching world. The two became fast friends despite their differences in personality; Keefe was quiet and studious, while Mickey was outgoing, jovial, and fun-loving. While Keefe was called "Sir Timothy" for his regal bearing, R. K. Munkittrick of *Puck* magazine called his pitching partner "Smiling Mickey," a nickname that stuck because it succinctly described Welch's character. Mickey Welch loved playing baseball and being a sports hero in the nation's largest city. "I can't complain," he once said. "I never learned how."

Mickey was always clean-shaven (while most of his teammates sported handlebar moustaches) and did not smoke, swear, or drink hard liquor, but he loved drinking beer. He enjoyed his beer so much that he composed little poems about the brew and recited them for sportswriters and fans, often during the carriage rides to the ballpark each day. One sample: "Pure elixir of malt and hops, beats all the drugs and all the drops." Another: "A mug of ale without a question, when drunk on top would aid digestion." The pitcher sometimes recited poems that advertised bars and restaurants owned by friends and acquaintances, probably in exchange for free mugs of beer. The New York fans ate it up, and "Smiling Mickey" Welch's outgoing nature made him one of the most popular men on the team.

A studio portrait of Mickey Welch, taken during the 1880s. (National Baseball Hall of Fame Library, Cooperstown, N.Y.)

He was friendly with his opponents, but was tough when he needed to be. The rivalry between the Giants and Cap Anson's Chicago White Stockings was a fierce one during the 1880s, and Mike (King) Kelly was one of Anson's most formidable players. "He didn't look tough or talk tough, but he was tough," said Welch. "When I was pitching against him I used to shy the first one up around his ears. He would say in his rich Irish brogue, 'Now, now, Mickey, me bye, I'm just after getting' me chin shaved this morning.' I'd usually let him alone after that mild warning because if I didn't, he'd throw the bat at me."[10]

Welch continued his fine pitching in 1886, but Tim Keefe slowly supplanted his partner as the number one pitcher for the Giants. Keefe's 1886 season, in which he won 42 games and led the league in wins, innings pitched, and complete games, was every bit as outstanding as Mickey's the year before. Welch, with 33 wins, was relegated to second place and would remain there for the next few seasons. They were still a formidable one-two combination, the best in the league, but Keefe was now the main man, with Welch in a supporting role.

The Giants, after challenging down to the wire in 1885, fell short in the next two campaigns, but the Keefe-Welch combination kept producing wins. By 1887, when the Giants fell to fourth place, some feared that the team's moment had passed. However, the National League batters had prospered in 1887 when the rules committee decreed that four strikes, not three, would constitute a strikeout. The number was restored to three in 1888, and pitchers once again gained the upper hand. The Giants, with the best pitching duo in the league, surged to the forefront in 1888. Keefe won a record 19 games in a row, surpassing Mickey's record set two years earlier, and the Giants rode the arms of Keefe (35–12) and Welch (26–19) to its first National League flag. Mickey split two decisions against St. Louis in the October "World's Series," as Keefe allowed only two runs in four games and pitched the Giants to victory.

The 1889 campaign was much more difficult for the Giants. Keefe held out in a contract dispute for the first three weeks of the season, but Mickey picked up the slack with help from second-line pitchers Cannonball Crane and Hank O'Day. Welch and Keefe were more evenly matched that season, with Keefe posting a 28–13 record and Welch an almost identical 27–12 log. They battled all season long with Boston, and only on the final weekend did the Giants clinch their second flag in a row. The World's Series against Brooklyn was almost an afterthought, as Keefe and Welch, exhausted from the pennant race, pitched in only one game apiece. Crane and O'Day won six games between them and gave the Giants their second consecutive post-season championship.

Mickey gained a distinction of his own on August 10 of that year. Hank O'Day started the game that day against Indianapolis, but manager Jim Mutrie took him out after five innings and instructed Mickey to warm up. The Giants scored six runs in their half of the inning, and O'Day's turn at bat unexpectedly came up. Mutrie put Welch in to bat in O'Day's place, and because Mickey batted before taking the mound, he became the first pinch-hitter in National League history. He struck out, though the Giants won the game by a 9–6 score.

While successfully defending their pennant, the Giants were at the forefront of baseball's greatest crisis to date. Four years earlier, Mickey Welch and eight other Giants had formed baseball's first trade union, the Brotherhood of Professional Base Ball Players. With John Ward as president and Tim Keefe as secretary-treasurer, this organization opposed the reserve clause, salary limits, and restrictions on player movement. The Brotherhood offered to represent the players in negotiations with the owners, and by 1887 more than 100 National Leaguers had joined. By late 1889, after ownership had ignored the Brotherhood and adopted a restrictive salary-classification plan, Ward and his new trade union struck back. The Brotherhood members quit the National League *en masse* and declared their intention to create and operate a competing circuit, to be called the Players League, in 1890. John Ward managed a new team in Brooklyn, while Keefe and others set up a franchise in New York and filled the roster with almost all of the Giants stars such as Keefe, Roger Connor, and Buck Ewing.

The advent of the Players League threatened all the National League owners, but none more so than John B. Day. His Giants had won the league title the past two seasons, and his players carried unprecedented fame and popularity both in New York and around the league. The migration of talent to a rival team in New York would spell disaster for Day and his Giants. Specifically, Day's ballclub would be no better than an expansion team if he lost both of his star pitchers. He might be able to survive with either Keefe or Welch in uniform, but not if he lost both men.

Day recognized that Tim Keefe, who was not only the secretary of the Brotherhood but also John Ward's brother-in-law, would never turn his back on the new circuit. Mickey Welch, however, might be receptive to a deal. In December of 1889 Day tempted both Welch and first baseman Roger Connor with generous offers to leave the Brotherhood and remain with the Giants. One report stated that Day promised Welch a three-year contract worth $4,000 per annum, a huge raise from the $2,000 or so that the pitcher had received in previous seasons. The contract was unusual for the time in that Day promised to honor the agreement for the full three years, regardless of injury or ineffectiveness.

Connor, who had been told by Day to "name your price," turned the Giants down, but Welch was intrigued by the offer. Though Mickey was one of the founders of the Brotherhood, he already had more than 280 wins and 450 complete games behind him, and had no idea how long his arm would last. He had passed his 30th birthday, a date that marked the beginning of the end for many hurlers in that era, and the financial well-being of his growing family in Holyoke weighed on his mind.

Welch considered the offer for two weeks, and by mid-January 1890 had made his decision. He told *The New York Times* that he had chosen to remain with the Giants. The contract length was the deciding factor. "I offered to play with the new club for a salary of $2,000 less than that offered me by Mr. Day," explained Mickey. "The figure suited the leaders of the movement, but the financial men would only guarantee me my salary for 1890. Some time ago Mr. Day made me a big offer, and said that he would sign a three years' contract, he to assume all risks.

"I am in the business for dollars and cents, and as the offer made by the old League was the better one, I accepted it."[11]

Mickey resigned from the Brotherhood a few days later. John Ward, president of the movement, bitterly denounced the "traitors" who chose to remain in the National League, but Tim Keefe was remarkably understanding. "Mike, you are your own boss," said Keefe, and the two men remained friends.

The Giants reeled from the loss of Keefe, Ewing, Connor, and others, but Day arranged for several men from the defunct Indianapolis franchise to join the team. Pitchers Amos Rusie and Jesse Burkett, shortstop Jack Glasscock, and four other Hoosiers helped keep the Giants afloat during the critical campaign. Burkett soon moved to the outfield, but the 18-year-old Rusie burst upon the New York baseball scene and surpassed Mickey Welch as the number one starter. Rusie, who threw the quickest fastball in the game, started more than half of the games for the Giants that year, ending up with a 29–34 record. Mickey, thrust into a supporting role, managed a 17–14 mark in 37 games, and earned his 300th victory with a shutout against Brooklyn on August 11. He was the third pitcher to win 300 major league games, following Jim (Pud) Galvin and Keefe, who had won his milestone game two months earlier.

The New York Players League entry drew more fans than the National League team, but when the new league collapsed that fall, Keefe, Ewing, and Connor rejoined the Giants. Keefe and Welch were reunited, but both men were aging, and Keefe had not recovered fully from a broken finger suffered the year before. Keefe pitched poorly during the early stages of the 1891 season, and the Giants released him at the end of July. Mickey Welch battled injuries as well, but remained on the team due to his three-year, no-cut contract. Mickey was relegated to the third position among Giant starters, behind Rusie and right-hander John Ewing, and compiled a 5–9 record.

After one appearance in 1892, in which he gave up 9 runs and 11 hits in five innings against the Orioles on May 17, the Giants sent Welch to Troy of the Eastern League. Mickey won 17 and lost 14 there, but his career was winding down. His fastball had slowed significantly, and it did not bode well for Mickey's future when the National League rulemakers decided to add 10 feet to the distance between batter and pitcher for the following season. When his contract expired at the end of the 1892 season, Mickey decided to call it quits. He occupied fourth place on the all-time win list with 307 at the time of his retirement, and today, more than 110 years later, he still stands in 20th place on the victory log.

If he harbored any desire to make a comeback, the Giants dashed it early the next year. When Mickey returned to his home in Holyoke and joined a local semipro team, he arranged for his new ballclub to play an exhibition match against the Giants in early April of 1893. Mickey took the mound against his old teammates, but found himself behind by a score of 11–0 after one inning of play. While Amos Rusie mowed down the Holyoke batters, the Giants roughed up Mickey for 21 runs and 19 hits in only five innings. Though Mickey pitched a few more games for Holyoke that summer, his career was virtually over at the age of 33.

The retired ballplayer operated a saloon, served as a steward of the Elks Club, and raised his family in Holyoke over the next few decades. He and his wife Mary produced nine children, seven of whom survived infancy, and in 1908 Mickey and his large brood appeared in a photograph in the sports section of the *Boston Globe*. The old ballplayer had sold his saloon and stated that he was involved in a milk-production business with his oldest son Frank. He appeared to be enjoying life as he approached his 60th birthday, spending his days hiking and talking baseball with Jack Doyle, a fellow old-time player and resident of Holyoke. Several of his children had married, and Mickey was now a grandfather.

He still loved baseball, traveling to Boston and New York several times a year to see games, and in 1912 New York Giants manager John McGraw offered Mickey a job as a night watchman at the Polo Grounds. Mickey lived in Manhattan during the summer months and worked for McGraw for more than 20 years, along with Amos Rusie, Dan Brouthers, and other old-time stars for whom McGraw had a soft spot. Mickey also served as a gate keeper and press-box attendant for the Yankees after they left the Polo Grounds and built Yankee Stadium in 1923. The old curveball pitcher maintained friendships with Tim Keefe and other teammates, but by the mid-1930s he had outlived most of them. When former second baseman Dasher Troy died in 1938, only Mickey Welch survived from the original New York Gothams of 1883.

Welch remained, in the words of *The New York Times* reporter John Kieran, "hale and hearty and lively as a cricket" into his old age. He was always well dressed in a suit and tie, and appears in photographs of the period as a distinguished-looking, gray-haired gentleman, never weighing much more than he had in his playing days. He attended a game at either the Polo Grounds or Yankee Stadium almost every day during the 1930s, and enjoyed talking to reporters about the old days. In 1939 the 80-year-old Mickey selected his all-time all-star team for the *New York Sunday News*, weighting his selections toward the old-time stars of the game. Welch named a few 20th-century players such as Ty Cobb and fellow screwball pitcher Carl Hubbell, but neither Babe Ruth nor Honus Wagner made the team.

Mickey told reporter Jimmy Powers that "most experts make a mistake. They ignore brains and go for brawn ... whenever brains clashed with brawn, brains always won." He named his old friend Tim Keefe as one of his pitchers, asserted that old Chicago shortstop Ed Williamson was superior to Wagner, and bypassed Ruth and Tris Speaker to select an outfield of Cobb, Hugh Duffy, and Willie Keeler. He admitted that "my all-time team might sound kind of silly to fans of 1939," but nominated his old catcher, Buck Ewing, as the greatest baseball player of all time. "I like a team that has pep and balance," he said. "That's the kind of club I'm going to pick, a team that would just rip the heart out of any club you could put against them."[12]

Mary Welch died in 1936, but Mickey enjoyed good health for several more years. In the summer of 1941 he traveled to Nashua, New Hampshire, to visit his grandson William Welch. While there, he fell ill and was taken to a hospital in Concord, where he died of heart failure on July 30, 1941 at the age of 82. He was buried in Woodside Cemetery in Queens, in the same plot as his parents, a sister who died in childhood, and his wife Mary. The tombstone displays both his original family name and his baseball moniker. The stone shows his name as "Smiling Mickey Walsh."

Mickey Welch far outlived his baseball fame. In 1942, a year after his death, *The Sporting News* took a poll to determine which players, both moderns and old-timers, deserved induction into the Hall of Fame in Cooperstown. Pitcher Lefty Grove led the balloting with more than 2,700 votes, while 19th-century stars Ed Delahanty and Hugh Duffy gained more than 1,700 apiece. Tim Keefe, Mickey's old pitching partner, was named on 1,040 ballots, but Mickey trailed far behind. Only 136 fans remembered "Smiling Mickey" well enough to vote for him.

His name was often mentioned during Veterans Committee meetings, but not until 1963 did the electors conclude that the pitchers who won 300 games during the 19th century deserved membership in the Hall. Charley Radbourn, elected in 1939, was the only such inductee until John Clarkson, Tim Keefe, and Pud Galvin joined him during the mid-1960s. Mickey Welch, the only 300-game winner not yet inducted, was left outside the Hall and forgotten until the early 1970s, when Early Wynn and Warren Spahn gained election. Wynn and Spahn were also members of the 300-win club, and their selections focused renewed attention on Welch and, most likely, led to his belated enshrinement.

The Sporting News has frequently criticized the Hall of Fame electoral process, especially the selections of the Veterans Committee, and has expressed dissatisfaction with the results of the election of 1973. However, the paper stated, "certainly there could be no quarrel with the selection of pitcher Mickey Welch." Though he is almost forgotten today, Welch played on two pennant-winning teams, compiled one of the best pitching records in his era, and made his mark on the sport as it was played more than 100 years ago. His election to the Hall was a well-deserved, if long overdue, honor.

11

Sam Thompson

> "This magnificent specimen of manhood serves numerous noble purposes. Indiana is proud of him because he is her honored son; Michigan is proud of him because he is fighting under her banner; Illinois is proud of him because he is maintaining the glory of the league to which she belongs; men everywhere are proud of him because he so splendidly illustrates well-applied virility, and women all adore him because there is combined with his superb athletic qualities a modesty that is inexpressibly charming."
> —*from an 1887 newspaper clipping*[1]

Baseball statistics are nearly as old as the game itself. When amateur teams played during the 1850s and early 1860s, scorekeepers usually kept track of outs made and runs scored by each player. Record-keeping grew along with the game, and before long hits, times at bat, and bases on balls became part of the statistical record. By the mid-1870s batting average, the ratio of hits to times at bat, became the sport's standard measure of ability and performance. Newspapers printed lists of player statistics in descending order of batting average, a custom that continues to this day, and the man with the highest average at season's end was considered the "champion batsman" of his league.

In 1880 the *Chicago Tribune* introduced a new measure of offensive production, dubbed "runs batted in." This effort was short-lived, but in 1920 the major leagues decided to record runs batted in, or RBI, in their official statistics. Since then, researchers have studied box scores and game accounts to determine RBI totals for pre–1920 players. Though many experts consider RBI an overrated measure of performance (since it depends on a team's ability to put men on base, which the batter cannot control), most people agree that a hitter who drives in lots of runs is a valuable man to have on a ballclub. Many players have won Most Valuable Player awards mainly by leading their league in RBI.

No player in history has ever managed to drive in a run per game over a significantly long career, but the greatest run producers come close. In fifth place on the all-time list of RBI per game is Babe Ruth, with a figure of .884. Joe DiMaggio (.885) is fourth, Hank Greenberg (.915) is third, and Lou Gehrig (.922) holds second place. All these great players are well-known to

Sam Thompson with the Detroit Wolverines, 1887. (National Baseball Hall of Fame Library, Cooperstown, N.Y.)

fans of the present day, and all easily earned election to the Baseball Hall of Fame.

On the other hand, the name of the top man on the list of RBI per game is virtually unknown to the present generation of fans. Sam Thompson performed for the Detroit Wolverines and the Philadelphia Phillies in the National League from 1885 to 1898, coming out of retirement to play eight games for the American League's Detroit Tigers in 1906. A slugger in an era of bunts, hit-and-run plays, and stolen bases, Thompson hit for both power and average, with a .331 career batting mark and 127 home runs, the pre–1900 National League record.[2] His average of .923 RBI per game is the highest figure ever recorded, and he was the first man to stroke 200 hits in a season. Despite his batting excellence, Thompson fell quickly into obscurity after his career ended, and his death in 1922 drew little notice in the sporting press. Not until 1974, when he was elected to the Hall of Fame by the Veterans Committee, did Sam Thompson emerge from anonymity to take his place with the game's greatest players.

The future ballplayer was born Samuel Luther Thompson on March 5, 1860 in Danville, Indiana, a town of fewer than 1,000 people just west of Indianapolis. Sam was the fifth child and fifth son of Jesse Thompson, a Quaker from North Carolina who found work as a carpenter in Danville, the seat of Hendricks County. He and a Danville girl named Rebecca McPheeters, a granddaughter of one of the county's earliest settlers, married in 1849 and began producing a family that eventually boasted 11 children.

Though Jesse was born a Southerner, during the Civil War he joined a unit of the Indiana Volunteers, serving on the Union side while Sam was a toddler. He guarded Southern prisoners at a camp in Indianapolis, but contracted an eye infection and was unable to go into battle with his unit. Blind when he was mustered out on a medical discharge in 1865, his eyesight gradually returned. At war's end, Jesse's fellow Union veterans returned to Danville, bringing baseball with them. The new sport swept the nation in the years following the war, spread by the enthusiasm of returning soldiers who played the game in military camps.

The six Thompson boys, all of whom were tall and strapping young ballplayers, pursued a variety of occupations. One became a druggist and one opened a bakery, another went into farming, and two others learned the carpentry trade from their father. Sam also trained as a carpenter, but his interest lay in Danville's town baseball team, the Browns, of which he became the star in his late teenage years. Sam, a left-handed batter and thrower,[3] stood six feet and two inches in height. His powerful build, at 207 pounds, made him the hardest hitter in Danville. People in neighboring towns chattered about the young man from Danville who "did nothing but hit home runs."

Sam's older brother Cyrus was also a fine ballplayer, and fans of the Danville Browns claimed that Cy was actually a better hitter than Sam. Cy hit for a higher average, they said, but Sam could hit the ball farther than Cy or anyone else in town. This was not always looked upon as an advantage, because Sam's wallop sent the ball so far over the fence that it might not easily be found. Games at this time were usually played with only one ball, and if Sam lost it with a long home run, the game was over.

Cy Thompson's prowess drew notice from professional teams, and in 1884 a scout came to Danville to watch him play. However, Cy, at age 26, was not interested in abandoning his career as a druggist. He recommended that the scout look up his brother Sam in Stinesville, 12 miles away, where Sam and his father were doing carpentry work. The scout found Sam working on a roof and offered him $2.50 per game to play for a new Northwest League team in Evansville, more than 150 miles from Danville. Sam readily accepted, over his father's objections, and thus began his professional baseball career in July of 1884.

The Northwest League, a loose confederation of Midwestern teams located in the Great Lakes states, was struggling to stay afloat. The club from Bay City, Michigan, had disbanded on July 22, and backers from Evansville scrambled to assemble a team to take Bay City's place on the schedule. They succeeded, and the Evansville nine played its first game on July 30. Unfortunately, many of the Northwest League clubs were also experiencing severe cash flow problems, and Evansville played only five games before it, and the rest of the league, collapsed during the first week of August. Four of the twelve teams, not including Evansville, continued to play through August, but ceased operations in early September, when the Northwest League went officially out of business.

Sam played in each of Evansville's five games and hit well, batting .391 and making only one error in the outfield. Despite his abbreviated introduction to professional ball, Sam attracted the attention of a nearby team, the Indianapolis Hoosiers of the Western League, which offered him a position for the following season. This development made news in Danville, where the paper reprinted an *Indianapolis Times* report on the local hero. "Sam Thompson, left fielder for the Evansvilles," stated the paper, "has promised to sign with the Indianapolis club when the Evansville club disbands—an event that is believed to be near at hand. Thompson is wanted to strengthen the battery of the Indianapolis club."[4] Sam was an outfielder, not a pitcher or catcher, but his hometown was excited about his rapid ascent up the baseball ladder.

Sam Thompson was not a young man, having turned 25 before the 1885 season began, but he quickly established himself as the best prospect on the ballclub. He batted .316 for Indianapolis and scored more than a run per game, and while his fielding average was a dismal .765, he displayed a powerful throwing arm in right field. Sam's hitting powered the Hoosiers to 27 wins in their first 31 games, but he and the other players soon discovered that the six-team Western League was financially unstable. The money-losing Cleveland and Toledo clubs folded in early June, while the failing Omaha nine moved to Keokuk, Iowa in a desperate attempt to stay in business. These moves merely delayed the inevitable. On June 15 the Indianapolis board of directors disbanded the first-place team, releasing the Hoosier players from their contracts. For the second year in a row, Sam's season had ended prematurely due to the fiscal woes of his team.

Luckily, Sam did not stay idle for long, as he and several other Indianapolis players had impressed Frederick Stearns, a pharmaceutical magnate and baseball enthusiast who served as president of the Detroit Wolverines of the National League. Stearns hired Bill Watkins as manager of the Wolverines, then decided to sign nine Indianapolis players, including Sam, to strengthen his Detroit club. Under the rules of organized ball at the time, the nine men were not allowed to sign contracts for ten days after their release, during which time they would be permitted to entertain offers from other ballclubs. Stearns did not want any competitors scooping up his best prospects, so he hit upon a novel way to keep the former Indianapolis players away from other teams. He chartered a fishing boat for a trip on the Great Lakes and invited the players along, with all expenses paid. Once the boat left the dock, it did not return for ten days.

"We didn't touch land during the time," remembered Thompson years later, "and no boat was allowed to come near us. We were prisoners, but well cared-for prisoners. Anything in the line of creature comforts you could find packed away on ice. We lived on the best in the market, and spent the rest of the time in fishing and playing poker, chips having very thoughtfully been provided. On the night of the tenth day, at midnight, we were all taken ashore, where Watkins met us and signed us to our contracts."[5] Only afterward did some of the players learn that other teams had made offers during their enforced absence.

Sam sat on the bench for a few days while his former Hoosier teammate Gene Moriarty played right field for the Wolverines. Moriarty was completely overmatched by National League pitching, batting .026 in 11 games, so Watkins finally decided to give Thompson a trial. Wearing a uniform that was noticeably too small for him, Sam made his major league debut with the Wolverines on July 2, 1885. He ignored the inevitable ribbing from fans and opponents, and belted a single in his first plate appearance against star pitcher Tim Keefe in a 4–0 win over the New York Giants. An oft-repeated story states that Sam's pants split open as he rounded first, and his good-natured reaction to the resulting laughter started Sam on the road to popularity with the Detroit fans.

Sam had joined one of the most woeful clubs in the National League. The Wolverines had won only eight of their first 42 games and were mired deeply in last place, 27 games behind the league-leading Chicago White Stockings. The Wolverines had struggled since joining the league in 1881, finishing in last place in 1884 with a 28–84 record. Attendance was poor, and not solely due to the bad showing of the ballclub. Detroit was, at the time, the least populous city in the circuit, and most observers considered it too small to host a profitable team. Nonetheless, Frederick Stearns was an optimist. He figured that if he built a championship ballclub, fans in other cities would flock to the opponents' ballparks to see his Wolverines. He would make most of his profit not from home attendance, but from the Detroit team's cut of the gate receipts on the road.

Thompson, unlike Gene Moriarty, found National League pitching to his liking. He pounded out 11 hits in his first 23 times at bat for a .423 average, and stayed above the .300 mark all season long. The right field job was his, and in mid-July Watkins moved his new slugger to the third spot in the Detroit lineup. Sam's hitting lit a fire under the formerly wretched Wolverines, who subsequently won 12 of their first 13 games with Sam in the outfield. One of his best performances came on July 28, when he scored five runs and belted three hits, including a homer, off Tim Keefe in a 12–6 win over the second-place Giants.

None of the other former Indianapolis players made an impression in the National League, but Sam Thompson quickly became a star. Only two National Leaguers hit more home runs than Sam in 1885, despite the fact that he played only half the season, and his .500 slugging average was the second-best mark in the league. His .303 batting average led the Wolverines, who improved markedly with the addition of Thompson and a left-handed pitcher, Charles (Lady) Baldwin, also a refugee from the Western League. Baldwin, who stabilized the pitching staff, and "Big Sam" Thompson, baseball's newest slugging star, gave reason for optimism to the long-suffering Detroit fans.

The Wolverines, buried in last place on July 1, crept up to sixth position by season's end, and Frederick Stearns was convinced that his instincts were sound. He resolved to spend top dollar to make his Wolverines a champion, and the collapse of the Buffalo Bisons after the 1885 season provided that opportunity. Buffalo's lineup contained some of the league's most powerful hitters, and on September 16, 1885, Stearns bought the Buffalo club outright for $7,000 and payment of all the team's debts. This made Buffalo's "Big Four"—first baseman Dan Brouthers, left fielder Hardy Richardson, shortstop Jack Rowe, and third baseman Jim (Deacon) White—the property of the Detroit Wolverines. The addition of these outstanding batters, combined with the presence of emerging star Sam Thompson, turned the Wolverines into instant contenders.

In retrospect, it appears that Stearns and Watkins valued players for their character as well as their talent. Charles Baldwin earned the nickname "Lady" because he did not drink, smoke, or curse, while Deacon White's moniker was the result of his habit of going to church every Sunday. Sam Thompson, a handsome man who sported one of the most impressive handlebar mustaches in the game, was also a sober, well-balanced individual whose only vice was a lifelong fondness for chewing tobacco. He could have intimidated others with his size, but rarely argued with anyone, and when his career was over the papers reported that Sam had never been suspended, fined, or ejected from a game by an umpire. He was a quiet, almost taciturn Midwesterner, and sportswriters called him the "silent outfielder" of the Wolverines. Sam was content to concentrate on his hitting and let the "Big Four" garner most of the headlines.

Sam worked diligently to make himself into a passable outfielder, but was already a powerful hitter when he arrived in the major leagues. Few, if any, batters swung as hard as Sam, but his bat control was so keen that only once did he strike out as many as 31 times in a season. His power was enhanced by his unusual batting stance. He crouched at the plate, giving the pitcher a small strike zone at which to aim, but rose quickly to an upright position as he lashed at the ball. This upward motion increased the power behind his swing and accounted for the incredible speed of his line drives and the length of his home runs. He "violated every rule when it came to taking his stance at the plate,"[6] said the *Indianapolis Times*, but his liners often found the gaps in the outfield. Despite his size, Sam ran well enough to hit lots of triples, leading the National League twice in that category.

The 1886 Wolverines were a good team, and boasted more talent in addition to the "Big Four" and "Big Sam" Thompson. Left-hander Lady Baldwin and right-hander Charlie Getzien comprised one of the best pitching duos in the league, while Charlie Bennett, a fixture in Detroit since the franchise began play in 1881, was perhaps the outstanding defensive catcher in the game. Center fielder Ned Hanlon was a mediocre hitter, but a fine defender and one of the league's smartest players. Hanlon was the captain of the Detroit team, directing the club on the field, and managed the pennant-winning Baltimore Orioles of the 1890s. The Detroit lineup, with Thompson and the Big Four supplying the offense, was now formidable enough to challenge for the pennant.

An old baseball adage states that a team cannot buy a pennant, but the Wolverines nearly did so in 1886. All the Big Four performed well for Detroit, with Richardson (.351) and Brouthers (.370) leading the way. These two men tied for the league lead in homers with 11, while Richardson also went 3–0 as a substitute pitcher. Sam Thompson, in his first full major league season, led the team in runs batted in with 89 and hit a credible .310. The rejuvenated Wolverines used a fearsome attack to forge a 15-game winning streak and vault to the top of the league in May. The more experienced White Stockings kept pace, and manager Cap Anson's decision to divide the pitching load among three men instead of the customary two proved the difference. Chicago's trio of John Clarkson, Jim McCormick, and Jocko Flynn combined for 90 wins, while Detroit's Lady Baldwin and Charlie Getzien posted 72 victories. Chicago, with its superior pitching, won the flag by two and a half games.

The 1887 campaign was an altogether different story. The owners of the White Stockings traded or sold several of their stars, leaving a void at the top of the National League and clearing the way for the Wolverines to mount a challenge for the pennant. The league rule-makers had decreed that four strikes, not three, would constitute a strikeout, thereby ensuring that 1887 would be a hitter's year. The hard-hitting Wolverines took advantage, leading the league in nearly every offensive category and holding off the Philadelphia Quakers for the pennant. It was Detroit's first, and only, championship in the National League. They capped the season with a victory in the 15-game World's Series against the American Association champion St. Louis Browns in October. Sam led the Wolverines with a .362 average and whacked two homers as the Wolverines won ten of the 15 contests.

Though the Big Four grabbed the headlines, Sam Thompson was the team's most dangerous hitter, and his 1887 season ranks as one of the greatest offensive explosions of all time. Sam set a new record for hits in a season with 203, leading the league in triples (23) and slugging percentage (.571). Runs batted in was not yet an official statistic, but later researchers determined that Sam was the most prodigious run-producer in the game. He drove in 166 runs in 1887, setting a record that lasted until 1921, when Babe Ruth of the Yankees drove in 171 men. On May 7 Sam set a new standard when he smacked two bases-loaded triples in an 18–2 win over Indianapolis. Other major league players have matched Sam's feat, but no one has since surpassed it.

Sam in a studio picture during his Detroit days. (Library of Congress)

Sam's batting average was officially listed as .407, third best in the league behind Cap Anson (.421) and Dan Brouthers (.419), during a year in which walks were counted as hits. Though Anson was awarded the batting title for

1887, most modern statisticians prefer to subtract the walks from the hit totals and revise the list of averages accordingly. When compiled in this manner, Thompson's average is recorded as .372, with Anson at .347 and Brouthers at .338. Most modern reference works list Sam Thompson, not Cap Anson, as the 1887 batting champion.

Though the Wolverines enjoyed their most successful season that year, tensions between the players and manager Bill Watkins began to surface. Watkins, a hot-tempered autocrat, was quick to criticize, and his mercurial manner made him unpopular with the Detroit players. Sam Thompson, who was usually an easygoing sort, soon grew tired of Watkins' negativity, criticizing him during a conversation with team president Frederick Stearns late in the season. Among other complaints, Sam grumbled that his average would be high enough to pass Cap Anson for the batting title had not Watkins recorded some of his hits as errors. The surprised Stearns assured his slugger that the manager was not, in fact, the official scorer, a revelation that caught Sam unawares. Still, the acrimony between the team and its manager was palpable, affecting morale during the championship season.

The 1888 campaign proved as disastrous for the Wolverines as the prior one was successful. Sam Thompson left the lineup with a sore arm, playing only 56 of the 134 games and leaving Detroit without its leading run producer for most of the season. Manager Watkins then tried to cut Sam's salary, a move that angered the other Wolverines and contributed to the field leader's unpopularity. Amid all the turmoil, only Dan Brouthers managed to hit .300 in 1888 after six Detroit players had done so the year before, and injuries to Thompson, Lady Baldwin, Hardy Richardson, and others decimated the ranks. Despite all the problems, Detroit led the league by one game on July 27, but then embarked on a 16-game losing streak and dropped out of the race. Stearns fired the reviled Watkins in late August, and the Wolverines finished in fifth place, 16 games behind the pennant-winning New York Giants.

The best thing that happened to Sam Thompson in 1888 was his marriage to a Detroit girl named Ida Morasha, seven years his junior. Sam and Ida set up housekeeping in Detroit, and remained there even after Sam's tenure with the Wolverines was finished. Though Sam often returned to Danville, Indiana to visit friends and relatives, the Thompsons resided in Detroit for the rest of their lives.

The Wolverines' failure to defend their championship put the team in a financial bind, but a league policy regarding the distribution of gate receipts actually hastened the end of National League baseball in Detroit. Visiting teams had always received a percentage of the gate, but in 1887 the league mandated that each visiting team would receive a fee of $125 per game regardless of attendance. The financial success of the Wolverines was based on drawing large crowds on the road, since home attendance was not significant enough for the team's survival, and this new policy negated any hope for the Wolverines to turn a profit. The team struggled to make ends meet during the 1887 championship season, but 1888 was a monetary disaster. In October of that year, the team board of directors dissolved the club, selling its stars around the league. Sam Thompson, perhaps the most coveted Wolverine despite his injury-marred 1888 season, went to the Philadelphia Phillies for $5,000.

The Phillies, who were also called the Quakers during the 1880s, played in a ballpark well suited for Sam's talents. The Huntingdon Street Grounds (which was later known as the Baker Bowl) was one of the newest parks in the National League, having been constructed two years earlier. Shoehorned into a single Philadelphia street grid, it had a huge left field area, but the right field fence stood only 300 feet from home plate.[7] The field configuration was made to order for a left-handed belter like Sam Thompson. On defense, Sam's powerful throwing arm came in handy. With much less ground to cover, he played closer to the infield and saw his assist totals rise dramatically. He perfected the art of throwing the ball to the plate on one bounce, which catchers found easier to handle than the usual throw on the fly. Some baseball historians credit Sam Thompson with introducing this type of throw to the major leagues.

Sam soon realized that the Phillies were not the easiest team to play for. Owned by Colonel John I. Rogers, a local banker, and former player and sporting goods magnate Al Reach, the Philadelphia club was noted for its penny-pinching management. Rogers and Reach strove to spend as little money as possible on hotels, meals, and transportation, and many Philadelphia players grew to dread road trips. The manager was Harry Wright, perhaps the most respected figure in the game, having managed the first professional team, the fabled 1869 Cincinnati Red Stockings. The aging Wright was a strict authoritarian who insisted on grueling practices at home and on the road, though his disciplinary measures were sometimes overruled by Rogers and Reach. The Phillies had finished in the first division for several years, but many believed that money disputes and inconsistent team discipline kept the team from making a sustained challenge for the pennant.

Healthy again in 1889, Sam Thompson took advantage of the short right field fence to belt 20 homers, leading the league for the first time in that category. He was the first left-handed batter in the National League to hit 20 four-baggers in a season, and his total stood as a team record until Gavvy Cravath hit 24 in 1916. The Phillies finished in fourth place as Sam led his new team in nearly every batting category. However, along with every other National League team, the Philadelphia ballclub faced a challenge to its survival after the close of the 1889 season. The National League players, after numerous disputes with management, had organized a trade union called the Brotherhood of Professional Base Ball Players several years before. The Brotherhood now created a new circuit, called the Players League, and invited all disgruntled National Leaguers to join.

Sam, who had become a member of the Brotherhood (along with several of his Detroit teammates) in May of 1886, expressed support for the new league. He was one of the game's underpaid stars, having earned a salary of $1,850 for leading the league in homers in 1889. Soon after the season ended, Thompson was one of the first players to quit the Phillies and sign with the Players League. However, Phillies team owner Colonel Rogers made Sam an proposal that nearly doubled his 1889 salary. Rogers offered his star slugger a salary of $3,000 per year on a three-year contract, with a $1,000 bonus added. Sam, whose confidence in the success of the Players League was shaky, hired a lawyer to scour his Players League contract for loopholes. He apparently found one, for in late December 1889 Sam quit the Brotherhood and rejoined the Phillies.

The Players League, recoiling at Thompson's defection, sued the Phillies, but failed in its attempt to make Sam honor his previous contract. Sam endured a great deal of criticism for his turnabout (as did New York pitcher Mickey Welch and Indianapolis shortstop Jack Glasscock, both of whom had also reneged on Players League agreements), but Phillies fans were happy to retain their cleanup hitter. In all, three teams, one in each league, vied for supremacy in the Philadelphia baseball market, but Sam's presence helped the National League Phillies draw the biggest crowds and win the most games. He hit only four homers in 1890, but led the league in hits and doubles and batted .313 as the Phillies finished third.

The new league collapsed after the 1890 campaign, leaving the Phillies and the Athletics of the American Association to vie for the loyalties of the fans. The 1891 Phillies finished in third place once again while the Athletics struggled at the gate, and by the beginning of the 1892 season the American Association was gone, leaving the Philadelphia baseball market solely in the possession of the Phillies.

The National League now owned a monopoly on major league baseball, and salaries fell across the board. Sam Thompson, whose contract calling for a salary of $3,000 per year expired after the 1892 season, soon learned the harsh realities of the baseball business. "They used an ax on my contract, cutting it to $1,800," lamented Sam years later. "It was an awful blow, but there was nothing to do but take it.... They cut us deep in those days, and they didn't bother about hurting our feelings a little bit."[8] Sam gained a bit more money over the next several years, but his yearly pay never exceeded $2,400, the league-mandated maximum salary during the 1890s.

By 1892, the Phillies possessed the best hitting outfield in baseball, and perhaps the hardest-hitting outfield of all time. Billy Hamilton, a speedy base-stealing specialist, patrolled center, while left field belonged to Ed Delahanty, a fast-rising star who led the league in triples with 23. The outfield of Thompson, Delahanty, and Hamilton took another step forward in 1893, as all three men batted .368 or better, finishing in the top three spots in the batting race.

Hamilton won the batting crown at .380, while Thompson led the league in hits and doubles and Delahanty topped the lists of homers, runs batted in, and total bases. Despite their offensive firepower, Philadelphia pitching was never more than mediocre, and the team finished in fourth place once again in Harry Wright's final season as manager.

Sam was frustrated by this failure to challenge for a pennant, and also by the excessive frugality of management. He wearied of the bad food, poor hotels, and rough transportation on road trips, and at the age of 34 Sam considered either retiring from the game or forcing the Phillies to trade him. "I shall not play again in Philadelphia," declared Thompson in October 1893, "and I told Harry Wright it would be a waste of time for him to write me about signing. The cheese-paring methods of the management, together with the fact that for five years I have had to face the sun in right field, have been the causes leading to my resolution.... The management [has] made a barrel of money, but they grind the players into the dirt."[9] Sam did not sign his 1894 contract until March of that year, after Rogers promised to improve the team's travel accommodations.

No season in the history of baseball saw more offense than the 1894 campaign, and the hard-hitting Phillies provided the greatest offensive fireworks ever seen in the game. The team as a whole, pitchers included, batted a record .349, and all four Philadelphia outfielders (Thompson, Delahanty, Hamilton, and substitute Tuck Turner) batted .400 or better. Sam hit .407, his highest average ever, while Delahanty hit .400, Hamilton .404, and Turner .416. The Phillies regularly scored in double figures during their games, and on August 17 the team belted a league record 36 hits in a 29–4 walloping of Louisville. Sam had six hits in seven trips to the plate that day, hitting for the cycle for the only time in his career, while three other Phillies stroked five hits apiece. A finger injury limited Thompson to 99 games, but he still drove in an incredible 141 runs and whacked a career-best 27 triples.

This injury proved the most serious of Sam's career. He played with pain in the little finger of his left hand for the first month of the season, and doctors determined that a few of the digit's smaller bones were dead. They recommended amputation, but Sam refused to consider such a drastic measure. Instead, the doctors operated on Thompson on May 17, removed the dead matter and sewed the finger back up. The operation alleviated the pain, and Sam was back in the lineup, hitting better than ever, by late June.

As usual, the Philadelphia offensive juggernaut could not make up for poor pitching, and the Phillies finished fourth for the third season in a row. The 1895 season brought more of the same, as Sam compiled perhaps his finest hitting performance with a .392 average and led the league in homers for the second time with 18. The 35-year-old drove in 165 runs, falling one short of his record total of eight years earlier with Detroit, and late that season Thompson won a newspaper poll as the most popular ballplayer in Philadelphia. Sam was so proud of the honor, and the silver cup that accompanied it, that he brought the trophy home to Danville to show the citizens of his hometown. "This beautiful present could not have been voted to a more worthy gentleman that Sam," said the local paper, the *Hendricks County Republican*, "and to say he is proud of it is putting it rather light."[10] Sam put the trophy on display at the drug store owned by his older brother Cyrus.

Despite Sam's stellar hitting, the Phillies finished fourth again and never challenged for the pennant. Colonel Rogers, growing increasingly frustrated with his team's performance, fired manager Arthur Irwin at season's end and traded center fielder Billy Hamilton to Boston for third baseman Billy Nash, who became the new field leader of the Phillies. Nash's tenure, which lasted only one year, proved a disaster for Philadelphia baseball. The Phillies missed Hamilton, the offensive sparkplug of the ballclub, and dropped all the way to eighth place in the 12-team National League. Sam Thompson also began to slow down. He endured pain in his back and abdomen that became so severe that he feared a serious kidney disease. Sam's average fell to .298, with 12 homers and 100 RBI, and his baseball future was in jeopardy.

Colonel Rogers decided that the team needed stricter discipline, so he hired George Stallings, a successful minor league manager, as his field leader for 1897. Stallings was a Southern gentleman off the field, but a biting, sarcastic man on it; as future Hall of Fame inductee Johnny Evers later wrote, Stallings "will crab and rave on the bench with any of them." Thompson harbored a distinct aversion to managers like Stallings (and Bill Watkins, his leader at Detroit many years earlier), and the two men did not get along. Sam, still struggling with acute pain, was clearly not interested in dealing with Stallings. He played only three games in 1897, then remained on the sidelines for the remainder of the season as the Phillies dropped to 10th place without him.

In late 1897, Sam asked the Phillies for his release so he could manage the Detroit Tigers of the Western League, but Colonel Rogers refused. Sam then reluctantly tried once more to continue his playing career. He reported to spring training camp at Cape May, New Jersey, in March of 1898, intent on putting his physical problems and differences with management behind him. The Phillies, not wanting to be caught short if Sam could not perform, signed a new outfielder named Elmer Flick, a speedy left-handed batter who hit .386 at Dayton the year before. Though Flick was poised to take Thompson's job, the veteran tutored the younger man in the art of playing right field at the Huntingdon Street Grounds. However, the tension between Sam and manager Stallings continued unabated, and many observers wondered how long Sam's 1898 season would last.

The 38-year-old slugger hit well at the start, driving in more than a run per game with an average well over .300, but his back pain grew worse, and Flick caddied for Sam in right field through April and early May. Flick hit well, showing promise of future stardom, but the Phillies fell to the bottom half of the league amid general dissatisfaction with Stallings' management. The situation annoyed the proud Thompson, and on May 18 the veteran ballplayer decided that he had had enough. He abruptly announced his retirement from the game, taking the next train home to Detroit.

Perhaps Sam should have waited a few weeks, as Stallings drew his walking papers in early June. At any rate, Sam put baseball behind him and began selling real estate in his adopted hometown of Detroit. He had always been a frugal ballplayer; as umpire Tim Hurst once stated, "[Sam has] got the first dollar he ever earned nailed up to his wall alongside the 'God Bless Our Home.'"[11] He had managed his money well, and, unlike too many ballplayers, was able to live in comfortable circumstances after his exit from the game. Best of all, the pain in Sam's back and abdomen gradually abated. He did not have a serious kidney ailment after all, and within a year his pain was gone.

With his health apparently restored, the 40-year-old Thompson was ready to play once more. He listed his occupation on the 1900 United States census as "base ball player," and made it known that he wished to continue his playing career. When the Western League changed its name to the American League in early 1900, Sam once again offered his services to the Detroit Tigers. The Tigers would have loved to sign him, but the Phillies still owned Thompson's playing rights and were unwilling to let go. Since the rules of organized ball dictated that Sam could only play for Philadelphia, he reluctantly dropped his plan to return to the professional game. Instead, he signed with a leading local semipro nine, the Detroit Athletic Club, where he starred for the next eight seasons. He could still belt the long ball, even past 40 years of age, and Sam's presence made the team so popular that the Detroit AC often attracted more fans than the Tigers.

Though the Phillies finally dropped Sam from their reserve list in 1901, he was not yet finished with the major leagues. In 1906 the Detroit Tigers suffered a crippling rash of injuries to their outfielders. Ty Cobb, the 19-year-old future superstar playing in his first full season, was felled by stomach problems in July and underwent abdominal surgery later that month. Regular left fielder Matty McIntyre and key substitute Davy Jones battled a series of ailments, and by late August the Tigers were reduced to using pitchers in right field. Sam Thompson, still in fine playing condition at age 46, offered to play for the club during a homestand in late August, and manager Bill Armour quickly accepted. After an absence of more than eight years, Sam was back in the major leagues.

Thompson's return, though only temporary, prompted excitement in Detroit. When he played his first game on August 31 against the St. Louis Browns, a group of fans stopped the contest by presenting Sam with an enormous floral horseshoe ("as big as a washtub," claimed *The Sporting News*) before he took his first turn at bat. Unfortunately for Thompson, Browns pitcher

Harry Howell threw a spitball, a pitch that Sam had never seen before, and struck him out. "That spitball that [Howell] was using was all Greek to me," remarked Sam afterward. "In my day there was no such ball, and though I had heard considerable discussion of it, I was completely fooled when I first attempted to connect with it."[12]

Sam lifted a fly ball for an out in the third inning, and came up in the fifth with the bases loaded and the Tigers down by a run. He belted one of Howell's spitballs down the right field line, and though Sam was thrown out at second trying to stretch his single into a double, he drove in two runs, putting the Tigers ahead for good. Detroit won the game by a 5–4 count, and Sam Thompson was the batting hero of the day. Though New York Highlanders manager Clark Griffith, whose team was involved in a pennant race against Chicago, criticized the Tigers a week later for putting Thompson in the lineup against the White Sox, Sam acquitted himself well. He participated in eight games for the Tigers, playing errorless ball in the outfield and managing seven hits in 31 times at bat for a .226 average.

Ty Cobb returned to the lineup in early September, and when Matty McIntyre rejoined the team, Sam Thompson retired from the major leagues for the second time and returned to the Detroit AC. Sam continued to dominate the semipro competition, and did not hang up his spikes for good until he was nearly 50 years old.

A popular figure around Detroit in his later years, Sam and wife Ida lived on Trumbull Avenue near the Tigers' ballpark, Bennett Field, which was named after Sam's old Wolverines teammate Charlie Bennett. Sam always appeared at the park for opening-day ceremonies and special occasions such as the flag-raising celebrations for the Tigers' pennant-winning teams of 1907, 1908, and 1909. In 1912, the Tigers razed Bennett Field and built a new park, then called Navin Field and later known as Tiger Stadium, at the corner of Michigan and Trumbull Avenues. Sam was a frequent guest at the new ballpark, and served as an unofficial advisor to Tigers owner Frank Navin. He also retained local celebrity status in his hometown of Danville, Indiana, returning often to visit friends and hunt and fish with relatives. The local paper, the *Hendricks County Republican*, ran a news item announcing Sam's presence whenever he came to town.

The old ballplayer, who counted many Detroit politicians and businessmen as friends, worked as a United States marshal and, later, as a bailiff and court crier in the Federal Court building downtown. He and Ida, who had no children, lived well while Sam dabbled in local Republican politics and kept a close eye on the baseball scene. Though many retired players believed that the athletes of their youth were greater than those of later generations, Sam did not agree. He modestly joked that his homers "looked like bunts" compared to those hit by Babe Ruth, and stated, "I am inclined to believe that the players of today are the better taken as a whole. We had some great stars in the old days, and we also have some now."[13]

Thompson kept in touch with many of his former teammates and opponents, who unanimously held "Big Sam" in high regard. In the fall of 1921 he traveled to New York for the World Series between the Yankees and the Giants. Sam looked up his friend Hugh Jennings, the Baltimore shortstop of the 1890s and later manager of the Tigers, who by 1921 was coaching for the Giants. Sam asked for a ticket, and expressed surprise when Jennings pressed six free passes into his hand. "Go on," said Jennings. "You're entitled to them. Baseball wouldn't be much of a game today, Sam, if it had not been for such fellows as you."[14]

Though Sam appeared to be in fine physical condition long after his retirement from baseball, his heart began to falter as he passed his 60th birthday. November 7, 1922 was an election day in Detroit, and the old ballplayer was assigned to serve as an election official and poll monitor. While performing his duties at a polling place early that morning, he suffered a heart attack and collapsed. Emergency workers treated him at the scene and transported him to his home on Trumbull Avenue, where he was stricken with a second, more serious attack a short time later. Sam Thompson died later that morning at the age of 62.

Thompson's passing was mourned by his many old friends and teammates. Charlie Bennett, the Detroit catcher whose career had ended in a crippling train accident many years before, told the *Detroit News*, "He was a wonderful friend. No one ever quarreled with Sam. No one ever knew him, with all his strength, to be rough of brutal. He was always even tempered, and simple, and plain."[15] Even Bill Watkins, the former Wolverines manager with whom Sam had quarreled so many years before, called Thompson "one of the finest gentlemen I ever knew" and "the greatest natural hitter of all time."[16] He was buried at Elmwood Cemetery in Detroit under a small marker that said only, "Sam Thompson 1860–1922." Ida Thompson, who lived for another three decades, was nearly 90 years old when she died in the mid-1950s.

Elmwood Cemetery contains the graves of senators, congressmen, mayors of Detroit, and Civil War generals, but Sam Thompson's final resting place became the cemetery's most popular attraction after his election to the Hall of Fame in 1974. Baseball fans and family members alike expressed their disappointment in the humble stone that marked the grave of the baseball legend, so the Thompson family decided to install a more appropriate gravestone. In 2000, the large marker, which displays Sam's baseball statistics and details his accomplishments, was unveiled. A ferocious-looking wolverine, copied from an 1887 World Series program, dominates the center of the stone. Another honor came Sam's way in June of 2006, when the Indiana Historical Bureau dedicated a marker in a park on East Main Street in Danville to commemorate his accomplishments. This tribute stands near a baseball diamond that also bears his name.

Though Sam Thompson was born in Indiana and played most of his career in Philadelphia, he will always be remembered as Detroit's first great baseball hero. It seems odd that a man who compiled a .331 lifetime batting average, led the National League in home runs and runs batted in twice apiece, and was the greatest slugger in the game during his era never received a single vote in the annual Hall of Fame balloting that began in 1936. Fortunately, the Veterans Committee did its homework in 1974 and selected Sam Thompson to an honored place in the Cooperstown museum, 53 years after his death. His enshrinement was a fitting testimonial to the memory of one of the greatest hitters, and finest gentlemen, of 19th-century baseball.

12

Amos Rusie

> "I'm not exaggerating when I say that [Amos Rusie] was the National League—the whole works. He was to baseball then what Babe Ruth was to baseball later. When anybody talked baseball, they just naturally talked about Rusie.... Rusie isn't in the Hall of Fame, but he belongs there."
>
> —*Clark Griffith, 1943*[1]

Nolan Ryan was 19 years old when he appeared in his first major league game with the New York Mets in 1966. A Texan with a lanky build and quiet manner, he possessed the ability to throw a fastball at a speed of 100 miles per hour and more.

Ryan was plagued by wildness and inconsistency with the Mets, and his career did not take off until they traded him to the California Angels prior to the 1972 season. Inserted into the starting rotation, Ryan learned to harness his incredible speed, winning 19 games for the Angels and striking out a league-leading 329 men. During one game, he threw a pitch in the ninth inning that was clocked at 101 miles per hour. Ryan was the fastest pitcher of his era, and finished his stellar career with 324 major league wins and more than 5,700 strikeouts.

Nolan Ryan was the latest in a line of fastball artists who struck out a multitude of batters, walked almost as many, and dazzled fans and opposing batters alike. Sandy Koufax was one such pitcher early in his career, and so was Bob Feller, who tied the major league record with 17 strikeouts in a game when he was only 17 years old. Walter Johnson, who pitched from 1907 to 1927, threw the ball so fast that opposing batters claimed that they could hear it, but not see it. All these great fastball pitchers easily gained election to the Baseball Hall of Fame.

Baseball's first fastball phenomenon could best be described as the Nolan Ryan of the 1890s. Amos Rusie of the New York Giants was a powerfully built right-hander, six feet and one inch tall and 200 pounds, who won 246 games and led the National League in strikeouts and walks five times each. He threw with such speed that baseball magnates were compelled to change the configuration of the field. In 1893, the National League moved the pitching rubber ten feet farther away from the plate to its present distance of 60 feet and six inches. Amos Rusie's nearly unhittable fastball was the main reason for the adjustment.

However, Rusie was almost completely forgotten by the time the Hall of Fame held its first elections in 1936. He never gained more than nine votes from the Baseball Writers Association of America in their annual balloting, and his name rarely came up before the Veterans Committee. Perhaps Nolan Ryan's strikeout exploits in the 1970s focused attention on his hard-throwing counterpart from eight decades before, for on January 31, 1977, the Veterans Committee elected Amos Rusie to the Hall of Fame.

Amos in a Giants uniform, wearing a tie. (National Baseball Hall of Fame Library, Cooperstown, N.Y.)

Amos Wilson Rusie was born on May 30, 1871 in Mooresville, Indiana, the second son of William Rusie, a brickmason, and the former Mary Donovan, a housewife. Mooresville was a town of about 1,000 people that lay 20 miles southwest of Indianapolis, and the Rusies lived in a large house with Mary's extended family. A few years later, William Rusie moved his family to Indianapolis, where work in his trade was available, and the 1880 United States census found the Rusies settled in the city's 8th ward.

Amos, a fair-skinned, red-haired boy, possessed talent for the game that evolved as he developed physically. He grew into a powerfully built lad, with exceptionally strong arms, shoulders, and legs. These attributes gave him the ability to throw a baseball harder and faster than anyone around, and his potential was apparent to all as early as his younger teenage years. By age 16, the stocky right-hander was six feet tall, and much more interested in baseball than in class work. He quit school, found a job at a local furniture factory, and played semipro ball in and around Indianapolis. He labored at the factory six days a week and played for a team called the Grand Avenues in the City League on Sundays. Before long, Amos Rusie was the most talked-about semipro player in town.

He began his career as an outfielder, mostly due to his hitting prowess, but his strong throwing arm soon attracted attention. One day his manager waved Amos in from the outfield and put him on the mound in the late stages of a blowout. Amos dazzled the opposition and teammates alike with a fastball that traveled faster than anyone had ever seen, and Rusie's career as an outfielder was over. He was a pitcher from that day forward, and the legend of the Rusie fastball began.

The teenaged Amos Rusie may already have been the fastest pitcher in the United States. He used his muscular legs and arms to put so much force behind the baseball that opposing players complained that they could not see it on its way to the plate. Amos caused a sensation everywhere he pitched, and although his wildness resulted in a large number of walks allowed, he compiled unbelievable strikeout totals. Some observers refused to believe the hype surrounding Rusie, and only when they saw him in action did they allow themselves to be convinced. The Grand Avenues paid him a reported $50 per month, a large amount of money at the time for a semipro ballplayer, but Amos Rusie was well worth the investment.

Indianapolis was then the home of the Hoosiers, a struggling National League team, and the Hoosier players often attended the City League semipro games because the professional leagues did not play on Sundays. Jack Glasscock, the team's veteran shortstop, saw Amos pitch and appealed to team president John T. Brush to sign the teenager before any other National League club found out about him. Brush agreed, and in late 1888 Amos Rusie, 17 years old, signed his first major league contract.

The Hoosiers were then entering their third National League season, and the future of baseball in Indiana's capital was still an open question. Brush, a Civil War veteran, was a local businessman who brought a major league team to Indianapolis as a vehicle to advertise his clothing store. The team finished last in the league in 1887 and managed to draw only about 1,000 people per game to its park on the corner of Seventh and Tennessee streets. The 1888 team moved up a notch to seventh position, mostly due to the ineptitude of the last-place Washington Senators, but attendance remained stagnant. The team was losing money, and perhaps Brush believed that the sensational local pitcher might put some more fans in the seats.

Amos Rusie, still three weeks shy of his 18th birthday, made his major league debut in relief on May 9, 1889, in the fifth inning of a 13–2 loss at Cleveland. One oft-told tale says that two of the Hoosier catchers refused to catch the young fastballer that day. Many years later, Jack Glasscock said that Dick Buckley refused to catch "that blankety-blank kid," while second stringer Con Daily also stalked off the field. A third catcher was pressed into service that day under threat of release.[2] The box score for that game shows only one catcher, Daily, but the apparently exaggerated story contained a kernel of truth. The Indianapolis backstops hated catching Rusie, because he threw so hard that his fastball made their hands red and sore.

Before long, the catchers demanded that manager Frank Bancroft assign Rusie to pitch batting practice for a half hour before each of his starting assignments, in an attempt to tire the youngster and reduce his amazing speed. This ploy didn't work, as Rusie was strong and thrived on extra labor. One of the Hoosier catchers, Dick Buckley, caught with a thick piece of lead and a sponge inside his glove to lessen the impact of Rusie's fastball. Amos had trouble finding the strike zone early in his career; as Clark Griffith said years later, "[Rusie] had awfully short arms and was wild as the devil when he was with Indianapolis."[3] The young pitcher walked more men than he struck out, but his fastball crackled, and, with the Indianapolis starters performing poorly, Bancroft gave Rusie many opportunities to pitch.

Bancroft used Rusie as the team's main reliever for several weeks while the teenager learned the ropes of the major leagues. He was a prime target for pranksters, as were all rookies at the time. One day, the Indianapolis team made an overnight trip from Boston to New York on a steamboat. Amos had never been on such a large craft, and Glasscock and the other Hoosiers convinced him that one wore a life preserver at all times on board, even in bed. Amos slept that night with the bulky round preserver strapped across his chest, much to the amusement of his teammates. The veteran Hoosiers also informed the wide-eyed Midwesterner that thieves were lurking, intent on stealing his possessions during overnight train rides. When a porter appeared in the wee hours to shine Rusie's shoes, Amos, so the story goes, went after him with a bat.

Bancroft moved Rusie into the starting rotation, and on June 22 he won his first start in a 16–11 win against Pittsburgh. Attendance picked up a bit, though the seventh-place team was still losing money, and in July Glasscock replaced Bancroft as manager. Rusie was too wild for Glasscock's taste, and though the Hoosiers considered Rusie a future star, the team figured that Amos needed some experience in a less pressured environment. Rusie's won-lost record stood at 3–5 in late July when the Hoosiers loaned him to Burlington, Iowa of the Central League. He pitched only four games there before the Hoosiers recalled him in mid-August, and the teenager responded by winning nine of his 14 starts during the last two months of the season. Amos finished 1889 with a 12–10 record.

Amos Rusie's future looked bright, but the Hoosiers were fading fast. After three money-losing seasons, the National League realized that the team could not survive the coming war with the new Players League. In late 1889, most of the established National League players quit their teams and signed on with the new league. However, John T. Brush grabbed some of the more valuable Hoosiers, including Amos Rusie and Jack Glasscock, before the Players League could get them. Brush intended to use these players, not to strengthen the Indianapolis team, but to reinforce the New York Giants, which had been decimated by Players League defections. In March of 1890, Brush turned the Indianapolis franchise back to the ownership of the National League, bought an interest in the Giants, and arranged for Rusie, Glasscock, and six other players to transfer to New York. Amos Rusie, a small-town boy from Indiana, was now a New York Giant.

Rusie blossomed in New York. Still only 18 years old at the start of the season, he quickly became the ace of the Giant pitching staff. He started nearly half the team's games in 1890, completing 56 of his 63 starts, and his 29–34 record was more a reflection of the weak Giant hitting attack than Rusie's pitching. He used his extraordinary fastball and a rapidly improving curveball to lead the National League in strikeouts with 341, while his wildness caused him to issue 289 walks, a major league record that has never been surpassed. "I was wilder'n a hawk," admitted Rusie later, "but then it took a lot of pitchin' to strike a man out in those days. The foul-strike rule hadn't come in. A guy had to miss three of 'em clean before he was out."[4] Foul balls were not considered strikes at the time, and would not be until the 20th century.

Rusie, always a good hitter, played 14 games in the outfield that season, batting .278 and contributing 13 doubles and six triples. He also took a huge step forward in his personal life. On November 7, 1890, Amos married an Indiana girl named Susie May Sloan, whom everyone called May, at the county courthouse in Muncie, his new wife's hometown.

One of Rusie's greatest performances of 1890 came on May 12 at New York's Polo Grounds against the Boston Beaneaters. In that game, Rusie and Boston rookie right-hander Kid Nichols mowed down the batters in inning after inning, and at the end of twelve frames the score stood at 0–0. The Players League team was in action at the same time in their ballpark, which stood next to the Polo Grounds, and fans in both parks cheered the duel between two of the best young pitchers in baseball. The battle raged until the thirteenth inning, when New York's Mike Tiernan walloped a homer over the center field fence, giving Rusie a 1–0 shutout win. *The New York Times* was impressed enough to state that the contest was "the finest game ever played between two professional teams and will go down on record as such."

The Giants nearly folded in August due to poor attendance and competition from the Players League, but a league bailout enabled them to survive to season's end. Fortunately for the franchise, the Players League collapsed in the fall of 1890, and former Giants stars such as Roger Connor, Tim Keefe, and Buck Ewing rejoined the team. Keefe and Mickey Welch, both 300-game winners, were on their way out, but Amos Rusie took over as the pitching idol of New York. He led the Giants to a third-place finish in 1891 with a 33–20 record, pacing the league once again in strikeouts, walks, and shutouts. He threw a no-hitter against Brooklyn on July 31, and on September 26 pitched an entire doubleheader by himself, beating Brooklyn by scores of 10–4 and 13–5. Keefe, who combined with Welch to pitch the Giants to two pennants in the late 1880s, taught Rusie how to throw a changeup, and the youngster's arsenal gained another potent weapon.

Amos was best known for his fastball, but Baltimore shortstop Hugh Jennings credited Rusie with the widest, and best, curveball in the National League. Jennings' teammate John McGraw marveled at Rusie's command of the pitch. "He had the nerve and confidence to whip his curve over the plate when in a hole. As a rule, pitchers do not dare try a curve when the count is two strikes and three balls ... [but] Rusie had no such misgivings. If in such a hole he would deliberately pitch his curve ball with every ounce of steam he could put on it."[5] Rusie had powerful fingers and hands, and his strength enabled him to grip the ball tightly and maximize the amount of spin imparted on it.

There were several other hard-throwing young pitchers reaching for stardom in the National League at the time, including Cy Young of Cleveland and Kid Nichols of Boston, but no one had ever seen a pitcher like Amos Rusie. "Words fail really to describe the speed with which Rusie sent the ball," said Chicago outfielder Jimmy Ryan. "He was a man of great height, great width, prodigious muscular strength and the ability to put every ounce of his weight and sinew on every pitch. The distance was shorter then, Rusie had the whole box to move around in, instead of being chained to a slab; and the giant simply drove the ball at you with the force of a cannon. It was like a white streak tearing past you." Fans and newspapermen attempted to find him a suitable nickname, but no ordinary moniker would do. Finally, someone came up with an appropriately grand nickname, and Amos Rusie became "The Hoosier Thunderbolt."

Thus inspired, bars in Manhattan named drinks after New York's brightest new star, while famous actress Lillian Russell demanded an introduction, and vaudeville comedians included Rusie's name in their routines. Amos enjoyed the attention, though he distrusted sportswriters, who portrayed him as a late-night carouser in their columns. Amos almost always refused to speak to the writers, but he quickly developed a taste for New York's night life. Everyone in the city, it seemed, wanted to buy a drink for the "Hoosier Thunderbolt," and Amos was not inclined to reject the generosity of his many admirers. By all accounts, May Rusie would have been perfectly happy to leave New York behind and live year-round in Muncie, Indiana. She never felt comfortable in a large city, but Amos was having the time of his life, so the Rusies lived in New York during the summer and returned to Indiana each year at season's end.

Rusie's hard-partying ways seemed have no effect on his pitching, at least in his first few seasons with the Giants. In 1892 he once again pitched nearly half of the innings for the New Yorkers, leading the league in walks and finishing second in strikeouts to another fireballer, Chicago's Bill Hutchison. Both Hutchison and Rusie threw more than 500 innings that season, becoming the last major league pitchers to work that many frames. The Giants finished in the middle of the pack in the split-season of 1892, but Rusie reached the 30-win plateau once more with a 32–31 record and 59 complete games.

Rusie was earning one of the league's top salaries at a reported $4,500 a year by 1892, but National League club owners were still claiming huge losses from the Players League war of two years before. Since the National League was now the only major circuit (after the American Association folded in 1891) the magnates owned a monopoly on American professional baseball. The era of high salaries was over, and in mid-1892 many teams demanded that their players, stars and bench-warmers alike, accept new contracts for lower pay. Rusie, outfielder Mike Tiernan, and shortstop Shorty Fuller refused to renegotiate, and on October 6, 1892 all three were given notice of release. Rusie's dismissal was delivered only two days after he pitched and won both ends of a doubleheader, defeating the Senators 6–4 and 9–5.

Amos was indignant, as his contract was not due to expire until the end of the 1893 campaign, but was powerless to do anything about it. Each contract contained the dreaded ten-day clause, which allowed the team to terminate the agreement, for any reason at all, with ten days notice. Since the National League teams had agreed among themselves not to sign each others' players, Rusie had no choice but to renegotiate with the Giants. He took a huge pay cut, signing for $2,500 per year in early 1893. The league bosses claimed victory in what was called a "crusade" against high salaries, but Amos Rusie would not forget this humiliating defeat.

Still the king of National League pitchers, Rusie, along with other fastballers like Chicago's Bill Hutchison and Cleveland's Cy Young, were so dominant during the early 1890s that the baseball magnates feared for the art of offense. League batting and slugging averages had plummeted during the preceding several seasons, and it appeared that pitchers held an insurmountable advantage over batters in the National League. Pitchers were getting bigger and stronger, and men such as Rusie, Hutchison, and Young fired their fastballs from a box only 50 feet from the plate. The familiar baseball expression, "You can't hit what you can't see," was most likely first uttered by someone who had to face Amos Rusie during this era.

In early 1893, the National League owners took a break from their salary-cutting and made the last major rule change in the game until the introduction of the designated hitter in 1973. Beginning with the 1893 season, the pitching box was eliminated and replaced with a slab of rubber, set into the ground at a distance of 60 feet and six inches from home plate. The pitcher would now be required to deliver the ball with one foot touching the rubber at all times. The magnates hoped that the extra ten feet of pitching distance would negate the advantages enjoyed by several fastballers, most notably Amos Rusie, and stimulate offense in a game where the art of batting had suffered.

The new pitching distance proved a greater offensive boost than any of its proponents could have imagined. The league batting average, which had dropped to .245 by 1892, jumped to .280 in 1893 and to .309 in 1894. The slugging average took a similar bounce, from .327 in 1892 to .435 in 1894. Oddly enough, fireballers such as Young and Rusie continued as big winners, though Bill Hutchison soon fell from the ranks of elite pitchers. The brunt of the offensive explosion was borne mostly by marginal major league hurlers who were not talented enough to keep pitching after 1892. The new field configuration hastened the demise of veterans from the 1880s, such as Tim Keefe, John Clarkson, and Tony Mullane, to name but a few. Their arms were worn out from years of pitching, and their fading fastballs were now much easier to hit.

Amos Rusie, like almost every pitcher in the National League, saw his earned run average rise (from 2.83 in 1892 to 3.23 the following year) but he adapted well while other pitchers struggled. His strikeouts fell to 208 in 1893, 80 fewer than the year before, but his total was enough to lead the league for the third time. His walks fell also, indicating that his control was improving with age, and he was still the workhorse of the league with 50 complete games. Rusie's 33–21 record paced the inconsistent Giants to a fifth-place finish.

Physically, 1893 was Rusie's most demanding season to date. In one game, he split the skin between two fingers of his right hand while pitching in the eighth inning. Blood covered the hand, his uniform shirt, and the ball, but Amos managed to finish the game. He kept the blood-stained ball as a souvenir for the rest of his life. In another contest, Brooklyn batter Mike Griffin rifled a shot that struck Amos in the head, spinning him around. The blow damaged Rusie's hearing and led to eventual deafness in his left ear.

The Giants were hobbled during the early 1890s by a lack of starting pitching aside from Rusie, but in 1894 right-hander Jouett Meekin (like Amos an Indiana lad) joined the club and provided the needed support. With Rusie having one of his greatest seasons with a 36–13 record and an astounding (for the era) 2.78 earned run average, Meekin nearly matched him with a 33–9 record. Rusie and Meekin were the best one-two pitching combination in baseball, and they boosted the team all the way to second place despite a mediocre Giant offense. The team finished only three games behind first-place Baltimore as Rusie led the league once again in wins, strikeouts, and shutouts. Amos dominated the Beaneaters so thoroughly in a 5–1 victory on August 31 that Boston outfielder Tommy McCarthy complained to the newspapers after the game. "It's no use," said McCarthy. "There are pitchers, very good pitchers, but Amos is the kingpin of all."[6]

When John Clarkson announced his retirement in August of that year, the 24-year-old Amos became the active career leader in strikeouts in only his sixth major league season. Rusie stood alone atop the pitching world, and the post-season Temple Cup series merely solidified his reputation. During the mid-1890s, the first- and second-place National League teams met in an October series for possession of the Temple Cup, a silver trophy donated by a Pittsburgh businessman named William Temple. The Giants entered the seven-game set as underdogs to the champion Baltimore Orioles, but Rusie mowed the Orioles down 4–1 in the first game, and Meekin defeated them by a 3–0 count in Game 2. Rusie returned and pitched a 4–1 win in the third contest, and Meekin closed out the series with a 16–3 thrashing of the Orioles. Amos pitched two complete games, allowed only one earned run, and batted .429 in the four-game sweep.

The Orioles, having already won the pennant, did not appear to take the Temple Cup seriously, as each Baltimore player paired up with a Giant, agreeing to split their winnings no matter the outcome. Amos made a pact with Baltimore outfielder Joe Kelley, and at series' end Amos left $204—the difference between a winning and a losing share—for Kelley at his hotel before leaving for home in Indiana. Amos was probably surprised to discover that he was the sole member of the Giants to keep his promise. His teammates, delighted with their unexpected victory in the series, reportedly reneged on their agreements. Each Giant earned $768, while each Oriole's share came to $360.[7] The apparent "welshing" by the Giants caused friction between the teams that lasted for several years, and led to several serious on-field brawls and beanball wars during the 1890s.

The 1894 Temple Cup victory was the high point of Amos Rusie's career, for a few months later the Giants entered the most turbulent era in team history. On January 17, 1895, a Tammany Hall politician named Andrew Freedman bought controlling interest in the Giants for $54,000. Freedman was a mercurial, hot-tempered businessman and political fixer who quickly put his mendacious stamp upon the New York baseball scene. He quarreled with manager John Ward, who resigned before the season started rather than work for his difficult new boss. Freedman picked fights with sportswriters, actually trading punches one day with a reporter from the *New York Sun*, and banning negative writers from the Polo Grounds. He dictated lineups and pitching changes to his managers and sometimes charged onto the field to bully umpires into favoring the Giants at home. Worst of all, Freedman appeared to care more about making money than winning games, and he was determined to slash salaries right and left. Amos Rusie, his biggest star and highest-paid player, became the new owner's prime target.

Freedman alienated fans, sportswriters, and players alike with his high-handed methods, and plunged the Giants into turmoil almost immediately. Shortstop George Davis was appointed manager to succeed Ward, but after 33 games Freedman fired him, putting first baseman Jack Doyle in charge. Doyle lasted until August, but with the Giants stuck at the .500 mark, Freedman made perhaps the worst managerial appointment in baseball history. He dismissed Doyle and replaced him with a Broadway actor and political hanger-on named Harvey Watkins. The Giants ignored their clueless new field leader and continued to play mediocre baseball, finishing the 1895 season in ninth place, one game above the break-even point.

Rusie led the league in strikeouts and shutouts again, but his 23–23 record was his worst since his 1889 season in Indianapolis. He and the other Giants played passive, disinterested baseball, and team discipline all but collapsed by mid-season. In July Freedman fined Rusie $100 for an alleged incident of drunkenness in Baltimore, and during the last game of the season Rusie made what Freedman claimed was a "threatening gesture" toward the owner. Freedman penalized Rusie another $100 for that offense. When Amos received his last pay envelope for the 1895 season, his check was $200 short.

Freedman appointed veteran field leader Arthur Irwin as his new manager for 1896, but spring training began without Amos Rusie. Still smarting over the fines from a year before, Amos refused to report for spring training unless the $200 was returned to him. He also balked at signing a contract for less than $3,000, which Freedman adamantly refused to pay. Rusie held firm, remaining at home in Indiana while the season began without him. If Freedman believed that Rusie would eventually capitulate and rejoin the team on the owner's terms, he was in for a surprise. Rusie stayed in Indiana for the entire 1896 season.

Amos Rusie (misspelled Russie on the caption) on an 1895 card from Mayo Cut Plug tobacco. (Author's collection)

Rusie may not have been blameless in the dispute, for it appears that the pitcher regularly broke curfew and ignored training rules. Sportswriter Sam Crane, who had been a teammate of Rusie with the Giants and was perhaps the only writer Amos trusted, stated, "Starting out life with everything in his favor, Rusie went through his active pitching days as though on a continuous joy ride. He broke training when he felt like it and never looked upon life as a serious matter."[8] Andrew Freedman may richly deserve his designation as the worst baseball owner in history, but Amos Rusie was not always a model citizen. Still, Amos insisted that he was in his room at 11 o'clock on the night that Freedman claimed he was out on a bender in Baltimore. The fines were nothing but an attempt to cut his salary, claimed Rusie, and he would not stand for it.

The Giants finished the season only two games behind their 1895 pace, even without their star pitcher, so Freedman may have been unconcerned about Rusie's absence. However, the New York fans were furious. They sided with Rusie when he applied to the National Board of Arbitration, the four-man committee that decided contract matters for the National League. Rusie demanded his release from his New York contract and the return of the $200 deducted from his paycheck. On June 8, 1896, the board declined to hear the case, referring him to the National League's board of directors. This panel met on June 29, 1896, and heard testimony from Freedman and John Ward, the former Giants manager who had left baseball after a dispute with Freedman and taken up the practice of law. Rusie was not present at the hearing.

The proceedings proved a disaster for the Giants pitcher. Ward merely presented an affidavit, sworn by himself, that described how Amos' teammates considered him a gentleman and that his behavior was above reproach. Freedman responded that Rusie caused problems for the team all during the 1895 campaign with his heavy drinking. Amos had drunkenly insulted the wife of the mayor of Jacksonville, Florida, at spring training there, said Freedman, and had instigated other embarrassing incidents during the season. Ward tried to refute the accusations, but the board of directors had heard enough. The panel upheld the fines, denying Rusie's petition for release from his contract. Ward and Rusie then played their next, and potentially most powerful, card. They filed a suit in federal court in Chicago for $5,000 in back pay and damages against the National League. That suit was dismissed on jurisdictional grounds, but Rusie and a new slate of attorneys refiled it in Trenton, New Jersey, in November of 1896.

The league power brokers feared this very development, as Rusie sought to overturn his contract with the Giants, and by extension every contract in major league baseball, by challenging the legality of the reserve clause. This provision had been introduced in 1879, and at first allowed each National League team to reserve five players from one year to the next. Two decades later, all teams claimed ownership of every man on its roster until that player was traded or released, forever if the team so chose. Though the reserve clause remained an integral part of baseball contract language until the birth of free agency in the 1970s, the magnates knew as early as 1896 that it might not withstand a court challenge. The New Jersey court accepted the case and scheduled opening arguments to commence on March 15, 1897.

Andrew Freedman was ready to fight Rusie in court, but the other owners took the long view and opted to settle with the recalcitrant pitcher. Over Freedman's fiery objections, the other 11 teams raised $5,000 and offered it to Rusie to drop his suit and return to the Giants. Rusie, for his part, would agree to a $2,400 salary for 1897 and drop his objection to the $200 fine. Rusie accepted the offer, and in March signed his contract and rejoined the New York club. Amos dropped the suit, but considered himself ultimately victorious.

"That $5,000 I received for not playing," said Rusie many years later, "was almost $2,000 more than I would have received for playing all season."[9]

Freedman was not a man to surrender gracefully. He refused to let Rusie appear in uniform at the beginning of the season, so Amos watched the first game from the stands. He rode the bench for the next few days, because Giants manager Bill Joyce was under strict orders not to put Rusie on the mound. The fans booed Freedman mercilessly, but the owner did not relent until the Giants dropped their first four games of the season. On April 27, Rusie took the field and defeated the Senators by a score of 8 to 3. Eleven more days passed before Rusie saw action again, when he beat Brooklyn 9–5, and only then did he begin to take his regular turn on the mound.

The 1897 campaign was a fateful one for Amos Rusie. He nearly killed Hugh Jennings with a pitch on June 29, when one of his swift "in-shoots" struck the Baltimore shortstop on the side of the head. Jennings, who was known for standing close to the plate, dropped unconscious to the ground. Amazingly, Jennings woke up, went to first base, and managed to play for several more innings, but was later removed from the game and diagnosed with a severe concussion. Jennings was beaned again by Jouett Meekin in October of 1898, as well as several other times during his career, and the repeated head blows may have contributed to his mental problems in later life. Rusie's greatest trouble, however, came in a game against Chicago. He tried to execute a fancy pickoff move in an attempt to catch Bill Lange off first base, but tore the muscles in his right shoulder in the process.[10]

Though Rusie stated in later years that he was unable to pitch for five weeks after the injury, a study of the 1897 game log of the Giants reveals that he was not out of the lineup for any length of time. He finished the campaign with a 28–10 mark and led the league in earned run average, though his strikeout total fell to 135 in 322 innings. However, when he began preparing for the 1898 season, Rusie found that he could not lift his arm above his head. His shoulder throbbed with pain whenever he tried to throw a fastball, putting the 27-year-old's baseball future in jeopardy. "I coulda lasted as long as old Cy Young, what with my strength and all," complained the pitcher long afterwards. "That's what happens when you try to act smart."[11]

While Rusie tried to salvage his career, the Giants played in more of a circus atmosphere than usual during 1898. After an ugly brawl in May between manager Bill Joyce and Cincinnati's Jake Beckley, Freedman came under pressure to discipline his field leader. He did, by dismissing Joyce as manager (while retaining him as a player) and hiring Cap Anson, recently dismissed as Chicago manager after 19 years. Anson was a disciplinarian, instituting morning workouts and strict curfews, and the players rebelled against his leadership. Rumors circulated that many of the Giants were purposely performing poorly in a bid to get their new manager fired. Joyce retained the loyalty of the players, and after three weeks Freedman fired Anson and reinstated Joyce.

All the while, Rusie tried to pitch without his legendary fastball. He participated in only one of the first 10 games on the schedule, and thereafter alternated good performances with poor ones. On June 8, he threw four shutout innings against Chicago, then allowed six runs in the fifth and left the game. On September 2, after one inning against Pittsburgh, he was unable to continue. He compiled a credible 20–11 record that season, but his 300 innings pitched and 33 complete games were the lowest totals of his career as a Giant. When Andrew Freedman, citing Rusie's injury, proposed to cut his salary to $2,000 for 1899, the ailing pitcher rebelled once again. He refused to report for spring training, threatening to file suit again to gain his release from the Giants.

The lawsuit never materialized, because Amos Rusie became embroiled in marital difficulties. May Rusie, accusing her husband of habitual drunkenness and abusive behavior, filed for divorce on January 9, 1899. The two reconciled, and Amos spent the entire 1899 baseball season at home in Indianapolis. In November of that year Rusie, still threatening to take the Giants to court over the reserve clause, signed a contract with the New York team of a new league, a revived American Association headed by Cap Anson. That league quickly collapsed, and in March of 1900 Rusie pronounced his arm sound and signed a new contract to pitch for the Giants.

Amos was willing to return to New York, but May Rusie was not. Amos hurriedly left the team on April 16, citing "personal business," and traveled by train to Indiana. Two days later, the newspapers revealed that May had, once again, filed for divorce, asking for $5,000 in alimony and property. Since Mary Rusie, the pitcher's mother, had recently died and left property to Amos in her will, the financial implications of the divorce became entangled with the will, complicating a potential divorce settlement. Amos could not play ball and attend to his legal problems simultaneously, so he spent the 1900 season on the sidelines.

May Rusie told the court that the marriage had been rocky for many years, and that Amos had threatened to kill her and then himself during his drunken rages. She stated that their latest crisis erupted when she asked a local saloonkeeper to stop serving liquor to her husband. Amos, she said, had promised to shoot her at the courthouse if she went through with the divorce. On May 9, 1900, the court awarded May a divorce and $1,000 in alimony, along with household goods and attorney fees.

Amos, frightened at last by the loss of his marriage, appeared to make a sincere attempt at staying sober and behaving himself. He promised to quit the Giants, since May had grown to detest New York and the effect the major league lifestyle had on her husband, and offered to settle down in Indiana permanently. May agreed, and in August of that year the couple were married for the second time. This union lasted for the rest of their lives and resulted in the birth of a daughter a few years later. Amos put the Giants behind him, and spent the summer umpiring semipro games and looking for a new line of work.

Most observers figured that Rusie's baseball days were over, but not before he became one of the principals in perhaps the most lopsided trade in baseball history. John T. Brush, the man who owned the Indianapolis Hoosiers so many years before, was both a stockholder in the Giants and the main owner of the Cincinnati Reds in 1900. Involved in negotiations to take control of the Giants at that time, Brush wanted to protect the best players on the New York roster. The Giants owned one of the most promising young pitchers in baseball, Christy Mathewson, a 20-year-old from Bucknell University who had won 20 games at Norfolk that season. Brush wanted to prevent the other National League teams from drafting the coveted Mathewson off the New York roster, so he devised a scheme to protect the young pitcher. He arranged for the Reds to claim Mathewson in the draft, then quickly traded him back to the Giants in exchange for Amos Rusie.

Mathewson became one of the greatest pitchers of all time, winning 373 games and gaining further distinction as one of the first five men elected to the Hall of Fame. Amos Rusie's best years were behind him, and at the age of 29 he was "pitched out," in the parlance of the day. The only man who refused to believe that Rusie's career was finished was Rusie himself. After two years out of the game, Amos was not yet ready to hang up his glove. He knew his wife would never stand for a return to New York, but Cincinnati might be an acceptable alternative. In early 1901 Amos, with his wife's blessing, reported for spring training with the Reds.

While Mathewson embarked on his first 20-win season for the Giants, Rusie made only two starts for Cincinnati and watched his career end in ignominy. In his first game for the Reds, on May 8, 1901, Rusie gave up 19 hits and lost to St. Louis by a 14–3 score. His fastball was only a memory, and the former "Hoosier Thunderbolt" felt the effects of his two-year layoff and his still-painful shoulder. He pitched well on June 5, allowing one run and nine hits against Brooklyn in a game that ended in a tie, but on June 9 the Giants raked Amos for 15 hits and 10 runs in five innings of relief work. The Giants won the game by a 25–13 count, though the unruly crowd caused the game to end in a forfeit, and the final score convinced Amos Rusie that he was finished as a pitcher. A few days later, he quit the Reds and retired from baseball.

In only nine full seasons and part of a tenth, Rusie compiled 246 wins, 174 losses, and 1,950 strikeouts. He also allowed 1,707 walks, a major league record that stood until Bobo Newsom surpassed it in 1952. Most pitchers enter their prime in their late twenties and early thirties, but Amos Rusie won his last game at age 27 and was out of baseball at 30. He returned to Indiana, and before the year was out the papers reported that the onetime baseball star had found employment as a laborer, earning $1.50 a day from the Muncie Water

Works. "I am leading a good, clean life," said the former pitching star, "and I am the last to need anyone's pity. I guess, though, my baseball days are over."[12]

Rusie was tempted to return to the game many times, and in July of 1906 New York Giants manager John McGraw expressed interest in giving Rusie another chance at major league stardom. However, Rusie's shoulder pain, which began in that fateful game in Chicago in 1897, never left him. He busied himself with unskilled labor, farming, and even a stint at pearl-diving. When clams in the Wabash River were found to contain the gems, Rusie traveled to Vincennes and tried his hand at harvesting the valuable nuggets. The pearl craze lasted for only a short time, and by 1907 Rusie was back in Muncie, digging ditches and working as a laborer for the local power company.

In 1909 Rusie moved his family to Seattle, Washington, where he worked as a steamfitter in a shipyard, but in 1921 John McGraw, still manager and vice-president of the New York Giants, offered him a position as an assistant superintendent at the Polo Grounds. Perhaps McGraw, an old Baltimore Oriole, remembered Rusie's honesty in the distribution of Temple Cup winnings nearly 30 years before. Rusie accepted the offer and moved back to New York, where he lived in a small apartment and went generally unnoticed by a new generation of fans and players. He was something of a curmudgeon, and still refused interview requests, once slamming his door in the face of a local reporter. Like most old ballplayers, he pronounced himself unimpressed by the new crop of stars. "It'd be like having a vacation if I were playing ball today," harrumphed the old pitcher. "I used to pitch every other day and twice hurled both ends of a doubleheader. A pitcher had a lot harder time in the old days."[13]

Rusie tired of New York after eight years, and in 1929 he and his wife returned to Seattle. He bought a chicken farm near Auburn, Washington, that went under during the Depression, and a serious auto accident in July of 1934 left him unconscious for four days and subsequently unable to work. His farm was repossessed in 1936, but a Seattle newspaper reporter saw the foreclosure notice and organized an effort to assist Rusie and his family. They raised enough money to buy a house for the old pitcher and provide for his needs for the rest of his life.

Rusie, who had always spurned interviews and treated reporters with disdain, was touched by the gesture. He became more accessible in his old age, and in December 1939 a reporter for *The Sporting News* interviewed the 68-year-old baseball legend and his wife at their new home. The writer found Rusie in fair health, still bothered by pain from his 1897 shoulder injury, but in good spirits. His daughter was married and living in Seattle, and wife May, though partially paralyzed by then, was talkative and quick-witted. Amos, shown petting his Labrador dog in a photo, still followed baseball closely by reading *The Sporting News* every week.

Ignored and forgotten by the Hall of Fame electors—he received only one vote in 1937, eight in 1938, and six in 1939—Amos Rusie lived his final days in near-total obscurity. May Rusie died in September of 1942, and Amos suffered a heart attack only two months later. He died on December 6, 1942 at the age of 71, and was buried at the Acacia Memorial Park in Seattle, more than 3,000 miles from the Polo Grounds, the scene of his greatest baseball triumphs.

Amos Rusie's career trajectory bears a strong resemblance to that of a later pitching star, Bob Feller. Both men burst on the major league scene at the age of 17 with incredible fastballs. Both led their leagues several times in both strikeouts and walks. Feller holds the post–1900 record for walks issued by a pitcher in a season, while Rusie is the pre–1900 standard bearer. Each man threw an excellent curveball as well as a blazing fastball, and both improved their control after a few seasons. Each lost three or more full seasons in their prime pitching years, Feller to military service in World War II, Rusie to holdouts and personal problems. Both were proud, often difficult men who fought numerous contract battles, but Feller was never a drinking man, while Rusie's alcohol abuse played a significant role in his career.

Bob Feller pitched for 18 seasons and retired at age 37, while Amos Rusie won his last major league game when he was only 27 years old. Had Rusie managed to avoid injury and alcohol-related off-the-field problems, his statistical line might have been one of the greatest ever compiled. Though he barely qualified for the Hall of Fame under the ten-year rule (to be eligible, a player must participate in 10 major league seasons, and Rusie pitched nine full seasons and a small part of a tenth), Rusie was the best pitcher in baseball at his peak during the 1890s. His total of 246 wins puts him ahead of many other Cooperstown inductees with longer careers. He was the fastest pitcher of his time, the first in a line of speed kings that includes Walter Johnson, Bob Feller, and Nolan Ryan, and as such Amos Rusie deserves his place in the Hall of Fame.

13
Arky Vaughan

> "For a fellow who lasted as long as he did in the big league, there just are no Arky Vaughan stories. He never said anything quotable or did anything worth mentioning. More has been written about the colorful Willie Mays in one year than was said of Vaughan in a lifetime."
>
> —*Arthur Daley, 1952*[1]

The career of Joseph Floyd (Arky) Vaughan can be summarized by his performance in the 1941 All-Star Game, which was held at Briggs Stadium (later Tiger Stadium) in Detroit. Vaughan, the starting shortstop that day for the National League, put on a hitting show that ranks with the greatest ever in All-Star competition. Vaughan led all players that day with three hits, and his two-run homer in the seventh inning off Sid Hudson gave the National League a 3–2 lead. He came up in the eighth and belted another two-run homer, this one off Eddie Smith, giving the senior circuit a seemingly insurmountable 5–2 margin. He was the first man to hit two home runs in an All-Star game, and sportswriters were already planning their profiles of Vaughan as the hero of the day.

However, Vaughan's achievements on that sunny afternoon in Detroit are barely remembered today. The American League scored a run in the eighth and another in the ninth, making the score 5–4, before Ted Williams of the Boston Red Sox stepped up to the plate with two on and two out. With more than 54,000 people cheering, Williams walloped a pitch from Chicago's Claude Passeau into the right field upper deck for a game-ending three-run homer that gave the American League a 7–5 win. Today, Williams' blast is recalled as one of the most dramatic home runs of all time, while Arky Vaughan's sensational hitting barely rates a footnote in baseball history. The game was a microcosm of the career of the quiet, efficient, but largely forgotten Vaughan, who did not gain election to the Hall of Fame until 1985, more than 30 years after his death.

Arky Vaughan's nickname derived from a state in which he lived only briefly. He was born Floyd Ellis Vaughan on March 9, 1912 in Clifty, Arkansas, the fourth of six children of Robert and Laura Vaughan. When Floyd was seven months old, the family relocated to Potter Valley, California, near the city of

Ukiah in Mendocino County about 80 miles north of San Francisco Bay. Robert Vaughan operated a farm, raising corn, wheat, and alfalfa. Floyd's school friends called him "Arky" after the state of his birth, as well as a nod to the Arkansas accent he inherited. When he reached adulthood, Arky changed his name to Joseph Floyd Vaughan, but noted that he had been called by his nickname for so long that no one remembered that his original name was Floyd.

Whenever they could find the time, he and the other area farm kids got together to play ball. Robert Vaughan loved the outdoors and athletic pursuits and, unlike many farming fathers, encouraged his children to play sports. He purchased balls, bats, and gloves for his three sons, and all grew into enthusiastic players. When Arky became a teenager, Robert decided to move several hundred miles south to Fullerton, near Los Angeles in Orange County, so the children could attend a good public high school. Robert sold the farm and found work with the Standard Oil Company, though Arky returned to Potter Valley each summer, earning money by working as a farm hand. He milked cows, pitched hay, and plowed fields, and the intensive work turned him into a strong, strapping young man.

Arky attended Union High School in Fullerton (where future president Richard Nixon was a classmate during his freshman and sophomore years), excelling in baseball, track, and football. He was such a talented running back that he received college scholarship offers after graduating in 1930, but baseball was his favorite sport, and he dreamed of a professional career on the diamond. He soon joined a semipro team in Fullerton and played in and around the Los Angeles area that fall and winter. In December of 1930, a scout named Art Griggs took in a game and noticed Arky at shortstop. Griggs was the owner and manager of the Wichita Aviators of the Western League, a farm team of the Pittsburgh Pirates, and was impressed enough to hustle onto the field and introduce himself to the teenager. Recognizing Vaughan's potential, Griggs went to the Vaughan home and convinced Arky and his father to agree to a contract to play for Wichita. Only later did Arky learn that Bill Essick, chief scout of the New York Yankees, had also been following his progress. By the time the Yankees were ready to make an offer, Arky was on his way to Wichita.

Griggs arranged for Arky to attend spring training with the Pirates in Paso Robles, California in the spring of 1931. Arky had just turned 19 years of age, but was unfazed by the competition. His fine hitting was a good indicator his potential. After reporting to Wichita in April, Arky quickly earned a position as the starting shortstop. Though new to professional ball, he batted .338, hit 21 homers, and led the league in stolen bases and runs scored. He formed a hard-hitting keystone combo with another future major leaguer, second baseman Tony Piet, who hit .336 and drove in 100 runs. Wichita, led by Vaughan and Piet, won the first half of the split-season pennant race and finished second in the final half, losing in the playoffs to Des Moines.

The Wichita club was affiliated with the Pittsburgh Pirates of the National

Arky Vaughan in 1932, his rookie season in Pittsburgh. He was 20 years old at the time. (National Baseball Hall of Fame Library, Cooperstown, N.Y.)

League. The Pirates had won the World Series in 1925 and the National League pennant in 1927, but seemingly had never recovered from a blowout loss in four straight games to the New York Yankees in the 1927 Series. The Pirates had finished fifth in 1930 and 1931, partly because of an unsettled infield situation aside from third base, where Pie Traynor starred. Their 1931 shortstop, veteran Tommy Thevenow, batted only .213 and suffered a broken leg in September, while Gus Suhr and George Grantham shared first base. Grantham,

Bill Regan, and Howdy Groskloss rotated at second base, and the constant lineup shuffle kept the Pirate infield from achieving consistency. However, the Pirates held both Tony Piet and Arky Vaughan in high regard, and tabbed them as the future keystone combination for the franchise.

Piet, four years older than Vaughan, was further along in his development. He was ready for the big leagues in 1931, but the parent team opted to leave him in Wichita for one more year to play alongside Vaughan. Both men impressed the Pirate management with their play in Wichita, and by the middle of the 1931 campaign the Pirates decided that Piet and Vaughan were seasoned enough to figure in Pittsburgh's future. Piet, called up to the parent club in August, claimed the second base position, while Vaughan, with his outstanding hitting in the Western League, emerged as a candidate to play shortstop for the Pirates in 1932.

Arky's precociousness served him off the field as well. On October 31, 1931, while still in his teens, he married Margaret Allen and started a family that would eventually produce four children. Margaret had been his high school sweetheart back in Fullerton, and a fine athlete in her own right, especially in basketball. She, too, had been born in Arkansas and moved to California at a young age, so they had much in common. Both enjoyed hunting and fishing, and both wanted to make their home in Mendocino County, despite the fact that Arky's career was about to take him to Pittsburgh. They bought a ranch in Potter Valley outside of Ukiah early in their marriage, and while spending six months of the year in Pittsburgh, began to develop their California property as a permanent home.

Arky reported to spring training in March of 1932, shortly after his 20th birthday. Though his contract still belonged to the Tulsa minor league team (the Wichita club had moved there after the 1931 season), the young shortstop was called upon to replace Thevenow, who was still recovering from the broken ankle he suffered the previous season. Arky hit so well that he convinced the Pirates to buy his contract from Tulsa and place him on the Pittsburgh roster. He began the year on the bench, but when Thevenow hit only .198 in April, Arky took the shortstop job and never relinquished it. He slumped in midsummer, but manager George Gibson kept him playing every day, boosting his confidence. With Tony Piet, his minor league teammate, beside him at second base, Arky batted a solid .318 as a rookie, with the promise of future stardom.

Despite his fine hitting, it was clear to all that Arky (whom the papers called Floyd Vaughan early in his career) was not yet a good, or even a passable, major league shortstop. His total of 46 errors led the league in 1932, and his range was wanting. He seemed to have a problem fielding grounders hit right at him, as most of his errors came on fumbled grounders, not on throws or pop flies. The Pirates, with Piet at second and Vaughan at short, turned only 124 double plays, the lowest total in the league, and their questionable infield play was one reason that the team gave up ten more runs than it scored. In retrospect, it appears that Pittsburgh's surprising second-place finish in 1932 was due in large part to the weakness of the league as a whole.

The Pirates were willing to be patient, since Arky was only 20 years old and already the best-hitting shortstop in the National League. Moving him to another position was out of the question, as third base was occupied by all-time great Pie Traynor and three other future Hall of Famers, Fred Lindstrom and brothers Paul and Lloyd Waner, patrolled the outfield. Pirate manager Gibson preferred to keep Vaughan's bat in the lineup while he learned to play shortstop, rather than return the slick-fielding but weak-hitting Tommy Thevenow to the position.

In an attempt to facilitate Arky's transition from promising newcomer to full-fledged star, the Pittsburgh team hired its greatest all-time player, 59-year-old Honus Wagner, as a coach for the 1933 season. Wagner, who played for the Pirates from 1900 to 1917, led them to four pennants, and won a record eight National League batting titles, is still almost unanimously considered the greatest shortstop of all time. His main assignment, besides interacting with the fans, was to help Arky Vaughan learn to play shortstop on the major league level. "They wanted me to coach one man, nothing else," said Wagner. "That's all I had to do. They said if I couldn't make a shortstop out of Arky Vaughan, nobody could."[2]

Wagner, a friendly man much beloved by the fans, immediately began tutoring Arky in the finer points of shortstop play. Though the long-retired star had once managed the Pirates for a brief time, coaching was a new experience for him, and his instructions were not always clear. One day manager Gibson asked Arky how the lessons were going. "I'm not sure," replied Vaughan. "When I asked Mr. Wagner what to do, he said, 'You just run in fast, grab the ball, and throw it to first base ahead of the runner.' But he didn't tell me how."[3]

Wagner was an intuitive athlete, and tried to convince Arky to trust his instincts on the field and not burden himself with overanalysis. "There ain't much to being a ballplayer, if you're a ballplayer," Wagner liked to say. Perhaps the message got through, as Arky improved in the field in 1933. Though he led the league in errors again, he helped the Pirates hold their opponents to 619 runs, 72 fewer than the year before, as the club moved from last place to sixth in double plays while repeating their second-place finish. In addition, the gregarious Wagner and the reserved Vaughan became close friends. They roomed together on the road for the next nine seasons, the remainder of Vaughan's career in Pittsburgh.

By no means the best fielding shortstop in the National League (Leo Durocher of the Cardinals and Dick Bartell of the Phillies were much better performers with the glove), Arky was nonetheless becoming one of the best hitters in the league at any position. He hit .314 in 1933 and used his speed and base-running ability to lead the league in triples with 19. "Could he ever fly around those bases!" said Rip Sewell. "I never saw anybody who could go from first to third or from second to home faster than Vaughan. Like we used to say, when he went around second his hip pocket was dipping sand. That's how sharp he cut those corners."[4] He followed his sophomore season with an even better one in 1934, hitting .333 while leading the circuit in walks, but the Pirates fell from contention. Tony Piet was traded to Cincinnati after a dispute with manager George Gibson, and his absence weakened the infield as the Pirates dropped to fifth place. In June of 1934, third baseman Pie Traynor succeeded Gibson as field leader.

Vaughan managed to post high batting averages due to his outstanding bat control. He swung so hard that one New York Giant remarked, "He'll rupture himself one of these days," but he rarely struck out. He had a bright future, and Vaughan's fellow Pirates encouraged him to set his sights high. One day Arky suggested to his teammates that he was "satisfied" with his average in 1934, but veteran outfielder Fred Lindstrom quickly registered his objection to such an attitude. "You're wrong to be satisfied with one hit out of three times at bat," suggested Lindstrom. "A fellow who can hit as well as you can ought to get as many base hits as possible, and even shoot for that .400 figure. I'm willing to bet that you can make it some day."[5]

Lindstrom nearly saw his prediction come true in 1935, as Arky Vaughan compiled one of the greatest offensive seasons by a shortstop in baseball history. Though the Pirates never threatened to enter the pennant chase, Arky began hitting the ball hard in spring training and barely let up all season long. In late August his average peaked at .407, leading the league by more than 35 points over the second-place hitter, Joe Medwick of the Cardinals. On August 31 Vaughan's average stood at .398 as he threatened to surpass the .400 mark for the season, a feat that not even Honus Wagner had achieved. Wagner was proud of his pupil, and though the old-timer kept tutoring Arky in fielding, he stopped giving batting advice. "It would not be common sense," said Honus late that season, "to tell any player how he might improve his hitting when he already ranks as the leading batsman of both big leagues."[6]

Arky slumped a bit in September, batting only .317 for the month to drop his final average to .385, but he still won his first (and only) National League batting title by a comfortable margin. His average is the highest ever posted by a shortstop in the league during the 20th century, and even surpassed Wagner's highest mark of .381, set in 1900. In fact, no National Leaguer has since bettered Vaughan's average in a full season; the only man to exceed the mark was Tony Gwynn, who hit .394 in the truncated 1994 campaign. Though Arky was not known as a home run hitter, his 19 round trippers set a new Pittsburgh team record. He finished third behind Gabby Hartnett of the Cubs and Dizzy Dean of the Cardinals in the Most Valuable Player balloting, but *The Sporting News* honored Vaughan with its Player of the Year award, at the time an equivalent prize.

Despite his success, Arky was probably the most under-the-radar star in the game during the 1930s. He rarely spoke to sportswriters, more out of shyness than anything else, and many were frustrated by their inability to elicit colorful quotes from of the Pirates' best player. "Sitting and talking in a one-on-one situation, he was great," said Bob Vaughan, Arky's younger brother. "He just didn't care for crowds. And he would probably avoid an interview if he could. He would just rather let his playing do the talking."[7]

Though Arky's demeanor was quiet, he was by no means a pushover. He argued with the arbiters, was ejected from games on occasion, and fought a memorable on-field battle against Brooklyn catcher Babe Phelps in 1940. His fielding improved after he learned to stand his ground and not give way to sliding baserunners. One day he hit a runner, Dick Bartell, with a throw on a double play ball, and Bartell swore revenge to the newspaper writers afterward. Before the next day's game, Vaughan approached Bartell and offered to settle the matter under the stands. Bartell wisely backed down.

The Pirates sailed along on the fringes of the pennant race for the next two seasons, finishing fourth in 1936 and third in 1937 as Arky Vaughan cemented his status as one of the game's best hitters. He did not improve quickly enough in the field to satisfy some of the fans, however, and by 1937 many questioned the wisdom of keeping Arky at shortstop. Pie Traynor had retired as a player by then, leaving third base open, but the Pirates continued to play Vaughan at short despite his perceived shortcomings. Traynor complained to the papers that other managers ridiculed the situation by calling Vaughan the best left fielder in the game who happened to be playing shortstop. "They all knock him," said Traynor, "but every one of them has tried to trade me out of him."[8] Still, Traynor, keeping his options open, put Arky in left field for 12 games late in the 1937 season. Vaughan made the All-Star team in 1937 for the fourth time, but manager Bill Terry of the Giants played him at third base with Dick Bartell at short.

In early 1938, Honus Wagner told Pittsburgh sportswriter Charles Doyle, "If they will let Arky alone, he will turn out to be a good shortstop." His prediction came true that season as the Pirates, with Vaughan at short and Pep Young at second base, led the National League in double plays. Arky, at the age of 26, made a sudden improvement in his shortstop play, leading the league for the first time in both putouts and assists. Though Arky was never as flashy in the field as a Durocher or a Bartell, he might have won the Gold Glove that season had the award been available at the time. He fielded at a high level for the next three seasons, leading the league in putouts each year and in assists twice, and finally earned recognition as a complete player. Although he finished third in the Most Valuable Player voting in 1938, Arky may have been the most complete player in the game during this era.

His best chance at reaching a World Series with Pittsburgh came during the 1938 season. The Pirates began slowly, but went on a winning streak in early July, wresting first place from the Cubs and Giants and holding it for most of the campaign. Pittsburgh stumbled slightly in late August when Arky was forced to sit out with a bruised thumb on his throwing hand, but although they went 16–16 for the month, they held a seven-game cushion over the Cubs and Reds on September 1. The Cubs pared the lead down to three and a half games by September 18, then won their next seven in a row to creep to within one and a half games with a three-game series against the Pirates in the offing.

At Chicago's Wrigley Field, the Cubs, behind their recently acquired pitcher Dizzy Dean, defeated the Pirates on September 27 to slice the Pirate margin to half a game. The following afternoon, Arky Vaughan batted cleanup for the Pirates and managed only a single, though he walked twice as the Chicago hurlers pitched carefully to him. The score was tied at 5 in the bottom of the ninth with darkness approaching, and if the Pirates could secure three outs, the game would end in a tie and preserve Pittsburgh's hold on first place. It was not to be, as Chicago's Gabby Hartnett hit a game-ending homer that vaulted the Cubs into the league lead. A 10–1 Pittsburgh loss the next day sealed the pennant for the Cubs, as the Pirates finished second for the third time in Arky's six years with the club.

The pennant loss seemed to demoralize the Pirates, and after a sixth-place finish in 1939, Pie Traynor was fired as manager and replaced by former Cardinals boss Frankie Frisch. Arky continued his fine play, as the sabermetric researchers from *Total Baseball* rate him as the National League's top performer in both 1938 and 1940, with a second-place ranking in 1939, but the team's stars were aging. Paul and Lloyd Waner were now on the downside of their careers, and the pitching staff was weakened by age and injury. The Pirates went into rebuilding mode, not to win another pennant until 1960.

Still an outstanding hitter, Arky began to experience knee and leg problems as he approached his 30th birthday. He had played nearly every game on the schedule for the Pirates each season, but in mid-1941 he suffered a spike wound in his left leg from an infield collision and left the lineup for two weeks. On August 30, during an exhibition game under the lights in London, Ontario, he was hit in the head by a pitch, resulting in a concussion. Arky tried to play again soon afterward, but his severe headaches prompted the Pirate team doctor to order him to bed. He batted above the .300 mark for the 10th year in a row, but appeared in only 106 games in what would be his last season in Pittsburgh.

The Pirates were in a cost-cutting mode during the early 1940s, releasing veteran Paul Waner and trading Lloyd Waner, while Arky remained as the longest-tenured and highest-paid member of the ballclub. The team owned a fine minor league shortstop prospect named Billy Cox, and since Arky was aging, management began entertaining offers for its star player. Several teams entered the bidding for Vaughan's services, but on December 12, 1941, the Pirates traded Arky to the league champion Brooklyn Dodgers for four players. They were pitcher Luke Hamlin, infielder Pete Coscarart, catcher Babe Phelps, and outfielder Jimmy Wasdell.

The Dodgers already possessed one of the best young shortstops in baseball in Harold (Pee Wee) Reese, a 23-year-old from Kentucky who hit only .229 in 1941 but performed well in the field. There was no place for Arky in the outfield, where Dixie Walker, Pete Reiser, and Joe Medwick all batted .311 or better the year before, so manager Leo Durocher decided to use him at third base. Harry (Cookie) Lavagetto had held that position in 1941, but his departure for military service late that year left a hole on the infield for Vaughan to fill. All in all, the addition of the perennial all-star Vaughan for four second-line players, two of whom (Hamlin and Phelps) had fallen out of favor with Durocher, appeared to strengthen the Dodgers and increase their chances of repeating as pennant winners in 1942.

Predictably, the New York and Brooklyn writers found the quiet Vaughan maddeningly inscrutable. "Vaughan is a loner," complained New York writer Tom Meany. "Writers have been trying to interview him since the Dodgers arrived, but they've had no success. Arky is polite, but not garrulous. Ask him a leading question and a veil appears to cover his eyes. He doesn't barber with the players, either. Arky's idea of a good time is to sit in a comfortable chair in a hotel lobby and stare into space.

"Dodger fans aren't likely to go into any raves over Vaughan. He has no more color than the guy behind the cage in a loan agency, but his bat speaks with authority."[9]

Arky had not participated in a real pennant chase since 1938, and the 1942 race was one of the closest and hardest-fought in National League history. The Dodgers won more than 70 percent of their games during the first four months of the season, and on August 10 Brooklyn led the league by nine games over the St. Louis Cardinals. Durocher's crew cooled off only slightly after that, but the Cardinals, powered by young stars such as Enos Slaughter and Stan Musial, put on one of the greatest pennant charges ever seen. They won 41 of their final 48 games, chipping away at the lead until passing Brooklyn on September 13. The Cardinals led by two on September 20, and although the Dodgers closed the season with eight consecutive wins, St. Louis refused to surrender. The Cardinals won the flag by two games, and once again Arky Vaughan was denied the chance to play in a World Series.

Arky's 1942 season was a disappointment, as he batted only .277 and failed to crack the .300 mark for the first time in his 11 seasons in the majors. He was named to his ninth consecutive All-Star team that summer, but did not hit his first home run until September 5. He seemed to play his best baseball against his former team, the Pirates. Arky's steal of home against Pittsburgh on July 24 embarrassed his ex-teammates and keyed a 4–3 win for the Dodgers.

Vaughan was only 30 years old at the end of the 1942 season, but was unhappy in Brooklyn, and told the newspapers that he was thinking of retiring and returning to his busy ranch in Potter Valley, California. He had hired his brother Glenn to oversee the spread during his absence, but Glenn was called into military service late in 1942, placing the management back in Arky's hands. Vaughan's baseball salary of $17,000 per year was good, but not spectacular, and operating a ranch on a full-time basis would probably have been as profitable as playing for another season. "I haven't made up my mind," said Arky in November of 1942. "It is hard to run a ranch nowadays because of the help problem. You can't get any one to work on a ranch. And I may buy 1,100 acres more to get into cattle raising. I have an Eastern transportation problem also with my three children and I wouldn't want to leave my family here while I played baseball."[10]

Vaughan with the Brooklyn Dodgers late in his career. (National Baseball Hall of Fame Library, Cooperstown, N.Y.)

The Dodgers had already lost Pee Wee Reese to the war effort, and the only other experienced shortstop on the Brooklyn roster was Durocher, who was nearly 40 years old and rarely put himself in the lineup. The Dodgers did not want to lose the entire left side of their infield, so new general manager Branch Rickey convinced Arky to play at least one more season. Vaughan reported to spring training as usual in March 1943 and prepared to resume his career, playing exhibition games at both third base and shortstop.

The roster was in a state of flux all year long, with players leaving for military service being replaced by minor leaguers and young prospects. Ten different men played third for the Dodgers that year, while eight players (including Durocher) saw action at shortstop. The ballclub never found its rhythm, and the Cardinals ran away with the flag while the Dodgers finished a distant third, 23 games out of first place. Arky, who played 99 games at short and 55 more at third, rebounded at the bat, hitting .305 and leading the league in runs scored with 112 and stolen bases with 20, his career high.

However, the 1943 season is most notable for a clubhouse explosion that pitted Durocher against the rest of his team, with Vaughan caught in the middle. On July 9, pitcher Bobo Newsom and catcher Bobby Bragan started an argument on the field that carried over into the dugout. Durocher turned furiously on Newsom, suspended him for "insubordination," and ordered him to turn in his uniform. The manager had angered the Dodgers a few days before by publicly castigating outfielder Joe Medwick, and the players resented Durocher's increasingly erratic leadership as the team fell out of the pennant race. On July 10, with tensions rising in the clubhouse before a game against Pittsburgh, Arky rolled up his uniform and handed it to Durocher. "Here," said Arky, "if you want [Newsom's] uniform, you can have mine too." Some say that Vaughan followed with an uncharacteristically off-color suggestion of what the manager could do with it.

Durocher, taken aback by the sudden revolt, screamed, "I don't know what this is all about, but if that's the way you feel, Arky, keep it off!" He shouted, "You're suspended too!" to Vaughan, whereupon outfielder Dixie Walker offered to surrender his uniform as well. Within seconds, the clubhouse was in an uproar. The rest of the players sided with Vaughan and threatened to walk out, and only after a personal plea by Branch Rickey did the Dodgers play that day, walloping the Pirates by a 23–6 score with Vaughan watching from the stands. Durocher offered to resign, but Rickey smoothed things over, with Arky rejoining the lineup the next day.[11] Five days later Rickey traded Newsom to the American League and released Medwick, ending the controversy and bringing a modicum of calm to the clubhouse. Arky's role in the blowup may have surprised most baseball people, but not his family. "My father never said much, but when he got mad, watch out," recalled his daughter Patricia years later.[12]

Arky completed the season on a high note, compiling his best statistics in years, but he was worried about his ranch. The Dodgers were so concerned that Arky might not return for the 1944 season that Durocher traveled to Potter Valley to meet with his veteran infielder that December. The manager declared that there were no hard feelings left over from the mid-season blowup, and Arky stated in a letter to Rickey that the matter was "forgiven and forgotten and Leo feels the same." However, Vaughan also told Rickey that his chances of playing ball in 1944 did not look promising. Not only was no one else available to manage the ranch, but the local draft board had informed Arky that he might be eligible for induction, despite his status as a married man with four dependent children.

The board dropped the idea of drafting the 32-year-old Vaughan, but in late March of that year, Arky wrote again to Rickey stating that he could not join the team until July at the earliest. Though the Dodgers carried Arky on their 25-man roster that season, waiting for him to change his mind, Vaughan did not return for three years. He remained on his ranch in California and, though he played some semipro ball, withdrew from major league baseball. In 1945 the Dodgers placed Arky on the voluntarily retired list, making it appear that one of baseball's greatest performers had played his final game.

Most observers connected Arky's sudden retirement with the revolt against Durocher in mid-1943, but in later years his daughter Patricia denied that the tiff had compelled her father to quit baseball. "My father was 31 years old, he had bad knees and four children and he didn't have to go into the service," she said. "But when my uncle Glenn was called into the service, there was nobody to run the ranch, so my father stayed home and did it. They didn't make those big salaries in baseball in those days, so it wasn't that big a deal. I've always felt badly that Leo Durocher was blamed for my father staying home."[13]

American soldiers, including Arky's brother Glenn, returned from military service in 1945 after the war ended. Vaughan could once again put the management of his growing ranch in good hands, and in late 1946 made inquiries about returning to the Dodgers. Though Arky had not played major league ball for three years, Brooklyn general manager Branch Rickey answered in the affirmative, and on November 20, 1946 Arky signed a contract to return to his old team. Many believed that he was hired as a coach to replace Charlie Dressen, who had left the Dodgers and joined the Yankees that year, but Vaughan was intent upon re-starting his playing career at third base. Since Leo Durocher was still managing the Dodgers at the time, Arky's willingness to return dispelled the rumors that Vaughan had quit due to a personality conflict with his field leader. "Arky looks just as he did three years ago," said Durocher at spring training. "He has that same flat swing, hits the ball hard, and I can't see any difference."[14]

Arky disliked turmoil, but the Dodgers experienced more of it than any other team before the 1947 season even began. Jackie Robinson, the first African American to make a major league roster in the 20th century, drew national headlines during spring training, bringing the issue of baseball integration to the forefront. Robinson had been penciled in to play third base, but Vaughan's return left him without a position until Durocher and Rickey decided to install him at first base ahead of a rookie named Gil Hodges. The level of commotion surrounding the Brooklyn team only increased on April 9, when baseball commissioner A. B. (Happy) Chandler suspended Durocher for the entire 1947 season after a series of incidents, both on the field and off. Burt Shotton, a much calmer presence than Durocher, took over as manager nine days later.

Despite the tumult, Shotton's steady hand guided Robinson through a successful rookie season, while Arky Vaughan settled in after his absence to excel as a part-time player. Arky played in 64 games and batted .325, with a .385 mark as a pinch hitter, and provided valuable help as the Dodgers rolled to the pennant over the defending champion St. Louis Cardinals. Vaughan finally received the chance to play in the World Series and made the most of it, pinch hitting three times and reaching base twice on a walk and a double. The Dodgers lost a hard-fought Series to the Yankees, but at least Arky could say, finally, that he played for a pennant winner.

Both Vaughan and the Dodgers took a step backward in 1948. Durocher returned as manager, but the team floundered, and by mid-season was mired in fifth place. On July 11 Durocher resigned and surprised everyone by signing on with the Giants, with Shotton taking the Brooklyn reins once again. Vaughan, now 36 years old, struggled with leg and knee problems and batted only .244 in 65 games. The Dodgers took first place briefly in late August, but fell apart in September, finishing in third place behind the surprising Boston Braves. On September 22, Arky hit a pinch single in the ninth inning against his old team, the Pirates, in what proved to be his final major league game.

Arky recognized that his career as a major league player was over. "I'm going home to California tomorrow," he told the sportswriters on September 28. "Maybe I'll hook on to something in the Pacific Coast League next year. If not, I'll try something else."[15] He would only continue playing if he could find a team much closer to his Potter Valley home, so in February of 1949 Arky signed with the San Francisco Seals of the Pacific Coast League as an outfielder. He hit .288 in 97 games, but knee problems and a gall bladder inflammation bothered him all season long, and on September 2 he decided that he had played enough ball. He announced his retirement from the game, this time for good, and returned to his ranch.

Sadly, only three years later an impromptu fishing expedition brought Arky Vaughan's life to a premature end. On August 30, 1952, Arky's friend Bill Wimer invited him to go fishing on Lost Lake in nearby Eagleville, California. They set out on the lake, which was actually the water-filled crater of a dormant volcano, stopping the boat about 220 feet from shore. Wimer, a much larger man than Vaughan, stood up to cast his line and capsized the boat, after which the two men decided to swim for shore in the cold water. Arky was a good swimmer, but Wimer was not, and began to sink about 25 feet from shore. Arky tried to assist him, but the two struggled, and before long both disappeared under the surface. Their bodies were recovered the next day. Arky Vaughan was dead at the age of 40, leaving his wife Margaret and four children.

A few days following the accident, the *Fullerton Daily News* attempted to put his career in perspective. "He lacked only one thing—a colorful personality," stated the paper. "Those who knew him best believe he would have been one of the game's greatest heroes had he been endowed with the sparkling personality that made lesser players great."[16] Another moving tribute came from his old Brooklyn Dodger teammate, Jackie Robinson. "He was one of the fellows who went out of his way to be nice to me when I came in here as a rookie," said Robinson. "Believe me, I needed it. He was a fine fellow."[17]

Memories of Arky Vaughan faded away so quickly after his untimely death that many were surprised by his election to the Hall of Fame in 1985. Nonetheless, his reputation as a player has increased sharply during the past few decades. Vaughan never won a Most Valuable Player award, but baseball researchers John Thorn and Pete Palmer, authors of *Total Baseball*, identified him as the best player in the National League in four of his 10 seasons with the Pirates. Bill James rated the top 100 men at each position in baseball history for his *New Historical Baseball Abstract* in 2000, astonishing many by ranking Arky as the second-best shortstop of all time, behind Honus Wagner and ahead of Cal Ripken. These belated accolades prove that the members of the oft-criticized Veterans Committee made an excellent choice when they named Arky Vaughan to the Hall of Fame.

14

Joe Williams

> *"[Joe Williams] was the Satchel Paige of his day. Before Satchel it was all Smokey Joe Williams. He was the best thing going. All us kids on the lots down in semipro, we wanted to be like Smokey even though we weren't pitching. We wanted to emulate Smokey Joe Williams; his name was a household word."*
> —*Josh Johnson, Negro Leagues player of the 1930s*[1]

The seven-member Hall of Fame induction class of 1999 was one of the most diverse in the institution's history. Honored that day were recently retired stars George Brett, Robin Yount, and Nolan Ryan, umpire Nestor Chylak, 19th-century manager Frank Selee, 1960s-era slugger Orlando Cepeda, and a legendary pitcher of pre-integration African American baseball named Smokey Joe Williams.

Perhaps it was fitting that Joe Williams and Nolan Ryan entered the Hall together. Both were tall, lanky fastball pitchers from Texas who were justly famous for their strikeout totals, their no-hitters (Ryan threw seven of them, while Williams reportedly tossed many more), and their longevity. However, the contrast between the two was apparent on the day of the induction ceremony in Cooperstown. Ryan was cheered on by dozens of family members, thousands of fans, and even by former Texas Rangers owner and future President of the United States, George W. Bush. Williams, on the other hand, was represented by no one. He and his wife Beatrice had no children, and as he had been dead for 48 years, the Hall was unable to locate any surviving relatives.

To even the most informed observers, Smokey Joe Williams is a barely recognizable name from baseball's distant past, but a look at his accomplishments reveals much more. He was almost unanimously considered the best African American pitcher of his era, and many regard him as the greatest of all.

Knowledge of Joe's early life is sketchy. He was born in Seguin, Texas, a town in Guadalupe County about 40 miles south of Austin and 20 miles east of San Antonio. James, his father, was African American, and his mother Lettie was of Indian heritage, possibly Choctaw. Minority children were not

Smokey Joe Williams in uniform for the New York Lincoln Giants, around 1915. (National Baseball Hall of Fame Library, Cooperstown, N.Y.)

required to have birth certificates in Texas at the time, but most sources say that Joe was born on April 6, 1886 (though others give the year as 1885). One of the few known facts about the young Joe Williams is that he dreamed of becoming a baseball player. "Someone gave me a baseball at an early age," said Joe in a rare interview near the end of his life, "and it was my constant companion for a long time. I carried it in my pocket and slept with it under my pillow. I always wanted to pitch."[2]

Joe grew to about six feet and five inches tall in young adulthood. With dark skin and Native American facial features, he weighed over 200 pounds and towered over most of his opponents on the Texas sandlots. By age 19 he was playing for semipro teams in the San Antonio area, where he reportedly compiled a record of 28 wins and only four defeats in 1905. He spent the following year in Austin, returning to San Antonio in 1907 as a member of the Black Bronchos, the fastest black team in the city. He won 20 or more games and spent some time in the outfield. Joe may already have earned the name "Cyclone" by this time, for his fastball was the talk of the Texas semipro baseball scene. He was credited with a 20–2 record in 1908 and split the 1909 campaign between San Antonio and Birmingham, Alabama, racking up a 32–8 mark. Though he left Birmingham late in 1909 and returned to San Antonio, reportedly due to homesickness, he spent the winter of 1909–10 in California with a Los Angeles-based club called the Trilbys.

Joe Williams was the epitome of the power pitcher. He threw his fastball with an easy overhand motion, but the ball fairly jumped out of his hand as he used his tall body and long arms to generate a tremendous amount of force behind it. "He threw overhanded," said Arthur Hardy, who faced him in 1908 while a member of the Giants of Kansas City, Kansas, "and he had a terrific drop ball, and you never could tell whether the ball was going to drop or whether it was his fastball because he threw them both with the same motion—and that ball looked like a pea coming up there."[3] Joe also studied the various tricks of the pitching trade. He always denied throwing a spitball, which was legal at the time, but learned to use tobacco juice to darken the ball, making it difficult for the batters to see. Later in his career, a reporter asked if he used the emery (sandpaper) ball. "Did I use the emery ball?" Joe said with a smile. "I'd have won every game." Joe explained that he stuck to his fastball and curve, "except when the other guy started using tricks."[4]

Joe was ready for the top level of black baseball in 1910, and his opportunity came when the Leland Giants of Chicago took a spring training tour through Texas. They soon faced the San Antonio Black Bronchos, with Cyclone Joe Williams on the mound. Frank Leland was the founder and primary owner of the club, but the field manager was Andrew (Rube) Foster, a great right-handed pitcher who became the leading entrepreneur of black baseball history. Leland and Foster had assembled the top African American ballclub in the nation, with legendary players such as Grant (Home Run) Johnson and Pete

Hill in the lineup. The Leland Giants had won the tough Chicago City League pennant for several years running, defeating some of the leading semipro clubs in the Midwest (including one headed by Cap Anson, the old Chicago White Stockings first baseman and manager). They looked forward to playing a few easy games in Texas to get in condition for the upcoming 1910 season.

The San Antonio ballclub would have been easy pickings for the fabled Leland Giants, had anyone other than Joe Williams been on the mound that day. Joe blanked the Leland Giants from one inning to the next as the Chicagoans spent the entire afternoon trying, and failing, to catch up to the Williams fastball. Joe and the Bronchos won the game by a score of 3–0, and Foster later sought out the 24-year-old pitcher. "Slow down a little there," remarked Foster.

"Do you really want me to throw hard?" asked Williams. "If I really throw hard, they won't see it at all."

"What's your name, boy?" demanded Foster.

"Just call me Cyclone," said Joe. Foster quickly signed Williams to a contract and brought him north to play in Chicago.[5]

Frank Leland was equally impressed with Foster's new pitching discovery, and hyped the young man's appearance to the Chicago newspapers. "If you have ever witnessed the speed of a pebble in a storm," claimed Leland, "you have not even seen the speed possessed by this wonderful Texan Giant. He is the king of all pitchers hailing from the Lone Star State and you have but to see him once to exclaim, that's a-plenty."[6]

However, a dispute between Leland and his financial backers caused him to lose control of his team. Shortly thereafter, he formed a rival unit called the Chicago Giants. Joe Williams spent the 1910 campaign with the Chicago Giants, where he gained experience while Foster's nine, which still employed the name Leland Giants, dominated their competition, compiling an incredible 123–6 mark against all comers in 1910. Foster dropped the Leland name the following year, renaming his club the Chicago American Giants. Joe remained with the Chicago Giants in 1911, then pitched again in California that winter and reportedly struck out 19 men in a single game.

Joe did not remain long in Chicago, for during this time a white promoter named Jess McMahon created a team in New York, the Lincoln Giants, and signed several stars away from Foster. With John Henry (Pop) Lloyd, Louis Santop, Bruce Petway, and other greats, the Lincoln Giants quickly became one of the leading teams in the East. Late in 1911, McMahon offered Joe Williams $105 per month to leave Chicago and join the Lincoln Giants. That was a fine salary for the time, as the other Lincoln Giants earned a reported $40 to $75 per month, so Joe followed the money to New York. He shared the pitching chores with "Cannonball Dick" Redding, an illiterate Georgian who also possessed an outstanding fastball. He and Joe would become teammates and, later, rivals for the next two decades.

During the winter of 1911–12, Joe played in Cuba, where he won 10 of his 17 decisions against tough competition. He then accompanied Foster's American Giants on a tour of the western states the following spring, and legend says that "Cyclone Joe" went 9–1 and defeated every Pacific Coast League team except Portland. His reputation grew as he proved his talent against major leaguers, as shown on October 27, 1912 when he shut out an all-star team headed by Larry Doyle of the New York Giants on a four-hitter, winning by a 6–0 score. Two weeks later he defeated a team made up mostly of New York Highlanders (later called the Yankees) with another four-hit shutout. Joe took another trip to Cuba that winter, where he and Cannonball Dick Redding joined the Fé team and pitched it to the Cuban Winter League title, with Redding posting a 7–2 log and Williams a 9–5 mark.

"Cyclone Joe" and "Cannonball Dick" comprised the greatest one-two punch in segregated baseball history, leading the Lincoln Giants to the national black championship in 1912 and 1913. Joe and the Lincoln Giants finished the 1913 season by playing five games against white major leaguers, winning four of them. On September 28 Joe struck out 15 men while defeating former New York Giant Mike Donlin and his All-Leaguers on a four-hitter, then split two games against another All-Star team led by Earle Mack, son of the fabled Athletics manager Connie Mack. Williams lost a 1–0 contest when Mack threw out Pop Lloyd at the plate in the ninth inning, but soon afterward Joe beat Mack's club by a 7–3 score, striking out 14. A week later, Joe took on a future Hall of Famer, Chief Bender of the Athletics, throwing a three-hitter for a 2–1 win.

Perhaps Joe's most dynamic victory against white competition came in a duel with Grover Cleveland Alexander, then the top pitcher in the National League, and the Philadelphia Phillies on October 5, 1913. At Olympic Field in New York, Williams allowed the Phillies eight hits and struck out nine men, while Alexander, who posted 22 wins that season, gave up 12 hits and fanned six. Williams defeated the future 300-game winner by a 9–2 score, belting a homer and scoring two runs himself. That same day, another black team, the Mohawk Giants, beat an all-star aggregation led by Washington's Walter Johnson in Schenectady, New York. The *New York Age* declared that the twin defeats of white teams by black ones "set the fans to arguing as to the relative strength of some of our colored baseball teams as compared with the big league teams."[7] On March 27, 1914, while pitching for the Chicago American Giants on another spring tour, Joe no-hit the Portland Beavers of the Pacific Coast League.

Though Redding, too, was a gifted pitcher, having once struck out 24 men in a nine-inning game and 15 in a six-inning contest, Williams gradually supplanted him as the leading hurler for the Lincoln Giants. As Negro League pitcher Bill Holland told historian John Holway, "[Joe] didn't have a lot of different stuff, but he had a terrific fastball and perfect control. If he caught you swinging at a ball down here at the knees, he'd raise it up to the belt, then up to the letters, pitch you outside, things like that." Another pitcher, Sam Streeter, claimed that Joe regularly wore out his catchers. "They talk about Satchel [Paige] and them throwing hard," said Streeter, "but I think Joe threw harder. It used to take two catchers to hold him. By the time the fifth inning was over, the catcher's hand would be all swollen. He'd have to have another catcher back there the rest of the game."[8]

Some wags dubbed Cyclone Joe Williams "the black Walter Johnson," and the similarities between the two men were striking. Both were tall and lanky with noticeably long arms. They were quiet individuals who never argued with the umpires, as well as workhorses who threw well over 300 innings per year during the regular season, then pitched many more contests every October and November. Each threw a fastball that had batters reaching for superlatives, while some claimed that neither man bothered to throw a curveball because their fastballs were so overpowering. Williams was highly popular with black fans, but so, surprisingly, was Johnson. "Sadie and I loved Walter Johnson," said Elizabeth Delany, an African American who wrote a best-selling memoir with her sister after both passed their 100th birthdays. "If he was pitching in New York, we were there!"[9]

Johnson was the fastest pitcher in white baseball, while Williams was the swiftest in the African American game, and controversy arose over who was faster. Sportswriter Sam Lacy saw both men pitch and stated that they were equal in speed, while Chester (Red) Hoff, a former New York Yankee who faced Johnson in the American League and Williams in semipro play, said that Williams "could throw almost as hard" as Johnson. The most reliable testimony comes from Robert Berman, a New York semipro catcher who batted against Williams many times, then joined the Senators briefly in 1918 as a teammate of Johnson. He said that Johnson was faster than Williams, but Williams was faster than anyone else. "It gripes me when the papers claim that Satchel Paige was the fastest black pitcher who ever lived," he told historian John Holway. "Smokey Joe Williams, in my mind, was the fastest."[10]

Did Johnson and Williams ever face each other on the playing field? Legend has it that Williams defeated Johnson by a 1–0 score sometime in the late 1910s, but no box score of such a contest has ever been discovered. Henry Thomas, Johnson's biographer (and grandson), could find no documentation, and doubts that it ever occurred. Johnson kept voluminous scrapbooks of his career, which Thomas scoured for information, and one would think that such a memorable game would have been included therein. Cyclone Joe, nonetheless, became famous for his numerous victories against all-white aggregations, both major and minor leaguers, in exhibition play. "It seems like pitching against the major leaguers brought out the best in him," said Negro Leagues historian James A. Riley. "Against the semipro teams he could coast, scatter a few hits and still strike out 10 or 15."[11]

He was already becoming a legendary figure. An oft-repeated claim that

Joe posted a 41–3 record in 1914 may be exaggerated, but not enough statistical evidence exists to prove or disprove the assertion. A broken arm, and later a cracked wrist, slowed Joe down the following year, but by fall he put the injuries behind him and resumed his dominance of white teams. He defeated Buffalo of the Federal League, then considered a major circuit, by a 3–0 score, then pitched several contests against the New York Giants and Philadelphia Phillies. Information on many of these games is hard to unearth, since the mainly white newspapers rarely mentioned them, but all appeared to be close, well-pitched games, and the legend of Cyclone Joe Williams continued to grow. Ty Cobb, star of the Detroit Tigers, was quoted as saying that Joe would be a certain 30-game winner if he pitched in the major leagues.

One of Joe's better-documented pitching performances came on October 17, 1915 against the National League champion Philadelphia Phillies. The Phillies, vanquished by the Boston Red Sox in the World Series a week earlier, were barnstorming through the Eastern Seaboard and arrived at Olympic Field in New York to take on the Lincoln Giants. Joe Williams faced George Chalmers, an eight-game winner for the Phillies that season. Both men proceeded to mow the batters down for seven innings of scoreless baseball. The Lincoln Giants finally scored in the eighth to take a 1–0 lead, but the Phillies nearly won it in the ninth when Bert Niehoff led off with a single and Joe Judge, a Washington Senator filling in at first base, blasted one of Cyclone Joe's pitches to deep center field.

The ball ricocheted off the front of the bleachers and bounded high into the air, but the scoreboard operator caught it in the stands and threw it in to the center fielder. Niehoff had crossed the plate, but the Lincoln Giants protested that Judge's hit should be ruled a ground-rule double and not a homer. The umpire agreed, sending Niehoff back to third and keeping the score at 1–0. The Lincoln Giants then threw Niehoff out at the plate on a grounder, and Joe retired the last two batters to preserve a 1–0 win. He struck out 10 Phillies, walked three, and allowed only five hits.

His most famous performance is so shrouded in mystery that it may never have actually happened. The story goes that in 1917, or perhaps in 1919, Joe and the Lincoln Giants faced the National League New York Giants in an historic contest. Williams dominated so thoroughly that day, they say, that he pitched a 10-inning no-hitter in which he struck out 20 major leaguers. Joe lost the game by a 1–0 score on an error, but afterward outfielder Ross Youngs clapped him on the back. "Hell of a game, Smokey," chirped Youngs, giving Joe Williams a new nickname that lasted for the rest of the pitcher's life. No box score or newspaper clipping of this game has ever been found. This oft-repeated tale may be an amalgam of several other outstanding pitching performances, but the legend persists to this day.

In truth, the nickname Smokey probably came from another famous fastball pitcher, Smokey Joe Wood, who won 34 games, 16 of them in succession, for the Boston Red Sox in 1912. Wood, a fine hitter like Williams, briefly rivaled Walter Johnson as the speed king of major league baseball before his arm gave out in 1913, bringing his pitching career to an end. Smokey Joe Williams, however, proved much more durable than Smokey Joe Wood. The sore-armed Wood managed to extend his career by playing the outfield and pinch-hitting, but Williams continued to defeat all comers, white and black, for many years after Wood's retirement from the game.

The Lincoln Giants enjoyed a healthy rivalry with Rube Foster's Chicago American Giants, and the two teams played many hard-fought games to determine the "national colored championship." The Lincoln Giants visited Chicago at least once a year, and Foster in turn brought his club to New York on a regular basis. During the late 1910s the teams played each other in Florida during the spring months, and on February 27, 1918 Joe pitched a masterful one-hit shutout against the American Giants in Palm Beach to kick off the black baseball season. Joe frequently lived in Florida over the winter, working as a waiter or bartender at a resort hotel while also playing for hotel-sponsored baseball teams.

Joe's main pitching rival during this era was Dick Redding, a former teammate who joined the New York Lincoln Stars in 1915 and played many hard-fought games against Williams and the Lincoln Giants. Joe gained the upper hand on May 8, 1919, when he opened the campaign with a 1–0 no-hitter against Redding and his new club, the Brooklyn Royal Giants. Redding allowed only two singles of his own that day, and Joe later regarded that performance as one of the greatest thrills of his career. Redding apparently still harbored resentment from earlier in the decade, when Joe took over as the pitching star of the Lincoln Giants, and when a photographer asked the two pitchers to pose, they refused to shake hands. "I'll stand beside him," offered Redding. "I don't want to shake his hand," replied Joe.[12] Redding got his revenge on July 17, 1920, by defeating Joe and the Lincoln Giants 5–0 in one of the first black baseball games ever held at Ebbets Field in Brooklyn.

The Jazz Age was in full swing during the early 1920s, and Joe Williams, who came from a small town on the Texas prairie, was dazzled by the night life. He loved the theaters and vaudeville houses of Harlem, becoming something of a "stage-door Johnny" and leaving flowers and gifts for showgirls who caught his eye. In 1922 Joe married one such chorine named Beatrice, who had performed in several all-black musical revues on Broadway. Unlike many contemporary pairings between athletes and entertainers, this union was a successful one that lasted for the rest of Joe's life.

Joe was a quiet, soft-spoken man who gave off an air of intelligence and dignity, not unlike Walter Johnson, and perhaps it was inevitable that the Lincoln Giants would appoint him manager of the team in 1922. He was already earning the highest salary on the squad, and his status as the premier pitcher in the African American game gave him the authority he needed to direct the club. In 1923 the Lincoln Giants gave up their independent status and joined the Eastern Colored League, but finished a disappointing sixth in an eight-team circuit.

Though African American baseball stars regularly bounced from team to team during this era, Williams spent 12 consecutive seasons with the Lincoln Giants. Still considered one of black baseball's greatest stars, he was stunned when the team embarked on a youth movement and released him at the conclusion of the 1923 season. He spent 1924 with the Brooklyn Royal Giants, where he reportedly struck out 25 men in a 12-inning game against a strong white semipro team, the Brooklyn Bushwicks. "It didn't matter if he was playing minor-leaguers, major-leaguers, semipros or the players from the black leagues," said historian Phil Dixon. "He just struck everybody out."[13] Managed by Joe's old rival, Cannonball Dick Redding, the Royal Giants scuffled all year as Joe won only three of his seven decisions in league play.

In 1925 Smokey Joe signed with the Homestead Grays, perhaps the leading independent (non-league) black team in the eastern part of the country. Based in Homestead, Pennsylvania, near Pittsburgh, they played many of their games at Forbes Field when the Pirates of the National League were on the road (though black players were not allowed to use the locker rooms). Owned and operated by promoter W. Cumberland (Cum) Posey, the Grays played more than 100 games a year against white and black teams alike, piling up prodigious records and beating all challengers. Posey regularly raided Negro National League clubs for talent in his quest to build the most powerful all-black team in the east, and the acquisition of Smokey Joe Williams cemented Homestead's dominance. The Grays, with Joe, Charles (Lefty) Williams, and Sam Streeter sharing pitching duties, compiled a 43-game winning streak in 1926 and reportedly won 140 of their 153 decisions.

Joe Williams barely slowed down after passing his 40th birthday. He pitched for the Grays against a white All-Star team on October 8, 1927, winning a three-hit shutout against a lineup that included American League batting champions Harry Heilmann and Heinie Manush, both of the Detroit Tigers. In 1928 Smokey Joe no-hit an Akron semipro club and, later that year, met an All-Star team that featured Heilmann and Philadelphia A's slugger Jimmie Foxx in Sharon, Pennsylvania. Joe held Foxx to a single in four trips to the plate as the Grays defeated the All-Stars 8 to 4. "He played his best in those games," said James A. Riley. "It was like he was proving to himself what he would have done if he'd been allowed [to play in the majors]."[14]

The Grays joined the Negro American League for the 1929 season, and the 43-year-old Joe Williams went 8–2 in league play as the team finished in third place. The circuit folded at season's end, with the Grays returning to independent play for the 1930 campaign. To strengthen the team, Cum Posey signed Oscar Charleston, the best center fielder in the black game. In mid-season he discovered a rawboned 19-year-old catcher named Josh Gibson, who soon became the greatest home-run hitter in black baseball history. Gibson bashed a reported 72 homers in 1931 as the Grays retained their position on top of the black baseball world, winning 136 games and dropping only 17.

One of Homestead's most famous games took place in Kansas City on August 7, 1930, when the 44-year-old Joe Williams faced the Kansas City Monarch ace, Chet Brewer, under the lights. The Kansas City team owned a portable lighting system, which enabled them to play night games several years before the majors, and the lights increased attendance and profit margins for the Monarchs during the Depression. However, artificial illumination was then in its infancy, and the Monarch system was not very good. Night games usually turned into pitching duels, especially since spitballs, emery balls, and the like were still legal at the time in the African American baseball world. When Williams and the Grays opposed Brewer and the Monarchs on that Thursday evening in August, the two pitchers made history.

Brewer was notorious for cutting the surface of the baseball to make it dip and sail in all directions, and when Grays manager William (Judy) Johnson complained about the practice, the umpire ignored him. Johnson then ordered Joe to hit the first Monarch batter. Joe did so, and Johnson resumed the argument. "See, ump?" said the manager. "Brewer's been cutting the ball, and now Joe doesn't know where he's throwing it!" The arbiter refused to intervene, so Brewer and Williams both took advantage of the poor lighting and dominated the batters, inning after inning. Joe began throwing with a sidearm delivery as the game wore on, frightening the Monarch batters who could barely see the ball on its way to the plate. Neither side scored in the first 11 frames as Williams and Brewer mowed down their opponents. "The outfielders were standing with their hands in their pockets," recalled Johnson years later.[15]

The Grays finally broke through in the 12th, when Oscar Charleston walked and scored on a hit by Chaney White. Joe set the Monarchs down in the bottom of the inning for a 1–0 win, completing a 12-inning one-hit shutout while striking out the incredible total of 27 men. Brewer was no slouch either that day, fanning 10 in a row from the seventh to the tenth and finishing with 19 strikeouts of his own.

By 1930, Smokey Joe Williams had been pitching for 25 years and had already assumed legendary status. He had played so well for so long that he took to exaggerating his age, telling reporters that he was born in the mid-1870s and had been pitching non-stop since 1890 or so. The Grays billed him as the "ageless wonder" many years before Satchel Paige followed the same script by claiming to be much older than he really was. Some news reports of Joe's 27-strikeout game referred to him as the 57-year-old marvel of the black baseball world. He was 44 years old, not 57, but his performance at an advanced baseball age is still remarkable. "Throwing aspirin tablets at that age!" said sportswriter Ric Roberts. "... He was still throwing the ball out of sight. Just changing the size of the ball! He pitched as long as Paige did. A power pitcher. He was just absolutely magnificent!"[16]

Like Nolan Ryan many years later, Joe Williams kept throwing his outstanding fastball well beyond his 40th birthday. With Oscar Charleston and Jud Wilson in the outfield and Josh Gibson behind the plate, Joe helped the Grays defeat the Lincoln Giants in a post-season series for the 1930 black baseball championship. After another good season the following year, the 45-year-old Joe and the Grays defeated the Kansas City Monarchs for the 1931 title. However, black baseball suffered dearly during the Depression, and the high-salaried Williams drew his release from the Grays in 1932, presumably for financial reasons. Posey placed Joe on a new team, the Detroit Wolves of the East-West League, but the new circuit failed to complete the campaign, and Joe's career appeared to be over after 28 seasons. He pitched two final exhibitions against white teams that fall, both of which ended in losses. Joe dropped a 7–6 decision to Lefty Grove and the Philadelphia Athletics, and lost by a 20–8 score to "Casey Stengel's Stars" with Fred Frankhouse of the Boston Braves on the mound.

He returned to his home in New York and obtained a job as a bartender at the Harlem Grill on Lenox Avenue in Manhattan, though he still pitched every now and then over the next few summers. In 1934 Joe rejoined the Homestead Grays as a part-time pitcher and gate attraction, mostly playing exhibition games in small towns where people still wanted to see the great Smokey Joe Williams. Nearing the age of 50, Joe could still beat most semipro and town teams. Josh Johnson, a young reserve catcher with the Grays, recalled that Joe helped him learn the hitters and call the correct pitches. Johnson said that Williams would never shake off a sign, lest the fans get the idea that the rookie catcher did not know what he was doing. "You just go ahead and call your game," said Williams. "If I don't agree with [the call], I won't toe the rubber." When Joe finally agreed with the catcher's selection, he would take his position and pitch. "That helped me over a lot of humps," said Johnson.[17]

The Grays celebrated "Smokey Joe Williams Day" at Pittsburgh's Forbes Field on August 5, 1934, and the fans watched Joe pitch two shutout innings against a semipro team from Indiana. Williams made his final pitching appearance in a 1938 old-timer's game, losing 5–0 to the 49-year-old Dick Redding (according to historian John Holway), and eventually retired to his bartending job in Harlem. He mixed drinks, talked baseball, and signed autographs for his many fans. Despite his naturally quiet nature, Joe was successful in his new career. "He was very quiet, didn't say much," said his wife Beatrice Williams, "unless you got him on baseball. Then he didn't know when to stop."[18]

Joe was also a fine judge of talent. In 1934 Walter (Buck) Leonard, a 27-year-old first baseman from North Carolina, struck up a conversation with Joe at the Harlem Grill. Williams, who had seen Leonard play the year before for the Brooklyn Royal Giants, asked, "Why don't you get on a good team?"

Williams contacted Cum Posey and talked him into signing Leonard, who played first base for the Grays for the next 17 seasons. In 1972, Buck Leonard, the "black Lou Gehrig," and Josh Gibson became the second and third Negro League players inducted into the Hall of Fame.

Baseball integration finally became a reality in 1947, when Joe Williams was in his sixties. According to historian Robert Smith, Joe sometimes joked that he did not play in the majors because his hair was "too curly," though the injustice of the color line must have rankled such a talented performer. However, Joe professed no bitterness that others had received the opportunity to play in the major leagues while he was too old to do so. "But there were many Negro League players just as good as them, they just never had a chance to prove their greatness," he said. "The important thing is that the long fight is over. I praise the Lord I've lived to see the day." Joe was not completely forgotten, as he was honored by the New York Giants before a Sunday afternoon game during the 1950 season, when the 64-year-old pitcher was in failing health. "My heart is weak now," said Joe to the media. "I've got to ride elevators. No more bouncing up and down stairs."[19]

Joe Williams died in New York on February 25, 1951, and was buried at Lincoln Cemetery in Suitland, Maryland. His passing prompted sports editor Joe Bostic of the Harlem newspaper *People's Voice* to be the first to advocate the addition of Negro League stars to the Hall of Fame in Cooperstown. Bostic wrote a column in March of 1951 that read, in part:

... The immortal Cyclone Joe Williams passed away some three or four weeks ago and fully nine-tenths of the baseball fans of the country knew nothing about it. Ask any informed baseball authority or any pro who had to bat against the man and you'll be told quickly that the Cyclone could throw with any man who ever tossed the little round pellet plateward. Still, despite this great talent, the present Jim Crow setup at Cooperstown can't accommodate Mr. Williams' name even though he were nominated. This is an injustice that cries to be wiped out.[20]

In 1952, a leading African American newspaper, the *Pittsburgh Courier*, conducted a poll of knowledgeable baseball writers and other experts to rank the greatest black players of all time at each position. Joe Williams edged Satchel Paige, 20 votes to 19, for the top spot among pitchers. Despite this honor, Joe was overlooked by the Hall of Fame's Committee on the Negro Leagues, which selected nine men to the Cooperstown shrine between 1971 and 1977. On March 2, 1999, nearly half a century after his death, Smokey Joe Williams was finally elected to the Hall of Fame by the Veterans Committee.

Bill James, in his *New Historical Baseball Abstract*, ranked the top 100 players of all time at each position and proclaimed Walter Johnson the greatest pitcher in baseball history. James did not include Negro Leaguers in his ratings, as he based his list on mathematical formulae derived from major league statistics, but Joe Williams, the "black Walter Johnson," certainly deserves a place near the top of the list. James' top five right-handed pitchers were Johnson, Grover Alexander, Cy Young, Tom Seaver, and Christy Mathewson. Smokey Joe Williams, who might have surpassed them all had he been allowed to play major league ball, fits comfortably in that elite company. He fully deserves his reputation as one of the greatest pitchers of all time, black or white.

15

Hilton Smith

> *"If I had to compare Hilton's stuff with somebody in the game today, I'd probably say [Roger] Clemens. It's not whether Hilton Smith has Clemens' stuff; I'd hope Clemens has Hilton Smith's kind of stuff. Good stuff is good stuff. Every era has outstanding pitchers, and Hilton Smith was right at the top in his era."*
> —Buck O'Neil, 2001[1]

When one thinks of the Negro Leagues, the name of Satchel Paige usually comes immediately to mind. The talented Paige played his first Negro League game in 1927 and used his incredible fastball, pinpoint control, and personal magnetism to establish himself as the greatest pitcher and biggest drawing card of segregated ball. After moving from team to team during the late 1930s, Paige joined the powerful Kansas City Monarchs in 1940, and wherever they played for the next eight seasons, the fans clamored to see Paige.

No hurler, not even the great Satchel Paige, could pitch every day, but the Monarchs did not want to leave their biggest gate attraction on the bench and disappoint their fans. The solution was simple. The team would send Paige out to pitch the first three innings, and then another great right-handed pitcher, Hilton Smith, would come in to finish the game. Together they formed a nearly unbeatable pitching tandem which some called "Paige/Smith" as if the two men were one. Paige, a born showman who enjoyed clowning for the fans, received the lion's share of the press attention, while Hilton Smith did his job quietly and efficiently, using his devastating curveball to great effect. "I just took my baseball serious," said Smith many years later. "I just went out there to do a job."[2]

Though Paige was, deservedly, the first Negro Leaguer elected to the Baseball Hall of Fame in 1971, many of his contemporaries believed that the reticent Smith was as good, if not better, than the legendary Satchel. "You better get your runs early [against Paige]," warned Gene Benson of the Philadelphia Stars, "'cause you ain't gonna get any runs after Smith came in."[3] Lefty Bryant, a fellow Monarch, said, "Hilton never got the credit he deserved. We never told him, but Hilton was the best pitcher we had, including Satchel."[4] Despite such accolades, Smith was passed over for the Hall of Fame by the original Committee on the Negro Leagues, which named nine men to the Cooperstown shrine between 1971 and 1977. Not until 2001, 18 years after his death, did the Hall admit the man whom Negro Leagues historian John Holway has labeled "the invisible man of black baseball."

Hilton Smith in a Kansas City Monarchs uniform. (National Baseball Hall of Fame Library, Cooperstown, N.Y.)

Many reference books give Hilton Smith's year of birth as 1912, but information culled from the United States Census reveals that he was actually five years older than his "baseball age." He was born on February 27, 1907 in Giddings, Texas, the first of six children of John and Mattie Smith. The future ballplayer's birth name was Alvis, or Elvis, and he appeared in the census under that name in 1910 and again in 1920. In 1930, while still living with his parents and siblings in Giddings, the 23-year-old identified himself as Hilton Smith to the census enumerator, and used that name for the rest of his life.

Giddings, the county seat of Lee County in east-central Texas, lies about 50 miles from the state capital of Austin and about 100 miles from Houston and the Gulf of Mexico. Like almost every Southern city and town at the time, Giddings was strictly segregated. Whites and blacks lived in separate but parallel worlds, rarely interacting with each other. Hilton Smith played ball as a young man on town and sandlot teams, learning the game from his father and two uncles who were outstanding local players. He became a very good teenaged pitcher, and once threw a 2–0 victory against the local high school team.

John Smith was a schoolteacher (though he is identified in the federal census as a farm laborer) who believed in the value of an education. He sent Hilton to Prairie View A&M College, the oldest historically African American institution of higher learning in Texas. Hilton studied there for two years, but found his calling while playing for the college baseball team. He was a tall, stringy right-handed pitcher, six feet and three inches in height, and weighed about

170 pounds. Hilton had already drawn notice for his pitching on Giddings town teams. He pitched infrequently for the Prairie View A&M Panthers as a freshman, but performed so well in his sophomore year that he received offers from local semipro teams. In 1931, after defeating one of the leading teams in Texas, the Austin Black Senators, the club promptly signed him.

The Black Senators had proved to be a steppingstone to success in higher-level black leagues. Shortstop Willie Wells, who grew up in Austin, and catcher Raleigh (Biz) Mackey, among others, had started their careers there and gone on to star in the highest levels of segregated ball. Hilton Smith pitched against several barnstorming teams that came through central Texas, and all were impressed with the former college pitcher. Late in 1931, Hilton defeated the Chicago American Giants, one of the best teams in the Midwest, by a 5–4 score, and his reputation grew.

In the fall of 1931, he accompanied the Black Senators on a barnstorming trip through Mexico and saw relief action one day after the Mexican team batted the Austin starting pitcher out of the box. Hilton threw six solid innings, but performed poorly the next afternoon due to a tired arm. Four days later, however, a well-rested Smith pitched a complete game to win by a 5–1 count. Smith, always a good hitter, drove in all five runs himself. As Hilton put it years later, "I struck out so many of them, they didn't think I was the same pitcher." [5]

Later that year, the Monroe Monarchs of the Negro Southern League played a home-and-home series against Austin and experienced Hilton Smith first hand. "Monroe, Louisiana, had a real good Negro team then," recalled Smith. "... They came out to Austin and played us two games. They were talking about they heard of this little schoolboy up there and said, 'Well, we came to work him over.' But we had a great big ball park and I beat 'em 2–1. They couldn't believe it. They said, 'Well, this big old park, no wonder you won. When you come to Monroe'—Monroe had a small park—'we'll hit so many home runs off you ...' So I went to Monroe the following Sunday and beat 'em 4–2."[6] Soon afterward, Monroe signed Hilton to pitch for them the following year.

Hilton had a fine fastball, but the curve was his calling card. As a youngster, he practiced for hours, learning to throw the pitch by throwing curves against a fence until he could make the ball go where he wanted. Perhaps this constant practice in his youth caused his strong right arm to grow crooked, as the left arm of New York Giants star Carl Hubbell appeared to be oddly bent due to throwing the screwball. Teammates and opponents immediately noticed Hilton's unusual right arm, but marveled at the curveballs that he delivered with it. He used both overhand and sidearm deliveries, confusing batters with different speeds and arm angles.

The Monroe Monarchs belonged to the Negro Southern League, a loosely-knit circuit that played most of its games in Texas and Louisiana. It had served as a minor league for the key Midwestern and Eastern nines in the Negro National League, but when that circuit collapsed after the 1931 season many of the nation's best players joined the Negro Southern League. The talent level thus rose sharply in 1932, and Hilton Smith was tested against some of the greatest black players in the country. More importantly, he showcased his talent to players and managers from all over the nation. Hilton claimed in later years that he won 31 games without a loss that season, but whatever his true record may have been, he was clearly the star of the team.

Rosters in black baseball were more fluid than those in the white leagues, and in 1933, while still pitching for the Monroe Monarchs, Smith appeared for lower-level teams such as the New Orleans Crescent Stars and the New Orleans Black Creoles. The 1934 season found Hilton back with Monroe, and in 1935 he joined an integrated independent team in Bismarck, North Dakota, the Bismarck Churchills, for a salary of $150 per month. The Churchills already had a pitching star in Ted "Double Duty" Radcliffe, who also managed the team, so Hilton played the outfield most of the time and exhibited his skill as a hitter. That fall, Hilton and his Bismarck ballclub played in the National Baseball Congress tournament in Wichita, Kansas. Radcliffe did most of the pitching, but Hilton Smith batted .343 with four homers as Bismarck won the tournament. Remaining with the Churchills in 1936, Hilton joined the rotation and went 5–0, with four shutouts, in the NBC tourney, though the Churchills failed to repeat as champions.

Hilton Smith was a rising star, and set his sights on playing for the leading team in the Midwest, the Kansas City Monarchs. This ballclub, owned by a white entrepreneur named J. L. Wilkinson, was formed in 1920 as one of the original franchises of the Negro National League. It immediately became the most powerful team in the league, winning pennants or half-pennants in split season play five times during the 1920s and capturing the first Negro World Series in 1924. The Negro National League dissolved after the 1931 season, but the Monarchs played an independent schedule for several years afterward, retaining their dominant position in black baseball. "Everybody," said Hilton Smith years later, "everybody—anybody that played baseball wanted to play with the Monarchs."[7]

J. L. Wilkinson was a good judge of talent, and after watching Smith pitch for Bismarck in the National Baseball Congress tournament in 1936, he invited Hilton to join the Kansas City team for a barnstorming tour at the end of the year. Smith pitched against both white and black teams, impressing both Wilkinson and manager Andy Cooper enough to gain a contract for the following season. Hilton, at the age of 30 (though he told people he was only 25) was thrilled to be a member of the fabled Kansas City Monarchs. He and his wife Louise, whom he married in 1934, moved to Kansas City and established permanent residence there, eventually raising two sons named Hilton and DeMorris.

Life in segregated baseball was a difficult one, even for the most gifted players. Salaries were low compared to the white majors, usually between $100 and $200 per month, and many on the less prosperous teams did not receive all their wages. The crowds were often small, with the Depression in full swing, and many African Americans had little money to spend on ball games and other entertainments. As a consequence, the Monarchs played most of their games outside of Kansas City. They toured almost non-stop in those years, journeying across the United States as well as Canada and Mexico, and logging thousands of miles each season. The players subsisted on up to a dollar a day in meal money, which was not so easy to spend when many restaurants and stores refused service to black people. The playing schedule was tough as well, with a minimal roster of no more than 14 or 15 players putting on ten or more games in a week. Hilton Smith and the other Monarch pitchers were expected to complete their games, as the Kansas City staff usually contained only three or four hurlers.

Many black teams failed in these years, but the Monarchs found ways to survive. They carried their own portable lighting system, allowing them to play night games several years before the majors adopted the practice, which increased attendance. Exhibitions against major leaguers, which usually took place after the conclusion of the white World Series, drew large crowds and excited the Kansas City fans. In 1934 an All-Star team, headed by St. Louis Cardinals pitching star Dizzy Dean, faced the Monarchs in a short series that drew from 14,000 to 20,000 fans per game. These contests not only helped to turn a small profit for the season, but also showcased the talents of black players against their major league counterparts.

The Monarchs returned to league play in 1937, joining the newly-formed Negro American League, and immediately dominated that circuit as thoroughly as they had controlled the rival league a decade earlier. Kansas City boasted some of the greatest players in black baseball, including such future Hall of Famers as shortstop Willard Brown, pitcher Bullet Joe Rogan, and pitcher-manager Andy Cooper. At second base was Newt Allen, a fixture with the team since 1923 and perhaps the best in the game at his position. It was a solid ballclub, and the Monarchs won the first half of the split-season pennant race in the Negro American League that year. Hilton, an NAL rookie, announced his arrival on May 15 with a no-hitter against the powerful Chicago American Giants. Some sources credit Smith with a perfect game that day, but newspaper reports say he allowed one walk. Hilton compiled a 6–4 record in league play, and the Monarchs defeated the Giants that fall for their first NAL pennant.

The greatest showcase for black baseball, beginning in 1933, was the East-West All-Star Game held annually at Comiskey Park in Chicago. Drawing between 20,000 and 50,000 fans each year, this contest was the highlight of the season, surpassing even the pennant races and (later on) the Negro World

Series in prestige. During the 1930s, the players did not receive compensation for playing the game, aside from expenses, as selection to the contest was reward enough. Hilton Smith was the starting pitcher for the West in the 1937 game, losing by a 7–2 score, but in 1938 he was the victor in a 5–4 contest. Hilton was named to the All-Star team in six consecutive seasons from 1937 to 1942.

Baseball was nearly a year-round occupation for African American ballplayers of that era, and Hilton sharpened his skills in exhibition and Latin American play after the 1937 season. That October, he pitched against a team of stars from the white major leagues, led by Bob Feller of the Indians and Johnny Mize of the Cardinals. Hilton won all three games he pitched in the seven game series, holding Mize hitless and prompting Feller to remark that he was a better pitcher than the legendary Satchel Paige. Hilton then traveled to Cuba, where he posted a 6–3 record for Marianao in the Cuban Winter League. With this experience under his belt, Hilton returned to the Monarchs in 1938 and went 12–2 in league play, leading the Negro American League in strikeouts.

The Memphis Red Sox won the 1938 NAL pennant, but Smith led Kansas City to the next four league championships in a row. "Hilton Smith was unbeatable there for a spell, from '38 to '42," said first baseman Buck O'Neil, who joined the Monarchs in 1938. "Unbeatable! He had more natural stuff, a good rising fastball and an excellent curveball with good control. My land! He would have been a 20-game winner in the major leagues with the stuff he had."[8] His reputation grew as he gained success, not only against other NAL teams, but also in exhibition play against white major league stars. Said O'Neil, "We played against an All-Star team the year Stan Musial came up, in 1941. Satchel Paige and Bob Feller pitched three innings. Musial hit a home run on Satchel on the roof of the stadium. But Musial and John Mize said they'd never seen a curve ball like Hilton's curve ball."[9]

"As fine of a pitcher as he was, Hilton also was a great gentleman," recalled Monte Irvin, who preceded Hilton to the Hall of Fame. "He had one of the finest curveballs I ever had the displeasure to try and hit. His curveball fell off the table. Sometimes you knew where it could be coming from, but you still couldn't hit it because it was that sharp. He was just as tough as Satchel was."[10] O'Neil concurred. "With that crooked right arm of his, he'd throw some kind of a curve ball. He had the other pitches to go with it, too. He'd change speeds, do everything a great pitcher is supposed to do."[11] Never a showman, Hilton was businesslike, reserved, and modest about his accomplishments. He was not as popular a gate attraction as the gregarious Satchel Paige, but by the late 1930s Hilton had surpassed Paige as the greatest pitcher in black baseball.

Paige, who pitched for the Homestead Grays during the late 1930s, had fallen on hard times. Traded to the Newark Eagles in 1938, he quit the team in a salary dispute and joined a team in Mexico, but suffered an arm injury so serious that his career appeared to be over. He pitched in only three games in 1938, winning one. He remained black baseball's biggest drawing card, but many observers doubted that Paige would ever take the mound again. Unlike Hilton Smith, a strong hitter who sometimes played the outfield, Paige was weak at the bat and unable to play any other position passably. In early 1939, still unable to throw, Paige traveled the country seeking a job as a coach or manager.

J. L. Wilkinson, the owner of the Monarchs, decided to gamble on Paige's eventual recovery. He signed Satchel (eventually working out a deal with Newark for his services) and placed him on the Monarch "B" team, an outfit that played in smaller towns throughout the Midwest and served as a farm team for the parent club. Paige manned first base and pitched every now and then, an inning at a time, getting by on change-ups and trick pitches until the pain in his arm grew too great to continue. Wilkinson hyped the "B" team as the "Satchel Paige All-Stars," but the most famous player in black baseball could barely perform throughout 1939 and most of 1940.

While Paige struggled to salvage his career, the Monarchs continued their winning ways with Smith, Chet Brewer, Connie Johnson, and others on the mound. Hilton was the star, reportedly compiling an all-around record of 25–2 in 1939 with an 8–2 mark in NAL play. On October 6, 1939, he and the Monarchs faced Paige and his All-Stars in Kansas City with Hilton defeating his more famous opponent by an 11–0 score. In 1940, Hilton went 21–4 against all comers, then spent the winter months in Mexico and posted a 5–3 mark for Torreon. Hilton was now at his peak. "I was to the place then that I could just do anything," he said later. "I felt that good. I thought I could go out there and get anybody out."[12]

Paige's arm suddenly improved late in the 1940 season, and while his legendary fastball never recovered all of its speed, his control was still as great as ever. He also learned a curveball and, from veteran outfielder James (Cool Papa) Bell, a devastating knuckleball. Fully recovered, Paige joined the main Monarchs squad for the 1941 campaign and, though Hilton Smith compiled perhaps his greatest season, Paige garnered almost all the headlines, thrusting Smith into the background. Though Smith, by his own recollection, went 25–1 in 1941 and 22–5 in 1942, Paige reclaimed his status as the biggest star in the game. "I played 12 years with the Kansas City Monarchs, 1937–48, and I won twenty or more games every year," said Smith sadly. "Not counting exhibitions, I won 161 league games and lost 22, but most people never heard of me. They've only heard of Satchel Paige. That's because I was Satchel's relief.... He'd go two or three innings. If there was a big crowd, and we had to win it, I'd go in there and save it. Then the next day I'd look in the paper and the headline would say, 'Satch and Monarchs Win Again.'"[13]

Though Hilton had been the Monarchs' star pitcher for several years prior to Paige's arrival, he receded farther and farther into the background. On August 24, 1941, the Monarchs faced the Newark Eagles before 25,000 people in Yankee Stadium. Paige pitched five innings and got the win, while Hilton finished the 6–1 victory with four shutout frames. Predictably, the papers lauded Paige and barely mentioned Smith. On October 5 of that year, Bob Feller's All-Stars scored four runs off Paige and defeated the Monarchs 4–1. Hilton barely rated a mention, though he allowed no runs and struck out six in his four innings of work. Someone once asked why Paige's pitching arm was straight while Smith's was crooked. "I'll tell you why," said Hilton. "Satchel pitched three [innings]—I pitched six!"[14]

Though Hilton resented his sudden fall from attention—"I guess it really hurt me. I tried to get away [from the Monarchs] but there wasn't anything I could do about it," he said later[15]—a performance in a relief role turned into what Hilton later called "one of my greatest thrills." On May 28, 1942, the Monarchs played Dizzy Dean's All-Stars in front of 29,000 people at Chicago's Wrigley Field. The sore-armed Dean had retired from National League play, but headlined a team of major leaguers that included such names as Cecil Travis, Zeke Bonura, and other stars who were headed for military service. Paige pitched the first five innings, leaving with a 1–1 score and bringing Hilton Smith into the game. Smith dominated the major leaguers, allowing only one hit in four innings and retiring Travis on a double play ball to end the game. Though Paige's photograph was featured prominently in newspaper accounts of the game the next day, Hilton was the winning pitcher as the Monarchs defeated the All-Stars by a 3–1 score.

Paige, to his credit, realized the unfairness of his ascension at Smith's expense. During the 1942 Negro World Series against the Homestead Grays, Paige won the first game in Washington on September 9 with relief help from Jack Matchett, and Hilton started the second contest at Forbes Field in Pittsburgh on September 10. Paige had not been expected to pitch, but he approached Smith before the game. "Hilton, you've been relieving me all this year," said Satchel. "Let me relieve you, just see what we can do."[16] Smith threw five shutout innings, and Paige finished up to complete the win. That was the famous game in which Paige reportedly walked the bases full in the seventh inning to bring Josh Gibson, the greatest slugger in black baseball, to the plate with the contest hanging in the balance. With the crowd roaring, Paige struck out Gibson in the most celebrated confrontation in Negro Leagues history. Once again, Hilton Smith got the win while Satchel Paige garnered the headlines.

Hilton hurt his arm in 1943 and played mostly at first base and the outfield for the next two seasons as the Monarchs, even with Paige pitching, finished out of the NAL pennant race. Though salaries for Negro League players had risen due to the prosperous wartime economy, travel restrictions and curbs on night baseball threatened to deprive the Monarchs and other teams of their usual

Hilton Smith's delivery. (National Baseball Hall of Fame Library, Cooperstown, N.Y.)

sources of revenue. The Monarchs began playing more games in Kansas City, where the team drew both black and white fans, especially when Satchel Paige was pitching. During the war years, the Monarchs regularly outdrew the minor-league Kansas City Blues, a farm club of the New York Yankees. However, so many Monarchs were called into military service that for much of the 1944 campaign, the team made do with a playing roster of only nine men. Hilton fell to 2–5 in league play in 1944, as the Monarchs finished with the worst record in the NAL.

Demands for the integration of major league baseball were growing louder and more insistent by this time, and in 1944 Hilton Smith played a small, but important, role in the process. During the latter part of that season, Jackie Robinson, a former college football and track star recently discharged from the Army, approached Smith and asked the veteran pitcher to speak with Monarchs co-owner J. L. Wilkinson about a tryout. Robinson's exploits as a four-sport star at UCLA were well-known, and he had already made a name for himself as one of the leading all-around athletes in the nation. Robinson was a potentially valuable commodity, and Wilkinson and co-owner Tom Baird offered the 26-year-old $400 per month to play shortstop for the Monarchs in 1945. Robinson accepted, batting .345 in 45 league games and earning a spot in the East-West All-Star game. Though Hilton had his reservations about Robinson's baseball talent ("Jackie's arm was weak at shortstop. Willie Wells was better than Jackie at that position," he stated), Robinson impressed general manager Branch Rickey of the Brooklyn Dodgers. In October 1945, Rickey signed Robinson to a contract with the Dodgers' Montreal farm team, breaking the decades-old color line in organized professional baseball.

While most of the baseball world applauded Robinson's signing, it proved a mixed blessing for black baseball in general. Rickey had not bothered to negotiate Robinson's release from the Monarchs, declaring that the Negro Leagues were "simply a booking agent's paradise. They are not leagues and have no right to expect organized ball to respect them." The Monarchs could hardly object to the signing, opening the door as it did for the eventual integration of the major leagues, so the team received nothing in return for its star player. "[Wilkinson] used to talk to me quite a bit," said Smith. "The onliest thing that ever hurt him, he said, in baseball was for them to take Jackie Robinson from him without him getting compensated anything."[17]

Even without Robinson, the Monarchs won the NAL pennant in 1946 as Hilton Smith went 5–2 and won a game in the Negro World Series that fall, though the Monarchs lost the championship to the Newark Eagles. At season's end, Smith barnstormed with Satchel Paige against a white all-star team led by Bob Feller, then traveled to South America and pitched the Vargas team to the Venezuelan Winter League pennant with an 8–5 record. On March 1, 1947, he threw five shutout innings for Vargas against the New York Yankees in Caracas, giving up only one hit, a single to Phil Rizzuto. At age 39, he was still the best curveball pitcher in black baseball. Though the Monarchs suffered at the gate in 1947, as black fans followed the exploits of Jackie Robinson, Larry Doby, and others in the newly-integrated majors, Hilton Smith continued his fine pitching with a 7–0 record.

Integration was a huge step forward for American society, but the signings of Robinson, Doby, and the rest accelerated the demise of the Negro Leagues. Such stars as Willard Brown, Satchel Paige, and Roy Campanella left the world of segregated baseball and, although only three major league clubs employed blacks in 1947 and 1948, the Rubicon had been crossed. The best African American players quickly abandoned the Negro Leagues, draining the talent pool and driving attendance down to a fraction of what it had been prior to integration. Several of the leading all-black teams folded in 1948, including the Homestead Grays and the New York Black Yankees, while the formerly prosperous Newark Eagles were sold to out-of-town businessmen. J. L. Wilkinson, too, recognized that black baseball was effectively finished. He sold his share of the Kansas City Monarchs in early 1948, severing his connection to the team after 28 years.

Hilton Smith dreamed of playing in the major leagues, as did most of his teammates, but by 1947 he was 40 years old and his time was past. "Had I been three or four years younger," Smith once proclaimed, "I probably would have been the first Negro signed in organized baseball. Satchel figured it was his age, just like me."[18] The Brooklyn Dodgers offered him a contract, but Hilton knew he would have to prove himself in the minors, where his pay would fall from the $800 per month he was getting from the Monarchs to half that amount in Triple-A ball. Also, the competition with younger pitchers would be fierce, as the Brooklyn team was well stocked with prospects such as fellow Negro Leaguers Don Newcombe and Dan Bankhead. "I felt that it was too long a shot," he said. "And I could feel myself that I was beginning to lose a little. And I had always prided myself [in knowing] when I see myself over the hill that I was going to retire, get out of baseball."[19]

Smith, like J. L. Wilkinson, knew that black baseball was dying. Negro League fans were so excited that Robinson, Doby, and others had finally gained entrance to the majors that they began following major league ball, ignoring the all-black game. "You could see it in '46, the first year Jackie went to Montreal," said Smith. "Then in '47 Negro baseball began to go back. All the people started to go Brooklynites, everybody who had never known anything about baseball. Even if we were playing here in Kansas City, everybody wanted to go over to St. Louis to see Jackie. So our league really began to go down, down, down."[20] When the 1948 season ended, the 41-year-old pitcher left the Kansas City Monarchs after 12 seasons.

He pitched briefly for an integrated independent team in Fulda, Minnesota in 1949, after which he was offered a job with Armco Steel in Kansas City. He remained in Kansas City for the rest of his life, working as a teacher, a baseball coach, and a foreman at the steel plant, while doing some scouting for the Chicago Cubs. During the next several years, he rarely talked about his baseball career; Don Motley, later the executive director of the Negro Leagues Museum in Kansas City, coached Hilton's two sons and remarked that the retired ballplayer "never came down and meddled like most fathers." Many of his neighbors and fellow worshipers at the church where he taught a Bible class had no idea that the soft-spoken, dignified older man had once been one of the biggest stars of segregated baseball.

Still, Hilton was proud of his accomplishments on the diamond, and after Satchel Paige was elected to the Hall of Fame in 1971, the old pitcher became convinced that he, too, merited induction. He became more forthcoming about his career as he approached his 70th year, giving interviews to historians and appearing in several books on segregated baseball. The Hall of Fame's Committee on the Negro Leagues disbanded after its 1977 election without naming Hilton Smith, so the great curveballer decided to take matters into his own hands. Much to his family's surprise, he spent many evenings sitting at his dining room table, writing letters to Hall officials and voters. He sent a collection of newspaper clippings to the museum in Cooperstown, even including a short autobiography. "I asked him, 'Why are you doing this?'" recalled Hilton's son DeMorris Smith. "I've always been like my father. Quiet. Reserved. Never made a fuss. I simply could not understand it. I suppose that my father knew he was dying."[21]

The Veterans Committee took over the responsibility for Negro League candidates after 1977, so Smith corresponded with members of this panel. He rarely, if ever, received a reply. He saw a glimmer of hope in 1981 when his old friend and Kansas City teammate Buck O'Neil was appointed to a place on the committee, but after Negro National League founder Rube Foster was elected that year, no more players from the era of segregated ball were enshrined during Hilton Smith's lifetime. Like so many old ballplayers, black and white, Hilton did not live to see his election to baseball's highest honor. He died in Kansas City on November 18, 1983, at the age of 76. Survived by his wife and two sons, he was buried at Mount Moriah Cemetery in that city, not far from the grave of another Hall of Fame pitcher, Charles (Kid) Nichols.

Interest in the Negro Leagues rose again during the 1990s, and beginning in 1995 the Veterans Committee, spurred on by O'Neil, took a fresh look at the qualifications of performers from the pre-integration era. From 1995 to 2001, the committee selected one Negro Leaguer per year, putting shortstop Willie Wells, pitchers Bill Foster, Joe Williams, Joe Rogan, and Leon Day, and slugger Turkey Stearnes into Cooperstown. Once again Hilton Smith had to wait his turn, but on March 6, 2001, he was finally elected to the Hall. "Well, he would be excited," said his widow Louise. "But he was a very quiet person, someone who just took life as it came. He just played baseball because he loved it so much."[22]

Hilton Smith may have been the "invisible man" of the Negro Leagues, but he compiled an enviable record. Though statistics from the era of segregated baseball are highly fragmentary, Smith's accepted won-lost record of 161–22 in league play ranks with the very best. He was one of the greatest pitchers of all time, black or white, and though he spent much of his career in the shadow of Satchel Paige, Hilton Smith genuinely earned a place next to his more famous teammate in Cooperstown.

16

Cristóbal Torriente

> "We have never given Torriente the credit he deserved. He did everything well, he fielded like a natural, threw in perfect form, he covered as much field as could be covered; as for batting, he left being good to being something extraordinary."
> —*Martin Dihigo*[1]

The Baseball Hall of Fame appointed its first Committee on the Negro Leagues in 1971. This panel elected nine men to the Cooperstown shrine over the next seven years, after which the responsibility for pre-integration ballplayers passed to the Committee on Veterans, which selected 11 more men between 1981 and 2001. Interest in the Negro Leagues increased markedly during this time, largely due to the nine-part documentary film *Baseball* by Ken Burns, and the valuable historical research of John Holway and others. This boom brought the names and exploits of many great players to public attention for the first time, and by the late 1990s, many experts believed that the stars of segregated ball were still underrepresented in the Hall of Fame.

To rectify this imbalance, the Hall of Fame board of directors met in 2001 to appoint a three-man screening committee that reviewed statistics, box scores, and newspaper accounts of African American baseball from 1860 to 1960. Armed with a $250,000 grant from Major League Baseball, this committee, assisted by more than 50 researchers, assembled a detailed history and statistical database of segregated baseball. The group used that research to draw up a preliminary list of 94 candidates for election to the Hall, then spent more time paring that list down to a more manageable number. In July 2005, a new 12-member panel was charged with identifying and selecting worthy candidates for enshrinement, and in November of that year, after four years of effort, this committee released its final ballot of 39 candidates.

In February 2006, the panel members and their non-voting chairman, former commissioner Fay Vincent, met in Tampa, Florida for two days and reviewed the qualifications of those 39 players and executives. With nine votes of the 12 committee members necessary for a finalist to gain election to the Hall of Fame, most observers figured that perhaps four or five names would

The 1920 Chicago American Giants. Cristóbal Torriente is in the back row, first from the left, while team manager and founder Rube Foster is in the middle of the back row. (National Baseball Hall of Fame Library, Cooperstown, N.Y.)

emerge from the meeting. Instead, the committee stunned the baseball world by anointing 17 new Hall of Famers. The choices included twelve players and five executives, all deceased, who participated either in the Negro Leagues or in segregated baseball before the founding of the first successful African American circuit, the Negro National League, in 1920.

Much of the controversy which ensued revolved around the committee's failure to elect outfielder Minnie Minoso and infielder Buck O'Neil, the only living candidates on the ballot. Additionally, the enshrinement of Newark Eagles co-owner Effa Manley as the first woman elected to the Hall was met with dismay by many. Some commentators reacted negatively to the news that two of the 17 new honorees, Manley and Kansas City Monarchs founder J. L. Wilkinson, were Caucasian, while others decried the selection of Alex Pompez, a gambler and racketeer who nonetheless played a major role in bringing Latin-American stars to the major leagues. The 17 honorees joined with relief pitcher Bruce Sutter, selected a few weeks earlier in the annual balloting of the Baseball Writers Association, to form the largest induction class by far in Cooperstown history.

One new Hall of Famer who drew scant attention was the Cuban-born Cristóbal Torriente, a power-hitting outfielder who played professional ball in Cuba and the United States from 1913 to 1932. Though Torriente was one of the great hitters of the Negro Leagues, having won a batting title in 1923 as well as leading the Chicago American Giants to three pennants, few American fans had heard of him. On the other hand, Torriente's exploits are legend in his homeland. Torriente, the "Cuban Babe Ruth," was elected to the Cuban Baseball Hall of Fame in 1939 as one of its ten charter members.

Cristóbal Torriente was born in Cienfuegos, Cuba, on November 16, 1893, though many sources list his birth year as 1895. Cienfuegos is a seaport on the southern side of the island, about 155 miles from Havana. It was, and still is, an agricultural center, and though little is known of Cristóbal Torriente's early life, one would guess that he, like many other Cuban ballplayers, worked in the sugar cane and tobacco fields during his youth. A strong, broad-shouldered young man, he joined the Cuban army as a teenager and was assigned to an artillery unit, mainly because he was strong enough to hoist the heavy equipment onto the mules. He played baseball for the artillery team, and in early 1913 joined the Havana Reds of the Cuban Winter League, batting .265 at the age of 19.[2] He impressed a promoter named Tinti Molina, who signed Torriente to play that summer for a traveling ballclub, the Cuban Stars. The Stars played all over the United States, challenging the leading semipro teams, both black and white, and winning most of their games.

Baseball was popular in Cuba, though during its rule of the island the Spanish colonial government tried to clamp down on the sport. As author Roberto González Echevarría explained, "Baseball was a sport played in defiance of Spanish authorities, who viewed this American invention as vaguely secessionist and dangerously violent because of the use of sticks."[3] Though the Spanish tried to ban baseball as early as 1869, the sport grew and prospered, receiving a major boost after the Spanish-American War of 1898 ended colonial rule. American baseball promoters had already discovered Cuba, and in 1891 the first barnstorming team from the States, an "All-American" club that included infielder John McGraw, played five games against Cuban clubs and won them all.

Cuban baseball was segregated in its early days, but revolution against the Spanish during the 1890s brought the races together in a common cause, and by 1900 blacks and whites played side by side in the Cuban Winter League. In 1908, the Cincinnati Reds came to the island and faced pitcher José Méndez, the "Black Diamond," who stunned the major leaguers with a 1–0 one-hitter, losing a perfect game with two out in the ninth. He followed that gem with another 14 innings of scoreless ball over the next two games. Méndez became a national hero, and the Cuban people took great pride in the successes of island stars who proved themselves against the American major leaguers.

Méndez, whose dark skin kept him from crossing the major league color line that existed until 1947, was the main pitcher for the Cuban Stars, but Cristóbal Torriente quickly became the team's leading hitter. Not yet 20 years old, Torriente had already grown into a powerfully built ballplayer. Like another great slugger, Babe Ruth, Torriente was a left-handed batter and thrower with a large torso balanced on slender legs, though at five feet and ten inches in height he stood four inches shorter than Ruth. Despite his build, he was a fast runner who covered great amounts of ground in center field while displaying a strong throwing arm. Torriente was also an accomplished pitcher, and although he threw left-handed, his skill and agility allowed him to put in time at third base and shortstop as needed. Promoters liked to keep traveling team rosters as light as possible, necessitating the presence of multi-position players, but the sight of Torriente at third or short was nonetheless unusual for the era.

Torriente was the prototypical five-tool player, though he was not known as a home run hitter. Neither Torriente nor anyone else hit many home runs in the huge Cuban ballparks of the time, but his power manifested itself in doubles and triples. He was a notorious bad-ball hitter, but walked often enough to have a high on-base percentage, and was fast enough to be a stolen base threat. Also skilled as a left-handed pitcher, Cristóbal was soon recognized as the best, and most complete, player on the island.

He moved to the Almendares Blues for the 1913–14 winter season and helped his new team claim the pennant, while he raised his average to .337. He won his first Cuban batting title the next year with a .387 mark, and in 1915–16 batted .403 and led the Cuban Winter League in hits, triples, home runs (with two) and stolen bases. Already celebrated as the greatest hitter in Cuba, Torriente did not play in the winter league again until 1919–20, when he won another batting title at .360 and led the circuit in doubles, triples, and stolen bases. He hit only one homer, but no one else managed to hit more, so he tied for the league lead in that category as well.

In the United States, Cristóbal played for the Cuban Stars during the summer and then, beginning in 1917, for a Kansas City-based team called All Nations which employed Cubans, American blacks, Mexicans, and Asians, along with a few white players. The talent level was high, as the Cuban José Méndez and the African American John Donaldson were the star pitchers; several of the whites on this club later performed in the major leagues. The All Nations ballclub, with Torriente supplying the power, was good enough to defeat the Chicago American Giants, one of the leading all-black teams in the Midwest, in 1917. All Nations disbanded in 1918 after several of its players were drafted into military service during World War I, but during their existence they were, as *Sporting Life* magazine described them, "an outfit that baseball sharps claim is good enough to give any major league club a nip-and-tuck battle, and prove it is possible for blacks and whites to play on one team."[4]

In 1919 Andrew (Rube) Foster, the greatest organizer of black baseball, signed Torriente to play for his Chicago American Giants, the ballclub that had dominated the sport in the Midwest since 1910. The American Giants already employed Oscar Charleston, the segregated game's leading center fielder, but Foster put Torriente in center and moved Charleston to left. Charleston and Torriente led a fearsome hitting attack, with Torriente hitting .280 for the American Giants in his first full season of play in segregated American ball. He also posted a 5–1 record on the mound as Foster's crew went 17–9 against top-level black competition.

Torriente's hitting statistics might have been more impressive had he not played his home games in South Side Park, which was often referred to as "the worst hitter's park in the world." The American Giants home field was a wooden facility that stood about four blocks from Comiskey Park, home of the American League White Sox. The Sox had played in South Side Park from 1901 to 1909, an era in which the team was called the "Hitless Wonders" even when they won the 1906 World Series. The park seated about 7,500 in 1920, with outfield fences so far from the plate that most home runs were of the inside-the-park variety. The park put a premium on defense, and Torriente utilized his outstanding speed to cover the huge outfield and make diving catches. His powerful arm allowed him to throw accurately to the plate from the deepest part of the outfield, which was another plus for the American Giants. Cristóbal's reputation was growing, and before long he would challenge Oscar Charleston as the leading outfielder in the non-white game.

Torriente was a jovial, fun-loving individual, by all accounts a larger-than-life personality much like the American slugging star Babe Ruth. He accented his uniform with a red bandana around his neck to remind himself of his first professional team, the Havana Reds. Torriente also wore bracelets on his wrists and shook them at the pitcher when he stood in the batter's box. "When he'd shake those bracelets," said one observer to historian John Holway, "look for the ball up against the fence; that's where he was going to hit it."[5]

He never really succeeded in mastering the English language. He disliked the American federal income tax requirement, and when he received his paycheck he'd remark in disgust, "The ducks got it. Me going back to Cuba this winter. Don't want the ducks to get my money." The "ducks" were deductions.[6] The outgoing Cristóbal was "a big, strong fellow, with a good disposition," said pitcher Bill Foster. "We'd say, 'Torriente, you gonna get 'em?' He'd say, 'Me get 'em!' And he would, too. He could get wood on the ball."[7]

Post-season tours of Cuba by American teams had been interrupted by World War I, but the Pittsburgh Pirates ventured to the island in October 1919 for a 14-game series against Torriente and a Cuban All-Star aggregation. The Pirates won eight contests, but Cristóbal impressed the Americans with a long home run against Leon Cadore on October 12. On the 27th, Torriente's double and single helped Cuban starter Adolfo Luque, who played in America for the Cincinnati Reds, defeat the Pirates by a 2–1 count, and on November 10, Cristóbal won the last game of the series with a sacrifice fly in the seventh inning. Another American team, led by major leaguers Wally Pipp, Milt Stock, and Jack Quinn, then arrived to challenge the Cubans. Torriente belted two homers against them, leading his countrymen to seven wins in ten games.

Rube Foster understood that the growth of black baseball would continue only within a structured format, so in 1920 he founded the Negro National League. This new circuit was designed to bring order from the chaos of barnstorming ballclubs which made their own schedules and raided other teams for players. Foster's American Giants ballclub was one of the cornerstone franchises of the 8-team league, while others included the Kansas City Monarchs, the Indianapolis ABCs, and Torriente's old club, the Cuban Stars, which adopted Cincinnati as its American base of operations. Foster sent Indianapolis native Oscar Charleston back to the ABCs to strengthen the franchise in that city, leaving center field position for the American Giants firmly in Torriente's hands for the next several seasons.

Even without Charleston, an all-time great of the black game, the American Giants won the first Negro National League pennant in 1920 as Torriente batted .396. The NNL gave no Most Valuable Player award then, but many later researchers agree that Cristóbal's outstanding performance would have made him the likely winner.[8] As Homestead Grays owner Cumberland (Cum) Posey claimed, "Torriente could do anything." Posey also stated that Indianapolis ABCs manager and owner C. I. Taylor once said to him, "Mr. Posey, if I should see Torriente walking up the other side of the street, I would say, 'There goes a ball club.'"[9]

Torriente was certainly talented enough to not only play, but excel, in major league baseball. While no black American had done so since the Walker brothers, Moses and Welday, played in the American Association in 1884, the color line did not bar Cuban stars with light skin from participating in the major leagues. In 1911 outfielder Armando Marsáns and infielder Rafael Almeida, both Spanish-speaking Cubans, joined the Cincinnati Reds and made their debuts together on the Fourth of July. Several more Cubans appeared on major league rosters over the next few seasons, mostly with the Reds and the Washington Senators, and by the beginning of the 1920s several American and National League teams were dotted with Cuban players. However, the baseball magnates found it necessary to proclaim that such Cuban players were not black. One Cincinnati paper assured its readers that Marsáns and Almeida were "two of the purest bars of Castille soap that ever floated to these shores."[10]

John McGraw, manager of the New York Giants of the National League, kept an eye out for Cuban talent, and would have had no objection to hiring Afro-Cuban players had he been allowed to do so. In 1901 he had tried to pass off a talented black second baseman, Charlie Grant, as an Indian from Oklahoma Territory, but Chicago White Sox owner Charles Comiskey called him on it and forced McGraw to abandon the idea. Jelly Gardner, a teammate of Torriente's on the American Giants, said that one of McGraw's scouts followed the team around the circuit during the early 1920s. "He was watching Torriente," said Gardner.

Though he (like José Méndez) was a Cuban of African descent, Cristóbal Torriente's skin was not much darker than that of Marsáns, Almeida, and the rest, but his hair was another matter. "He was a light brown, and he would have gone up to the major leagues, but he had real rough hair,"[11] explained Gardner. Incredibly, it appears that McGraw and the Giants would have signed Torriente were it not for the kinky texture of his hair.

After the conclusion of the 1920 major league baseball season, McGraw took most of his New York Giants on a tour of Cuba for a series of games against the Havana and Almendares teams. Some team members passed up the trip, but McGraw filled the holes in his roster with players from other major league clubs. The most important addition to the team was Babe Ruth, the biggest star in the game, who belted a record 54 homers for the New York Yankees that season. Ruth received the then-stunning total of $1,000 per game from the Cuban promoters of the trip, and the Giants expected to clear more than $20,000 as their share of the gate. The Giants, with Ruth, arrived in Havana in late October and played two games against the Havana Reds, winning the first and losing the second. Ruth hit a single and a double in the first game, but Jose Acosta, a knuckleball pitcher who played for the Washington Senators, struck Ruth out three times in leading the Reds to a 7–1 win in the second contest.

On November 4, 1920, the Ruth-led Giants and the Almendares Blues met in the Cuban team's home park for the third game of the series. The Giants, low on pitching talent after an injury to starter Jesse Barnes, put first baseman George Kelly on the mound, with Ruth at first, Frankie Frisch at third, and two other future Hall of Fame selections (Ross Youngs and Dave Bancroft) in the lineup. The Blues, facing the traveling Giants for the first time on the tour, sent Isidro Fabre to the hill, with major leaguers Armando Marsáns and Merito Acosta playing first base and left field respectively. Cristóbal Torriente, whose exploits were as yet unknown to the Americans, batted fifth and played center field.

The Giants scored three times in the first inning as Ruth walked and came around to score, but Torriente whacked a long two-run homer to left center field in the second. This blow ignited a four-run outburst as the Cubans took the lead 4–3. In the third, Torriente belted an even longer opposite-field blow with the bases empty for a 5–3 advantage. Ruth hit a grounder in his second trip to the plate, though he was safe on an error, and the contest between the greatest slugger in American baseball and his Cuban counterpart proceeded in Torriente's favor.

Torriente came up again in the fifth inning, and, according to eyewitness accounts of the game, Ruth switched positions with Kelly and declared his intention to pitch to Torriente himself. Ruth had been a fine left-handed pitcher, winning 20 games in a season for the Red Sox before moving to the outfield, and in 1920 had started one game for the Yankees and won it. Now he wanted to test his pitching prowess against the "Cuban Babe Ruth."

Torriente was unfazed by the presence on the mound of baseball's greatest star. He hit a scorching line drive down the third base line that Frankie Frisch tried, and failed, to stop. "Look in the glove, it might be there," recalled Frisch. "But it wasn't in my glove. It dug a hole about a foot deep on its way to left field. And I'm glad I wasn't in front of it!"[12] Torriente steamed into second base with a double, and Ruth had seen enough. He retired the next three batters, then returned to first base and gave the pitching chores back to Kelly.

Ruth walked in the sixth, and in the Almendares half of the inning Kelly retired Torriente on a ground ball. In the eighth, with the Cubans leading by a comfortable margin, Torriente pounded his third homer of the contest, a solo shot that gave the Blues an 11–4 lead that they held until the end of the game. Ruth went hitless that day, while his Cuban rival belted four hits in five trips to the plate, compiling 14 total bases with three homers and a double. Said Frisch, "In those days Torriente was a hell of a player. Christ, I'd like to whitewash him and bring him up."[13]

To this day, Cuban baseball fans remember this game with pride and call Cristóbal Torriente "the man who defeated Babe Ruth." *The New York Times* took notice as well, razzing George Kelly a bit for his pitching. "The Cuban Babe Ruth," said the *Times*, "a chocolate-tinted chap named Torriente, or something like that, let [Kelly] down easy with only three home runs. That was professional courtesy."[14] Torriente's homers were most certainly all inside-the-park shots, as the right field fence of the gigantic Almendares ballpark stood more than 400 feet from the plate, with the left field barrier almost 500 feet away. Still, Cristóbal hit three round-trippers that day while Babe Ruth managed none, and his performance lives in Cuban baseball annals.

To be fair, some of the Giants may not have exerted much effort in an exhibition game that was as much a vacation for them as a test of their skill. The presence of first baseman George Kelly on the mound was one indication of such. As Cuban historian and diarist Ramon S. Mendoza wrote, "We admire the extraordinary power of the blasts by the great Almendares slugger ... but that does not mean that we should not admit also that he took advantage of the opportunity offered him when he was opposed by someone who may very well be a pitcher but does not play that position for his club."[15] The tour took a bizarre turn later on when Almendares hired several professional jai-alai players, who took the field with their wicker *cestas* and used them to catch and throw the ball.

Torriente continued his superlative hitting for the rest of the tour, and after Ruth and the Giants left Cuba, he and the Almendares team faced another traveling outfit, a leading Negro League team called the Bacharach Giants from Atlantic City, New Jersey. Torriente belted three triples in one game against them. Though Torriente batted only .296 in league play during the winter of 1920–21, his hot hitting against black and white American teams helped spread his fame and put him in the first rank of stars outside the all-white confines of organized baseball. Baseball historian John Holway has since determined that

Cristóbal compiled a career average of .436, by far the best in history, in 110 times at bat against white major leaguers.[16]

He was so talented that some of his recorded exploits in the Negro National League sound like tall tales. In one game in Kansas City against the Monarchs, he belted a rare homer over the faraway center field fence. According to witnesses, the ball struck the face of a clock above the fence, making its hands spin crazily while Torriente trotted around the bases. Another time, claimed teammate Jelly Gardner, "he hit a line drive in Indianapolis that hit the top of the right field wall and the right fielder threw him out at first base. That's how much power he had."[17]

The Negro National League was a pitcher's league, so Rube Foster demanded that all his players learn to bunt, advance runners, and execute the hit-and-run to perfection. The team manufactured runs for many of its wins, usually with Torriente in the middle of the action. On August 14, 1921, the American Giants played a typically low-scoring contest, winning 1–0 as Dave Brown pitched a shutout against the St. Louis Giants in Chicago. The game's only run crossed the plate in the eighth inning as Torriente singled, was sacrificed to second, stole third, and scored on a squeeze bunt by Gardner.

In 1922, when the American Giants captured their third pennant in a row, they faced the Bacharach Giants in one of the most famous games in Negro League annals. The two clubs played 19 innings of scoreless baseball before the American Giants pushed across a run in the bottom of the 20th for a 1–0 win. Torriente once again scored the winning tally, as he walked, was sacrificed to second, and came around on a single by Dave Malarcher. However, the American Giants sometimes exploded on offense, as they did against the Detroit Stars on June 26, 1923. Cristóbal homered and led the American Giants to a 20–0 rout of the Stars that afternoon.

Another wild game occurred on June 28, 1921, when the Chicagoans found themselves on the short end of a 10–0 deficit after seven innings against the Indianapolis ABCs. Rube Foster ordered his men to bunt their way on base, and the American Giants drove the ABCs crazy, bunting 11 times and loading the bases repeatedly during the last two innings. Cristóbal walloped a grand slam homer in the eighth, and the American Giants scored nine times to cut the margin to 10–9. The ABCs answered with eight more runs in the ninth for an 18–9 lead, but Foster ignited the bunting attack again, and Chicago scored nine times in the ninth to knot the score. After all that effort, the game ended on account of darkness as an 18–18 tie.

While Cristóbal gained recognition as perhaps the best hitter in the Negro National League, he returned to Cuba every fall to play a Cuban Winter League season. He shifted from Almendares back to his original team, the Havana Reds, in 1921–22, though he played only five games that winter. In 1922–23 he stayed with the Reds for the entire campaign and led the circuit in runs, hits, stolen bases, and homers (with four). After a brief fling with Marianao during the last half of the 1923–24 campaign, he returned to the Reds and continued his fine hitting. In all, Torriente batted .352 during his 12-year career in Cuba, starred on four pennant winners, and led the league in triples and home runs five times each.

In America, Cristóbal compiled one of his greatest seasons in 1923, batting .389 although his American Giants lost the pennant to the Kansas City Monarchs. In October 1923 he made another appearance against a major league club, the Detroit Tigers (who played the three-game series without star outfielder and manager Ty Cobb). The Tigers and American Giants tied the first contest 5–5, but the Detroiters won easily by a 7–1 score the next day. Torriente and Oscar Charleston, imported from the Indianapolis ABCs to strengthen Foster's team for the series, then left for Cuba, missing the third and final game. With outfielder Harry Heilmann pitching the final two innings for Detroit, the American Giants defeated the Tigers 8–6 without their two best hitters.

Cristóbal had no weaknesses as a ballplayer, but his off-the-field behavior became troublesome by 1924. Though Prohibition was the law of the land in the United States (but not in Cuba), it was not difficult to find alcohol in wide-open Chicago during the early 1920s. Chicago was a city of speakeasies, corruption, and vice during the Jazz Age, and Torriente apparently dove into the scene with great enthusiasm. Sadly, he developed a taste for liquor that appears to have evolved into alcoholism. Though Cristóbal was one of the American Giants' greatest stars, his love of nightlife was beginning to affect his performance. He hit .331 for the American Giants in 1924 and followed it up with a .360 mark in winter ball, but his Negro National League average fell all the way to .241 in 1925.

Torriente's career in the States faltered due to alcohol-related problems, and Rube Foster found himself unable to control his star center fielder. Cristóbal became undependable, often showing up at the park in no condition to play and sometimes missing games entirely. Foster was trying to rebuild his club after two mediocre seasons, so he reluctantly dropped Torriente, trading him

This Cuban baseball card of Torriente was issued in 1923. (Author's collection)

to another Negro National League team, the Kansas City Monarchs, for the 1926 campaign.

Managed by José Méndez, the Monarchs had won the NNL pennant in 1925, after which Méndez retired to Cuba, leaving the team in the hands of star pitcher "Bullet Joe" Rogan. The Monarchs, with Torriente batting in the cleanup spot, took up where they left off and won the first-half pennant in 1926. Cristóbal's old team, the American Giants, won the second-half flag, and the teams met in a nine-game playoff series in October. Torriente went 11 for 31 during the series, which was won by the American Giants when pitcher Bill Foster, Rube's half-brother, defeated Rogan in both ends of a doubleheader. Torriente batted a healthy .339 during the season, but angered team management by sitting out part of the season in a money dispute, and his nightlife escapades prompted another trade at season's end. He moved again, this time to the Detroit Stars.

The Stars already owned of the Negro National League's outstanding center fielders in Norman (Turkey) Stearnes, so Cristóbal spent most of his time patrolling left or right field, and taking an occasional turn on the mound. Playing in a better hitter's park, Torriente batted a reported .320 in 1927 as he and Stearnes formed one of black baseball's best slugging duos. However, poor second-line pitching behind future Hall of Famer Andy Cooper held the Stars to a fifth-place finish. The team improved to third in 1928 as Torriente once again batted over .300 and went 7–3 as a pitcher, but his alcohol abuse and increasingly erratic behavior frustrated manager Bingo DeMoss and the team owners. Despite his fine statistics, the Stars dropped Torriente after the 1928 campaign.

Prohibition proved disastrous for Cristóbal Torriente. Frustrated by the inability to buy liquor, his thirst was so great that he resorted to distilling it himself in his Chicago apartment. "Instead of going to Cuba to manage," said Rogelio Crespo, a former teammate, "he stayed in Chicago and made his own booze. The winter was cold, and he drank, drank, drank. His face swelled up from the booze. At spring training he couldn't stand up in the batter's box without falling. He was in such bad condition, no team wanted him."[18]

He had hit well for Detroit in 1928, but in 1929 dropped out of the Negro National League and wound up with a lower-level club, Gilkerson's Union Giants, based in Spring Valley, Illinois. The Union Giants were a virtual farm team for the Kansas City Monarchs, and it is possible that the Monarchs placed Cristóbal there to see if he could resurrect his career and rejoin the parent team. Instead, Torriente spent the next three seasons with the Union Giants, playing amateur and semipro teams in the Midwest and trying to reinvigorate his talent. Stints with the Atlanta Black Crackers and the Cleveland Cubs in 1932 were short-lived, and in 1933 he managed and played sparingly for an obscure ballclub called the Falcon Athletic Giants.

He tried repeatedly to resuscitate his career, but by 1934 Cristóbal Torriente was finished as a ballplayer. He had passed his 40th birthday the year before, and was overweight and out of condition. Lost to alcoholism, he lived his days in poverty in Chicago, where fellow Cuban baseball star Martin Dihigo found him in 1935 and brought him to New York. There the "Cuban Babe Ruth" spent the remaining years of his life alone and unnoticed as his health slowly deteriorated. Suffering from pneumonia, he entered a New York hospital in the fall of 1937 and never left. On April 11, 1938, Torriente died at the age of 44.[19]

A Cuban politician arranged for the ballplayer's body to be returned to the island for burial, and Torriente, his coffin wrapped in a Cuban flag, was interred at the Cuban national cemetery, the Cementerio de Cristóbal Colon in Havana. Though American fans soon forgot about Torriente, the Cuban people still revered him as one of their greatest players, and in 1939 he was one of the first 10 men elected to the Cuban Baseball Hall of Fame. In 1951, the Cuban professional baseball association installed a marker at the national cemetery for the "Pantéon" of island baseball, listing the names of all members of the Cuban Hall of Fame. Three players, whose images were carved into the top of the plaque, were honored above the rest. Those three men were José Méndez, 1890s-era slugger Antonio Garcia, and Cristóbal Torriente.

While Méndez is usually considered Cuban baseball's greatest pitcher and Martin Dihigo its top all-around player, Cristóbal Torriente is the island's most accomplished hitter. Later players such as Tony Oliva, Tony Perez, and Minnie Minoso made their mark on major league baseball, but Torriente is the man whom people called "the Cuban Babe Ruth." A poll of African American baseball experts, assembled by the *Pittsburgh Courier* in 1952, named Torriente to its all-time All-Star team, and Homestead Grays owner Cum Posey proclaimed him the top black outfielder in Negro League history. In 2006, 68 years after his death, the Baseball Hall of Fame finally gave Cristóbal Torriente the recognition he deserved as one of Cuba's, and baseball's, greatest players.

Notes

Chapter 1

1. *The Sporting News*, April 6, 1939.
2. *1939 Spalding's Official Base Ball Guide*, page 33.
3. James A. Vlasich, *A Legend for the Legendary: The Origin of the Baseball Hall of Fame* (Bowling Green, Ohio: Bowling Green State University Popular Press, 1990), pages 49–50.
4. *Washington Post*, November 21, 1915.
5. Harold Seymour, *Baseball: The Early Years* (New York: Oxford University Press, 1960), page 48.
6. *New York Clipper*, January 9, 1869.
7. *Washington Post*, November 21, 1915.
8. *1889 Spalding's Official Base Ball Guide*, page 55. A proposal to allow players to overrun second and third was made again, and rejected, at the 1888 rules meeting.
9. *Cincinnati Commercial*, June 15, 1870.
10. *Washington Post*, November 21, 1915.
11. *Boston Globe*, December 19, 2004.
12. From the Baseball Hall of Fame web site at http://www.baseballhalloffame.org.
13. *1889 Spalding's Official Base Ball Guide*, page 92.
14. *Boston Globe*, August 31, 1919.
15. *Boston Globe*, December 11, 1990.
16. *Dorchester Reporter*, April 12, 2001. The United Press article appeared in the nation's newspapers on February 23, 1926.
17. *Washington Post*, November 21, 1915.

Chapter 2

1. *The Sporting News*, March 11, 1943.
2. Ibid.
3. *Boston Globe*, November 10, 1895.
4. *Boston Globe*, March 10, 1901.
5. The name "Pilgrims" exists in many histories about the early days of the team, but the name did not appear until 1906, and then only on an infrequent basis in some newspapers. See "About the Boston Pilgrims" by Bill Nowlin in the 2006 edition of the SABR publication, *The National Pastime*, page 40.
6. *Sporting Life*, October 17, 1903.
7. The Pittsburgh player contracts ran until October 15, so Dreyfuss could afford to give his Pirates all the receipts, since he did not have to pay more money in salaries during the Series. The Boston management, however, were required to pay their players for an extra two weeks, and wanted the 50–50 split from the players to lighten the burden.
8. Fred Lieb, *The Boston Red Sox* (New York: G. P. Putnam's Sons, 1947), page 42.
9. Lieb, page 60.
10. *Boston Globe*, January 18, 1907.
11. *The New York Times*, January 16, 1943.
12. Ibid.
13. *The Sporting News*, March 11, 1943.

Chapter 3

1. From the Hall of Fame web site at http://www.baseballhalloffame.org.
2. From the Dan Brouthers page at http://www.baseballlibrary.com.
3. *Boston Globe*, June 16, 1889.
4. *Chicago Tribune*, August 19, 1882.
5. *Chicago Tribune*, July 21, 1890.
6. *The New York Times*, September 17, 1887.
7. *Chicago Tribune*, November 21, 1887.
8. *The New York Times*, June 9, 1888.
9. *Boston Globe*, November 22, 1888.
10. *Washington Post*, January 24, 1897.
11. *Brooklyn Eagle*, May 5, 1894.
12. *Washington Post*, May 14, 1895.
13. *Boston Globe*, August 6, 1896.
14. *Boston Globe*, July 6, 1899.

15. John McGraw, *My Thirty Years in Baseball* (New York: Boni and Liveright, 1923), page 68.
16. *1896 Spalding's Official Base Ball Guide*, page 76.

Chapter 4

1. From the Baseball Hall of Fame web site at http://www.baseballhalloffame.org.
2. McCarthy also played 53 games in the Union Association in 1884, batting .215, but the UA's claim to major status is disputed by many baseball historians. McCarthy, as of 2006, is the only member of the Hall of Fame to have played even one game in the Union Association.
3. Eddie Gold, "Tommy McCarthy," *Baseball Research Journal #24* (1995), page 88.
4. Bill James, *The Politics of Glory: How Baseball's Hall of Fame Really Works* (New York: Macmillan, 1994), page 371.
5. *The New York Times*, August 12, 1984.
6. Interview with Comiskey in the *Atlanta Constitution*, March 19, 1916.
7. *The Sporting News*, June 9, 1888.
8. Marty Appel and Burt Goldblatt, *Baseball's Best: The Hall of Fame Gallery* (New York: McGraw-Hill, 1980), page 288.
9. *Chicago Tribune*, July 1, 1877. The description was as follows: "Some chap stated the following conundrum, professing not to understand it: 'Why do batsmen strike a ball when a base-runner is half-way to second base on a clever steal?' The answer was found in Thursday's game, when McVey started to second base, and Anson hit the ball in the exact spot where McGeary had been standing before he ran to his base to catch McVey. It is really a clever batting trick to hit to right field when it lies all open."
10. Dean A. Sullivan (editor), *Early Innings: A Documentary History of Baseball, 1825–1908* (Lincoln, Nebraska: University of Nebraska Press, 1995), page 235. This passage is quoted from the *1896 Spalding Guide*.
11. *Boston Globe*, November 10, 1895.
12. *Brooklyn Eagle*, March 9, 1898.
13. Ken Smith, *Baseball's Hall of Fame* (New York: Grosset and Dunlap, 1962), page 144.

Chapter 5

1. *Boston Globe*, December 29, 1895.
2. *The New York Times*, January 31, 1961.
3. Robert L. Tiemann and Mark Rucker (editors), *Nineteenth Century Stars* (Kansas City, Missouri: Society for American Baseball Research, 1989), page 75.
4. *Brooklyn Eagle*, May 10, 1890.
5. *The Sporting News*, October 28, 1899.
6. John Phillips, *The 1898 Cleveland Spiders* (Cabin John, Maryland: Capital Publishing, 1997), page 94.
7. *Boston Globe*, August 26, 1910.
8. *Washington Post*, August 6, 1896.
9. *The Sporting News*, June 4, 1898.
10. *Boston Globe*, December 29, 1895.
11. *San Francisco Chronicle*, September 18, 1990.
12. From Billy Hamilton file, National Baseball Library, Cooperstown, New York.
13. Bill James, *The New Bill James Historical Baseball Abstract* (New York: Free Press, 2001), page 728.

Chapter 6

1. *Washington Post*, January 24, 1963.
2. Ibid.
3. "The Secrets of Sam," *Sports Illustrated*, July 19, 1993.
4. *Washington Post*, May 8, 1963.
5. "The Secrets of Sam," *Sports Illustrated*, July 19, 1993.
6. *Washington Post*, January 24, 1963.
7. *Washington Post*, October 25, 1974.
8. "The Secrets of Sam," *Sports Illustrated*, July 19, 1993.
9. *Sport*, July 1967, page 74.
10. *Washington Post*, July 20, 1932.
11. "The Secrets of Sam," *Sports Illustrated*, July 19, 1993.
12. The *Sports Illustrated* article from 1993 that appears in these footnotes gives the impression that Sam kept the tragedy a secret from his family for nearly 40 years, but such appears to be an exaggeration. Sam married Mary Kendall at age 69, not 39 as the article stated, and Christine Rice was Sam's stepdaughter, though the article implies that she was his biological daughter. The article does not mention Sam's second wife Edith, to whom he was married from 1920 to 1957, at all. Sam kept the secret from Mary for six or seven years at most. Also,

though most of Rice's teammates did not know about the family Sam lost in the tornado, the incident was not completely unknown in the baseball world. On October 13, 1925, during the World Series, Frank Butzow of the *Chicago Tribune* wrote a short biography of Rice that included an account of the tragedy.
13. "The Secrets of Sam," *Sports Illustrated*, July 19, 1993.
14. *Washington Post*, November 5, 1974.

Chapter 7

1. *Brooklyn Eagle*, July 19, 1896.
2. Many sources say that Patrick Keefe was imprisoned for more than four years and did not return to Cambridge until after war's end, but it appears that he may have been in custody for two or three years, not more. The 1880 United States census lists his children Daniel (age 25), Catherine (21), Mary (20), Margaret (16), Ellen (15) and Anne (13). If Margaret was born in 1864 and Ellen in 1865, then perhaps Patrick was repatriated long before the cessation of hostilities.
3. *Boston Globe*, May 5, 1895.
4. Jonathan Fraser Light, *The Cultural Encyclopedia of Baseball* (Jefferson, North Carolina: McFarland and Company, 1997), page 514.
5. Dean A. Sullivan (editor), *Early Innings: A Documentary History of Baseball, 1825–1908* (Lincoln, Nebraska: University of Nebraska Press, 1995), page 196. The ledger that Keefe kept, covering the years 1885 to 1889, was sold at auction in 2005 for $99,000.
6. *The Sporting News*, July 7, 1888.
7. *New York Clipper*, July 13, 1889.
8. Daniel M. Pearson, *Baseball in 1889: Players vs. Owners* (New York: Popular Press, 1993), page 92.
9. Ethan Lewis, "A Structure to Last Forever: The Players' League and The Brotherhood War of 1890," chapter 3, on http:/www.businessofbaseball.com. Lewis' article reproduces the quote in the text from *Players' National League Guide* (Chicago: W. J. Jefferson, 1890), pages 9–10.
10. *Sporting Life*, April 8, 1893.
11. *The New York Times*, July 9, 1896.
12. *Brooklyn Eagle*, July 19, 1896.
13. *Fort Wayne (Indiana) Sentinel*, December 11, 1912.

Chapter 8

1. Bill James, *The New Bill James Historical Baseball Abstract* (New York: Free Press, 2001), page 813. The quote first appeared in Baseball magazine in 1925.
2. *Chicago Tribune*, January 29, 1968.
3. F. C. Lane, *Batting* (New York: Baseball Magazine Company, 1925), page 38.
4. Lawrence Ritter, *The Glory of Their Times*, enlarged edition (New York: William Morrow, 1984), page 285.
5. Bill James gives a fine overview of this controversy in *The Bill James Guide to Baseball Managers from 1870 to Today* (New York: Scribner, 1997), pages 83–84.
6. *Atlanta Constitution*, October 16, 1927.
7. "Why Kiki Cuyler Was Benched," *Baseball Digest*, May 1968.
8. Ibid.
9. *Chicago Tribune*, October 8, 1927.
10. James, *The New Bill James Historical Baseball Abstract*, page 813.
11. *Chicago Tribune*, June 2, 1935.
12. Ibid.
13. James, *The New Bill James Historical Baseball Abstract*, page 813.
14. *The Sporting News*, February 22, 1950.

Chapter 9

1. John McGraw, *My Thirty Years in Baseball* (New York: Boni and Liveright, 1923), page 220.
2. *Boston Globe*, July 29, 1891.
3. *Boston Globe*, August 27, 1891.
4. *Baltimore Sun*, September 30, 1892.
5. Fred Lieb, *The Baltimore Orioles* (New York: G. P. Putnam's Sons, 1955), page 68.
6. Charles Alexander, *John McGraw* (New York: Viking Penguin, 1988), page 41.
7. *Washington Post*, May 17, 1896.
8. McGraw, pages 79–80.
9. Seven other players have stroked nine hits in a doubleheader (including Kelley's teammate Wilbert Robinson in 1892), but all needed more than nine times at bat to compile that total.
10. John Phillips, *Chief Sockalexis and the 1897 Cleveland Indians* (Cabin John, Maryland: Capital Publishing, 1991).
11. *Brooklyn Eagle*, July 25, 1897.

12. Alexander, page 89.
13. *Boston Globe*, July 1, 1902.
14. *Chicago Tribune*, March 21, 1920.
15. *The New York Times*, December 16, 1947.
16. Lawrence Ritter, *The Glory of Their Times, enlarged edition* (New York: William Morrow, 1984), page 213.

Chapter 10

1. *Brooklyn Eagle*, November 25, 1888.
2. Robert L. Tiemann and Mark Rucker (editors), *Nineteenth Century Stars* (Kansas City, Missouri: Society for American Baseball Research, 1989), page 170.
3. Tiemann and Rucker, page 171.
4. George H. Allyn, "Sketch of Holyoke" article at http://www.holyokemass.com.
5. *Washington Post*, May 9, 1880.
6. Bill James and Rob Neyer, *The Neyer /James guide to pitchers: an historical compendium of pitching, pitchers, and pitches* (New York: Fireside Press, 2004), page 421.
7. *The New York Times*, January 25, 1938.
8. Ibid.
9. *The New York Times*, August 27, 1884.
10. Allison Danzig and Joe Reichler, *The History of Baseball* (Englewood Cliffs, New Jersey: Prentice-Hall, 1959), page 176.
11. *The New York Times*, January 14, 1890.
12. Danzig and Reichler, page 176.

Chapter 11

1. This quote appears in a clipping dated October 20, 1887, found in the Sam Thompson file at the National Baseball Library, Cooperstown, New York.
2. Roger Connor hit 138 home runs from 1880 to 1897, but only 124 of them came in National League play. He hit 14 more in the Players League in 1890.
3. Some of Sam's relatives claim that Sam must have thrown with his right hand. He was an enthusiastic hunter and fisherman in later life, and family sources say that he shot a gun over his right shoulder and cast a rod with his right, not his left, hand. They also state that he never played catch with his younger family members, and none can ever remember him wearing a fielding glove. The author could find no photos of Thompson wearing a glove, and early issues of *Daguerrotypes*, a publication from *The Sporting News* that first appeared in 1934, do not state what hand he threw with. However, if the hard-throwing Sam was actually right-handed, one would think that he would have played third base at some point during his career.
4. *Hendricks County Republican*, September 4, 1884.
5. *Washington Post*, January 28, 1906.
6. *Indianapolis Times*, March 26, 1961.
7. The distance to the right field fence was listed at 300 feet in 1887. The park was rebuilt after it burned in 1894, and the fence was brought in to the distance of 272 feet.
8. *Washington Post*, January 28, 1906.
9. *Boston Globe*, October 8, 1893.
10. *Hendricks County Republican*, October 10, 1895.
11. *Brooklyn Eagle*, June 9, 1897.
12. *Washington Post*, September 16, 1906.
13. *Detroit Free Press*, November 8, 1922.
14. *Detroit News*, November 7, 1922.
15. *Detroit News*, November 8, 1922.
16. Ibid.

Chapter 12

1. "Amos Rusie: Daddy of the Fire-Ballers," *Baseball Digest*, March 1943.
2. *The Sporting News*, March 10, 1932.
3. "Amos Rusie: Daddy of the Fire-Ballers," *Baseball Digest*, March 1943.
4. *The New York Times*, December 7, 1942.
5. Bill James and Rob Neyer, *The Neyer /James guide to pitchers: an historical compendium of pitching, pitchers, and pitches* (New York: Fireside Press, 2004), page 368.
6. *The New York Times*, September 1, 1894.
7. Burt Solomon, *Where They Ain't: The Fabled Life and Untimely Death of the Original Baltimore Orioles, the Team That Gave Birth to Modern Baseball* (New York: Main Street Books, 2000), page 86.
8. From the Amos Rusie page at http://www.thebaseballpage.com.
9. *The Sporting News*, December 28, 1939.
10. The incident may have happened on June 5, 1897, a game in which Rusie carried a 4–3 lead into the ninth and gave up seven

runs to lose by a 10–4 count. Lange had two stolen bases in that contest, one of which was part of a double steal in the decisive ninth inning. Rusie lost his next two games, to Cincinnati on June 11 and to Cleveland on June 15.
   11. *The New York Times*, December 7, 1942.
   12. *Chicago Tribune*, December 6, 1901.
   13. *The Sporting News*, December 28, 1939.

Chapter 13

   1. *The New York Times*, September 3, 1952.
   2. Dennis DeValeria and Jeanne Burke DeValeria, *Honus Wagner: A Biography* (New York: H. Holt, 1996), page 289.
   3. DeValeria and DeValeria, page 289.
   4. From the Hall of Fame web site, http://www.baseballhalloffame.org.
   5. *The Sporting News*, August 29, 1935.
   6. *The Sporting News*, October 24, 1935.
   7. *Los Angeles Times*, August 31, 1985.
   8. *The Sporting News*, January 28, 1937.
   9. *The Sporting News*, March 12, 1942.
   10. *The New York Times*, November 20, 1942.
   11. A complete description of the controversy can be found in Roscoe McGowen's column in *The New York Times*, July 11, 1943.
   12. *The New York Times*, July 31, 1985.
   13. Ibid.
   14. *The New York Times*, February 22, 1947.
   15. *Chicago Tribune*, September 29, 1948.
   16. *Fullerton Daily News*, September 3, 1952.
   17. *The New York Times*, September 1, 1952.

Chapter 14

   1. Brent P. Kelley, *Voices from the Negro Leagues* (Jefferson, North Carolina: McFarland and Company, 1997), pages 39–40.
   2. John Holway, *Blackball Stars: Negro League pioneers* (Westport, Connecticut: Meckler Books, 1988), page 63.
   3. Robert Peterson, *Only the Ball Was White* (Englewood Cliffs, New Jersey: Prentice-Hall, 1970), pages 216–217.
   4. Robert Smith, *Pioneers of Baseball* (Boston: Little, Brown, 1978), page 100.

   5. Holway, page 65.
   6. Lawrence D. Hogan, *Shades of Glory: the Negro Leagues and the story of African-American baseball* (Washington, D. C.: National Geographic, 2006), page 119.
   7. *New York Age*, October 9, 1913.
   8. Thom Loverro, *Encyclopedia of Negro League Baseball* (New York: Checkmark Books, 2003), pages 313–314.
   9. Henry W. Thomas, *Walter Johnson: Baseball's Big Train* (Washington, D. C.: Phenom Press, 1995), page 390.
   10. Holway, page 62.
   11. Associated Press wire story, March 5, 1999.
   12. Hogan, page 149.
   13. *Austin American Statesman*, February 25, 1998.
   14. Ibid.
   15. Holway, page 74.
   16. Holway, page 75.
   17. Kelley, page 40.
   18. Holway, page 71.
   19. Holway, page 77.
   20. This article was posted on the Baseball Think Factory web site, http://www.baseballthinkfactory.org, on August 17, 2004, in a Hall of Merit discussion of Joe Williams.

Chapter 15

   1. From interview with Buck O'Neil on the Major League Baseball web site, http://www.mlb.com.
   2. John Holway, *Voices from the Great Black Baseball Leagues*, revised edition (New York: Da Capo Press, 1992), page 281.
   3. John Holway, *Josh and Satch: the life and times of Josh Gibson and Satchel Paige* (Westport, Connecticut: Meckler Books, 1991), page 144.
   4. Janet Bruce, *The Kansas City Monarchs: champions of black baseball* (Lawrence, Kansas: University Press of Kansas, 1985), page 95.
   5. Holway, *Voices from the Great Black Baseball Leagues*, page 285.
   6. Ibid.
   7. Bruce, page 24.
   8. John Holway, *Black Diamonds* (Westport, Connecticut: Meckler Books, 1989), page 96.
   9. Ibid.
   10. From the Baseball Hall of Fame web site, http://www.baseballhalloffame.org.

11. From interview with Buck O'Neil on the Major League Baseball web site, http://www.mlb.com.
12. Holway, *Voices from the Great Black Baseball Leagues*, page 285.
13. Holway, *Voices from the Great Black Baseball Leagues*, page 281.
14. Buck O'Neil (with Steve Wulf and David Conrads), *I Was Right On Time* (New York: Simon and Schuster, 1996), page 90.
15. Ibid.
16. Holway, *Voices from the Great Black Baseball Leagues*, page 291.
17. Bruce, page 112.
18. Bruce, page 113.
19. Ibid.
20. Holway, *Voices from the Great Black Baseball Leagues*, page 295.
21. *Kansas City Star*, March 6, 2001.
22. Ibid.

Chapter 16

1. Lawrence D. Hogan, *Shades of Glory: the Negro Leagues and the story of African-American baseball* (Washington, D. C.: National Geographic, 2006), page 147.
2. The Cuban League statistics referenced here come from Jorge S. Figueredo, *Who's Who in Cuban Baseball 1878–1961* (Jefferson, North Carolina: McFarland and Company, 2003), page 82. Torriente's Negro National League stats come from John Holway's *Blackball Stars: Negro League pioneers* (Westport, Connecticut: Meckler Books, 1988), though later research may change these numbers.
3. Roberto González Echevarría, *The Pride of Havana: A History of Cuban Baseball* (New York: Oxford University Press, 1999), pages 89–90.
4. *Sporting Life*, July 3, 1915.
5. John Holway, *Blackball Stars: Negro League pioneers* (Westport, Connecticut: Meckler Books, 1988), page 125.
6. Holway, page 131.
7. Holway, page 130.
8. The *2006 ESPN Baseball Encyclopedia*, edited by Gary Gillette and Pete Palmer, awarded both the 1920 and 1922 NNL Most Valuable Player awards to Torriente.
9. William McNeil, *Cool Papas and Double Duties: the all-time greats of the Negro Leagues* (Jefferson, North Carolina: McFarland and Company, 2001), page 195.
10. Eric Enders, "Armando Marsáns," from the SABR Baseball Biography Project web site at http://bioproj.sabr.org.
11. Robert Peterson, *Only the Ball Was White* (Englewood Cliffs, New Jersey: Prentice-Hall, 1970), page 245.
12. Holway, page 125.
13. Ibid.
14. *The New York Times*, November 20, 1920.
15. González Echevarría, page 161. Kelly only pitched once in major league play, throwing one inning for the New York Giants in 1917.
16. Holway, in *Blackball Stars*, gave Torriente credit for a .311 mark against white major league players, but his later work, *The Complete Book of Baseball's Negro Leagues: the other half of baseball history* (Fern Park, Florida: Hastings House, 2001) revised that figure upward as more data became available.
17. Peterson, page 244.
18. Holway, page 132.
19. This account of the end of Torriente's life comes from the *Chicago Defender*, April 23, 1938.

Bibliography

Books

Alexander, Charles. *John McGraw*. New York: Viking Penguin, 1988.
Appel, Marty, and Goldblatt, Burt. *Baseball's Best: The Hall of Fame Gallery*. New York: McGraw-Hill, 1980.
Bruce, Janet. *The Kansas City Monarchs: Champions of Black Baseball*. Lawrence: University Press of Kansas, 1985.
Danzig, Allison, and Reichler, Joe. *The History of Baseball*. Englewood Cliffs, New Jersey: Prentice-Hall, 1959.
DeValeria, Dennis, and DeValeria, Jeanne Burke. *Honus Wagner: A Biography*. New York: Holt, 1996.
Figueredo, Jorge S. *Who's Who in Cuban Baseball 1878–1961*. Jefferson, North Carolina: McFarland, 2003.
González Echevarría, Roberto. *The Pride of Havana: A History of Cuban Baseball*. New York: Oxford University Press, 1999.
Hogan, Lawrence D. *Shades of Glory: The Negro Leagues and the Story of African-American Baseball*. Washington, D. C.: National Geographic, 2006.
Holway, John. *Black Diamonds*. Westport, Connecticut: Meckler, 1989.
_____. *Blackball Stars: Negro League Pioneers*. Westport, Connecticut: Meckler, 1988.
_____. *Josh and Satch: The Life and Times of Josh Gibson and Satchel Paige*. Westport, Connecticut: Meckler, 1991.
_____. *Voices from the Great Black Baseball Leagues*. Rev. ed. New York: Da Capo, 1992.
James, Bill. *The New Bill James Historical Baseball Abstract*. New York: Free Press, 2001.
_____. *The Politics of Glory: How Baseball's Hall of Fame Really Works*. New York: Macmillan, 1994.
James, Bill, and Neyer, Rob. *The Neyer/James Guide to Pitchers: An Historical Compendium of Pitching, Pitchers, and Pitches*. New York: Fireside, 2004.
Lane, F. C. *Batting*. New York: Baseball Magazine Company, 1925.
Lieb, Fred. *The Baltimore Orioles*. New York: G. P. Putnam's, 1955.
_____. *The Boston Red Sox*. New York: G. P. Putnam's, 1947.
Light, Jonathan Taylor. *The Cultural Encyclopedia of Baseball*. Jefferson, North Carolina: McFarland, 1997.
McGraw, John. *My Thirty Years in Baseball*. New York: Boni and Liveright, 1923.
McNeil, William. *Cool Papas and Double Duties: The All-time Greats of the Negro Leagues*. Jefferson, North Carolina: McFarland, 2001.
Nemec, David. *The Great Encyclopedia of 19th-Century Major League Baseball*. New York: Donald I. Fine, 1997.
O'Neil, Buck, with Steve Wulf and David Conrads. *I Was Right on Time*. New York: Simon and Schuster, 1996.

Pearson, Daniel M. *Baseball in 1889: Players vs. Owners.* New York: Popular, 1993.
Peterson, Robert. *Only the Ball Was White.* Englewood Cliffs, New Jersey: Prentice-Hall, 1970.
Phillips, John. *Chief Sockalexis and the 1897 Cleveland Indians.* Cabin John, Maryland: Capital, 1991.
_____. *The 1898 Cleveland Spiders.* Cabin John, Maryland: Capital, 1997.
Pietrusza, David, et al., editors. *Baseball: The Biographical Encyclopedia.* Kingston, New York: Total Sports Illustrated, 2000.
Ritter, Lawrence S. *The Glory of Their Times: The Story of Early Days of Baseball Told by the Men Who Played It.* Enlarged ed. New York: William Morrow, 1984.
Rogosin, Donn. *Invisible Men: Life in Baseball's Negro Leagues.* New York: Atheneum, 1983.
Seymour, Harold. *Baseball: The Early Years.* New York: Oxford University Press, 1960.
Smith, Robert. *Pioneers of Baseball.* Boston: Little, Brown, 1978.
Sullivan, Dean A., editor. *Early Innings: A Documentary History of Baseball, 1825–1908.* Lincoln: University of Nebraska Press, 1995.
Tiemann, Robert L., and Rucker, Mark, editors. *Nineteenth Century Stars.* Kansas City, Missouri: Society for American Baseball Research, 1989.
Vlasich, James A. *A Legend for the Legendary: The Origin of the Baseball Hall of Fame.* Bowling Green, Ohio: Bowling Green State University Popular Press, 1990.

Newspapers

Atlanta Constitution
Austin American Statesman
Baltimore Sun
Boston Globe
Brooklyn Eagle
Chicago Defender
Chicago Tribune
Cincinnati Commercial
Detroit Free Press
Detroit News
Dorchester (Massachusetts) *Reporter*
Fort Wayne (Indiana) *Sentinel*
Fullerton (California) *Daily News*
Hendricks County (Indiana) *Republican*
Indianapolis Times
Kansas City Star
Los Angeles Times
New York Age
New York Clipper
The New York Times
San Francisco Chronicle
Washington Post

Magazines

Baseball Digest
Baseball Magazine
Baseball Research Journal
The National Pastime
Sport
Sporting Life
The Sporting News
Sports Illustrated

Internet sites

The Baseball Archive http://www.baseball1.com
The Baseball Page http://www.thebaseballpage.com
Baseball Reference *http://www.baseball-reference.com*
Baseball Think Factory http://www.baseballthinkfactory.org
The Business of Baseball http://www.businessofbaseball.com
Major League Baseball http://www.mlb.com
National Baseball Hall of Fame and Museum http://www.baseballhalloffame.org
Project Retrosheet http://www.retrosheet.org
Society for American Baseball Research SABR *http://www.sabr.org*
SABR Baseball Biography Project http://bioproj.sabr.org
The Sporting News *http://tsn.sportingnews.com*

Index

A.G. Spalding and Company 14–15
Aaron, Henry 33, 50
Acosta, José 230
Acosta, Merito 230
Adams, Charles (Babe) 112
Adams, Sparky 114
Alexander, Grover Cleveland 202, 210
All Star Game 117–118
Allen, Lee 89
Allen, Newt 215
Almeida, Rafael 229
Altrock, Nick 89
Anson, Adrian (Cap) 11, 13, 37–38, 40–41, 43, 52, 57, 62, 103, 144–145, 157–159, 179–180, 201
Appling, Luke 91
Armour, Bill 164

Bagley, Ed 144
Baird, Tom 220
Baker, Frank 30
Baldwin, Charles (Lady) 40, 156–157
Bancroft, Dave 230
Bancroft, Frank 170–171
Bankhead, Dan 221
Barkley, Sam 67
Barnes, Jesse 230
Barnes, Ross 10–12
Barnhart, Clyde 113
Bartell, Dick 188, 190
Baseball Writers Association of America (BBWAA) 3, 18, 64
Becannon, Buck 97
Beckley, Jake 126, 133–134, 136, 179
Bell, James (Cool Papa) 217
Bender, Charles (Chief) 202
Bennett, Charlie 14, 43, 60, 157, 165–166
Benson, Gene 211
Bergen, Marty 61, 72, 74
Berman, Robert 203
Bigbee, Carson 110, 112
Birdsall, Dave 10

Bluege, Ossie 84
Bonura, Zeke 218
Bostic, Joe 209
Bradley, Bill 31–32
Bragan, Bobby 193
Brainard, Asa 7
Brett, George 32, 198
Brewer, Chet 207, 217
Brock, Lou 74
Brotherhood of Professional Base Ball Players 42–43, 56, 98, 100–103, 146–147, 160–161
Brouthers, Annie 35
Brouthers, Dennis (Dan) 21, 33–47, 124, 126–127, 136, 143, 149, 156–159
Brouthers, Lillian 39
Brouthers, Margaret 39, 47
Brouthers, Mary Ellen 38–39, 45, 47
Brouthers, Michael 35, 39
Brown, Dave 232
Brown, Tom 70
Brown, Willard 215, 221
Brush, John T. 132, 170–171, 181
Bryant, Lefty 211
Buckenberger, Al 47
Buckley, Dick 170–171
Bulkeley, Morgan G. 3
Burke, Eddie 67–68
Burkett, Jesse 22, 28, 75–76, 148
Burnham, George 126
Bush, George W. 198
Bush, Owen (Donie) 83, 112–115
Bushong, Albert (Doc) 52

Cadore, Leon 228
Cammeyer, William 139
Campanella, Roy 221
Carey, George (Scoops) 45, 128
Carey, Max 64–65, 111–113
Carroll, Cliff 58–59
Caruthers, Bob 52
Cepeda, Orlando 198

Index

Chadwick, Henry 10
Chalmers, George 204
Chamberlain, Elton (Icebox) 52
Champion, Aaron 9
Chandler, A.B. (Happy) 195
Chapman, Jack 20
Charleston, Oscar 206–208, 227–229, 233
Chesbro, Jack 27
Chylak, Nestor 198
Clarke, Fred 108, 111–112
Clarkson, John 43, 93, 95, 99, 102, 122, 144, 150, 157, 175
Clemens, Roger 107, 211
Clemente, Roberto 111, 138
Clemente, Vera 138
Clements, Jack 67
Cleveland, Grover 19, 32, 37, 41
Cobb, Tyrus (Ty) 3, 18, 32, 65, 67–69, 76, 79, 83, 111, 115, 120, 149, 164–165, 204, 233
Collins, Alice 19
Collins, Anthony 19
Collins, Eddie 74, 83
Collins, Jimmy 18–32, 61, 72, 74
Collins, Sara 30
Comiskey, Charles 52–56, 229
Comorosky, Adam 113
Comway, Pete 42
Cone, Fred 10
Connolly, Tommy 132
Connor, Roger 36–37, 46, 94–95, 98, 103, 140–141, 143, 147, 172
Conroy, Wid 32
Coolidge, Calvin 85
Cooper, Andy 214, 234
Corcoran, Larry 95
Coscarart, Pete 191
Coughlin, Bill 31–32
Coveleski, Stanley 112
Cox, Billy 191
Crane, Ed (Cannonball) 102, 146
Crane, Sam 177
Cravath, Cliff (Gavvy) 160
Crawford, Sam 64, 92, 133–134
Crespo, Rogelio 234
Criger, Lou 27–28
Cronin, Joe 64
Cuban Baseball Hall of Fame 235
Cummings, William (Candy) 12, 139
Cuyler, Anna 108
Cuyler, Bertha 109, 120
Cuyler, George 108
Cuyler, Harold 116, 119
Cuyler, Hazen (Kiki) 108–120

Dahlen, Bill 130
Daily, Con 170
Daily, Hugh 51
Daley, Arthur 32, 65, 76, 184
Daugherty, Patsy 27
Dauss, George 82
Davis, George 176
Day, John B. 94, 97, 99–100, 142–144, 147
Dean, Jay (Dizzy) 189, 191, 215, 218
Delahanty, Ed 68–71, 150, 161–162
Delahanty, Jim 30
Delany, Elizabeth 203
Delany, Sadie 203
Demaree, Frank 117–118
DeMoss, Bingo 234
Dihigo, Martin 224, 235
DiMaggio, Joe 64, 151
Dineen, Bill 24–27
Ditson, Henry 12, 15, 17
Dixon, Phil 206
Doby, Larry 221
Dolan, Patrick (Cozy) 93
Donaldson, John 227
Donlin, Mike 133–134, 202
Dorgan, Mike 98
Dovey, George 134
Doyle, Charles 190
Doyle, Jack 73, 149, 176
Doyle, Larry 47, 202
Dressen, Charlie 118, 195
Dreyfuss, Barney 26, 112, 114, 133
Duffee, Clarence 56
Duffy, Hugh 20, 23, 30, 57–61, 63, 72–74, 149–150
Durocher, Leo 119, 188, 190, 192–196

East-West All Star Game 215–216, 220
English, Woody 117
Essick, Bill 185
Esterbrook, Tom (Dude) 95, 97, 144
Evers, Johnny 163
Ewing, John 103, 148
Ewing, William (Buck) 36, 94–95, 98, 103, 142–143, 147, 149, 172

Faber, Urban (Red) 91
Fabre, Isidro 230
Feller, Bob 79, 168, 183, 216, 218, 220
Ferguson, Bob 9, 36, 94, 139, 141–142
Fillmore, Millard 32
Flick, Elmer 48, 163
Flynn, Jocko 157
Ford, Whitey 90
Foster, Andrew (Rube) 200–202, 205, 222, 225, 227–228, 232

Foster, Bill 222, 228, 234
Foutz, Dave 44, 52, 62
Foxx, Jimmie 64, 206
Frankhouse, Fred 208
Freedman, Andrew 132, 176–180
Freeman, John (Buck) 24–25
Frisch, Frank 85, 230–231
Fuller, Shorty 56, 174

Gaffney, John 93, 100
Galvin, Jim (Pud) 37–39, 41, 106, 148, 150
Garcia, Antonio 235
Gardner, Jelly 229–230, 232
Gehrig, Lou 33, 79, 114, 117, 151
Gerhardt, Joe 98
Getzien, Charlie 157
Gibson, George 187–189
Gibson, Josh 206–209, 218
Gibson, Norwood 24–25
Gillespie, Pat 95, 143
Gilligan, Barney 93
Glasscock, Jack 103, 148, 161, 170–171
Gleason, Bill 52
Gleason, William (Kid) 67
Gold, Eddie 50
Goldsmith, Fred 55
González Echevarría, Roberto 226
Gore, George 71, 75
Goslin, Leon (Goose) 84, 86, 112, 120
Gould, Charlie 9
Gowdy, Hank 85
Grant, Charlie 229
Grant, Ulysses S. 143
Grantham, George 186
Greenberg, Hank 64, 151
Griffin, Mike 175
Griffith, Clark 81–83, 87, 165, 168, 171
Griggs, Art 185
Grimes, Burleigh 91, 119
Grimm, Charlie 117
Groskloss, Howard (Howdy) 187
Grove, Robert (Lefty) 85, 90, 150, 208
Gwynn, Tony 189

Hackett, Mert 93
Hackett, Walter 93
Hafey, Charles (Chick) 118
Haines, Jesse 48
Hamilton, Billy 23, 61, 64–77, 161–163
Hamilton, Dorothy 72
Hamilton, Ethel 72
Hamilton, Mary 66
Hamilton, Mildred 72
Hamilton, Rebecca 72–76
Hamilton, Ruth 72

Hamilton, Samuel 66
Hamlin, Luke 191–192
Hanlon, Ned 40, 42, 124, 126, 129–134, 137, 157
Hardy, Arthur 200
Harkins, John 143
Harrington, Joe 22
Harris, Joe 86
Harris, Stanley (Bucky) 83–86
Hartnett, Charles (Gabby) 114, 116, 189, 191
Hatfield, Gil 99
Healy, John 96
Heathcote, Cliff 114, 116
Heilmann, Harry 206, 233
Herman, Babe 136
Herzog, Buck 47
Heydler, John 124
Hill, Pete 200–201
Hodges, Gil 195
Hoff, Chester (Red) 203
Holbert, Bill 95, 97, 143
Holland, Bill 202
Holmes, Ducky 130
Holway, John 50, 202–203, 209, 231
Hoover, Herbert 87
Hornsby, Rogers 19, 111, 115–117
Howell, Harry 165
Hoy, William (Dummy) 52
Hubbell, Carl 118, 142, 149, 213
Huff, George 29
Huggins, Miller 91, 135
Hughes, Tom 24–25
Hulbert, William 13–14
Hurst, Tim 164
Husting, Bert 24
Huston, T. L. 135
Hutchison, Bill 173–175

Infield fly rule 54, 60, 63
Irvin, Monte 216
Irwin, Arthur 70–72, 163, 177

Jackson, Travis 85
James, Bill 50, 69, 76–77, 197, 209–210
Jennings, Hugh 21, 44, 124, 126, 128–131, 136, 166, 172–173, 179
Johnson, Andrew 6
Johnson, Byron B. (Ban) 3, 27, 131–132
Johnson, Connie 217
Johnson, Grant (Home Run) 200
Johnson, Josh 198, 208
Johnson, Walter 3, 65, 78–79, 81, 84–87, 90, 112, 168, 183, 198, 202–203, 205, 209–210

Index

Johnson, William (Judy) 207
Jones, Davy 164
Jones, Fielder 130
Joss, Adrian (Addie) 48
Joyce, Bill 179
Judge, Joe 82, 84, 86, 89, 204

Kaese, Harold 92
Kaline, Al 33
Keefe, Clara 101
Keefe, Mary 92
Keefe, Patrick 92
Keefe, Tim 36, 91–107, 122–123, 141–150, 155–156, 172, 175
Keefe and Becannon 97, 100, 103, 105
Keeler, Willie 21–22, 44, 124, 126–131, 134, 136, 149
Kelley, Joe 44, 93, 121–137, 176
Kelley, Joseph, Jr. 121, 129
Kelley, Margaret 129
Kelly, George 230–231
Kelly, Mike (King) 42–44, 123, 145
Kerr, Paul 89–92
Kieran, John 149
Killilea, Henry 26
Kilroy, Matt 67
Klobedanz, Fred 61, 72
Knight, Jack 30
Koenig, Mark 117
Koufax, Sandy 100, 168
Kuhn, Bowie 121

Lacy, Sam 203
Lajoie, Napoleon (Nap) 32, 45
Landis, Kenesaw Mountain 3, 86, 110
Lange, Bill 179
Larkin, Frank 141
Latham, Walter (Arlie) 47, 52, 55
Lavagetto, Harry (Cookie) 192
Leach, Tommy 27
Lee, Doc 80–81
Leibold, Nemo 84, 86
Leland, Frank 200–201
Leonard, Andy 7
Leonard, Walter (Buck) 208–209
Lewis, Ted 24, 72
Lindstrom, Fred 85, 118, 188–189
Lloyd, John Henry (Pop) 201
Loftus, Tom 74
Long, Herman 22, 57–59, 74
Lovett, Tom 52
Lowe, Bobby 22, 57–60
Lucas, Henry 14, 50
Luque, Adolfo 228
Lyons, Harry 52

Mack, Connie 3, 18, 23–24, 30, 74, 202
Mack, Earle 202
Mackey, Raleigh (Biz) 213
MacPhail, Larry 119
Maddux, Greg 107
Mahon, John J. 129, 131–132
Malarcher, Dave 232
Malone, Fergy 11
Manley, Effa 225
Mantle, Mickey 33, 90
Manush, Heinie 91, 206
Marberry, Fred (Firpo) 84
Marquard, Richard (Rube) 48, 99
Marsáns, Armando 229–230
Matchett, Jack 218
Mathews, Bobby 12
Mathews, Ed 32
Mathewson, Christy 3, 76, 133, 142, 181, 210
Mays, Willie 33, 50
McBride, George 83
McCarthy, Daniel 50
McCarthy, Joe 64, 114, 116, 119
McCarthy, Margaret 54, 62
McCarthy, Sarah 50
McCarthy, Tommy 20, 23, 48–63, 72, 175
McCloskey, John 20
McCormick, Jim 157
McGarr, James (Chippy) 70
McGraw, John 3, 18, 21, 32–33, 44, 46–48, 71, 74, 121, 124, 126–132, 134, 149, 173, 182, 226, 229–230
McIntyre, Matty 164–165
McKechnie, Bill 86, 90, 110–112, 118
McMahon, Jess 201
McNeely, Earl 84–86, 90
McPhee, John (Bid) 133
McVey, Cal 9, 12
Meany, Tom 192
Medwick, Joe 120, 189, 192, 194
Meekin, Jouett 175–176, 179
Mendéz, José 226–227, 229, 234–235
Mendoza, Ramon S. 231
Merkle, Fred 47
Merritt, Bill 60
Milan, Clyde 82–83
Milligan, Jocko 52, 54
Mills Commission 16
Minoso, Minnie 225, 235
Mitchell, Fred 24
Mize, Johnny 216
Molina, Tinti 226
Molitor, Paul 87
Moore, Eddie 112

Index

Morgan, Mike 33
Moriarty, Gene 155–156
Motley, Don 222
Mullane, Tony 175
Munkittrick, R. K. 144
Murnane, Tim 14, 21, 31, 51, 62
Murray, Billy 20
Musial, Stan 33, 48, 192, 216
Mutrie, Jim 93, 96, 143, 146

Nash, Billy 21–22, 45, 58–61, 72, 163
National Association of Professional Base Ball Players (NAPBB) 7–8
National Baseball Hall of Fame 3, 16–17, 18–19, 31–33, 48–49, 64–66, 79, 90–92, 120–121, 136–138, 150, 167, 169, 184, 196–198, 209, 211, 222–225, 235
Navin, Frank 165
Negro World Series 215, 218
Newcombe, Don 221
Newsom, Louis (Bobo) 181, 193–194
Nichols, Charles (Kid) 23, 57–60, 72, 74, 127, 172–173, 222
Niehoff, Bert 204
Nixon, Richard 185

O'Day, Hank 102, 146
Oliva, Tony 235
O'Neil, John (Buck) 211, 216, 222, 225
O'Neill, James (Tip) 96, 143
O'Neill, Mike 30
O'Rourke, Jim 10, 36–37, 39, 98
Orr, Dave 95
Ott, Mel 33, 64, 118

Paige, Leroy (Satchel) 121, 198, 207–209, 211, 216–218, 220–223
Palmer, Pete 196
Peckinpaugh, Roger 84
Perez, Tony 235
Pesky, Johnny 114
Petway, Bruce 201
Phelps, Ernest (Babe) 190–192
Phillippe, Charles (Deacon) 26–27
Phillips, Horace 35
Piet, Tony 185, 187, 189
Pike, Lipman (Lip) 139
Pipp, Wally 228
Plank, Eddie 24
Pompez, Alex 225
Pond, W. A. (Arlie) 128
Posey, W. Cumberland (Cum) 206, 208, 229, 235
Povich, Shirley 81
Preston, Walter 20

Quigley, Johnny 35
Quinn, Jack 228
Quinn, Joe 58

Radbourn, Charley 14, 96–97, 99, 142, 144, 150
Radcliffe, Ted (Double Duty) 214
Reach, Al 11, 67, 71, 101, 139, 160
Redding, Dick (Cannonball) 201–202, 205–206, 209
Reese, Harold (Pee Wee) 192–193
Regan, Bill 187
Reiser, Pete 192
Reserve clause 12–14, 42, 98, 178
Rice, Beulah 79
Rice, Charles 79–80
Rice, Christine 79, 89
Rice, Edgar (Sam) 78–90
Rice, Edith 83, 87, 89
Rice, Louise 79
Rice, Mary 79, 89
Richardson, Dan 98
Richardson, Hardy 36, 38–41, 43–44, 156–157, 159
Rickey, Branch 193–195, 220
Riley, James A. 203, 206
Ripken, Cal, Jr. 197
Ritter, Larry 120, 136
Rixey, Eppa 91
Rizzuto, Phil 220
Roberts, Ric 207
Robinson, Brooks 33
Robinson, Jackie 79, 195–196, 220–221
Robinson, Wilbert 124, 129–132, 136
Rodriguez, Alex 75
Rogan, Joe 215, 222, 234
Rogers, John I. 67, 71, 160–163
Rollins, Jimmy 71
Roush, Edd 91
Rowe, Jack 36, 38–40, 42–43
Ruel, Herold (Muddy) 84–85
Rusie, Amos 47, 105, 127, 133, 148–149, 168–183
Rusie, Mary 169, 180
Rusie, May 172–173, 180, 182–183
Rusie, William 169
Russell, Lillian 173
Ruth, George (Babe) 3, 18, 31, 33, 65, 74–75, 79, 84–85, 111, 114, 117, 119, 135–136, 149, 151, 158, 165, 168, 226, 228, 230–231
Ryan, Jimmy 173
Ryan, Nolan 168–169, 183, 198, 208

Santop, Louis 201
Schaefer, Harry 10

Schmidt, Mike 32
Scott, Pete 114
Seaver, Tom 143, 210
Selbach, Kip 69
Selee, Frank 20–21, 51–52, 56–57, 60–61, 72–74, 123, 129, 198
Sewell, Rip 188
Seymour, James (Cy) 133–134
Sharrott, George 44
Sheckard, Jimmy 131
Shindle, Billy 44, 124
Shotton, Burt 195–196
Simmons, Al 78, 85
Slaughter, Enos 192
Smith, DeMorris 214, 222
Smith, Earl 86, 112
Smith, Hilton 211–223
Smith, John 212
Smith, Ken 63
Smith, Louise 214, 222
Smith, Mattie 212
Smith, Robert 209
Somers, Charles 23–24
Spahn, Warren 138, 150
Spalding, Albert G. 6, 9, 11–12, 14–16, 57, 100–102, 105
Spalding, Walter 105
Speaker, Tris 78–79, 149
Stahl, Charles (Chick) 22, 24, 28–29, 73–74
Stallings, George 163–164
Stargell, Willie 111
Start, Joe 9
Stearns, Frederick 39–41, 155–156, 159
Stengel, Charles (Casey) 208
Stenzel, Jake 128–130
Stephenson, Riggs 114–115
Stivetts, Jack 56–58, 60–61, 127
Stock, Milt 228
Stone, George 28
Stovey, Harry 75
Streeter, Sam 203, 206
Suhr, Gus 186
Sullivan, John L. 23
Sutter, Bruce 225
Sutton, Ezra 12
Sweeney, Charlie 107

Tannehill, Lee 32
Taylor, C.I. 229
Taylor, Charles H. 28
Taylor, Charles I. 28–30
Taylor, Sam 117
Temple, William 175
Temple Cup 73, 127–129, 175–176

Tenney, Fred 22, 72
Terry, Bill 190
Thayer, Fred 12
Thevenow, Tommy 186–188
Thompson, Cyrus 153–154, 163
Thompson, Ida 159, 165–166
Thompson, Jesse 153
Thompson, Rebecca 153
Thompson, Sam 40–42, 45, 67–71, 90, 151–167
Thorn, John 196
Three-strike rule 40–41
Tiernan, Mike 172, 174
Titcomb, Ledell (Cannonball) 99, 102
Torriente, Cristóbal 224–235
Travis, Cecil 218
Traynor, Harold (Pie) 189–191
Treadway, George 44, 124
Troy, Dasher 149
Turner, Tuck 71, 162

Unglaub, Bob 27, 29
Union Association 14, 50–51

Valenzuela, Fernando 142
Van Haltren, George 123–124
Vaughan, Bob 190
Vaughan, Glenn 192–194
Vaughan, Joseph Floyd (Arky) 184–197
Vaughan, Laura 184
Vaughan, Margaret 187, 196
Vaughan, Patricia 194–195
Vaughan, Robert 184–185
Vickers, Rube 133
Vidmer, Richards 3
Vincent, Francis (Fay) 224
Von der Ahe, Chris 52–56
Von der Horst, Harry 44, 73

Waddell, George (Rube) 24
Wagner, John (Honus) 3, 27, 32, 149, 188–190, 197
Walker, Fred (Dixie) 192, 194
Walker, Moses 229
Walker, Welday 229
Wallace, Bobby 23
Walsh, Bridget 139
Walsh, Joseph 139
Waner, Lloyd 113–114, 188, 191
Waner, Paul 112–113, 188, 191
Ward, Helen Deauvray 100
Ward, John M. 42, 58, 91, 98, 101, 103, 143–144, 146, 176, 178
Wasdell, Jimmy 191
Waterman, Fred 7

Watkins, Bill 40–41, 67, 155–156, 159, 163, 166
Watkins, Harvey 176
Welch, Curt 52
Welch, Mary 140, 148–149
Welch, Mickey 36, 43, 47, 91–99, 102–103, 105–107, 123, 138–150, 161, 172
Wells, Willie 213, 220
Weyhing, Gus 66
Wheat, Zack 64, 91
White, Bill 52
White, Chaney 207
White, James (Deacon) 12, 36, 39, 42–43, 156
Wilkinson, J. L. 214, 217, 220–221, 225
Williams, Beatrice 198, 205, 208
Williams, Charles (Lefty) 206
Williams, James 198
Williams, Joe 198–210, 222
Williams, Lettie 198
Williams, Ted 74, 184
Williamson, Ed 107, 149
Willis, Vic 24
Wilson, Howard 24
Wilson, Jimmy 119
Wilson, Jud 208
Wilson, Lewis (Hack) 114–116
Wilson, Willie 85
Wimer, Bill 196
Winter, George 24
Wood, George 14
Wood, Joe 204–205
World Series 26–28, 40–41, 52, 54, 85–86, 90, 96–97, 100, 102, 112, 114, 117, 146, 158, 195
Wright, Abbaria (Abbie) 12
Wright, Annie Tone 4
Wright, Beals 16
Wright, George 3–17, 51, 101
Wright, Harry 3–4, 6–8, 10–11, 13–14, 16, 67–68, 70, 105, 160, 162
Wright, Irving 16
Wright, Samuel 4
Wright and Ditson 12, 14–16
Wynn, Early 150

Yastrzemski, Carl 33
Young, Denton (Cy) 24–27, 29, 69, 106, 173–175, 179, 210
Young, Nicholas 39
Young, Pep 190
Youngs, Ross 48, 204, 230

Zachary, Tom 84–85
Zettelein, George 9

www.ingramcontent.com/pod-product-compliance
Lightning Source LLC
Chambersburg PA
CBHW021402230426
43666CB00006B/615